CURZON AND BRITISH
IMPERIALISM IN THE
MIDDLE EAST
1916–19

Curzon and British Imperialism in the Middle East

1916–19

JOHN FISHER

FRANK CASS
LONDON • PORTLAND, OR.

First published in 1999 in Great Britain by
FRANK CASS PUBLISHERS
Newbury House, 900 Eastern Avenue
London, IG2 7HH

and in the United States of America by
FRANK CASS PUBLISHERS
c/o ISBS, 5804 N.E. Hassalo Street
Portland, Oregon, 97213-3644

Website http://www.frankcass.com

British Library Cataloguing in Publication Data

Fisher, John
    Curzon and British imperialism in the Middle East, 1916–19
    1. Curzon, George Nathaniel Curzon, Marquess, 1859–1925
    2. Great Britain – Foreign relations – Middle East –
    1910–1936   3. Middle East – Foreign relations – Great Britain
    4. Great Britain – Territorial expansion – History – 20th century
    I. Title
    325. 3'41'0956'09041

ISBN 0-7146-4875-2 (cloth)
ISBN 0-7146-4429-3 (paper)

Library of Congress Cataloging in Publication Data

Fisher, John, 1968–
    Curzon and British imperialism in the Middle East, 1916–19 / John
Fisher.
        p.   cm.
    Includes bibliographical references (p.   ) and index.
    ISBN 0-7146-4875-2 (cloth). – ISBN 0-7146-4429-3 (paper)
    1. Middle East – Foreign relations – Great Britain.   2. Great
Britain – Foreign relations – Middle East.   3. Curzon, George
Nathaniel Curzon, Marquis of, 1859–1925.   4. Great Britain – Foreign
relations – 1901–1936.   I. Title.
DS63.2G7F496   1998
327.56041 – dc21   98-17117
                                                                              CIP

Typeset by Regent Typesetting, London
Printed in Great Britain by
Bookcraft (Bath) Ltd, Midsomer Norton, Somerset

Contents

Maps

Appendices

Illustrations

(Photograph 1, from the Imperial War Museum, A.T. Wilson Papers; 2, reproduced by kind permission of the Oriental and India Office Collections of the British Library; 3 to 8, reproduced by kind permission of the *Illustrated London News*.) While efforts have been made to obtain permissions from all copyright holders, we apologise for any omissions; these can be rectified in later editions.

Abbreviations

AHR	*American Historical Review*
CJH	*Canadian Journal of History*
CUP	Committee of Union and Progress
EC	Eastern Committee
EC	*Minutes of a meeting of the Eastern Committee*
FO	Foreign Office
GOI	Government of India
HJ	*Historical Journal*
IHR	*International History Review*
IO	India Office
JCH	*Journal of Contemporary History*
JICH	*Journal of Imperial and Commonwealth History*
MEC	Middle East Committee
MEC	*Minutes of a meeting of the Middle East Committee*
MES	*Middle Eastern Studies*
OIOC	Oriental and India Office Collections
PID	Political Intelligence Department
PRO	Public Record Office
S/S	Secretary of State
TAPS	*Transactions of the American Philosophical Society*
TRHS	*Transactions of the Royal Historical Society*
US/S	Under Secretary of State
WO	War Office
W&S	*War and Society*

Acknowledgements

For permission to quote from material in their care or possession, I am grateful to the following: The Trustees of the National Maritime Museum for the Norris Papers; Dr Caroline Barron for the Hogarth Papers at St Antony's College, Oxford; The Syndics of Cambridge University Library for the Crewe and Hardinge Papers; The Warden and Fellows of New College, Oxford, for the Milner Papers; Professor John Charmley for the George Lloyd Papers; The Rt. Hon. The Viscount Esher for the Esher Papers and Diaries; The Master and Fellows of Churchill College, Cambridge, for the Hankey Papers and Diaries; Mrs Bridget Grant and The Somerset Record Office for the Diaries and Papers of Aubrey Herbert; The Trustees of the Imperial War Museum for the Sir Arnold Wilson Papers and Sir Henry Wilson Diaries and Papers; The Fellows of Pembroke College, Cambridge, for the Storrs Diaries and Papers; Sir Tatton Sykes for the Papers of Sir Mark Sykes; The London Library for papers of Sir Arnold Wilson; The Keeper of the Records of Scotland for the Lothian Papers; The Earl of Balfour for the Balfour Papers deposited at the Scottish Record Office; The British Library for the Balfour Papers and for the Bertie of Thame Papers; Professor A. K. S. Lambton for the Cecil of Chelwood Diaries and Papers; The Bodleian Library, Oxford, for the Asquith Papers; The Private Papers Collection, The Middle East Centre, St Antony's College, for the Hubert Young Papers; Crown copyright material in the Public Record Office is reproduced by permission of the Controller of Her Majesty's Stationery Office; quotations from Crown copyright material in Oriental and India Office Collections of the British Library appear by permission of the Controller of Her Majesty's Stationery Office. Every attempt has been made to contact the holders of copyright but if infringement has been made my apologies are due to the individuals or institutions concerned.

This book began as a doctoral thesis submitted to the University of Leeds. I am most grateful to my former supervisor, Dr Keith Wilson, and also to him and to Sally Wheeler for their hospitality on my visits to Leeds. Dr David Gillard and Professor Erik Goldstein kindly read the manuscript and made valuable suggestions, as did Professor Michael Dockrill and Dr Hugh Cecil at an earlier stage. The lectures of Dr Gillard and of Professor Keith Robbins on various aspects of International History at Glasgow University were inspiring and encouraged me to undertake research in this area. For support of various kinds I am most grateful to Michelle Tiernan, Jon Loken, John Edwards, to the Public Record Office, and to my family; and it is to my parents that I dedicate this book.

Introduction

The outstanding account of this period remains Professor Elie Kedourie's masterful book on *England and the Middle East*. I would not dissent from his main thesis, namely the tendency towards disingenuous behaviour among prominent officials and politicians in framing and executing British policy in the Middle East. Indeed, it is one of the underlying themes of this work also.

My preliminary research on British policies in the Middle East in the first years of World War I suggested that many civil servants, politicians and senior military figures aspired to expand British interests in the region. Their motives were several and their methods equally diverse. Chapter 1 draws these ideas together in the context of the ailing Dardanelles Expedition and amid speculations about the likely reactions to British expansion in Russia and France.

The advance of the Mesopotamian Expeditionary Force from the autumn of 1914 occurred in territories which were soon to be included in bilateral and multilateral agreements between Britain and her Allies. The political aspects of the expedition arising from this advance, and from the desire of the British Government to establish a permanent footing in Mesopotamia, were delegated to a sub-committee of the War Cabinet, the Mesopotamian Administration Committee, which met under Curzon's chairmanship. Chapter 2 traces the development of the acquisitive thinking which underpinned the expedition and which was most vividly displayed by India Office officials. Hitherto, the forward thinking of Lord Hardinge, Viceroy of India, has been emphasised but his instincts were in keeping with feelings in Whitehall.

Discussions connected with the Mesopotamian Administration Committee revealed from an early stage a crucial divergence between those who, in order to justify British involvement, focused on British military achievements there, and others who sought justification in the argument that the Arabs of Mesopotamia might only achieve self-fulfilment with British assistance.

British involvement in Mesopotamia entailed some consideration of how this embryonic dependency might be accommodated within the fabric of the British Empire. In turn, the Committee examined the foundations upon which some degree of civil administration might be established, consistent with Britain's commitments to her Allies and with conditions on the ground.

This relationship between Britain's ties with the Arab movement and the genesis of civil government revealed the methods by which prominent imperialists sought to obtain for Britain a predominant and lasting presence in the country. Friction between the civil and military authorities in Mesopotamia threatened this and proved a lasting pre-occupation of the Committee.

The desire of many British officials during World War I to maintain a traditional policy of aloofness in the Arabian Peninsula proved impossible. This was due partly to the intensification of the pre-war policy designed to exclude foreign competition from the Peninsula. The steadily growing ambitions of France and Italy and the sometimes distorted perception of these among British officials fuelled this. Furthermore, there was the apparent concession to France and Italy of a position of equality with Britain in the Peninsula provided by the Sykes–Picot Agreement of 1916 and St Jean de Maurienne Agreement of 1917. The persistence of Turkish intrigues and military activities in south-western Arabia and the continuing strategical importance of the Peninsula to Britain further ensured that some measure of British involvement was inevitable.

During 1916–17 determined efforts were made to obtain from France and Italy an acknowledgement of Britain's political predominance in the Peninsula. The circumstances in which these efforts were made rendered the question peculiarly sensitive. A detailed study of Britain's Arab policy, as it impinged upon the issue of the recognition of her primacy, is provided. Above all, emphasis is given to the difficulty faced by British officials in reconciling this much publicised policy with the need not to be outdone by her rivals.

An added worry was the opportunism of Curzon and others regarding the Hejaz. This debate occurred against a backdrop of on-going discussion about the future military and political control of the Peninsula and its component parts. Such matters were of special interest to Curzon and some assessment is made of his overall contribution to the question of British influence in the Peninsula, imbued, as it was, with decades of experience in the problems of the region.

By the beginning of 1918 Curzon was deeply frustrated with the conduct of British policy in the Middle East. He had failed to persuade the Cabinet to sanction an overwhelming advance in the Palestinian/ Syrian theatre and had been unable to muster support for an advance in Mesopotamia. Worse still, the Foreign and India Offices were formulating policy without reference to him. There were also fundamental constraints on British policy in Mesopotamia. France was unwilling to forego her claims in Mosul and there was an increasing and inescapable emphasis on self-determination.

Discussions about the relationship between Britain and the Vilayets of Basra and Baghdad were of considerable importance in 1918. Simultaneously, tensions arose between the policy-making departments in London and the men on the spot. Simply stated, these rested upon a divergence of opinion on the means by which Britain might justify to her Allies and associated Powers her retention of a predominant position in Mesopotamia. As Chairman of the Eastern Committee, Curzon was either unable or unwilling to grasp the point that it was no longer possible for Britain to justify her position on grounds of military conquest alone. Rather, according to some India Office officials, the administrative and commercial fabric of the country must be so arranged as to render the success of the country as an Arab State entirely dependent upon a strong and prolonged British presence. To an extent, officials were able to proceed with this policy in discreet defiance of Curzon. However, some India Office officials felt that by virtue of this policy Britain might unwittingly prejudice the case against her future predominance in the country; something which could only be assured by agreement with her Allies on the cessation of hostilities.

By the autumn of 1918, with peace imminent and with increasing pressure from international opinion, several senior officials favoured more circumspect methods. A growing discrepancy between the policy of the Foreign and India Offices was reflected in their respective interpretations of the Anglo-French Declaration of November 1918, for which the Foreign Office was primarily responsible, and which confirmed Britain in her role of disinterested patron of the Arab movement. By this time, both within the India Office and among other senior figures, the idea of a British protectorate in Mesopotamia appealed increasingly.

The debate surrounding the Anglo-French Declaration occurred against the backdrop of the Armistice of Mudros. During the preliminary discussions Curzon mounted a vigorous campaign to ensure that Britain would not have to discontinue her military operations in Mesopotamia and thereby be prevented from securing the Mosul Vilayet.

Denied immediate and substantial gains in Palestine or Mesopotamia, Curzon gazed on the Caucasus with evident relish. Britain's involvement there in the first eight months of 1918 was intended, primarily, as a response to Turco-German advances. Notwithstanding a broad consensus in the analysis of the problem by senior figures, British policy remained essentially cautious. A significant discrepancy arose between the portrayal of this threat and the action taken to forestall it. This was partly due to the considerable exaggeration of the immediacy of the threat posed by Turco-German arms. Quite simply it did not lead directly to the high-water mark of British imperial involvement in the Caucasus. Rather, British policy in the Caucasus at this time might be explained as much with reference to perceptions of the Bolshevik Russian regime among British officials.

Inevitably, as 1918 wore on and the actual threat posed by Turco-German advances diminished, a change of emphasis in British strategic thinking occurred towards a greater awareness of events in Bolshevik Russia. Efforts were made to maintain the spectre of Turco-German penetration, partly to disguise an increasingly obvious incompatibility between British and Bolshevik Russian interests in Asia. Paradoxically, as the extent of this incompatibility increased, the possibility of taking decisive action to remedy it diminished. However, as Curzon realised, such inactivity provided the genesis for the real battle for Asia. During the summer and autumn of 1918 Britain and France had negotiated and pledged themselves to a declaration in which they undertook to assist the Arab communities of the Middle East to achieve self-fulfilment. The Anglo-French Declaration, with its emphasis on self-determination, was intended to allay the fears of those who detected elements of traditional imperialist policy in the behaviour of the Western Powers. More specifically, it was felt that, in time, the Declaration might render untenable the concessions made to France in the Sykes–Picot Agreement.

By this time, however, although France had conceded that the Sykes–Picot Agreement was outdated, there had been no discussions aimed specifically towards its revision. By playing the self-determination card, it was hoped that the pressure of international opinion would encourage France to forego her claims in Syria and Mosul. However, to some officials the Anglo-French Declaration seemed to invite unwanted international scrutiny. More seriously, it emphasised the parity between

British and French interests, respectively, in Mesopotamia and Syria. When British policies in Mesopotamia had experienced considerable success and when informed opinion advised that Britain should attempt to obtain Syria and Mosul, the Declaration was perceived by some as a retrograde step.

Curzon and several of his colleagues were committed to using self-determination to oust the French from Syria. Simultaneously it was recognised that this was a dangerous weapon and that, in utilising the pressure of the United States, Britain must avoid giving her Allies any outward impression of this. There was also the question of the extent to which Britain must align herself with Hashemite ambitions in the Middle East. There was a growing awareness that in Central Arabia these ambitions might complicate British policy, whereas if they were harnessed and channelled in a more northerly direction they might instead serve British policy. By the end of 1918 Curzon and others tended increasingly to perceive in the growth of Hashemite power a potentially hostile element in a unified Moslem bloc stretching across the entire Middle East.

None the less, it was partly to avoid disappointing Britain's Arab allies and to avoid the creation of a land-locked Arab state that the idea of removing France from Syria began to appeal to some of Curzon's colleagues. Inducement might be offered in the form of a mandate for Armenia and the Caucasian States. An element of compulsion would be found in the manipulation of American opinion and French objectives in the West. Discussion of the first idea entailed the definition of Armenia, something which again raised the question of French territorial rights under the Sykes–Picot Agreement. In addition it raised the whole question of British policy towards pan-Islamism and pan-Turanianism.

In his emphatic opposition to this and to the possibility of any country other than Britain controlling the Caucasus, Curzon had a strong hand. For those who feared expanding British commitments, Curzon's belief in the indivisibility of the Armenian Vilayets and the Caucasian States presented the possibility of France controlling a vast wedge of territory on the flank of the Indian Empire with unlimited opportunity for intrigue. Equally, as Curzon argued, the possibility of America becoming involved was never more than wishful thinking.

Curzon believed that if left to their own devices the population of the Caucasus would favour the continuation of the British presence. Admittedly, it might be necessary to accept the status of a mandatory

power under the League of Nations but, at the end of 1918, this
appeared to Curzon as a distant hazard. This also explains Curzon's
relative optimism at this time regarding Britain obtaining a permanent
and controlling interest in Palestine. Although the Jews and Arabs
might manipulate the Anglo-French Declaration for selfish ends, the self-
determination card would, so Curzon believed, lead to demands for
British guidance. This was necessary on grounds of history, strategy
and economics. Why his views on the desirability of this changed as
rapidly as they did is explained in the final chapter.

At any rate, at the end of 1918, in spite of profound differences with
colleagues, Curzon used his position as Chairman of the Eastern
Committee to forge a sufficient consensus to establish for the Peace
Conference expansive and detailed imperialist desiderata for each of the
countries of the Middle East. Yet these were simply recommendations
and, in anticipation of the Peace Conference, the Committee, and therefore also its chairman, moved from an executive to an advisory role. In
spite of strenuous efforts to regain his executive functions as Acting
Secretary of State for Foreign Affairs from January 1919, Curzon was
unable thereafter to re-establish his ascendancy. The initial lustre of the
Foreign Office rapidly waned as the extent of the disorganisation arising
from the maintenance of dual Foreign Office establishments in London
and Paris became clear. Curzon's increasing pessimism was partly due
to his dissatisfaction with organisational difficulties. More significantly,
he was distressed by the division of work between himself and Balfour.
On too many issues Curzon found his often brilliant interventions
ignored and the Foreign Office being turned to peripheral concerns.
That, in the often serious divergence of opinions that emerged between
himself and colleagues in Paris, Curzon gained the support of Foreign
Office officials and, on occasion, that of members of the British
Delegation merely compounded his frustration. Among the latter group
was Sir Eyre Crowe, Assistant Under-Secretary of State for Foreign
Affairs, who spoke of 'the strong cool breeze blowing from London'.
The various currents which combined to shape Curzon's thought at this
time and the lingering death of War Imperialism during 1919 form the
subject of the final chapter.

∞ 1 ∞

Playing Babylon against Byzantium

EARLY IN FEBRUARY 1915, a light cruiser of the British East Indies Station might have been observed dropping anchor off Alexandretta. In the following days landing parties would proceed to liaise with Turkish troops and with the British Consul and to execute various reconnaissance tasks. Among the party, acting in an intelligence capacity, was Captain Aubrey Herbert MP,[1] a well-connected and linguistically gifted Turkophile of aristocratic stock. Although it was Herbert's first experience of Ayas Bay, in mid-December HMS *Doris* had already undertaken operations there against Turkish communications.[2]

Writing in January, Herbert had recorded his belief that France should not be permitted to fulfil her traditional imperial aims in Syria but that Syria should instead be independent.[3] If, however, as Herbert continued, Syria 'chooses to come to Egypt offering herself as a satrapy' then 'well and good'.[4] In any event Herbert felt that Britain should occupy Alexandretta. This conviction was strengthened by a rumoured French expedition to Syria and by suggestions that the Cilician Armenians who wanted British protection were, by default, turning to Russia.[5] Herbert was convinced that Britain should immediately occupy Alexandretta, a 'beautiful position', and that Russia, who, according to the British Consul at Alexandretta, a Mr Catoni, was seen by Turks as the real enemy, might instead have Mersina.[6] Herbert believed that the possession of Alexandretta was a vital calculation in St Petersburg, where, in all likelihood, it was realised that Constantinople would be hers anyway, and as developments might conspire to undermine her traditional preponderance in the Balkans.[7] This, Herbert argued, would 'produce a reactionary effect on Russian policy', and encourage Russian expansion elsewhere.[8] Whilst Constantinople could only ever be a

'passive and defensive' port for Russia, Alexandretta could not be sur-
passed as an 'active and offensive' Russian port.[9] Russia's difficulty was
justifying its acquisition. For Britain, however, as Herbert remarked, 'it
is almost an essential part of British strategy to seize the key hole of the
enemy's door'.[10] Failing an immediate British occupation while Turkish
attacks on the Suez Canal persisted then, Herbert argued, 'our opportunity is lost, for the occupation of Alexandretta would then become a
move against Russia instead of a move against Turkey'.[11] A temporary
British occupation would, in Herbert's view, at least afford Britain the
requisite bargaining power to render Alexandretta neutral.[12]

The despatch of HMS *Doris* to Alexandretta was part of a broader
strategy evolved at the end of 1914 by the Admiralty, undertaken concurrently with investigations on the possibility of sizeable landings at
Alexandretta. These would aim ostensibly to disrupt Turkish communications but might also save face should the initial bombardment of
the Dardanelles prove unsuccessful. Early in 1915 the General Staff
estimated that 13,000 men would be required to capture the Bailan Pass
and then secure field works in the surrounding area.[13] Should it then be
necessary to capture Aleppo, as a means of holding the Baghdad
Railway, more than a division would be necessary.[14]

Herbert was not the only British officer with experience of the Middle
East who enthused about the occupation of Alexandretta, yet there were
others whose strategic analysis, though similar to Herbert's, was more
fully developed.[15] To Ronald Storrs, Oriental Secretary at the British
Agency in Cairo, it seemed, early in February 1915, that Britain must
occupy Alexandretta to forestall the almost inevitable southward movement by Russia and the extension of French claims to areas outside the
Lebanon.[16] Although, as Storrs had previously acknowledged, France
would be a better neighbour for Britain than Russia, he also recognised
that the Entente might not last.[17] At the end of 1914 Storrs felt that
the inclusion within the Egyptian Protectorate of part of Palestine
might provide some protection from potentially hostile interests, but he
soon evolved more expansive desiderata.[18] A British occupation of
Alexandretta would be a legitimate undertaking by virtue of Turkish
operations against Egypt and British operations in Mesopotamia.
However, given French disinclination to substantiate her Syrian claims,
Storrs believed that the permanent occupation of Alexandretta by
Britain would also 'ensure the settlement of the Syrian question to our
advantage in due course of time'.[19] Writing later in February, Storrs
emphasised the importance of Syria to Britain, suggesting 'it is not only

a goal per se but also a necessity both with regard to Irak and the Arabian peninsula'.[20] On 8 March, while feigning innocence amid warnings from Sir Edward Grey, the Foreign Secretary,[21] that the encouraging of British ambitions in Syria would lead to 'a break with France', Storrs evidently cherished the idea of a 'Near Eastern Vice-royalty' under Kitchener, stretching from the Sudan to Alexandretta.[22] With France 'directed into channels of profit and consolidation in West Africa' and Russia installed in Constantinople, Britain, in Storrs's view, would have free scope for expansion.[23]

Taking up the cudgels at the War Council on 10 March, Kitchener opposed Grey's sensibilities about French ambitions in Syria by arguing that Alexandretta lay beyond areas of traditional French claims.[24] As Asquith, the Prime Minister, indicated, if, as was assumed, Russia was to obtain Constantinople, then there were, in the opinion of the Admiralty, strong reasons for a British Naval Base at Alexandretta.[25] Besides the importance to Britain of maintaining naval supremacy Kitchener was emphatic that, with Alexandretta controlled by another power, Britain could neither count on holding Egypt nor could she maintain her new dependency in Mesopotamia.[26] There was also, as suggested by Lord Fisher, First Sea Lord,[27] the question of Alexandretta as the outlet for the oil supplies of Mesopotamia and Persia.[28]

Kitchener believed that the possession of Syria by France and Constantinople by Russia would not lead inevitably to a permanent peace with Britain. In particular, he was convinced that traditional schemes of Russian expansion towards the Persian Gulf would continue. Developing his thoughts in a note entitled 'Alexandretta and Mesopotamia', Kitchener argued that it was precisely with the thwarting of such expansionism in mind that Britain should occupy Alexandretta. Similarly, Kitchener felt that if Britain did not 'take' Mesopotamia then Russia would and this, as he continued, 'would give them an outlet into the Persian Gulf, and enable them eventually to control the military situation and the greater part of its commerce'.[29]

Such a contingency arising on the division of the Ottoman Empire would, in Kitchener's opinion, fatally undermine British prestige.[30] Rather than ceding Mesopotamia to Russia, its possession by Britain was necessary for the creation of a great Arab kingdom 'bounded on the north by the valley of the Tigris and Euphrates, and containing within it the chief Mahommedan Holy Places, Mecca, Medina, and Kerbala'.[31] Precisely the same point about prestige or 'moral ascendancy' was developed in an Admiralty paper of 17 March. Given that Russia was being established 'in the most famous seat of Empire in the East' and that Britain was 'allowing her to clothe herself in all the majesty of Rûm', Britain, as the Admiralty paper suggested, must seek compensation elsewhere:

> And where can such compensation be found in anything like so much force as in reviving the still more ancient seat of empire in the Middle East? We must play Babylon against Byzantium. But this cannot be done by merely occupying and bringing to life again the old Mesopotamia. The ancient empire must not only be restored to its wealth, it must be brought to the shores of the Mediterranean. The war is teaching us that the Mediterranean is still, as it always was, the centre of world politics, and it is there we must establish the gate of our new acquisition as a counterpoise to the new weight that Russia is acquiring in the dominant area.[32]

At the India Office, Sir Arthur Hirtzel,[33] the formidable and highly regarded Secretary of the Political and Secret Department, though sharing Kitchener's reluctant belief that Britain would probably have to be coterminous with Russia, also wished, ideally, to be able to hold the Alexandretta–Mosul line.[34] A more realistic policy seemed to Hirtzel to attempt to control Alexandretta but not to contemplate the defence of that line.[35] The main purpose of such control would be to prevent the construction of the section of the Baghdad Railway between Alexandretta and Mosul should Britain complete the line between Mosul and the Persian Gulf.[36] This was vital not only with a view to preventing a Russian movement towards the Gulf but, as argued by Admiral Jackson, to impede both a revival of German designs on Persia and a hostile French movement on the Euphrates Valley.[37] Furthermore, Hirtzel felt that British possession of Alexandretta or the creation of a free port there would provide an outlet for Northern Mesopotamian trade without affecting, disadvantageously, the traditional orientation of Indian trade in the Persian Gulf.[38]

Kitchener attached such importance to the acquisition of Alexandretta because he believed that its possession represented the lynchpin in a broader strategy evolved by himself and Storrs, whereby the Khalifate would be transferred to Arabia and a substantial Arab Empire would emerge under British auspices. This, as Kitchener argued at the War Council on 19 March, would prevent the Khalif from falling into Russian hands, something with potentially disastrous consequences for British rule in India, and would render feasible the establishing of the Middle Eastern Viceroyalty in which Kitchener aspired to preeminence.[39] This would account for his opposition to the more restrained thinking of Major-General E.G. Barrow, Military Secretary at the India Office, who, responding to Hirtzel's remarks of 14 March, suggested that if Russia obtained Constantinople then Britain would seek to maintain Turkey in Asia and should therefore encourage the transfer of the Turkish capital and the Khalifate to Konia. Maintenance of Turkish sovereignty would, moreover, provide a buffer between Russian interests to the north and those of Britain in Mesopotamia. The latter, in Barrow's view, must be restricted to the Basra Vilayet, which Britain must annex, and the Baghdad Vilayet, in which Britain would conduct the administration under Turkish suzerainty. Although Barrow contemplated some restrictions on French gains in Syria, in that Britain might control a railway passing from Mesopotamia to Egypt via Damascus, he did not believe that Britain should or could undertake the defence of Northern Mesopotamia. On this basis, and because he felt that its possession would create friction with France and Russia, Barrow, ever the cautious thruster, argued against a British occupation of Alexandretta.[40]

Kitchener's scheme for an Arab Khalif and Empire emerged in the course of correspondence between Kitchener and Hussein, Sherif of Mecca, which commenced in the summer of 1914.[41] Whilst initially confined to Hussein's role in the war, by the summer of 1915 discussion had broadened by virtue of claims advanced by Hussein for the creation of an independent Arab Kingdom, under his rule, covering most of Arab Asia.[42] Hussein had discovered the intention of the Porte, the Turkish Government, to depose him at the war's end and his demands in the summer of 1915 reflected views of secret, anti-Turk societies in Damascus with whom Faisal,[43] Hussein's son, had negotiated, partly to establish his father's ascendancy in the post-war Middle East. Having been suppressed, the secret societies informed Hussein that as they could not revolt against the Porte he might be able to do so if he could obtain from Britain pledges of support.

British officials began to take Hussein's demands more seriously with the discovery that there might be considerable support for such a revolt throughout the region and by virtue of the need to get the Arabs actively involved on the Allied side to ease matters at Gallipoli. The negotiations which developed with Hussein were extremely ambiguous, not least because of the activities of a member of a secret society, al-Faruqi,[44] who acted as go-between under the pretence that he was the spokesman of both the British Government and the secret societies. It seems that, by virtue of al-Faruqi's misrepresentation of Hussein, senior figures in Cairo Intelligence were led to believe that, whilst Hussein was determined to maintain the independence of inland Syria, he would accept French predominance on the Syrian littoral. The division of those territories and the area that was to be Arab and independent was equally ambiguous. According to David Fromkin, in searching for a convenient boundary British officials may have turned to the 1910 edition of *Encyclopaedia Britannica* in which Damascus, Aleppo, Homs and Hama are given as the only towns in the Syrian interior.[45] When embodied in a telegram to London by Sir Henry McMahon, British High Commissioner in Cairo, the definition of those districts, the possession of which Hussein demanded, was unclear; one interpretation suggesting, as Fromkin notes, that Britain had accepted the notion of an Arab Palestine, another that Palestine had been excluded from the proposed Arab area.[46]

An examination of the War Council minutes in the first months of 1915 suggests that many of Kitchener's senior colleagues were at least mentally attuned to the possibility of Britain making substantial gains in the Middle East. This was exemplified in a remark by Asquith at the War Council on 19 March that, although he sympathised with Grey's suggestion that Britain already had 'as much territory as we are able to hold', 'we were not free agents'. As Asquith continued, Russia, France, Italy and Greece coveted parts of the Ottoman Empire:

> If, for one reason or another, because we didn't want more territory, or because we didn't feel equal to the responsibility, we were to leave the other nations to scramble for Turkey without taking anything for ourselves, we should not be doing our duty.[47]

Lloyd George,[48] destined to have a decisive influence on the evolution of the Middle East, seemed less obviously burdened with a rigid concept of this duty, expressing the typically more flexible view that Britain should acquire Palestine rather than Alexandretta. The latter place, as he implied on 19 March, might be left to Germany as a means of offsetting Russian power.[49]

More importantly, whilst there was no obvious dissension from Kitchener's view that Alexandretta lay outside, or was not essential to, French claims in Syria, his colleagues did not then insist on its acquisition by Britain. When it was revealed that France did claim Alexandretta and Cilicia, Balfour, First Lord of the Admiralty, who shared Kitchener's opinion on the inseparability of Alexandretta and

Mesopotamia, deemed the French claims 'excessive'.[50] At the Foreign Office, Sir Arthur Nicolson, Permanent Under-Secretary of State, anticipated 'considerable difficulty' with France over Alexandretta but, envisaging as he did limited British gains in the Middle East, he felt that the future of Alexandretta need not be discussed until the war's end.[51] The Secretary of State for India, Lord Crewe, was equally aghast at the scope of French claims, suggesting to Grey on 22 March 1915, that Britain 'may claim particular interest in the fate of the western half of Turkey in Asia and of Palestine'.[52] Early in April, when reflecting in a letter to Hardinge,[53] Viceroy of India and a prominent exponent of British expansion, on the vast changes which Britain contemplated by virtue of her support for an Arab Khalif and Empire stretching to the Mediterranean, Crewe foresaw trouble with France 'when the cutting of the cake begins'. Yet, concluding his letter, Crewe observed: 'I am not madly keen for Alexandretta, – another hostage to fortune. But I am open to conviction when I know more of its charms.'[54]

Concern about French susceptibilities was a factor in the equation, but it was insufficient to prevent a British occupation of Alexandretta; and this was implicit in that British policy ultimately became rooted in Hirtzel's idea of a free port. As stated in an Admiralty memorandum, French territorial acquisitions in North Africa should render her more amenable in Syria and, as the memorandum continued, would not Anglo-French co-operation be beneficial in presenting 'a counterpoise to Russian prestige' if France were to obtain Syria?[55] As Herbert suggested, British designs on Alexandretta in the spring of 1915 were inhibited chiefly by the possibility of Russian hostility in the event of Britain securing a defensive frontier between Alexandretta and Mosul as outlined by Kitchener. This was illustrated by the thoughts of Hardinge who, like many of his colleagues in England, was keenly aware of the inexorable movement of Russia towards the Gulf.

Assessing the strategic picture Hardinge fell between two stools. Like Hirtzel, he believed it necessary to come to terms with Russia in Asia and even recommended an eventual Anglo-Russian 'treaty of alliance'. More immediately, Hardinge felt that Britain might absorb the neutral sphere in Persia. In the case of Mesopotamia, however, Hardinge favoured Barrow's buffer theory. Whilst Britain might administer the Baghdad Vilayet she would neither assume responsibility for the defence of Northern Mesopotamia nor would she construct a railway from Alexandretta to Baghdad. However, unlike Hirtzel, Hardinge conceived an autonomous Armenia including the Vilayets of Bitlis and

Diarbekir and this, providing a buffer between Alexandretta and Russian territory, would allow Britain to occupy an enclave of territory stretching to Aleppo; purportedly to contain Turkey to the north.[56]

Policy-makers were anticipating the post-bellum world when Britain's rivals in Asia might direct their full energies to the pursuit of time-honoured goals.[57] Precisely this eventuality concerned Beauchamp Duff, Commander-in-Chief of India, to whom it seemed unlikely that Britain would have the resources to implement Kitchener's schemes and 'to annex the whole of Mesopotamia'. More crucially, Duff continued:

> Russia, on the contrary, will come out of the war a greater nation than she was when she entered on it. She is likely to progress, both in population and wealth, much more rapidly than either England or India can expect to do. Should she ever become our enemy, she will be a much more formidable one than we had previously reckoned on. It is the possibility of such enmity that has steadily to be borne in mind in considering the bearings of any extension of our territory.[58]

Accordingly, though resigned to a coterminous frontier with Russia in Persia, Duff opposed any further partition of the country. In Mesopotamia, though conscious of Hirtzel's argument that Britain must control the upper reaches of the Tigris and Euphrates, Duff was willing to risk the development of lower Mesopotamia rather than take Mosul. Equally, Duff held that Russia must not have it and for this reason, because 'our object is to keep them as far away as possible', Mosul and Alexandretta should be left to Turkey.[59]

The other striking aspect of British Middle Eastern policy at this time was the sheer scale of the changes that were being suggested. From a time when Britain had relatively modest strategic aims arising from her interests in the Persian Gulf, senior figures were proving receptive to fundamental change involving policies which would not only profoundly affect Britain's relations with her Moslem subjects but which would considerably expand the scope of her responsibilities in the region.

BUILDING WITHOUT BRICKS

None was more acutely aware of the nature of what was being proposed than the Earl Curzon of Kedleston,[60] who had played a particularly active role in establishing the edifice of Britain's eastern Empire and in thwarting Russian attempts to secure its demise. It was precisely these elements, and a continuing unease about Russian intentions, which combined to shape Curzon's contributions in the first years of the war.

For Curzon the war was a momentous struggle for the safety of the Empire. It was, moreover, one in which Curzon sought to attain a position in which his experience of the Empire might be used and which might atone for the years of enforced idleness on his return from India. With this in mind Curzon had written to Asquith on the outbreak of war offering his services. Leaving nothing to chance, he repeated the offer, by implication, in a letter to *The Times* at the end of August 1914.[61] Primarily, it was for Curzon a war of conquest in which the free peoples of the British Empire would fight for the good of mankind. Such, at least, was the grand scale in which Curzon conceived of the conflict on 10 September, when, according to *The Times*, he announced to prolonged cheering at St Andrew's Hall in Glasgow

> that the Indian troops, in coming to the Empire's assistance, were coming because the Empire of which they were members stood to them for something more than power; it stood for justice, uprightness, good government, mercy and truth. The Indians had no desire to change that rule for the Prussian sabre or the jackboots of the German infantryman. 'For my part,' said Lord Curzon, 'I venture to hope that these Indian troops, when they come to Europe, will be in at the death. I should like to see the lances of the Bengal Lancers fluttering down the streets of Berlin, and I should like to see the dark-skinned Gurkha making himself at ease in the gardens of Potsdam.'[62]

Elevation to the Cabinet as Lord Privy Seal in May 1915 did not satisfy Curzon's ambitions. Partly this related to Curzon's misgivings about serving in a coalition government and, ultimately, to the nature of Asquith's administration, whereby, according to Curzon, Cabinet Ministers were routinely denied information.[63] At the end of May Curzon wrote to Lloyd George expressing the hope that 'I may be found useful for any odd job that you or my colleagues may like to give me'.[64] Within a fortnight, however, Curzon confessed to Cromer that he was 'so tired with being turned on to all the odd jobs of Government, Munitions, Aircraft, Dardanelles and the Lord knows what, that I hardly know what to do'.[65] Such was Curzon's discontent that in August he suggested to Asquith that he might surrender the salary for the 'nominal office' of Lord Privy Seal.[66] By this time Asquith's unhappiness with aspects of Curzon's involvement in government work was evident. Writing to Crewe early in July about Curzon's description of the country as being in 'grave peril', Asquith observed that Curzon 'would have to have his comb clipped before long'.[67] Evidently Curzon's restlessness did little to commend him to Asquith when, having offered to surrender his salary, he proceeded to complain that, although he was supposed to know something of administration, he had been given the one office where there was nothing to administer.[68] That within several days of writing to Asquith in this manner Curzon was to refuse Asquith's offer that he might create and head a War Trade Department, supports the idea that Curzon was acutely anxious for involvement in imperial affairs.[69] Suggesting, repeatedly, that he might be found work on the Committee of Imperial Defence or on any of its sub-committees, Curzon observed: 'As one who was at the Foreign Office for three years, who served in India for seven, and who knows personally almost every country in Europe and Asia, I ought surely to be of greater use than I am now permitted to be.'[70]

Whether or not Asquith acted on Curzon's pleas is unclear. Early in August, Austen Chamberlain, the new Secretary of State for India, had written to Curzon at Grey's request offering him the chair of an inter-departmental committee on British policy in Persia. The Committee was Chamberlain's brainchild and in his view it 'should at least survey the position still further East and notably as regards Thibet'.[71] That both Lord Robert Cecil[72] and Chamberlain had expressed their willingness to receive any advice which Curzon might offer on the work of their departments added to Curzon's frustration when the Committee failed to meet.[73]

By this time, having obtained Foreign Office approval, Sir Henry McMahon had resumed his negotiations with Hussein. Apparently motivated primarily by a desire to leave Britain with room for manoeuvre, briefly McMahon agreed to Arab independence within a British protectorate.

According to Fromkin's analysis, McMahon proceeded with much evasion to eliminate all Arab territories from inclusion within this area of Arab independence.[74] Whilst territory west of Damascus, Aleppo, Homs and Hama could not, by virtue of French claims, be independent, the need for 'special administrative arrangements' for the Vilayets of Basra and Baghdad, in which Britain had interests, meant that Britain could not commit herself to their inclusion within the Arab Kingdom. In Syria and Palestine, McMahon stated that Britain was restricted by French interests and, as Fromkin alleges, given that France claimed both Syria and Palestine 'in their entirety . . . it followed that Britain could not pledge support for Arab claims with respect to them either – not even to Damascus, Aleppo, Homs, and Hama'.[75] Moreover, Britain's existing agreements with other leaders of the Arabian Peninsula entailed similar restrictions in the extent to which she could make pledges of independence with reference to the Peninsula. Neither in Cairo nor in London was McMahon believed to have committed Britain to anything.[76] Hussein remained bitterly opposed to any concessions to France in Syria and, in any case, the creation of an Arab Kingdom was held to be contingent upon the Arab rising against the Porte.

Curzon's anxiety to find a leading role was understandable. From the autumn of 1914, with the despatch of a British force to the Persian Gulf, events were afoot which might radically change the nature of Britain's eastern Empire. To Curzon it was, moreover, an opportunity to give expression to that strain of forward thinking with which his name had come to be associated. Confessing that he had not discussed the logistics of an advance on Baghdad with any soldiers, he informed Crewe in December 1914 that the distance from the Persian Gulf to Baghdad was roughly equivalent to that traversed by General Roberts on his march on Kabul and Kandahar in 1879. Recalling his own progression up the Tigris and Euphrates, Curzon thought it unlikely that a British force would encounter much resistance. As Curzon continued: 'Nor do I imagine that there would be much difficulty in holding Baghdad at any rate for the duration of the war. The effect of taking it would be *prodigious* throughout Asia and it would be a valuable piece when the game of chess begins.'[77]

The prospect of such gains in the east was tantalising. Crewe, reflecting that Britain did not have the troops to take and hold Baghdad, suggested that had Turkey declared war earlier then the Indian Army might have been assigned 'to carry out the conquest of Mesopotamia and even Asia Minor'.[78] This 'speculation' was, as Curzon observed,

> vastly interesting. But I should have liked had the men and the ships been forthcoming to have had a dash at Syria or Palestine and to have cut the Hedjaz Railway. Anyhow when the war is over keep an eye on Alexandretta. We always meant to have it in the old days. It is the complement to Cyprus and it would be agreeable to profit by the lavish expenditure of the Germans.[79]

Though Curzon accepted that Britain lacked the troops necessary to hold Baghdad, it seems that he was not deflected from his interest in a future British presence there.[80] Nor was he unduly perturbed by

Crewe's suggestion that any British landings on coastal Syria would impinge on the French sphere.[81] Curzon's mind was turning on the momentous changes in Anglo-Russian relations which were likely to arise as a result of British policies in the east. Writing to Crewe in mid-December 1914, on the subject of water sources north of Kurna, Curzon cast doubt on reports that the Russians were established on the Upper Euphrates. It was, however, conceivable, as Curzon continued, that they might be on the Upper Tigris:

> This left me thinking whether they might if they had a successful campaign in the mountains contemplate coming down into the plains. That would be rather inconvenient for us: as I imagine we don't want them putting in a rival claim to parts of Mesopotamia.[82]

By mid-March 1915, Curzon's concerns were mounting. To Cromer he confided his opposition to an advance on Baghdad and pointed out that recent Turkish attacks at Kurna and Ahwaz had demonstrated the dangers of such an undertaking. The difficulty, as Curzon observed, was that Basra had no obvious defensive frontier:

> I have been up the river, nay up both rivers, and I know the ground. We can make Mesopotamia pay a score of times over, and it will be a fine dumping-ground for Indian rayats. But it will be a big business holding and defending it. And what is much more serious . . . it involves the turning into a British sphere of the neutral zone in Southern Persia – which you have heard me denounce a dozen times in the House of Lords. This, of course, will not carry direct or administrative responsibility. But in the long run it means keeping order (as Persia has gone irretrievably to pieces); it means a coterminous frontier with Russia; and it means holding that frontier in the last resort with Indian troops.[83]

Curzon's unease was attributable to the poor showing of British troops in Egypt and to the lack of firm purpose behind the Dardanelles expedition.[84] Local intelligence suggested that Britain's position in Basra would encounter imminently fierce Turkish resistance. The outlook was bleak yet, as Curzon informed Crewe, local opinion was apparently 'united as to the necessity of an ultimate advance on Baghdad if we are to get the Arabs on our side'.[85] To facilitate this it had been put to Curzon that, ideally, the road between Tarsus and Bozante should be blocked.[86]

The success of British arms in Mesopotamia was, as Curzon realised, connected with the broader policy engineered by Kitchener of transferring the Khalifate to Arabia and of establishing an Arab Empire under British auspices. Curzon was hesitant in his acceptance of the scheme. Any announcement of British support must, in his view, await the psychological moment presented by the fall of Constantinople, yet in the spring of 1915 Curzon considered this unlikely.[87] Curzon was staggered by the scope of Arab territorial demands and failed to see any obvious candidate for the Khalifate or where it might be located. There was, moreover, the problem which troubled Curzon throughout the war that, having exerted considerable efforts to capture enemy territory in Mesopotamia, Britain proposed to give it to the Arabs who, as Curzon informed Cromer, 'are at this moment fighting against us as hard as they can, and are known to be in the pay of the Germans!' Equally, whilst exponents of Arab policy in Cairo made wide-ranging promises to the Arabs, they appeared to contemplate with equanimity the probable failure of the movement; something which Curzon felt must inevitably lead to Britain's embarrassment.[88]

Curzon's inclusion in the Dardanelles Committee provided relief from physical ailments and from the many aspects of government policy with which he disagreed. His exclusion from the bodies which replaced it, in spite of hints to Asquith, was something which Curzon found difficult to accept.[89] Having sought an interview with the Archbishop of Canterbury, Randall Davidson,[90] on 18 November, Curzon was apparently 'gravely disquieted about the whole position at home and abroad'. Though discounting much of what Curzon said in view of his 'objection to the Radical Government' and 'his own absence from the present War Council or Committee', Davidson recorded Curzon's outspokenness on the 'extraordinary difficulty' of having to assume responsibility for decisions taken by the War Council – such as Salonika – which were 'disastrously wrong'. Tempted to probe further, Davidson recalled:

> On my speaking of the value of his expert knowledge of Persia, Eastern Turkey and Afghanistan, he spoke rather bitterly. He says that never once since he has been in the Cabinet has he been asked one single question about one of these places or things. It has all been settled by the India Office or other people, most of whom, as he describes it, have not an idea where the places are, whereas he has written books about every bit of it and devoted years of his life to the study of this region.[91]

Though Davidson was equally inclined to discount Curzon's enthusiasm for the idea of Kitchener remaining in Egypt, on account of events in India a decade before, it seems likely that on this matter Curzon was sincere.[92] Aware of Asquith's low opinion of the Secretary for War, Curzon was to write to Asquith in December repeating his suggestion that Kitchener remain in Egypt and conveying his dislike of him.[93] Possibly rumour may have reached Curzon of his replacing Kitchener at the War Office.[94] Yet, while suggesting to Davidson that Kitchener lacked vision, Curzon admitted that in the matter of deciding where to make a stand against the German thrust on Baghdad his judgement was sound.[95] What Curzon actually meant was that having flirted with the idea of taking Baghdad for a year he had changed his mind and now positively advised its occupation by Britain.[96] On future occasions Curzon recalled with satisfaction that he alone of the War Cabinet[97] had rejected the proposed advance in the autumn of 1915.[98] Much has been made of the technical responsibility of General Nixon, Commander of the Mesopotamian Expeditionary Force, for that advance and the fact that, at best, as alleged by one author, he was at least unwilling to trust his intelligence sources.[99] Given the factors in play – the difficult terrain, poor communications, and limited intelligence – it would be astonishing if men of the calibre of Hirtzel, whose significance in encouraging the advance is often overlooked, would have so arranged matters as to leave the burden of responsibility at any door in Whitehall. As Hirtzel had written in December 1914 with reference to Mesopotamia, having invaded a country the natural tendency was to aim for its capital.[100] Accordingly, Britain might move at least to Baghdad, and Russia, in her move on Erzerum, might be expected to occupy Mosul.[101] At this early stage such thoughts were shared by, among others, Sir Louis Mallet, British Ambassador in Constantinople, and Hardinge and were at least implicit in Curzon's thinking.[102]

Of the early proponents of advance much will be made of Hirtzel, a man of remarkable percipience, who, in Mesopotamian affairs, exhibited a clarity of thought quite unequalled in any of his colleagues. This was partly owing to Hirtzel's success in grasping the true proportions of the interrelationship between British policy in the east and Moslem feeling. To this understanding of 'prestige' was added an acute awareness, again from an early stage, that the Arab Kingdom was a fantasy.

Late in 1915 Hirtzel felt that in his conversations with Hussein, McMahon had committed Britain too far.[103] Britain might be embarrassed if the scheme collapsed and Hirtzel was sceptical about the level of support among Indian Moslems for a change in the Khalifate.[104] More crucially, Hirtzel was perturbed by the strategic implications of a large Moslem entity established in proximity to British interests in the Middle East.[105] When commenting on a communication from Delhi on the dangers of an Arab State, Hirtzel observed in February 1916:

A strong Arab State might be more dangerous to Christendom than a strong Ottoman State, and Lord Kitchener's policy of destroying one Islamic State merely for the purpose of creating another, has always seemed to me disastrous, from the point of view no less of expediency than of civilization. The justification of the policy of HMG lies mainly in the fact that the Arabs have shown themselves incapable of creating or maintaining such a State; and, in as much as it will be to the joint interests of France, Russia and ourselves to prevent them from doing so in fact – while enabling them to present a suitable façade for the world – the policy is probably also free from practical danger. The danger of it, to my mind, lies in its disingenuousness.[106]

Unaffected by Hirtzel's momentary qualms about the moral propriety of policy, senior figures in Cairo saw things in similar terms. Writing in January 1916 Brigadier-General G.F. Clayton, Director of Intelligence in Cairo and an influential co-ordinating figure in eastern affairs, stated that Britain had never intended to create an Arab Kingdom as it 'might be a threat against [*sic*] British interests'.[107] Sir Reginald Wingate, Sirdar of the Sudan, had, when writing to Cromer in May 1915, referred to the Arab Empire as 'utopian'.[108]

As 1916 progressed Hussein's position became increasingly embattled and debate arose about the feasibility of sending him military assistance. Hirtzel argued that Britain was 'morally bound' to assist him and to sustain the Arab movement.[109] This formed part of strenuous efforts on Hirtzel's part to curb the more strident criticisms of Arab policy by the Government of India and India Office colleagues. Sir Thomas Holderness, the ever cautious Permanent Under-Secretary of State, felt that the conditions which had sustained the Ottoman Empire would never be reproduced in Arabia and Chamberlain considered a strong Arab State 'a creation of the imagination'.[110] By August, Chamberlain felt vindicated in the belief that Arab unity 'was a myth'.[111] A month later Holderness commented that 'a union of Kilkenny cats would be hardly less fanciful' and in December he uttered the damning observation: 'There can be no building without bricks: and there are no bricks, as far as we can see, for constructing an Arab Empire.'[112]

Moral obligations aside, Hirtzel supported the Arab movement because, like Clayton, Wingate and others, he realised that much could be achieved by supporting an Arab Empire. Much to Hirtzel's disgust the inter-departmental De Bunsen Committee,[113] established by Asquith in the spring of 1915 to define British desiderata in Asia, had pronounced against a simple partition of the Arab Middle East between the

Allies. Whilst there was much scepticism of the Arab movement at the Foreign Office, there was no driving impetus there to seek alternative means of securing British territorial gain in the Middle East.[114] To Hirtzel the acquisitive momentum might best be sustained by close involvement with the creation of the Arab 'façade' and the development of this policy throughout the war will be studied in detail.

Connected with this approach to the Arab movement was a feeling that the risk of Jehad or an easterly penetration by enemy agents was exaggerated. In Hirtzel's hands this proved a potent weapon in fomenting an atmosphere in which British military gains in the east were seen in the context of Moslem opinion. The contention that prestige was an important factor in policy formulation is plausible. On the outbreak of war and until the spring of 1917 it was Hirtzel's task to analyse the possibly deleterious effects of British policy on Moslem feeling in India. Though not amounting in severity to a full extraction, that policy was, at least, a thorough and uncomfortable probing involving a landing in Mesopotamia, plans for the partition of the Ottoman Empire, the supplanting of and revolt against the Khalif, and a military assault against the traditional seat of that potentate, presumably entailing all of the risks previously connected with the failure of such a policy.[115] Having monitored the effects of British policy Hirtzel was not perturbed by the possibility of Indian insurrection. A policy of education (propaganda), of rapid and ruthless suppression of insurrection, and, as David French concedes, of active counter-intelligence was sufficient to contain the danger.[116]

To many of Hirtzel's colleagues this atmosphere of sensitivity to Moslem feeling was an impelling factor in the forward policy adopted in Mesopotamia. Reflecting on continued stalemate at the Dardanelles, Hardinge wrote to Nicolson on 23 September 1915:

> Now, it has been our policy and intention not to advance in Mesopotamia beyond the limits of the province of Busrah, and we have always considered that Kut-el-Amara would be our advanced post. It seems to me, however, that if we are unable, for a long time to come, to force the Dardanelles, it becomes a question whether we should not strike a blow somewhere, and we could do this quite easily by taking Baghdad . . . The capture of Baghdad would, from our point of view and that of Persia and Afghanistan, have a far greater effect than the capture of the Straits and Constantinople, and I am not sure that it will not have to be done. Had the Dardanelles and Constantinople fallen, I always counted on Baghdad falling like a ripe plum into our lap.[117]

Proximity to the likely focus of Jehad in India influenced the judgement of many in their assessment of the potency of that threat and this was true throughout the war.[118] Whilst it is not proposed to discuss Gallipoli here, considerations of prestige did feature prominently in arguments against evacuation.[119] Yet the possibility of failure at the Dardanelles and the likely effect of this on Moslem opinion was not sufficient to prevent the expedition. Moreover, there was widespread sympathy for an advance in Mesopotamia and for the Arab revolt long before either policy, partly on grounds of prestige, was sanctioned.[120] Nor, in spite of the misgivings of many senior figures, did risings occur when Gallipoli was evacuated and when Britain was repulsed at Kut.[121] This may partly account for Hardinge's change of heart on the matter of Jehad. Writing in July 1916, with the perspective afforded from observing events from afar, Hardinge suggested that the time had come to grasp the nettle.[122]

Though Curzon argued eloquently against the evacuation of Gallipoli, on grounds of its deleterious effect among Indian Moslems, generally he refrained from the more cataclysmic assessments favoured by others.[123] When he did indulge in such speculations it was only in his blackest moods and, even then, he perceived full-scale Jehad as remote.[124] Whilst, like many others, in the autumn of 1915 Curzon believed occupation of Baghdad would have a salutary effect, though not apparently sufficient to offset withdrawal from Gallipoli, it is questionable to what extent either Curzon or Hardinge was aware of any notion of playing off Arab nationalism against pan-Islamism.[125] This was implicit in Curzon's role in policy formulation in the following years and was reflected in an interview between Curzon and Randall Davidson on 6 October 1916. Responding to the argument of Sir William Robertson, CIGS, that Britain should withdraw from Mesopotamia, Curzon felt that this would compound the impression of defeat created by withdrawal from the Dardanelles and by Britain's failure to press the advance in Mesopotamia. Now that occupation seemed possible, militarily, Curzon observed: '[G]o on – occupy Baghdad, show your strength and then if you think wiser to leave it in Arab hands (supposing the Arab revolt to succeed) good and well.'[126]

THE ADVANCE ON BAGHDAD

In the recriminations which followed the advance on Baghdad much was to be made of the culpability of Hardinge and E.G. Barrow in their support for the move.[127] Barrow argued subsequently that he was only one of a number of experts who had been similarly inclined.[128] Hirtzel and his deputy, J.E. Shuckburgh,[129] had been outspoken on possession of the city preventing the successful prosecution of enemy schemes of military and psychological penetration to the east.[130] Nicolson had written to Hardinge in this sense in October 1915, repeatedly expressing the hope that Britain might occupy Baghdad.[131] Curzon claimed with pride his dissent from the decision to advance but Randall Davidson recorded that on 18 November, several weeks after the Dardanelles Committee had provisionally sanctioned the move but before General Nixon had been rebuffed by Turkish forces, Curzon was 'distinctly in favour of our taking Baghdad'.[132] On the following day at the War Cabinet, presumably on the basis of Nixon's over-optimistic reports, Chamberlain passed Curzon the following note:

> I think that the Germans are now deliberately spreading exaggerated reports as to Turkish reinforcements whilst also discounting the prospects of the early fall of Baghdad. I *think* Nixon can both take and hold the place, I cannot say there is no danger that in time the Turks might not prove too strong for him. But I think it unlikely because of the difficulty they would have in concentrating and supplying such a force.[133]

Curzon later recalled that his stand against the advance at the Dardanelles Committee on 21 October was due to his anticipation of an enemy attack 'in strength' as part of Germany's 'scheme to drive us right back to the Persian Gulf'.[134] In fact, Curzon was equally concerned that a British occupation, if it were to be sustained, would entail military commitments beyond Baghdad itself, possibly extending to Alexandretta.[135] For Chamberlain, who seemed to attach some importance to Curzon's opinions on the subject, Curzon summarised his conclusions:

> though he would not be called an exponent of a forward policy, he would clearly like to go to Baghdad, but he was nervous. If we attempted to hold it for six months or a year, and if the Germans and the Turks pushed eastwards, our position would be precarious, and retirement would counteract our momentary advantage. As a layman he was diffident against going. His advice was 'don't go'.[136]

Lord Bertie, Britain's Ambassador in Paris, was to record Curzon's opinion that he alone of the Dardanelles Committee opposed an advance.[137] The issue was complicated by the possibility of Britain staging a temporary occupation and by the variety of reasons advanced in support of occupation. Like Curzon, many high-ranking officials and statesmen were clearly nervous. As Selborne[138] implied, this nervousness about the force necessary for the advance veiled a general consensus in favour of advance; and this dichotomy was embodied in the instructions transmitted to Delhi on 21 October.[139] By virtue of this communication, prepared jointly by Grey, Kitchener, Chamberlain and Balfour, Hardinge was informed: 'Unless you consider that possibility of eventual withdrawal is decisive against the advance, all other considerations seem to us to render it desirable, and we are prepared to order it.'[140]

The disingenuousness of Curzon's recollections must therefore be seen in the context of the hypocrisy of many senior officials. Also, until recently, historians have accepted at face value the interpretation of the advance presented by the Mesopotamia Commission and endorsed, with reservations, in a report prepared by Curzon, at the request of the Cabinet, on the culpability of those involved.[141]

According to Rothwell, in Mesopotamian affairs Curzon was as able as Hardinge to display an 'unpleasing Machiavellism'.[142] Perhaps, as Grigg has written, shiftiness would be more appropriate.[143] Certainly Hirtzel's Machiavellian credentials were superlative.[144] Although Douglas Goold admits that 'Hardinge was far from being alone in his imperial aspirations for Mesopotamia', in his analysis of Hardinge's 'policy of advance' he fails to place the Viceroy's views in context.[145] Like many contemporary policy-makers, Hardinge's thoughts on Mesopotamia were acquisitive, but they were also based on assessments of the inherent value of Mesopotamia which were current long before his Viceroyalty.[146] Goold identifies an extension of Hardinge's 'war aims' in 1915 and an awareness on his part 'that policies and proposals were emanating from too many centres and that there was a vast gap between hopes and their fulfilment'.[147] This may be accurate but they must be seen against the concept of 'duty' expounded by Asquith which led the De Bunsen Committee[148] to define desiderata far in excess of anything suggested by Hardinge.[149] They were not, however, in advance of the hopes, clearly defined in official memoranda or expressed at meetings of the War Cabinet, of men such as Kitchener, Hirtzel and Balfour.

Hardinge's thoughts must also be seen in the context of the expansionist designs which emerged in discussions surrounding the Baghdad advance. Whilst Curzon cited, as a reason against the advance, the possibility that operations at Alexandretta would be necessary, according to Hankey, Secretary of the War Cabinet, Grey contemplated this with equanimity.[150] Grey was convinced by arguments suggesting that negotiations with the Arabs had reached a critical stage and that a tangible demonstration of British strength was necessary to ensure their unity and loyalty. It was, moreover, unmistakable that the Arab claims to independence in inland Syria would inevitably lead to a clash with France. The Arab Kingdom, if it were realised, would be under British auspices whilst, if it failed, Britain, by virtue of her support of it, would have a strong moral claim to occupy and retain those territories pertaining to it.

Aubrey Herbert favoured the removal of French influence from inland Syria by the promise of territory elsewhere, feeling that the alternatives which remained much the same in 1918–19, of telling France that her intransigence would lead to trouble, or of encouraging her to accept 'a wider sphere of influence with a broader measure of autonomy for the inhabitants of that sphere', were unattractive. As Herbert argued, was it reasonable to expect Britain to prosecute major operations in the east to realise French claims which were 'after all a matter mainly of sentiment'?[151]

Curzon could not resist such opportunities and the possibility of ousting France from inland Syria presented by the Anglo-Arab negotiations was one element in his change of heart regarding an advance on Baghdad and an occupation of Alexandretta.[152] Certainly, Curzon's enthusiasm was sufficient for him to send Herbert's suggestions to Grey and was reflected in his disappointment when it emerged exactly what Britain had promised France in Syria and Mosul by virtue of negotiations initiated later in 1915.[153]

The question arises whether, in view of the strength of feeling within official circles about the desirability of occupying Baghdad in October 1915, Hardinge could reasonably be expected to have been preoccupied with the problems identified by Goold; problems which were as irrelevant at the time as Hardinge's belief that from a strategic perspective Mesopotamia, like the Dardanelles, East Africa and Salonika, was a blunder.[154] On 3 November Asquith spoke to Parliament of Force 'D' being 'within measurable distance of Baghdad'. Asquith continued: 'I do not think that in the whole course of the War there has been a series of operations more carefully contrived, more brilliantly conducted, and with a better chance of final success.'[155]

The disingenuousness exhibited by Curzon and others was, as Hirtzel freely admitted, the bedrock of his Mesopotamian policy. The importance of Mesopotamia as the show-piece of British imperialism in World War I and as the 'ganglion' of the Middle East is reflected in the following chapters. None was more acutely aware of this importance than the man who thus described it, Arnold Talbot Wilson,[156] who attained the position of Acting Civil Commissioner of Mesopotamia. None, equally, was more representative of the spirit of British imperialism in Mesopotamia, of the onward and 'immense momentum of the machine'.[157] For Wilson, war was a purifying experience in which the immensity of the undertaking of British policy in Mesopotamia was fully reflected in a robust ego.[158] To Hirtzel, in his eyrie in Whitehall, fell the task of channelling these currents and overseeing the warp and weft of policy in Mesopotamia, and frequent reference will be made to the relationship between Hirtzel and Wilson, embodying as it did the broader aspects of policy.

The timing of Bertie's remark that several Cabinet ministers wished Curzon to replace Kitchener suggests that it was partly Curzon's admittedly impressive role in the Baghdad advance at the Dardanelles Committee on 21 October that was responsible for this.[159] This experience of Mesopotamian affairs was an important factor in the decision in March 1917 to delegate to Curzon direction of British policy there.

In the short term Curzon's prominence in the Baghdad controversy served to compound his despair. His predicament in the following months was captured by Crewe, writing early in 1916 in response to a letter from Curzon in which he requested fair participation in the despatch of government business in the House of Lords.[160] Stating that he had spoken to Asquith and other colleagues on the matter, Crewe's description of Curzon resembling 'a Rolls-Royce car, with a highly competent driver, kept to take an occasional parcel to the station' caused mild consternation in Carlton House Terrace.[161] This was particularly so given Crewe's subsequent evasiveness when Curzon repeated his grievance.[162] A month later Curzon's restlessness took a new turning. Having requested a meeting with Hankey to discuss various aspects of aviation, the latter recorded that Curzon 'evidently wants to be the first Minister of the air, and gave me strong hints about his desire to be a member of the War Committee'.[163] Hankey was wrong on at least one point: that he had convinced Curzon of the impossibility of establishing an Air Department.[164] It was precisely on the possibility of undertaking such a department, as a Cabinet Minister, that Curzon wrote to Asquith in March. As Curzon observed, the work of the Shipping Committee, to which he had been assigned as Chairman but which had proved no more than a temporary diversion, was finished and he was feeling utterly useless in a Cabinet where I have nothing to do: I have greater administrative experience than most of my colleagues and could not have been in the India Office for a year, the Foreign Office five years, and head of the Government of India for seven years without having something. I feel quite ashamed at the position I occupy in the greatest crisis of our history when all my knowledge and experience, such as they are, are thrown away. I have often thought seriously whether I ought not to resign . . . As it is the Lord Privy Seal is a mere 'transient and embarrassed phantom' impotent for good or evil.[165]

Hardinge's remark that Curzon tended to poke his nose in everywhere had a ring of truth, yet Curzon's subsequent political marginalisation in the course of 1916 served to ensure that when he attained a position of authority, there was a prolonged and bloody retribution as his ego battled with a system which had excluded him for so long.[166] This was starkly displayed in the field of British policy in the Middle East.

By the end of 1915 Curzon was firmly in the forward school which had, a month previously, favoured advance in Mesopotamia. As we have seen, this school attracted considerable support from many quarters and was best exemplified by an analysis of British interests undertaken several months before by the De Bunsen Committee.[167]

THE DE BUNSEN COMMITTEE

Analysing the factors which bore upon the problem of the future of Ottoman territories in Asia, the De Bunsen Committee assumed the defeat of Germany and the demise of her schemes of economic and political penetration.[168] Furthermore, the Committee felt that French and Russian imperialism would receive a considerable fillip from the war and that, in the future, Britain would at least face rivalry if not outright hostility from these powers. Given the belief that Britain already had sufficient responsibilities, the Committee suggested that Britain's aim should be to safeguard her position in the Persian Gulf. Connected with this, however, was the need to safeguard the approaches to the Gulf and, irrespective of the scheme which might ultimately be devised to achieve this, the Committee was receptive to wide-reaching measures in defining basic desiderata. The first solution on which the Committee elaborated was the possibility of a partition of the Ottoman Empire between the Allies with the maintenance of a limited area of Turkish sovereignty in Anatolia. Under this scheme the defence of Britain's position in the Persian Gulf would involve the annexation of the

Vilayets of Basra, Baghdad and most of Mosul, the creation of a British port on the Mediterranean and the connection of this port with the Persian Gulf and Baghdad via Abu Kemal, with a branch line linking Baghdad and Mosul. The need for such a port, besides commercial considerations, was principally with a view to the rapid reinforcement of Mesopotamia in the event of a Russian invasion. In view of the proximity of Alexandretta to the proposed Russian sphere the Committee considered Haifa preferable. This would also obviate future difficulties caused by French claims in Syria and Cilicia. The extensive nature of the British sphere was attributable to three factors. Firstly, the Committee felt that a defensive frontier could only be found among the mountains to the north of Mosul. Secondly, the Committee tended to agree with Hirtzel's arguments about the interdependence and inseparability of the Vilayets of Mesopotamia in terms of navigation, irrigation, oil extraction and, generally, on the basis of commerce and development. This argument applied with equal force on strategic grounds, for Britain, established as the 'gate-keeper at Basra', must inevitably succumb to the forces of France and Russia in their inexorable southerly movement. Thirdly, it was felt that in view of the extent of international competition, Britain should 'ensure that the regions left to our trade shall be extensive, capable of development, and self-supporting, and that it shall be in our power to prevent all and any unfair competition'.

Vitally, in adopting a forward line of defence north of Mosul, Britain would to a considerable extent be abandoning the traditional policy of interposing a buffer between Russia and British possessions in Asia. In certain areas the presence of France might provide some security but the possibility of a hostile Franco-Russian combination had also to be considered.

The decision of the Committee to support the idea of an Ottoman Empire with decentralised areas of local administration, was influenced primarily by a desire to keep Britain's hands free for the future. As A.S. Klieman suggests, the Committee was also motivated by an awareness that partition would be a divisive factor among the Allies.[169] Whilst the scheme of partition, or the establishing of zones of Allied interest in the same areas, involved considerable extensions of responsibility, decentralisation would permit Britain to develop her economic interests in the sphere reserved for her in the partition scheme and would not preclude future extensions of British political control should the Ottoman Empire collapse.[170]

MAP 1.   SCHEME

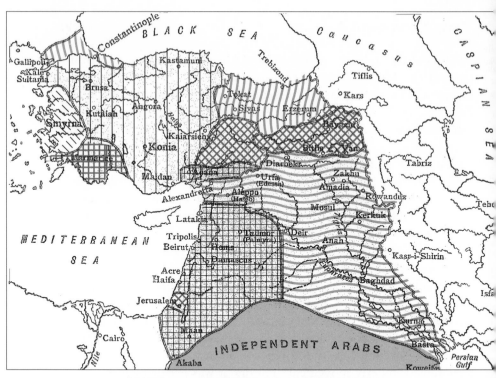

MAP I   1st SCHEME OF ANNEXATION
including Alexandretta in British Territory

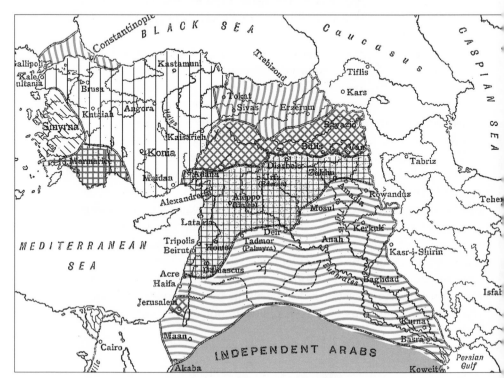

MAP II   2nd SCHEME OF ANNEXATION
replacing Alexandretta by Haifa

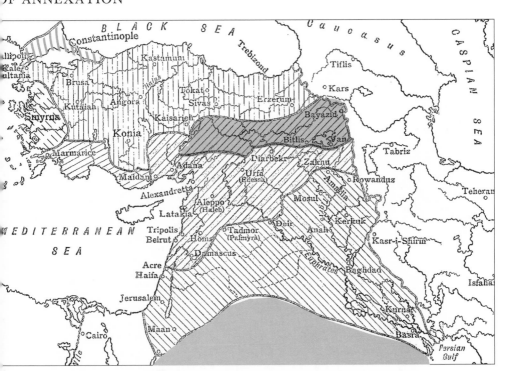

MAP III   ZONES OF INTEREST

		Zones
French		
Russian		
Greek (possible)		
Italian (possible)		
British		
Ottoman		
Independent Arabs		
Special administrations		

MAP 1 (continued)

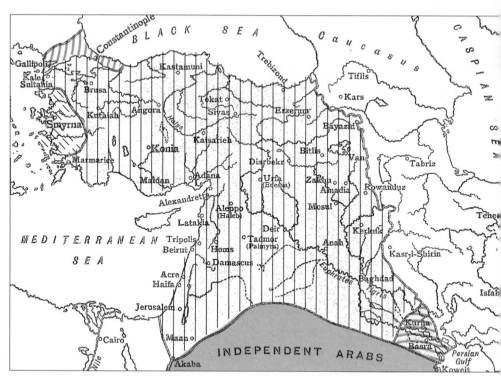

MAP IV   OTTOMAN INDEPENDENCE

		Zones
French		
Russian		
Greek (possible)		
Italian (possible)		
British		
Ottoman		
Independent Arabs		
Special administrations		

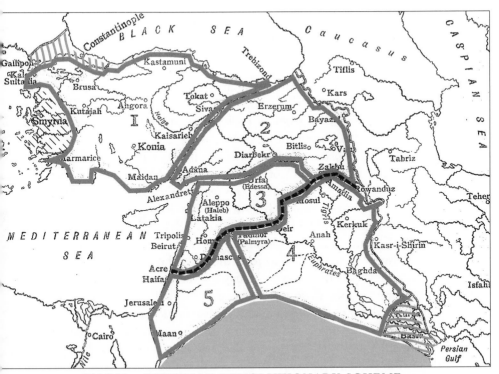

MAP V   OTTOMAN DEVOLUTIONARY SCHEME

Map showing the areas of the five Ayalets: 1. Anatolia   2. Armenia   3. Syria   4. Jazirah-Irak   5. Palestine

▬ ▬ ▬ ▬   Northern boundary of British sphere of enterprise

Source: PRO ref: CAB 27/1

Curzon's change of heart on the matter of Baghdad and a possible occupation of Alexandretta was undoubtedly influenced by consideration of the offensive intentions and capabilities of Germany and Turkey. In strategic terms, however, it seems likely that Curzon's mind was turning on the growing possibility that Russia would be unable to secure possession of Constantinople, Armenia and Kurdistan. This was a cardinal factor in the Anglo-French negotiations which commenced at the end of 1915, by virtue of which there emerged the Sykes–Picot Agreement of February 1916.[171] Named after its joint authors, Sir Mark Sykes[172] and Monsieur Georges Picot, the French representative, the Agreement, like the De Bunsen analysis, was designed with reference to a post-war world in which Britain and her Allies would compete for influence in the Middle East.[173] Implicit in Sykes–Picot, however, was that the Ottoman Empire would not survive the war and, accordingly, the division of territories which emerged, though stopping short of the partition scheme with a British outlet on the Mediterranean at Alexandretta, bore close resemblance both to the alternative partition scheme with an outlet at Haifa and to the zones of interest scheme. The main differences lay in the curtailing of the area of British influence in the Mosul Vilayet and in the considerable extension of the French area to include Sivas, Diarbekir and a considerable portion of the Mosul Vilayet extending east beyond Rowanduz. In addition, the areas of French and British influence would be divided between areas of economic priority and areas of direct or indirect control. Under Sykes–Picot, although Britain retained access to Haifa, Palestine was to be internationalised.

The Sykes–Picot Agreement was largely based upon the thinking with which Sykes had opposed the partition option at meetings of the De Bunsen Committee. It was, moreover, a perspective which Sykes, from his position on the periphery of officialdom, was to advance with some success in the following years, notwithstanding the resentment of several senior figures towards his activities as an 'amateur' diplomat. Although 'colonialist' in its general outline, the Agreement was bitterly opposed by proponents of partition for the reason that it appeared voluntarily to impose severe restraints on British gains while ceding considerable territories to France.[174] Whilst Hirtzel and others were attempting to establish an acquisitive momentum which would leave Britain in possession of Mosul and, if necessary, coterminous with Russia, British negotiators appeared to have reverted with a vengeance to a buffer theory which, as Hirtzel pointed out, it had never been the intention to sustain.[175] In opposing partition the De Bunsen Report suggested that, in seeking the liberation of Armenia, Cilicia, Syria, Mosul and lower Mesopotamia, Britain would be compelled to continue hostilities against Turkey for what the report implied were imperialist reasons.[176] There was, moreover, according to the report, the possibility that such gains would adversely affect Moslem opinion, that possible British commercial gains in Mesopotamia would not offset British losses in areas assigned to her Allies, and that in increasing her territorial responsibilities Britain would merely present her rivals with a bigger target.[177] Finally, as the report argued:

> We should have destroyed the political power of Islam represented by Turkey, and at the same time, by our annexation of Mesopotamia, have made it clear to all Moslems that any hope of an Arab Khalifate acquiring material wealth and prosperity sufficient to restore a Moslem State that would count among the Governments of the world was henceforth impossible.[178]

In their efforts to escape from the perversity of this logic and from the consequences of the failure to take Baghdad, Hirtzel and others were to see that much could be achieved by virtue of an opportunistic alliance with men like Sykes, who came to believe in the possibility of Arab independence.[179] Sykes–Picot did not attempt to define an area in which such independence might take root nor was it considered, other than by Sykes, to tie in with the arrangements which were being discussed concurrently between McMahon and Hussein. However, Sykes–Picot did provide for Damascus, Aleppo, Homs and Hama as falling within the area of indirect exclusively French influence.

Curzon, like Hirtzel, was aghast at the prospect of France obtaining so much territory and influence when Russia was sickening, when Britain appeared to get no more than was rightfully hers, and when Britain was apparently to get no quid pro quo for those additional territories destined for French control.[180] Curzon was similarly dismayed by the fact that he had not been consulted on the terms of the Agreement and that, according to his recollection, it had not been referred to the Cabinet for its approval.[181]

THE SYKES–PICOT AGREEMENT

The Sykes–Picot Agreement, 'that much abused instrument' as Hirtzel called it, provided an enduring stimulus to those who wished to expand

British territories in the east.[182] Essentially this was due to the discrepancies between it and the first partition scheme outlined in the
De Bunsen Report which was, as Klieman alleges, the solution most
widely supported at the time.[183] The passage of time compounded the
deficiencies of the Agreement in the eyes of many officials, not least
because France failed to take any steps to secure those territories allotted
to her. The story of British 'war imperialism' in the Middle East is
inextricably linked with the attitudes of senior figures towards Sykes–
Picot and with the limitations which it was seen to impose on British
gains. This was true of policy in Mesopotamia, Palestine, Syria and the
Arabian Peninsula and each will be discussed. Furthermore, it seems
likely that the frustrations of the imperialists by virtue of the Agreement
found some expression in schemes for permanent British involvement
in the Caucasus.

There was strong criticism of Sykes–Picot from its inception and this
developed into a deep cynicism. Grey was sceptical about the
Agreement ever being realised and Balfour objected to Russian gains in
Armenia as it would draw her closer to the Persian Gulf.[184] It is in fact
debatable whether, as Klieman seems to imply, many policy-makers
ever really abandoned their loyalties to the territorial divisions of the
partition scheme which provided for British retention of Alexandretta.[185]
The means by which it was sought to abandon the fetters of Sykes–Picot
disguised a fairly widespread consensus on the matter. Curzon's conviction of the need for physical occupation grew as Russian power
ebbed and, paradoxically, as America, with her ill-conceived notions of
self-determination, entered the war. Though publicly enthusiastic on
this matter, Curzon had an abiding suspicion of Woodrow Wilson, of
his motives, and of the 'very dangerous places' into which the 'world
worship of so-called democracy is leading us'.[186] To Curzon, Britain's
Arab policy was another symptom of the disease of democracy and it
was with considerable difficulty, and only partial success, that Curzon
was made to see that British gains might only be secured by the creation
at least of a façade of Arab independence.

From the summer of 1917, when an awareness of 'international'
opinion became a vital factor in policy formulation, Curzon's myopia
was a key factor in efforts by the Foreign and India Offices to minimise
his influence.[187] This was also a major factor in the serious and sustained
efforts made during 1918 to alter the nature of control of British policy
in the Middle East.[188] This fascinating and complex matter cannot be
discussed in detail except in so far as these efforts appeared likely to

affect Curzon's personal position as Chairman of the Eastern Committee.[189] That Curzon did feel threatened is made evident by his
recourse to a confidant, in this case Hankey, something that he rarely
did.[190] Yet Curzon's insecurity was justified, as a very poisonous brew of
departmentalism, traditions of authority, international trends, personal
animosity and ambition were at work. Robert Cecil's conviction that
Curzon should be by-passed altogether in the formulation of eastern
policy is best summarised in Cecil's description of the function of the
Assistant Secretary of State of a proposed Middle East Department of
the Foreign Office. This, as Cecil informed Balfour in August 1918,
amounted to 'founding an administrative department for dealing with a
new Empire'.[191] Some effort will be made to unravel this in the following chapters.

A further important consideration of the War Imperialists in
attempting to revise or abandon Sykes–Picot was the collapse of Tsarist
Russia. Like many of his colleagues Curzon was distressed by what he
considered to be the treachery of Britain's traditional rival in Asia but,
again like several colleagues, he perceived this temporary indisposition
at St Petersburg as an opportunity for a general advance in Asia.[192] This
was true of Persia, where Curzon pressed for the extension of the
Nushki Railway into the neutral zone created by the Anglo-Russian
Convention of 1907, and in Mesopotamia with the capture of Baghdad.
In both cases Curzon's thinking was shared by Hardinge who, for some
time before the fall of Baghdad, had been sensitive to Russian ambitions
in Mesopotamia.[193] Both men had considerable experience of Russian
policy in Asia and, even if the post-bellum arrangements which each
sought to create with Russia differed, their final preoccupation was with
a united and hostile Russia. This was masked by more immediate concerns, such as the unravelling of Sykes–Picot, by the rivalry of France
and Italy, and by criticism of Curzon's handling of such issues.

As we shall see such criticism was common during the period
1918–19, not only from Robert Cecil but from others who, like Sir
Mark Sykes, made plain their belief that Curzon's approach to the
problems of the Middle East was outdated.[194] Whilst it is difficult to
assess precisely to what extent the imperialists purposely exaggerated
the ambitions of Britain's Allies in the Middle East to justify tighter
control here or military advance there, that these threats, real or otherwise, sustained the forward impulse in some measure is beyond doubt.

A significant preoccupation for the forward thinkers was the
phenomenon of *Drang nach Osten*, the anticipated onslaught of Turco-

MAP 2. THE SYKES–PICOT AGREEMENT

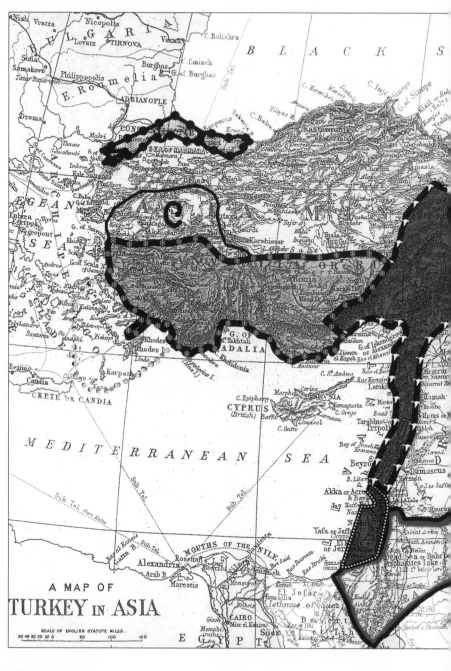

French sphere   Italian sphere

British sphere   Russian sphere

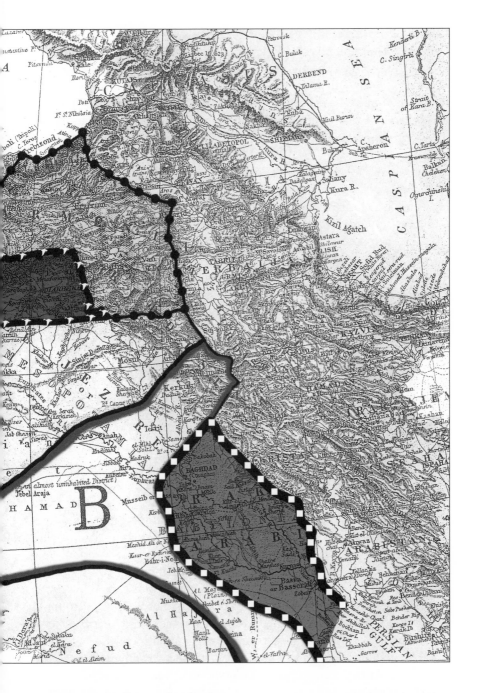

······· International sphere

C = Italian sphere of influence
A and B = Independent Arab State,
A being in the French, and B in the
British, sphere of influence

Source: PRO ref: FO 925/41157

German forces in the van of propaganda, sweeping first through Palestine, Mesopotamia and Egypt and then, with the collapse of Russia, in a northerly route through the Turkik Republics of Central Asia. The opportunities for advance presented by the development of that threat was something which Curzon, Hirtzel and others perceived from an early stage. From the spring of 1917, on the matter of German ambitions for world domination, Curzon would find an outspoken ally in Captain Leo Amery, MP.[195]

The significance of the relationship between Curzon and Amery is difficult to judge. Initially there was much suspicion of Amery, particularly in Conservative circles, and it may be that Curzon shared this.[196] Certainly, although there was some scope for collusion, he and Amery admired each other from afar. Partly this was due to the fact that Amery was by nature a forward planner and an innovator.[197] This led him to evolve plans for the defence of British possessions in the east which attracted the guarded support of many senior figures. The conceptual basis on which Curzon came to view the defeat of *Drang nach Osten* owed much to Amery's long and wide-ranging memoranda, yet, encumbered by *realpolitik,* senior figures were selective in the implementation of Amery's plans. This was true also of Milner[198] when Secretary of State for War, and of Sir Henry Wilson[199] as CIGS, both of whom, by virtue of their positions, were obliged unwillingly to reconcile ambitious imperial objectives with increasingly slender imperial resources. There was, moreover, the fact that whether writing about Palestine, Mesopotamia, Syria, or the Caucasus and beyond, Amery's ideas were invariably couched in a distinctively broad context either of Middle Eastern or world geopolitics. Fine tuning might render this framework acceptable to a wide audience but the lateral angle from which Amery assessed British interests in the Middle East was innovatory, perhaps rather too much so, for his views to synchronise with Curzon's. During 1917, however, there was some collaboration. The collapse of Russia led Curzon and Amery to champion forward policies in the Middle East without reference to 'the old gang'.[200] Curzon watched with fascination as Amery plotted the more northerly route of *Drang nach Osten,* yet with the extension of the scope of Curzon's executive authority on Middle Eastern matters, Curzon himself came under fire, albeit indirectly, from Amery.[201] With the development of *Drang nach Osten* Amery campaigned tirelessly for greater co-ordination in British policy and operations in the Middle East. It remains unclear what, if any, influence Amery had in the creation of the Eastern

Committee, but it is plain that Amery was keenly aware of the personal shortcomings which helped alienate Curzon from his colleagues.[202] Without access to the Amery papers it is difficult to assess the intrigue factor in Amery's conduct.[203] Amery could undoubtedly speak openly to Lloyd George about the removal of senior figures or even criticise Lloyd George himself.[204] Lloyd George was, of course, capable of contemplating the removal of Balfour without Amery's prompting and, in any case, his disenchantment with 'the old gang' was every bit as deep as Amery's.[205]

Curzon's satisfaction on the creation of the Middle East and Eastern Committees was short-lived and predictably failed to bring any significant remission in the perpetual struggle which characterised his involvement in official business. Ill-health, dissatisfaction with the transaction of Cabinet business, lingering frustration with his previous exclusion from high office, departmentalism among colleagues on the Eastern Committee and uncertainty about the future buttressed that prickliness and fullness of character which, as Montagu wrote in mid-June 1918, 'amuses me, interests me, irritates me'.[206]

NOTES

1. Herbert had travelled widely in the east and served in Flanders, Gallipoli, Mesopotamia, and in the Balkans. Regarded by some as a maverick figure, he attempted to broker a peace between Britain and Turkey in 1917.
2. See M. Gilbert, *The Challenge of War, Winston S. Churchill 1914–16* (London, 1990), pp. 222–3.
3. Entry for 15 January 1915, Diaries of Aubrey Herbert, reel 1, vol. 4; for an assessment of French interests in the Levant and in Syria see J. Nevakivi, *Britain, France and the Arab Middle East, 1914–20* (London, 1969), pp. 5ff., 30–1; H. Sachar, *The Emergence of the Middle East 1914–20* (London, 1969), pp. 161–4.
4. Ibid., Herbert Diaries.
5. Ibid. See also entries for 23 and 28 January and 5 February 1915.
6. Ibid. Entry of 16 February 1915. Catoni, who had acted as Consul at Aleppo for several years, became Vice-Consul at Alexandretta in 1877.
7. Ibid. Memorandum by Herbert, n.d., DD/DRU 35 part marked 'IIIb'.
8. Ibid.
9. Ibid. See also Herbert to Lord Robert Cecil, 22 June 1915, H.Q. New Zealand and Australian Division, Anzac Cove, Gallipoli Peninsula, DD/DRU 33. Cecil was Parliamentary Under-Secretary of State for Foreign Affairs.
10. Ibid. Memorandum.
11. Ibid.
12. Ibid.
13. Note on Mr Cheetham's Proposals for Operations in Syria, n.d., General Staff, War Office Papers WO 106/1570. Cheetham had been Counsellor in Cairo from July 1911.
14. Ibid.
15. See, for example, Memorandum by Lt. H. Pirie-Gordon, RNVR Intelligence Officer HMS *Doris*; enclosure no. 3 in East Indies letter no. 1081 of 22 March 1915, to Director of Intelligence, Cairo, Herbert Papers DD/DRU 35.
16. Storrs to Kitchener, 4 February 1915, The Residency, Cairo, Kitchener Papers, Public Record

Office Papers (hereafter PRO) 30/57, 47/QQ15. Storrs was Acting Oriental Secretary at the Agency in Cairo from 1909 and was on special service in Jerusalem from December 1917. Kitchener was Secretary of State for War and a member of the War Cabinet from 1914 and was Storrs's mentor. He had wide experience of the east gained in a distinguished military career. Between 1911–14 he was HM's Agent and Consul-General in Egypt.

17. Ibid. Storrs to Fitzgerald, 28 December 1914, British Agency, Cairo, 45/00 73.

18. Ibid.

19. See n. 16

20. Storrs to his parents, 22 February 1915, The Residency, Cairo, private, Storrs Papers II.3; quoted in J.K. Tanenbaum, 'France and the Arab Middle East 1914–1920', *Transactions of the American Philosophical Society (TAPS)*, vol. 68, pt 7 (1978), p. 7.

21. Grey, who was Foreign Secretary between December 1905 and December 1916, was considered by Aubrey Herbert, among others, to have little interest in or grasp of eastern affairs.

22. Storrs to Fitzgerald, 8 March 1915, The Residency, Cairo, private, Kitchener Papers, PRO 30/57 QQ 18; see also E. Kedourie, 'Cairo and Khartoum on the Arab Question', in *The Chatham House Version and other Middle Eastern Studies* (Hanover/London, 1984), p. 17. As will be seen, the fact that British gains in the region did not develop precisely in the manner envisaged by Storrs and Kitchener was no indication that their thoughts became redundant. Rather, international, regional and domestic political developments necessitated the evolution of other political configurations, albeit underpinned by an equally powerful commitment to imperial expansion.

23. See n. 20

24. Secretary's Notes of a Meeting of the War Council, 10 March 1915, secret, Cabinet Papers (hereafter CAB) 22/1/2. As Nevakivi suggests, early in 1915 Kitchener had little respect for French claims in Syria: J. Nevakivi, 'Lord Kitchener and the Partition of the Ottoman Empire 1915–16', in *Studies in International History: Essays Presented to W. Norton Medlicott*, ed. K. Bourne and D.C. Watt (London, 1967).

25. Ibid.

26. Ibid.

27. Fisher entered the Navy in 1854 and was First Sea Lord between 1904–10 and 1914–15.

28. See n.24, Meeting of the War Council. Nevakivi records Fisher's enthusiasm for the development of a 'great harbour' at Alexandretta with which, in Fisher's words, 'the oil fields of the Garden of Eden' might be connected. See Nevakivi, op. cit., p. 323. However, as Marian Kent argues, oil did not play a significant part in the considerations which led to the expansion of British interests in Mesopotamia: M. Kent, 'Asiatic Turkey, 1914–1916', in F. H. Hinsley, *The Foreign Policy of Sir Edward Grey* (Cambridge, 1977).

29. Memorandum by Kitchener, 'Alexandretta and Mesopotamia', 16 March 1915, secret, CAB 42/2/10 G.12.

30. Ibid.

31. Ibid. See Nevakivi, op. cit., p. 320.

32. Admiralty Memorandum, 'Alexandretta and Mesopotamia', 17 March 1915, CAB 42/2/11 G.13.

33. After Dulwich and Trinity College, Oxford, where he attained scholarly distinction, Hirtzel entered the India Office in 1894. He served as Private Secretary to Secretaries of State Brodrick and Morley before assuming control of the Political and Secret Department in 1909, where he remained until 1917. He was then, successively, Assistant, Deputy and Permanent Under-Secretary of State.

34. Notes and Private Telegram from the Viceroy regarding the future settlement of Eastern Turkey in Asia and Arabia, secret. Note by the Secretary, Political and Secret Department, India Office, 14 March 1915, CAB 24/1. Nevakivi fails to point out that Hirtzel had no qualms about a coterminous frontier with Russia and would have been prepared to make the Alexandretta–Mosul line a defensive line had Britain the troops to man it: J. Nevakivi, in Bourne and Watt, pp. 324–5. If Kent includes Hirtzel within her ambiguous phrase 'Indian opinion', then she also omits this distinction: M. Kent, op. cit., p. 443.

35. Ibid. See also comments on Sir Edmund Barrow's Note by Hirtzel, 17 March 1915.

36. Ibid.

37. Ibid. See also Note by Admiral Jackson, 'Remarks on the Importance of Alexandretta as a

Future Base', 15 March 1915, CAB/42/2/13, secret. Jackson entered the Navy in 1868 and was Chief of War Staff 1912–14 and First Sea Lord on Fisher's resignation in May 1915.

38. See n. 34.
39. Secretary's Notes of a Meeting of the War Council, 19 March 1915, CAB 42/2/14, secret.
40. Barrow was Military Secretary between 1914–17 and before this had a distinguished service record in the Indian Army. It was marred only by his involvement in the Curzon–Kitchener controversy. Note by Sir Edmund Barrow on the Defence of Mesopotamia, 16 March 1915, CAB 24/1.
41. This interpretation follows that of D. Fromkin, *A Peace To End All Peace: Creating The Modern Middle East 1914–1922* (London, 1989), ch. 23.
42. More accurately, the area was to extend from Mersin in the north, to the Persian frontier in the east, and from the Red Sea to the Indian Ocean in the south; see P. Mansfield, *A History of the Middle East* (London, 1991), p. 154.
43. Faisal was subsequently to lead the Arab revolt and, from 1921, was ruler of Iraq.
44. Little is known of Faruqi's background other than that he was a 24-year-old staff officer from Mosul with the rank of Lieutenant in the Ottoman Army.
45. As Fromkin states, the towns of Damascus, Aleppo, Homs and Hama were also the four stops of the rail-line connecting Syria with the Hejaz: Fromkin, op. cit., pp. 179–80.
46. Ibid., pp. 179, 182. McMahon's career had been spent mainly in political service on the frontiers of India before he became High Commissioner in December 1914, a post in which he remained until December 1916. Though enthusiastic about this appointment, Curzon, like many others at the time and since, developed strong reservations about McMahon's judgement. Curzon was to recommend McMahon's appointment to a roving international commission in the Middle East in 1919.
47. See n. 39; also Fromkin, op cit., p. 142; A.S. Klieman, 'Britain's War Aims in the Middle East in 1915', *Journal of Contemporary History (JCH)*, 13 (1968), p. 242.
48. Liberal MP for Caernarvon, 1890–1931; President of the Board of Trade, 1905–8; Chancellor of the Exchequer, 1908–15; Minister of Munitions, 1915–16; Secretary for War, 1916; Prime Minister and First Lord of the Treasury, 1916–22.
49. A.S. Klieman, *JCH*, 13. This rather than, as Klieman suggests, a desire to interpose a buffer between Britain and France was Lloyd George's primary motive. Nor was Lloyd George unduly perturbed by a fear of impinging on 'the French sphere'; J.S. Galbraith, 'British War Aims in World War I: A Commentary on Statesmanship', *Journal of Imperial and Commonwealth History (JICH)*, 13 (1984–85), p. 27.
50. See n. 39. Although he was Foreign Secretary, 1916–19, a figure of considerable influence and quite capable of advanced imperial thinking, if anything Balfour emerges as more restrained in his conception of British interests in the region.
51. Nicolson to McMahon, 31 March 1915, Foreign Office, Nicolson Papers, Foreign Office Papers, FO 800/377, f. 191. Nicolson, who became Permanent Under-Secretary in 1910, had served in Berlin, Peking, Constantinople, Athens, Tehran, Hungary, Morocco and St Petersburg.
52. Crewe to Grey, 22 March 1915, India Office, private, Crewe Papers I/20/5. Crewe was a Liberal Peer who had previously held a number of government posts. He was to replace Grey at the Foreign Office during the latter's illnesses.
53. Both before and after his Viceroyalty, which lasted from November 1910 to April 1916, Hardinge served as Permanent Under-Secretary at the Foreign Office. His distinguished overseas service included postings in Constantinople, Berlin, Washington, Sofia, Bucharest, Paris, Tehran and St Petersburg.
54. Crewe to Hardinge, 2 April 1915, India Office, Whitehall, private, Crewe Papers C/24.
55. See n. 32. French susceptibilities and Britain's awareness of these are detailed by Tanenbaum who, nevertheless, arrives at rather different conclusions as to their significance: J.K. Tanenbaum, *TAPS*, 68, pp. 5–7.
56. Hardinge to Nicolson, 8 April 1915, Viceroy's Camp, India, private, Nicolson Papers, FO 800/377.
57. See Nevakivi, in Bourne and Watt, p. 322.
58. Note by Beauchamp Duff, 20 April 1915, Crewe Papers C/25/3.
59. Ibid.

60. Earl Curzon of Kedleston (1859–1925): Assistant Private Secretary to Salisbury (Foreign Secretary), 1885–86; Under-Secretary of State for India, 1891–92; Parliamentary Under-Secretary, Foreign Office, 1895–98; Governor General of India, 1898–1904, 1904–5; Lord Privy Seal, May 1915; Lord President of the Council, December 1916; Acting Foreign Secretary, January 1919; Foreign Secretary, October 1919. Curzon had travelled in and written extensively on the Middle East.

61. See D. Gilmour, *Curzon* (London, 1994), p. 432; Ronaldshay, *Life of Curzon*, vol. 3 (London, 1928), pp. 121–2.

62. *The Times,* 11 September 1914; Gilmour, op. cit., p. 432.

63. Rider Haggard to Curzon, 21 May 1915; W. Long to Curzon, 5 June 1915, Local Government Board; Long to Curzon, 19 June 1915; all in Curzon Papers F112/115; see also Ronaldshay, op. cit., p.125; Gilmour, op. cit., p. 439.

64. Curzon to Lloyd George, 26 May 1915, 1 Carlton House Terrace, SW, Lloyd George Papers D/16/10/1.

65. Curzon to Cromer, 9 June 1915, 1 Carlton House Terrace, Cromer Papers FO 633, vol. 24, f. 115.

66. Curzon to Asquith (draft), 5 August 1915, Curzon Papers F112/114a, f. 26; see Gilmour, op. cit., p. 440.

67. Asquith to Crewe, 4 July 1915, Esher Place, Surrey, confidential, Crewe Papers C/40.

68. See n. 66.

69. Ibid. Curzon to Asquith, 10 August 1915, f. 30.

70. Ibid.

71. Chamberlain to Curzon (?1) August 1915, 9 Egerton Place, Curzon Papers F112/114a, f. 112. Chamberlain moved to the India Office in May 1915.

72. Cecil was subsequently Minister for the Blockade and, from July 1919 until January 1919, Assistant Secretary of State for Foreign Affairs. As such, and in view of Balfour's lack of interest in anything but the broadest lines of policy, he was able to exert a significant influence on the transaction of Foreign Office and interdepartmental activity on the Middle East

73. Chamberlain to Curzon, (?1) August 1915; Cecil to Curzon, 2 June 1915 (reply), f. 103; Chamberlain to Curzon, n.d. (reply), f. 107, F112/114a. Quite why the Committee failed to meet in 1915 is difficult to judge. It would seem that Asquith was at least prepared to contemplate the notion of Curzon's inclusion in the overall direction of the war. Two days after writing to Asquith, hinting that he should like to be included in the body which succeeded the Dardanelles Committee (see note 89), Curzon's name appeared in a rough note of eight names for a 'suggested War Conduct Committee' (J. Grigg, *Lloyd George, From Peace to War 1912–16*, London, 1985, p. 319). More broadly, it is an interesting speculation that Curzon's doubts about serving in a Liberal controlled coalition related partly to a belief that promotion to the highest posts would be unlikely. If a Conservative ministry were to succeed a failed coalition, Curzon might be excluded by virtue of his association with its predecessor. Recording a conversation with Curzon in April 1916, Bertie, Britain's Ambassador in Paris, observed:

> I said that I hoped that if Grey resigned the Foreign Secretaryship he [Curzon] would take the post if well enough. He doubted the resignation and the succession. Asquith had suggested to Grey that he should hand over to Curzon the *management* of Middle East and Egypt affairs he having local experience. Grey would not hear of it. Asquith, said George, is a very clever party leader and means to keep all the chief posts in Liberal hands.

Record by Bertie of a conversation with Curzon on 12 April 1916, London, Bertie Papers Add. Ms 63041, f. 193 (British Library). Bertie's ambassadorship stretched from 1905 to May 1918 and he was a close friend of Curzon. It is, of course, possible that Asquith deliberately presented Grey with this option in the knowledge that if Curzon's involvement were presented in these terms it would be refused out of hand. At any rate, by 17 August, Foreign Office delegates had already been chosen and memoranda for the Committee were in process of preparation. All that remained was for Curzon to summon his Committee. It is also possible that Asquith perceived the need for a more active policy in the east which would give effect to his ideas on Britain fulfilling her 'duty'.

74. See Fromkin, *A Peace to End All Peace*, p. 183.

75. Ibid.

76. See Kedourie, *The Chatham House Version*, p. 19.
77. Curzon to Crewe, 3 December 1914, Hackwood, private, Crewe Papers I/20/3.
78. Ibid. Crewe to Curzon, 4 December 1914, India Office, private; see also D. Goold, 'Lord Hardinge and the Mesopotamia Expedition and Inquiry, 1914–1917', *Historical Journal (HJ)*, 19, 4 (1976), n. 87.
79. Ibid. Curzon to Crewe, 5 December 1914, Hackwood.
80. Ibid.
81. Ibid. Crewe to Curzon, 20 January 1915, India Office, private, C/12.
82. Ibid. Curzon to Crewe, 17 December 1914, 1 Carlton House Terrace.
83. Curzon to Cromer, 19 March 1915, Hackwood, Basingstoke, Cromer Papers FO 633, vol. 24, f. 61; see Gilmour, *Curzon*, p. 476. Cromer had been Private Secretary to the Government of India, 1872–76, and British Agent and Consul-General, Egypt, 1883–1904. He was to chair the Dardanelles Commission in 1916–17.
84. Ibid.
85. Curzon to Crewe, 27 March 1915, Hackwood, private. Curzon wrote on the basis of a conversation which he had with Arthur Tod, Manager of Lynch & Co., Baghdad, Crewe Papers I/19/3.
86. Ibid. See also P. Landon to Curzon, 27 March 1915, 83 Charlwood Street, SW, Curzon Papers F112/115, f. 51.
87. Curzon to Cromer, 22 April 1915, 1 Carlton House Terrace, SW, Cromer Papers FO 633, vol. 24, f. 77; see Gilmour, op. cit., p. 476; Kedourie, op. cit., pp. 14–15.
88. Ibid. See also Curzon to Cromer, 17 May 1915, f. 100.
89. Curzon to Asquith, 22 September 1915, Asquith Papers, vol. 10 /28, f. 181.
90. Davidson held the position between 1903–28.
91. Entry of 18 November 1915, Davidson Papers, vol. 13. Davidson was to become a confidant of Curzon in times of acute troubles. The relationship was initiated by Davidson requesting a meeting in August 1915 in order to obtain information on the war which, ordinarily, he gleaned from Lord Stamfordham, the King's principal private secretary. On 18 November 1915, Curzon sought out Davidson and appeared to the latter 'most unreserved and evidently glad to pour out his soul'. On 27 June 1916, in an entry marked 'most private', Davidson recorded that Curzon had telephoned asking urgently for a talk. Davidson continued: 'He began by saying that, strange to tell, the fate of the Government, and possibly of National affairs, seemed to turn upon a decision which he must make within the next two hours. The person whose advice he wanted was myself.'
    Curzon's association with Davidson does not appear to have pre-dated 1915 and, although they continued to meet later in the war and to discuss politics, it seems that Curzon's immersion in eastern affairs, turbulent though it was, rendered his confessor redundant. However see n. 190; ibid., Davidson Papers, entries for 23 August, 18 November 1915 and 27 June 1916.
92. Ibid. According to J. Charmley, Curzon informed Churchill, Chancellor of the Duchy of Lancaster, on 14 September that the Unionist members of the Government had reached a point 'at which they would demand conscription and Kitchener's removal': J. Charmley, *Churchill: The End of Glory* (London, 1993), p. 134; see also Gilmour, *Curzon*, p. 443.
93. Asquith to Curzon, 8 December 1915, 10 Downing Street, Whitehall, SW, most secret, Curzon Papers F112/114a, f. 19; Curzon to Asquith, 8 December 1915, 1 Carlton House Terrace, confidential, Asquith Papers, vol. 10 /15. The timing of these letters is interesting. It seems that Curzon's letter, 'written long after midnight', was a reply to Asquith's letter in which the latter confessed that Kitchener was 'not a source of confidence or strength'. (See Gilmour, op. cit., p. 446.) Gleefully twisting the knife, Curzon took the opportunity to scotch Kitchener's ambitions to succeed Hardinge as Indian Viceroy.
94. Note by Bertie, 24 October 1915, Bertie Papers, Add. Ms 63039, f. 83 (British Library).
95. See n. 91.
96. Ibid. This, rather than simply support for an advance in principle, is implied by Davidson.
97. It was, in fact, the Dardanelles Committee that discussed the question on 21 October 1915.
98. Minute by Curzon, n.d., Curzon Papers F112/163. At the Dardanelles Committee on 21 October, Crewe, attempting to simplify matters, suggested that the question on which the Committee must pronounce was whether or not to advance on Baghdad. The issue was more

complicated, not least because Kitchener, who shared Curzon's political objections to a prolonged British occupation, favoured a raid on military grounds. This distinction is over-looked by Goold, *HJ*, 19, p. 933. It was, moreover, a distinction which Curzon was himself to blur albeit in a different sense. See, for example, record by Bertie of a conversation with Curzon, 12 April 1916, London, Bertie Papers Add. Ms 63041, f. 193 (British Library). Bertie's record is unsatisfactory but the reason for this must surely lie with Curzon's economy with the truth sharpened, as it was on this occasion, by physical pain. Whilst one might assume that Curzon based his remarks on a recollection of the discussion of 21 October 1915, as Crewe and later Goold suggest, as one of advance or the adoption of a defensive posture, the grounds upon which, according to his recollection, he opposed the advance were, in fact, shared by Kitchener at that meeting. There is no mention of this in Bertie's notes. Admittedly, Curzon spoke with the intention of disabusing Bertie of Hardinge's belief that 'the military' were responsible for the disastrous miscalculations about Turkish capabilities, and he may therefore unintentionally have overestimated the unanimity among his colleagues for an advance on 21 October. However, the terms in which Curzon couched his remarks, in which there are several derogatory references to Kitchener bearing on Mesopotamian and other matters, suggest that Curzon had no wish to share the plinth with him. Needless to say there is no mention in Bertie's account of Curzon's alleged volte-face on the advance. That Curzon did wish to maximise his political gain from the episode is unmistakable. Incidentally, Curzon's description of the (full) meeting of the Dardanelles Committee of 21 October is given by Bertie as 'a small committee of the Cabinet'. Writing later on 21 October Hankey, by then a firm proponent of advance, recorded that Curzon and Kitchener had both opposed the advance. It was, as Hankey continued, 'the usual shilly-shallying, no grip, no courage'; entry of 21 October 1915, Hankey Diaries 1/1 (Churchill College, Cambridge). Hankey was Secretary of the War Cabinet.

99. See J.S. Galbraith, 'No Man's Child: The Campaign in Mesopotamia, 1914–1916', *The International History Review (IHR)*, 6, 3 (August 1984), p. 371. Of course, Nixon has received much less generous treatment by other authors and Galbraith/Huttenback are to be commended for their portrayal of Nixon as a scapegoat: J.S. Galbraith and R.A. Huttenback, 'Bureaucracies at War: The British in the Middle East in the First World War', in E. Ingram, *National and International Politics in the Middle East, Essays in Honour of Elie Kedourie* (London, 1986), p. 111; H.V.F. Winstone provides a more balanced view than most authors in assessing responsibility for the advance: H.V.F. Winstone, *The Illicit Adventure: The Story of Political and Military Intelligence in the Middle East from 1898–1926* (London, 1982), p. 206.

100. Minute by Hirtzel, n.d. (December) 1914, L/P+S/11/87 P342.

101. Ibid.

102. Ibid. Mallet to Foreign Office, 4 September 1914, L/P+S/10/462 P3497. Mallet had previously served in Egypt and was Acting Assistant Under-Secretary at the Foreign Office from May 1918; Hardinge to Crewe, 8 October 1914, private, Viceregal Lodge, Simla, Crewe Papers C22; ibid., Hardinge to Crewe, 5 November 1914, Viceregal Lodge, Delhi.

103. Minute by Hirtzel, 2 November 1915, L/P+S/10/523 P4024.

104. Ibid. Also minute by Hirtzel, 4 January 1916, P4774.

105. Minute by Hirtzel for Holderness, 18 July 1916, L/P+S/10/599 P352. This view was shared by Hardinge, who termed the Arab Kingdom 'visionary'. Hardinge to Nicolson, 28 December 1915, Viceroy's Camp, India, private, Nicolson Papers FO 800/381, f. 106; ibid., Hardinge to ?(Wingate), 28 December 1915, Viceroy's Camp, India, private, copy, FO 882/12, f. 160.

106. Minute by Hirtzel, 23 February 1916, L/P+S/10/586 P705; see B. Westrate, *The Arab Bureau: British Policy in the Middle East 1916–1920* (University Park, c. 1992), p. 82. According to Tanenbaum, similar fears of Arab unity breeding a hostile Moslem alliance in French North Africa led France to support, albeit half heartedly, the Arab Revolt: Tanenbaum, *TAPS*, 68, p. 15.

107. Clayton to Wingate, 28 January 1916, FO 882/12. Clayton displayed great consistency in his disingenuousness; see Westrate, op. cit., passim. Clayton subsequently became BGGS, Hejaz Operations, CPO EEF, 1917–19, and Adviser to the Ministry of the Interior in Egypt, 1919–22.

108. Wingate to Cromer, 14 May 1915, Governor-General's Office, Khartoum, Cromer Papers FO 633, vol. 24, f. 104; see Kedourie on Clayton and Wingate: Kedourie, *The Chatham House Version*, pp. 17, 22. Wingate became High Commissioner of Egypt in January 1917.

109. See n. 105.
110. Minutes by Holderness, 25 February, and Chamberlain, 28 February 1916, L/P+S/10/586 P705. Holderness joined the Indian Civil Service in 1872 and transferred to the India Office where he became Secretary of the Revenue, Statistics and Commerce Department from 1901–12.
111. Minute by Chamberlain, 4 August 1916, L/P+S/10/598 P3054.
112. Minutes by Holderness, 18 September 1916, L/P+S/10/600 P3762; 30 December 1916, L/P+S/10/601 P5408.
113. See n.167.
114. Minute by Hirtzel, L/P+S/10/523 P3935. Grey's enthusiasm for an advance on Baghdad in October 1915, according to his statements at the Dardanelles Committee, was owing to a belief that the Arab movement, based as it was on notions of British prestige, was at a turning point and required a demonstration of Britain's commitment to its success. Yet, as Kent demonstrates, Grey apparently felt comfortable supporting advance behind the mask of the Arab movement – something which, according to Chamberlain, Grey believed 'was a castle in the air which would never materialize'; ibid., minute by Chamberlain, 27 October 1915. By March 1916, Grey's cynicism had not abated (M. Kent, in Hinsley, p. 451) and it is tempting to wonder if besides Grey's apparent disinterest in eastern affairs, his mind was working along similar lines to that of Hirtzel and figures in Cairo. This would certainly tie in with Grey's belief that Sykes–Picot would never fructify and that Britain, in this eventuality, would be in a strong bargaining position with at least Baghdad in her possession.
115. On the views of Grey and of the Admiralty/General Staff in, respectively, 1913 and 1906, see D. French, 'The Dardanelles, Mecca, and Kut: Prestige as a Factor in British Eastern Strategy, 1914–1916', *War and Society*, 5, 1 (May 1987), nn. 11, 17. Although as far as Kitchener was concerned the political consequences of failure did weigh in his mind when considering Gallipoli rather than Salonika; when conditions on the Western Front demanded greater British efforts Kitchener saw such consequences in perspective; see K. Neilson, 'Kitchener: A Reputation Refurbished?', *Canadian Journal of History (CJH)*, 15 (1980), pp. 213, 223. Hardinge's thoughts also underwent a considerable change. See S.A. Cohen, 'Mesopotamia in British Strategy, 1903–14', *Middle Eastern Studies (MES)*, 9 (1978), p. 175.
116. Ibid. D. French, op. cit., p. 57. T.G. Fraser places German insurgency in proper perspective: T.G. Fraser, 'Germany and Indian Revolution, 1914–18', *JCH* 12 (1977), p. 268; for a similar assessment see J. Brown, 'War and the Colonial Relationship: Britain, India and the War of 1914–18', in M.R.D. Foot, *War and Society: Historical Essays in Honour of J.R. Western, 1928–1971* (London, 1973), p. 95; R.J. Popplewell, *Intelligence and Imperial Defence: British Intelligence and the Defence of the Indian Empire, 1904–1924* (London, 1995), p. 180. Popplewell correctly notes that British policy in the Near East was affected by fears of Indian terrorism. However, he greatly underestimates the extent to which it was manipulated by the forward thinkers to justify territorial gains in the region; ibid., pp. 4–6, 187–8. However, see ibid., p. 228, n. 64.
117. Hardinge to Nicolson, 23 September 1915, Viceregal Lodge, Simla, private, Nicolson Papers FO 800/379, f. 82. Whilst it is not intended to examine in detail the question raised by D. E. Lee as to whether pan-Islamism 'was a genuine reaction to Western encroachment or merely a weapon of imperialism', this study tends to confirm Lee's suggestion that British officials did manipulate it: D. E. Lee, 'The Origins of Pan-Islamism', *American Historical Review (AHR)*, 47 (1942).
118. This was true, among others, of Sir (later Lord) George Lloyd; see p.106, n. 82.
119. See Neilson, op cit., pp. 225–6.
120. See French, op. cit., pp. 54–5 and Popplewell, op. cit., p. 6, who omit this point. That prestige was a factor in the support for an Arab kingdom, at least by Kitchener, is shown by Nevakivi: J. Nevakivi, in Bourne and Watt, pp. 319–20.
121. French, op. cit., p. 56.
122. Hardinge to McMahon, 12 July 1916, Foreign Office, private, copy, Hardinge Papers /23, f. 291.
123. That Curzon's contributions to the Gallipoli debate were frequently praised must have rendered his subsequent exclusion from eastern affairs difficult to bear. See, for example, McKenna to Curzon, 26 November 1915, at Cabinet, on Curzon's first Gallipoli paper; Stamfordham to Curzon, 1 December 1915, Buckingham Palace, both in Curzon Papers

F112/115; also, entry of 26 November 1915, Hankey Diaries 1/1 (Churchill College, Cambridge).

124. Records of conversations with Curzon on 23 August and 18 November 1915, Davidson Papers, vol. 13. On the first occasion Curzon reflected that if Britain were forced to abandon the Gallipoli Peninsula then '[t]he effect on Egypt, on Persia, on India of a Mahommedan triumph or apparent triumph in repelling the infidel from Constantinople cannot be measured in words'. Failure to reach Constantinople probably would not, in Curzon's view, be regarded 'as betokening the triumph of Islam . . . but it is of course difficult to judge how long the inability to effect our aim can be regarded without scorn'. However, when asked as to the probability of Allied success, Curzon summoned the chilling prospect of the collapse of France and Russia. This, in Curzon's view, would not in itself be fatal: 'But then there arises in the background of my mind the disturbing vision of India. Suppose we were in that condition and India were to rise. These, however, are contingencies impossible to formulate in any useful way at present.' Similarly, on 18 November, though able to conceive of a rising from Persia along the Indian frontier, Curzon, according to Davidson, felt this 'a long way off and he does not seriously apprehend it'. Davidson Papers, vol. 13.

125. Ibid. Conversation of 18 November 1915; see D. French, op. cit., p. 56. As Kedourie notes, this argument was used by Wingate: E. Kedourie, *The Chatham House Version*, p. 17.

126. Ibid. Record of a conversation with Curzon at Hackwood, Basingstoke, 6 October 1916.

127. They were, respectively, second and fourth in the list of officials named in the section of the report which referred to the advance on Baghdad: Mesopotamia Commission, vol. 1, Report, L/MIL/17/15/65/1, pt. xii.

128. Statement of Major-General E.G. Barrow to Mesopotamia Commission, 17 July 1917, Barrow Papers E420; see Gilmour, *Curzon*, p. 480, who makes the point that in the debate on the report in the House of Lords, Curzon defended Barrow, with whom, of course, he had had a close and significant association in India.

129. Shuckburgh replaced Hirtzel as head of the Political and Secret Department in the spring of 1917 and moved to the Colonial Office to head the Middle East Department in 1921. Curzon considered him unsurpassed in his drafting of official documents.

130. Note by Political Department, India Office, 'Advance to Baghdad – Political Considerations', 6 October 1915, L/P+S/18/B220.

131. Nicolson to Hardinge, 7 October 1915, Foreign Office, Nicolson Papers FO 800/380, f. 87; ibid., Nicolson to Hardinge, 14 October 1915.

132. See n.91.

133. Chamberlain to Curzon, 19 November 1915, at Cabinet, Curzon Papers F112/114a, f. 129.

134. Curzon to Asquith, 8 December 1915, 1 Carlton House Terrace, confidential, Asquith Papers, vol. 10 /15, f. 179.

135. Secretary's Notes of a meeting of the Dardanelles Committee, 21 October 1915, CAB 42/4/22/2.

136. Ibid. The manner in which Curzon presented his case to the Dardanelles Committee and the basis on which he framed his support for an advance in conversations with Randall Davidson and when writing to Asquith, suggests that he vested considerable importance in the views of the Joint Chiefs of Staff expressed in a paper of 19 October. Ibid., Appendix 3; see also n.91. The paper endorsed the inter-dependence of a British occupation of Alexandretta with a permanent or prolonged occupation of Baghdad established by Kitchener. However, having supported the idea of a raid, provided the military authorities could withdraw at will, the paper continued:

> A strong argument in favour of temporarily occupying Baghdad is the probability that a failure to push on now might create nearly, if not quite, as bad an impression in the East as would a withdrawal after occupation. But if there are such strong political objections to a withdrawal from Baghdad – after having once got there as to make it in the least doubtful whether the military authorities would be permitted to withdraw the troops at their discretion, however desirable it might be to do so on military grounds, then the opinion of the Combined Staffs is definitely against either occupation or raid.

137. Record by Bertie of conversation with Curzon, 12 April 1916, Bertie Papers Add. Ms 63041, f. 193 (British Library); see also n.135.

138. Selborne, who was President of the Board of Agriculture, lost a brother in the Mesopotamian Campaign in January 1916.

139. S/S to Viceroy, 21 October 1914, private, L/MIL/5/753, vol. 4.

140. Ibid.

141. Report of Mesopotamia Commission, memorandum by Curzon as to proposed disciplinary action, written after consultation with A. Chamberlain, Derby, Secretary for War, and George Barnes, Labour member of the War Cabinet, 18 June 1917, G.T. 1108, CAB 24/17.

142. See V.H. Rothwell. 'Mesopotamia in British War Aims, 1914–1918', *HJ*, 2 (1970), pp. 274–5.

143. J. Grigg, *From Peace to War*, p. 483, describes Curzon as 'a self-conscious grandee, as shifty as he was brilliant'. However, in the context in which Grigg makes the remark – the fall of Asquith – Gilmour provides a different interpretation and absolves Curzon from charges of devious conduct: Gilmour, *Curzon*, pp. xii, 459–60.

144. See Rothwell, op. cit., p. 275.

145. See Goold, *HJ*, 19, n. 79 and p. 920.

146. In particular, India Office officials spoke on the basis of investigations conducted by Sir William Willcocks, former head of the Egyptian Irrigation Department, in the first years of the century. See L/P+S/10/87 P2972.

147. See Goold, op. cit., p. 930.

148. See n. 167.

149. See n.135. The Report of the De Bunsen Committee may be found at CAB 27/1, and is reproduced in J.C. Hurewitz, *The Middle East and North Africa in World Politics 1914–45*, vol. 2 (New Haven, CT, London, 1979), document 12.

150. Secretary's Notes of a Meeting of the Dardanelles Committee, 21 October 1915, CAB 42/4/22/2; entry of 21 October 1915, Hankey Diaries 1/1 (Churchill College, Cambridge).

151. Notes by Aubrey Herbert, 20 October 1915, P. and O. Karmala, Herbert Papers DD/DR 35.

152. That Curzon may already have been considering such matters is suggested by a letter from a Col. Faber, MP, in which the latter suggested a landing at Alexandretta coinciding with an attack in Mesopotamia and that, in conjunction, and possibly with Japanese help, British troops might move on the Black Sea: W. Faber to Curzon, 2 November 1915, Barradus, Weedon, Curzon Papers F112/110, f. 59. Faber was a Unionist MP from 1906–18.

153. Ibid. Grey to Curzon, 9 November 1915, Foreign Office, f. 89; record by Bertie of a conversation with Curzon, 12 April 1916, London, Bertie Papers Add. Ms 63041, f. 193 (British Library). Bertie shared Curzon's disgust with the handling of the Anglo-French negotiations by the Foreign Office: Crewe to Bertie, 17 December 1915; Bertie to Crewe, 21 December 1915, draft, Paris, Bertie Papers FO 800/162, respectively, Eg/15/6, Eg/15/17 (PRO).

154. Hardinge to ?(McMahon), 28 November 1915, Viceregal Lodge, Delhi, FO 882/4, f. 82.

155. *The Times*, 3 November 1915; quoted in Galbraith, *IHR*, 6, p. 360. Asquith was another candidate for the 'unpleasing Machiavellism', not only with reference to Mesopotamian policy but the Middle East as a whole. It is difficult to square his ideas on 'duty' expressed at the War Council of 19 March 1915 (see n.39) with his diary entry of 25 March 1915, in which he stated that it was Churchill who had been most enthusiastic that 'we should be able to appropriate some equivalent share of the spoils . . . [while] at the moment Grey and I are the only two men who doubt and distrust any such settlement. We both think that . . . at the end of the War we could say that we had taken and gained nothing, and this not merely from a moral and sentimental view.' Quoted in Klieman, *JCH*, 13, p. 243. As Asquith implied, his views might change. Clearly they did (see n.116, also J.S. Galbraith, *IHR*, 6, 12). It is interesting to note, as Kent does, that at the end of December 1915, Grey and Balfour renewed their support for an occupation of Baghdad: M. Kent, in Hinsley, p. 442; also Galbraith, *JICH*, 13, p. 26.

156. Joined army, 1903; transferred to Indian Political Service, 1910; on special duty S.W. Persia, 1907–9, 1911–13; Consul for Arabistan, 1909–11; Deputy British Commissioner Turco-British Frontier Commission, November 1913, then Commissioner; Assistant Political Officer with Indian Expeditionary Force, December 1914; Deputy Chief Political Officer, 1916; Deputy Civil Commissioner, 1917; Political Resident Persian Gulf and Acting Civil Commissioner, March 1918.

157. A.T. Wilson to his mother, 17 October 1915, Basra, A.T. Wilson Papers, vol. 2.

158. Writing to his father from Basra at the end of August 1915, Wilson expressed himself in lines worthy of Rupert Brooke:

> When officers complain to me – as they do sometimes – that 'all war is cursed rot – what do we want to be fighting the Turks for?' I sometimes liken the process through which the world is passing to a human body stricken with disease – disease perhaps due to self-indulgence. Millions of bacteria, we are taught, must live and fight and die in the process. We get well, and we don't think of the struggles or the privations of the millions of the microcosms that go to make up our life. So with the world – as long as it gets well we must not complain if bacteria or corpuscles by the million are slain. I do not feel that war, here at all events, is degrading or demoralising, but the reverse, for men who are in Brigades and Divisions hard at work under arduous conditions – they are the better men for it.

159. Note by Bertie, 24 October 1915, Bertie Papers Add. Ms 63039, f. 83 (British Library). The context of these remarks, in which Bertie stated that Curzon was the only Cabinet member entirely for conscription, suggests that Curzon's role in that controversy may also have been a factor. Curzon's involvement in the affair may also account for his subsequent appointment to investigate the culpability of those named in the report of the Mesopotamia Commission. The accusations of vindictiveness which surrounded Curzon's role in this post-mortem reflected the fact that the Mesopotamian expedition reopened many wounds; some of which dated from the Curzon–Kitchener controversy.

160. Curzon to Crewe, 6 January 1916, Crewe Papers C/12; see Gilmour, op. cit., p.448.

161. Crewe to Curzon, 7 January 1916, Crewe House, Curzon Street, Curzon Papers F112/116, f. 53; see Gilmour, op. cit., p.449.

162. Ibid. Crewe to Curzon, 9 January 1916, f. 55.

163. Entry of 9 February 1916, Hankey Diaries 1/1 (Churchill College, Cambridge).

164. Ibid.

165. Curzon to Asquith, 23 March 1916, 1 Carlton House Terrace, confidential, Asquith Papers, vol. 10/16, f. 111; see Gilmour, op. cit., pp. 449–50.

166. Curzon's feelings at the time were exemplified by his confession to Asquith of feeling 'quite ashamed at the position I occupy in the greatest crisis of our history when all my knowledge and experience, such as they are, are thrown away'. Typically, the subsequent birth of an Air Department with Curzon as its head, failed to satisfy his ambitions; entry of 12 May 1916, Hankey Diaries 1/1 (Churchill College, Cambridge); see Gilmour, op. cit., pp. 451–2. Developments in the remainder of 1916 did little to improve Curzon's temper. Writing to Lord Lamington on 7 December Curzon noted that he was 'to be the Conservative watchdog in the War Committee of four'. His other duties – Lord President of the Council, Leader in the House of Lords and 'a few other things' – were, in Curzon's words, 'Quite enough to break me down'. The addition of the chair of a Restrictions on Imports Committee later in December was evidently seen by Curzon as yet another scrap swept from the table of high politics, designed to tether him to largely monotonous and time-consuming detail; see Ronaldshay, *Life of Curzon*, vol. 3, p. 122.

167. Chaired by Sir Maurice De Bunsen, Assistant Under-Secretary at the Foreign Office, the Committee consisted of representatives from the Foreign, India and War Offices, the Admiralty and the Board of Trade. De Bunsen had no special expertise in eastern affairs but had extensive overseas experience. Colonel Sir Mark Sykes attended as Kitchener's representative and the Committee met on thirteen occasions between 12 April and 28 May 1915.

168. See n.149. All material in this section is based on the De Bunsen Committee Report unless otherwise specified.

169. Ibid. See Klieman, *JCH*, 13, pp. 247–8.

170. Ibid. See n.168.

171. See Appendix 1. The negotiations and correspondence embodying the Agreement spanned the period January to May 1916.

172. Sykes had travelled in the east from an early age. He served in South Africa and was subsequently Hon. Attaché in Constantinople. From 1911 he was a Conservative MP and from the spring of 1915 he worked in the War Office. In June 1916 he moved to the CID Secretariat and later to the War Cabinet Secretariat. From the end of 1917 he was Acting Adviser on Arabian and Palestinian Affairs at the Foreign Office.

Playing Babylon against Byzantium

173. For details of Picot's background see Fromkin, *A Peace to End All Peace*, pp. 189ff.
174. J.E. Mack, *A Prince of Our Disorder: The Life of T.E. Lawrence* (Boston/Toronto, 1976), p. 125.
175. Minute by Hirtzel, 15 March 1916, L/P+S/10/526 P953. Presumably Hirtzel spoke with reference to his own ideas and those of Kitchener expressed in the spring of 1915 and with regard to the partition scheme with a British outlet at Alexandretta. Nevakivi attributes the creation of a buffer zone to Kitchener's change of heart: Nevakivi, in Bourne and Watt, pp. 325–7; see also Fromkin, op. cit., p. 191. The oil deposits of Mosul were therefore of secondary importance; see Rothwell, *HJ*, 2, pp. 287–8; also Kent, in Hinsley, p. 444.
176. See n.168.
177. Ibid. Similar arguments against partition had been advanced some time before; see S.A. Cohen, 'Mesopotamia in British Strategy, 1903–14', *MES*, 9 (1978), p. 174.
178. Ibid. As Klieman suggests, Sykes–Picot was a 'calculated division in advance of territorial spoils of war' and bore the hallmarks of imperialism. A narrow conception of Arab sovereignty was assumed and as the 'protectors' of the Arab State, Britain and France would devise such administrative systems 'as they may desire and as they may think fit to arrange' with the Arabs. The fatal flaw, as Klieman notes, was that, regardless of historical precedent, Sykes–Picot assumed future Anglo-French co-operation in the region: Klieman, *Foundations of British Policy in the Arab World: The Cairo Conference of 1921* (Baltimore/London, 1970), p. 13.
179. See Rothwell, op. cit., p. 295; H. Mejcher, 'British Middle East Policy 1917–21: The Inter-departmental Level', *JCH*, 8, 4 (1973), p. 84.
180. Curzon to Grey, 3 February 1916, 1 Carlton House Terrace, SW, Grey Papers FO 800/106, f. 526.
181. Ibid. Curzon to Grey, 20 February 1916, private, 1 Carlton House Terrace, SW, f. 535. To Curzon's complaint that the Agreement had been concluded without reference to the Cabinet, Grey replied that the papers relating to the Agreement had been circulated to the Cabinet at a Cabinet meeting; that a committee had met, at the request of the Cabinet, to discuss the question, but that their meeting had taken place on the day on which Curzon had gone to Belgium. According to Grey, Curzon's objections had been read to the Committee but, with minor alterations, the Agreement was adopted and it was decided to submit it to the Russians. As Grey hastened to add, the terms of the Agreement would only become effective 'if and when the Arabs throw in their lot with us' and pleaded pressure of business to excuse the lack of discussion of the Agreement by the Cabinet.
  Though sharing Grey's doubts about the likelihood of an Arab revolt, Curzon was not entirely mollified, suggesting, on 26 February, that the question had never come before the Cabinet but that it had been referred to a committee by the War Council – from which Curzon was excluded – and that the matter was then settled 'during the only five days I have been out of England since the Government was formed'.
182. Memorandum by Hirtzel, 'The French Claims in Syria', 14 February 1919, Montagu Papers AS4/4/26 (Trinity College, Cambridge). That it was so is reflected in the following selection of remarks made by senior figures about the Agreement. To Sykes, co-author of the Agreement, to whom aspects of the arrangements had appeared regrettable soon after its con-clusion, the Agreement appeared 'dead' by July 1918; Minutes of the Eastern Committee, 18 July 1918, *EC* 21, secret, CAB 27/24. In October 1918, Curzon was to suggest that the Agreement was 'out of date and unscientific'. Ibid., *EC* 34, 3 October 1918. To Macdonogh, Adjutant-General, it was 'a positive source of danger'; Memorandum by Macdonogh, 'A Note on Policy in the Middle East', 28 October 1918, EC 2133, CAB 27/35. Early in November, T.E. Lawrence, fresh from Damascus and attempting to reconcile British policy with con-ditions on the ground, spoke of the 'geographical absurdities' of Sykes–Picot; EC 2207, CAB 27/36. Towards the end of November Sykes–Picot was, in Curzon's words, 'that unfortunate Agreement, which has been hanging like a millstone round our necks'; *EC* 39, 27 November 1918, CAB 27/24. To Smuts, early in December 1918, it was a 'hopeless blunder in policy', a view endorsed by Robert Cecil when speaking on 5 December of 'The evil of the Sykes–Picot Agreement'. Memorandum by Smuts, 'Our Policy at the Peace Conference', 3 December 1918, 39 CAB 29/2. Smuts was South African representative on the Imperial War Cabinet and was generally receptive to limited imperial expansion; *EC* 41, 5 December 1918, CAB 27/24. In February 1919, Kidston of the Eastern Department of the Foreign Office spoke of 'that intolerable instrument' and, when writing to Derby on the same day, Curzon referred

to Sykes–Picot as being 'impossible and out of date'; Minute by Kidston, 12 February 1919, FO 371/4148; Curzon to Derby, 12 February 1919, FO 371/4178, pp. 597ff. Finally, Balfour, while remarking in June 1919 that the Agreement was 'dead', felt that 'its ruins still encumber the earth'. Memorandum of interview in Mr Balfour's Apartment, 23 Rue Nitot, between Balfour, Mr Justice Brandeis, Lord Eustice Percy and Mr Frankfurter, 24 June 1919, strictly confidential, FO 800/217, f. 187ff; see also E. Goldstein, 'British Peace Aims and the Eastern Question: The Political Intelligence Department and the Eastern Committee, 1918', *MES*, 23, 4 (1987), p. 424; E. Kedourie, *The Chatham House Version*, pp. 29–30.

183. See Klieman, *JCH*, 13, p. 247. This stimulus was provided in equal measure by the determination of French politicians in maintaining that the Agreement was 'definitive and final'; J.K. Tanenbaum, *TAPS*, 68, p. 14, n. 64.

184. See Kent, in Hinsley, p. 450.

185. Klieman states that partition 'was the scheme most widely advocated at the time and, contrary to the De Bunsen Report, became the policy adopted and pursued thereafter by the government'. Of course, while closely resembling the partition scheme with Britain established at Haifa, with regard to the definition of Anglo-French spheres, Sykes–Picot owed as much to the zones of interest scheme; see Klieman, op. cit.

186. Curzon to Cecil, 1 June 1917, 1 Carlton House Terrace, SW, private, Cecil Papers FO 800/198 (PRO). Although Curzon was speaking with reference to events in Greece and Russia, in view of the reverberations of events in Russia, especially, his remarks had wider application. However, as Rothwell demonstrates, Curzon was quite capable of turning 'democracy' to Britain's advantage as a justification for the annexation by her of the German Colonies: Rothwell, *HJ*, xiii, p. 282; see also Galbraith, *JICH*, 13, p. 30.

187. See ch. 3, section 4.

188. On this see Mejcher, *JCH*, 8 (1973).

189. Although there were more fundamental matters involved, essentially Cecil and Montagu wished, in Cecil's words, 'to convert the Eastern Committee into a Middle East Department'; Cecil to Montagu, 5 September 1918, Cecil Papers FO 800/207 (PRO); quoted in Mejcher, op. cit., p. 94. Montagu was Secretary of State for India, 1917–22, and was profoundly sceptical of the arguments used by Curzon and others to justify substantial imperial gains. It is clear that Cecil wished to replace Balfour, that he resented Curzon's personal shortcomings, his interference in policy formulation and the system of Cabinet Committees vested with executive powers. See also n.201.

190. Entry of 20 August 1918, Hankey Diaries 1/5 (Churchill College, Cambridge).

191. Cecil to Balfour, 23 August 1918, Balfour Papers Add. Ms 49738, ff. 225–30 (British Library); quoted in Mejcher, op. cit., p. 95.

192. See n.186, Curzon to Cecil, 1 June 1917.

193. See for example Bell to Hardinge, 27 April 1917, GHQ, Basra, Hardinge Papers /22. Bell, who had a considerable knowledge of the Middle East, was then an Assistant Political Officer in Baghdad; Hardinge to Nicolson, 18 February 1916, Viceregal Lodge, Delhi, private, Nicolson Papers FO 800/381, f. 137.

194. See ch. 3, section 4. Yet, as Tanenbaum has suggested, Sykes had suspicions of the spur provided to French imperialism by Sykes–Picot soon after its conclusion: Tanenbaum, *TAPS*, 68, p. 12.

195. Hon. Fellow, All Souls, Oxford; 1899–1909, *Times* Editorial Staff; served Flanders and Middle East, 1914–16; Assistant Secretary War Cabinet and Imperial War Cabinet, 1917; on staff of War Council, Versailles, and personal Staff of Secretary of War, 1917–18; temporary Lt. Colonel GS; Parliamentary Under-Secretary of State for the Colonies, 1919–21.

196. Entry of 10 January 1917, Hankey Diaries 1/1 (Churchill College, Cambridge). Hankey recorded Walter Long, the Colonial Secretary, as saying that Amery was 'quite untrustworthy' due to his close links with *The Times* and that this was strongly felt in the Commons. On the following day, writing in connection with Amery's plans to have secretaries at his disposal at the Cabinet Office, Hankey described Amery as 'a scheming little devil'; ibid., entry of 11 January 1917. Apparently Hankey's opinion of Amery changed; see Grigg, *From Peace to War*, p. 489.

197. Evidence suggests that Amery was important in the creation of the War Policy Committee. *The Leo Amery Diaries*, vol. 1, 1896–1929, eds J. Barnes and D. Nicholson (London, 1980), pp.

157–8; Amery to Hankey, 1 June 1917, Offices of the War Cabinet, 2 Whitehall Gardens, SW, enclosing Amery to Milner, same date, CAB 21/88, f. 478. Amery's letter to Milner may also be seen at Milner Papers 358, ff. 53–4 (Bodleian Library, Oxford). Having drummed up support, Amery then tackled Lloyd George: Amery to Lloyd George, 5 June 1917, Offices of the War Cabinet, 2 Whitehall Gardens, SW, Lloyd George Papers F/2/1/4. It is interesting that, when writing to Milner and Hankey, Amery did not include Curzon in the proposed Committee, mentioning only Milner, Smuts and Lloyd George. There is also evidence to suggest that Amery was active in efforts to create the Supreme War Council.

198. Private Secretary to Goschen (Chancellor), 1887–89; Under-Secretary for Finance, Egypt, 1889–92; Chairman Board of Inland Revenue, 1892–97; Governor Cape of Good Hope, 1897–1901; Governor of Transvaal and Orange River Colony, 1901–5; High Commissioner, South Africa, 1897–1905; Member of the War Cabinet (without portf.), 1916–18; Secretary of State for War, 1918–19; Colonial Secretary, 1919–21.

199. Wilson was commissioned in 1884 and by 1914 was Assistant Chief of General Staff to Lord French. He was then, successively, Corps Commander, Liaison Officer with the French, Commander of the Eastern District, British Military Representative at Versailles, 1917, and, from February 1918, CIGS and member of the War Cabinet.

200. Amery to Lloyd George, 12 January 1918, Offices of the War Cabinet, 2 Whitehall Gardens, Lloyd George Papers F/2/1/11.

201. The Mesopotamian Administration Committee was created as a result of a meeting of the War Cabinet on 16 March 1917. Its remit was gradually extended and at the ninth meeting of the Committee on 22 August 1917, the Committee resolved to recommend to the War Cabinet that it be renamed the Middle Eastern Administration Committee. The Middle East Committee, as it became known, met only twice in the format of the Mesopotamian Administration Committee before convening in its new composition on 19 January 1918. Curzon had also chaired the interdepartmental Persia Committee which met frequently from the summer of 1917 until its functions, together with those of the Middle East Committee and some of those pertaining to the Russia Committee (see ch. 5, n. 19) were subsumed in the Eastern Committee created by the War Cabinet on 11 March 1918. The Eastern Committee continued to meet until 7 January 1919. At its final meeting it was agreed to recommend to the Cabinet that the labours of the Committee should be undertaken by an occasional Inter-Departmental Conference, again chaired by Curzon. In his account of the origins of the Eastern Committee, Galbraith is inaccurate: Galbraith, *IHR*, 6, p. 381. His errors are repeated in Galbraith/Huttenback, n. 73 in E. Ingram.

202. See ch. 5, n.61 for evidence indicating some such connection. For Amery on Curzon see, for example, Amery to his wife, 25 September 1917, Barnes and Nicholson, *The Leo Amery Diaries*, vol. 1, p. 172. According to Amery, Smuts favoured Curzon as Foreign Secretary 'in spite of his defects, because he can administer, knows the Empire, and knows what he wants'.

203. The late Lord Amery's secretary has informed the author that no date has been set for the intended transfer of the Leo Amery papers to Churchill College, Cambridge, but that this will not be until a biography has been written.

204. Amery to Lloyd George, 14 April 1918. Offices of the War Cabinet, 2 Whitehall Gardens, SW, Lloyd George Papers F/2/1/17; ibid., Amery to Lloyd George, 8 June 1918, Offices of the War Cabinet, 2 Whitehall Gardens, SW, F/2/1/24.

205. Entries of 2 January, 3 February 1918, Hankey Diaries 1/3, 1/4 (Churchill College, Cambridge).

206. Montagu to Chelmsford, 15 June 1918, India Office, private, Montagu Papers D523/2 (OIOC). Montagu prefaced his remarks on Curzon with praise of Chamberlain and it seems that Montagu was feeling the strain of attempting to reconcile Chelmsford, Indian Viceroy, 1916–21, with Persian policy as defined by the Eastern Committee and for which Chelmsford held Curzon personally responsible. In April 1918, when, as Amery implied, Curzon's gaze was fixed with envy on the Foreign Office, it seems that Curzon was attempting to gain ascendancy in imperial affairs by virtue of his leadership of the House of Lords. See n.204, Amery to Lloyd George, 14 April 1918; also, Curzon to Bonar Law, 16 May 1918, 1 Carlton House Terrace, Bonar Law Papers 83/3/30. Bonar Law was Chancellor of the Exchequer and Unionist leader.

2

The Mesopotamian
Administration Committee

THE PROCLAMATION

T HE OCCUPATION OF Baghdad in March 1917 by a British Military
Expedition marked the culmination of a process which began in the
autumn of 1914 with the despatch of a military force from India to protect British interests in the Persian Gulf. Occupation necessitated an
examination of the means by which Britain, in accordance with the
Sykes–Picot Agreement, might exercise a predominating influence in
the Baghdad Vilayet.[1] Accordingly, in March 1917, the War Cabinet
created an interdepartmental committee to consider this question and
that of the administration of the Basra Vilayet, in which, by virtue of the
correspondence between King Hussein and Sir Henry McMahon,
Britain was to exercise a permanent influence.

Occupation presented dangers as well as opportunities. This symbolic
victory, if it were to become a bargaining counter, had to survive
interdepartmental and personal frictions. Curzon's appointment as
Chairman of the Mesopotamian Administration Committee, though
unsurprising in view of his reputed expertise on eastern affairs, was
unlikely to diminish scope for disagreement in its deliberations. Since his
return from India and a Viceroyalty marked for its alternating brilliance
and tempestuousness, Curzon, as we have seen, had not only failed to
fulfil the 'Balliol prophecy' by becoming premier, but had also been
unable to impose his distinctive views on policy formulation. Denial of
high office had neither deprived Curzon of his powers of work nor had
it altered, materially, his conception of the Pax Britannica.

The question of what should be done immediately on occupation,
though ultimately a Cabinet matter, was not dealt with initially by
Curzon, but by the India Office, and, in particular, by Sir Arthur
Hirtzel. Hirtzel, and his colleagues, Sir Thomas Holderness and J.E.

Shuckburgh, soon to succeed Hirtzel at the Political and Secret Department, had been prominent architects of British policy in Mesopotamia and all three attended the Mesopotamian Administration Committee.[2]

Hirtzel, especially, had been a prominent and consistent advocate of advancing on Baghdad. In this respect he differed from Curzon but he nevertheless possessed imperial goals which, in the case of Mesopotamia, were comparable if not greater in scope than those of Curzon. When, in February 1915, Lord Kitchener had expressed a preference for withdrawing Force 'D', the Mesopotamian Expeditionary Force, unless India could reinforce it with two Divisions, Hirtzel maintained that guarantees given to the Sheikhs of Mohammerah and Koweit[3] rendered impossible an honourable withdrawal except after a defeat: 'Withdrawal would thus have all the present disadvantages of defeat, with the added disadvantage that it would destroy our future in that region.'[4]

Prestige with the Arabs was important to Hirtzel precisely because of his views about Britain's future in Mesopotamia. In an undated memorandum, probably written in December 1914, Hirtzel noted: 'From the point of view of this department the eventual occupation of Bagdad is so desirable as to be practically essential.'[5]

On that occasion Hirtzel had to defer to military advice in postponing an advance. Already, however, he had conceded the essential point which, it might be said, rendered all other considerations secondary, namely the primacy of Baghdad.

> It may indeed be doubted – though this is a matter for Sir Edmund Barrow – whether our temporary occupation of Basra can be regarded as secure so long as Bagdad remains in the hands of the enemy. For whereas nothing threatens Bagdad (Mosul is too far off), Bagdad will always be a threat to Basra.[6]

There were, perhaps, too many uncertainties for Hirtzel to express himself freely. Occupation of Basra was, he alleged, temporary and undertaken simply 'in order to obtain status in the final settlement', to detach the Arabs from the Turks and to minimise the risk of a Turkish attack on British commercial interests in Arabistan.[7]

The relationship between Hardinge, who, as Permanent Under-Secretary at the Foreign Office, attended most of the meetings of the Mesopotamian Administration Committee, and Curzon, was complicated. Shared interest in and experience of the east had not equipped them with an entirely similar approach to its problems. Unlike Curzon, Hardinge struggled to attain the Anglo-Russian Agreement of 1907. As Viceroy of India, Hardinge reversed the partition of Bengal and championed the removal of the capital from Calcutta to Delhi, moves which, perhaps, identified Hardinge in Curzon's mind as a threat to his own legacy in the east.

The meetings of the Mesopotamian Administration Committee were to take place against this back-drop and with a bitterness which intensified with the events surrounding the publication in June 1917 of the Report of the Mesopotamia Commission.[8] However, Curzon's active involvement in these events could not hide a substantial degree of common ground. Both men, as Viceroy of India, had exhibited on occasion a tendency to delegate matters to subordinates which ignored policy directives from Whitehall. Hardinge, writing to Curzon in 1915, perhaps divined future possibilities for co-operation in British policy in Mesopotamia: 'when the time comes to make peace with Turkey, Baghdad, Busra and perhaps even Mosul must be lopped off, and while we remain at Busra some kind of protectorate over the rest of Mesopotamia must be established.'[9]

In Hirtzel's view, British interests would not be secured by a protectorate over the Baghdad Vilayet. Annexation, even of the Baghdad and Basra Vilayets, left a perceptible gap in Britain's defences and one in which Hirtzel, now less guarded in his public utterances than Hardinge, could find scope to satisfy his annexationist urges:

> all the considerations that make the detachment from Turkey of the Bagdad Vilayet necessary to Basra, apply also to the detachment of Upper Mesopotamia. They apply, but not perhaps with quite so much force, because Bagdad is more dangerous to Basra than Aleppo and Mosul would be to Bagdad; and therefore whereas we must, in my opinion, annex Bagdad, we may be content with 'protecting' Upper Mesopotamia.[10]

By the autumn of 1915 there was broad support for an advance on Baghdad. Hirtzel and Shuckburgh stood apart from this body – which included the Foreign Office and an interdepartmental committee on which Holderness represented the India Office – in their belief that a temporary occupation, even by default, was preferable to no occupation.[11] Holding this view they differed also from the combined General Staff and from Curzon.[12] The prevailing feeling at the India Office, though composed of many shades of opinion, was to support the looser grip over the Baghdad Vilayet envisaged by Hardinge. Holderness spoke in very different terms from Hirtzel when he argued thus:

> The taking of Bagdad would undoubtedly impress the middle East, and would be an appropriate first step to the predominant position which is sought to be acquired for Great Britain in Lower Mesopotamia. But as a *desideratum* it is nothing compared with the expulsion of the Turks from Constantinople and Europe.[13]

By March 1917, there was at least consensus on one point: that the psychological moment should not be allowed to pass and that a proclamation, announcing the intentions of the British Government, should be issued.

Awaiting a copy of the proclamation which Sir Percy Cox, Chief Political Officer, had been asked to prepare, Hirtzel received a dispatch from General Maude, General Officer Commanding, Force 'D', in which the latter expressed a hope that civil administration in the Baghdad Vilayet would be embarked upon in sufficient scale.[14] Hirtzel regarded this as interference by the military in the civil domain and it alerted those on the Mesopotamian Administration Committee to future difficulties in this regard. More seriously, if, as he hoped, Hirtzel might guide the Committee towards annexation of the Baghdad Vilayet and a protectorate over the Mosul Vilayet, then such ill-timed outbursts by men on the spot would have to be discouraged. Hirtzel insisted that,

> whatever may be the ultimate decision, the existing administrative machinery is as far as possible to be preserved for the present with the substitution of Arab for Turkish spirit and personnel. The façade must be Arab. While therefore the Vilayet should remain under martial law for the security of the occupying force, the inhabitants should be formally invited to assume control of the civil administration with British co-operation. Every effort should be made to induce representative men to come forward for this purpose and the British Officers to be lent should be strictly limited to the minimum necessary as advisers.[15]

Cox's draft proclamation arrived on 9 March and Hirtzel, on the same day, noted despairingly that 'the whole argument . . . leads up to this: "mind your own affairs, and leave us do the governing" '.[16] This, Hirtzel continued, was unacceptable, as '*vis à vis* both of King Hussein and of the Allies they [His Majesty's Government] are irretrievably committed to the policy of the Arab State, until, at all events, the Arab State has been tried and proved a failure'.[17]

This was an important qualification. Hirtzel was impatient with the delay in publishing a suitable proclamation and one which, as he implied, acknowledged that Britain had not claimed nor had King Hussein granted the right of a British administration for Baghdad.[18]

Hirtzel regarded a premature annexation of Baghdad as dangerous: firstly, because 'expediency and honour require us to give the Arabs a fair chance', and, secondly, because Britain might thereby jeopardise her long-term position in Mesopotamia.[19] Support for an Arab State had weaned the Arabs from the German–Turkish Alliance. More importantly, it held French territorial ambitions in check physically and morally. Britain's presence in Baghdad gave her the opportunity of ingratiating herself further with Arab opinion, something denied to the French in Syria, whilst when peace was restored it would leave her in physical occupation of Baghdad, similar to her position *vis à vis* Basra on the eve of the McMahon–Hussein correspondence. Hirtzel perceived that physical occupation alone might not be sufficient to secure Britain's future in Mesopotamia. Another possibility had taken root in his mind:

> before the war Great Britain had a rather unenviable reputation for giving pledges and then receding from them owing to force of circumstances; and it is important now to avoid uttering words which we may hereafter have to eat if the Arab State proves a failure. In that event we shall almost certainly have to annex Bagdad, and we ought not to tie our hands now.[20]

The task of improving Cox's proclamation[21] fell to Sir Mark Sykes, joint author of the Inter-Allied Agreement of 1916, who sat on the Mesopotamian Administration Committee in an unofficial capacity and acted as its secretary.

Hirtzel's interpretation of British commitments to France was considerably more cynical than that of Sykes but Hirtzel was none the less careful to render Sykes's alternative proclamation harmless as gently as possible. In fact, Hirtzel objected to one line only: 'It is the desire of the British Government that the Arabs of Irak and Bagdad shall in future be a free people, enjoying their own wealth and substance under their own institutions and laws.'[22]

Hirtzel, overstating the matter to make his point, saw this as a 'direct and unconditional promise of independence to the vilayets of Basra and Bagdad'.[23] Chamberlain shared Hirtzel's concern about future charges of breach of faith should the Arab State prove to be a failure and submitted an alternative wording which avoided Sykes's incautious formula.[24]

Sykes advanced many arguments in favour of his draft proclamation

Source: Imperial War Museum, A.T. Wilson Papers

1. Lieutenant-Colonel Arnold Talbot Wilson

2. Sir Arthur Hirtzel

against that of Chamberlain, whose aim was not, as Sykes's biographer Roger Adelson implies, to Indianise Mesopotamia.[25] Both Chamberlain and Sykes were inclined to refrain from forward moves in Meso-potamia. With Chamberlain this was due to the counsel of outspoken advisers and to the lack of any definite policy. With Sykes, besides his Arabophile tendencies, there was the protection afforded by the Sykes–Picot Agreement against unlimited French expansion and the benefits arising from adherence to it: 'if we play our cards properly by means of "advisers" instead of "rulers" and back Arab nationalism, we shall have a permanent footing at little cost'.[26]

There was in fact sufficient mutual ground for Hirtzel to steer a common path, but the proclamation in its final form was drawn up neither by Sykes nor by Chamberlain alone, but by a Cabinet commit-tee consisting of Curzon, Milner, Hardinge and Chamberlain created by the War Cabinet on 12 March.[27]

The disputed section of the proclamation was diluted further by this committee to remove the possibility of misconstruction by Britain's Allies. However, subsequent prevarications by Maude and Cox were more likely to afford the proconsular figures – Curzon, Milner and Hardinge – scope to interfere.

General Maude claimed that the revised proclamation did not 'touch on subjects [with] which [the] feelings of communities in Baghdad and Irak are immediately concerned'.[28] Austen Chamberlain suggested a reply of which the crucial section read:

> There is no objection to subsidiary proclamations dealing with matters of local interest provided that they do not suggest permanent incorporation of the Baghdad Vilayet in the British Empire which it is the desire of His Majesty's Government to avoid.[29]

Anxious lest the psychological moment pass, Chamberlain's telegram was submitted to Curzon, Hardinge and Milner as 'very urgent'.[30] Curzon, like Hirtzel, had no wish to tie Britain's hands. Nor, however, was he willing to adopt Chamberlain's reply in the sense in which it was meant. Instead, Curzon apparently gained the concurrence of Hardinge and Milner to Chamberlain's reply precisely because the wording was sufficiently vague not to preclude the permanent incorporation of the Baghdad Vilayet.[31] Time and authority were on Curzon's side, and Hirtzel, who perceived that Britain must retain the Baghdad Vilayet by virtue of moral argument rather than physical occupation, could only register disappointment that a tighter wording had not been adopted.[32]

The events surrounding publication of the proclamation were indicative of much that was to follow. Often difficult to detect, Curzon's influence was none the less, in theory at least, unassailable, given that all matters of policy had first to be referred to him for approval. This enabled him to disregard departmental advice when it conflicted with his own views about the best means of strengthening Britain's position in Mesopotamia.

LAYING THE FOUNDATIONS

The provisional recommendations of the Mesopotamian Administration Committee arising from its first meeting on 19 March marked the first attempt by an executive body to define British interests in Mesopotamia.[33] On certain points on which past experience rendered fulfilment obvious and necessary there was agreement among the Committee members and, additionally, with the Government of India and Sir Percy Cox when at the end of March their concurrence was sought to a revised set of these proposals.[34] It was assumed by all parties that Basra would remain under permanent British occupation and that the Vilayets of Basra and Baghdad, if the latter were to remain under British occupation, should be administered by the Foreign Office, not the Government of India, and by a civil service which would amalgamate with that of the Soudan and the Levant.[35] On other points important differences arose, inevitably perhaps, as a result of established interests and conflicting interpretations of Britain's commitments to the Arabs and her other Allies.

Having witnessed at first hand the inefficiencies of Government of India control in Mesopotamia, Mark Sykes was anxious to transfer authority there, in Aden and in Muscat, to the Foreign Office. Sykes had raised the issue in a statement and accompanying memorandum to the War Committee in July 1916,[36] when he argued that 'circumstances, atmosphere and tradition' had rendered the Government of India 'incapable of handling the Arab question'. To attain 'unity and co-ordination', Sykes argued that 'the political affairs of Mesopotamia, Aden and Muscat' should be placed directly under the Foreign Office with Sir Percy Cox as High Commissioner to Mesopotamia, equal in rank to Sir Henry McMahon. Furthermore, Sykes intended that Cox should be based in Cairo.[37]

Curzon's immediate reaction to Sykes's proposal was to endorse his choice of Cox whom he himself had appointed Resident in the Persian

Gulf. Sykes's tour of the Middle East had revealed weaknesses in British administration there to which senior figures such as Balfour, Lloyd George and Curzon readily admitted. However, the scope of Sykes's solution was unacceptable and Curzon played on this at the meeting of the War Committee at which it was discussed claiming that: 'This was not only the solution of an immediate question but a great change of policy that they were asked to approve.'

Not only were Mesopotamia, Muscat and Aden involved but the disruption of a tradition of influence which, Curzon noted, extended throughout Arabia and along the southern and western shores of the Persian Gulf. It was, moreover, an influence which Curzon had been instrumental in fostering. As the Minutes of the War Committee recorded:

> There again was the question whether the Foreign Office could do what had been built up in India in the course of many years. Would they take the same interest? . . . When he himself left India, he left all these things in a strong and stable condition. He doubted if they would get anyone here to take the same interest, and to give the same attention and eager enthusiasm.[38]

It was decided that Grey, Chamberlain, Curzon and Hardinge should discuss the question of Arab policy and it was, perhaps, only when this had occurred, and at a subsequent meeting of the War Committee, that Curzon directly questioned the feasibility of administering Mesopotamia from Cairo.[39]

A year later military conditions in Mesopotamia remained unpredictable but the occupation of Baghdad enabled the members of the Mesopotamian Administration Committee to reach some tentative conclusions about the occupied territories, and, more broadly, about the future division of responsibilities between London and Delhi.

In accordance with the provisional recommendations of the Committee, the occupied territories of Basra and Baghdad were to be administered by the Foreign Office, not the Government of India, and a special service was to be formed for this purpose. Koweit, owing perhaps to its proximity to Basra, would be included henceforth in the new administration. Essentially there were to be no changes of the nature recommended by Sykes in July 1916. The Government of India was to retain control of Southern Persia, Muscat and the southern and western sides of the Persian Gulf and there was to be no alteration of the 'Cairo sphere of influence'.[40] In fact, the only scope for change lay in the control of Aden where, according to Curzon and many others, British prestige was being seriously undermined by the failure of the Government of India to repel Turkish military advances.[41]

Curzon's hesitancy, even where Aden was concerned, was indicative of his distaste in articulating, prematurely, the specific parameters of Britain's new Middle Eastern interests. Tampering with established methods of control was worsened by the knowledge that revision was intended to buttress Sykes's vision of Britain's future in Mesopotamia, involving little in the way of direct British administration. Consequently, Curzon insisted on imbuing the provisional recommendations regarding the physical extent of the Baghdad Vilayet with vagueness. The Committee decided, and Sykes was unable subsequently to alter this, that 'the region to be controlled from [Baghdad] should be approximately that coloured in the map attached to the Anglo-French-Russian Agreement of 1916'. Also, and more significantly, the Committee resolved:

> That it would be premature to determine at present what should be the precise form of Arab government to be ultimately set up in the Baghdad Vilayet and contiguous Arab sphere, but that the provisional British administration to be established in the occupied territories outside of the Basra Vilayet should be formed with a view to such a development in the future.[42]

The meaning of this rather vague clause was clear enough to Sykes, and by the time of its transmission to Delhi and Baghdad, the nature of Britain's proposed presence in the Baghdad Vilayet had hardened.[43] Baghdad was to be an Arab State with a local ruler or government under a 'British Protectorate in everything but name'.[44]

However, on the issue of the division of authority between Mesopotamia and India Curzon was forced to compromise. A sub-committee of the Mesopotamian Administration Committee, to which that matter had been referred, recommended that Arabia, and with it control of Haudramaut, South Arabia and the Arabian littoral, should go to the Foreign Office.[45] This decision was based partly on the recent extension of the territory under Bin Saud to the Arabian coast as far as Bahrein and on the need to cultivate good relations with him and the tribes under his authority which were located on the border of the occupied territories.[46] Also, it was felt that previous staffing difficulties encountered by the Government of India might be overcome if this area fell within the remit of the proposed new civil service which, the sub-committee anticipated, might amalgamate with that of the Soudan and, later, possibly, with that of Egypt.[47] The creation of such a service stretching from Mesopotamia to the Soudan reflected views shared by Hirtzel and Sykes that, in Hirtzel's words, 'if Mesopotamia is not to be administered by India, a new dependency will be created which will include the whole of Arabia, Egypt and the Soudan – a unilingual and unicultural area, from Sollum to the Turco-Persian frontier'.[48] Moreover, given Sykes's preference that this dependency should be controlled from Cairo and his association with officialdom there, there may in Sykes's case have been an unconscious urge to resuscitate the idea of a Middle-Eastern Viceroyalty, the brainchild of Ronald Storrs.

The sub-committee further proposed, assuming Basra was to be permanently incorporated, that the chief of the administration should be 'termed "Governor of Basra and High Commissioner of Mesopotamia," with his titular headquarters at Basra; although it would be understood that he would usually reside at Bagdad, where his most important duties would lie'. He would be assisted in his absence by two deputies residing in Basra and Baghdad. This scheme was apparently accepted by Curzon, as was the recommendation that 'The policy of His Majesty's Government should be to administer the Vilayet (Bagdad) as an Arab province, so far as possible by indigenous agency in accordance with existing laws and institutions'.[49] This rendered undesirable the extension of the Irak Code, under which Basra was governed, to Baghdad, and it was in response to this proposal, and that relating to the head of the administration, that Cox revealed a markedly different vision of Britain's presence in Mesopotamia.

Cox's views, simply stated, were that the two administrations 'should be so similar as to be indistinguishable in the making', that they were 'inseparable', and that in judicial matters they should be assimilated.[50]

The separation of the administrative arrangements envisaged in the provisional recommendations of the Mesopotamian Administration Committee was intended partly to stem the process of Indianisation. This intention was stated unequivocally in the instructions sent to the Government of India at the end of March, whereby the employment of Indians and non-Arabic or Persian Asiatics in the Baghdad Vilayet was 'to be strictly discountenanced' and, in the Basra Vilayet, where Indianisation had already occurred, discouraged.[51]

By 1917 the Government of India was prepared to forgo Indian settlement in the Baghdad Vilayet if an alternative 'field for expansion' could be found. However, the issue remained emotive and the

Government of India claimed that if alternative provision were not made then 'bitter and legitimate resentment' would arise.[52]

The crux of the issue was that labour shortages in Mesopotamia rendered essential the use of at least some Indian personnel, in whatever capacity, if the legendary wealth of Mesopotamia was to be exploited. In reply to a request for information about remaining executives and administrators, in April 1917 Cox reported that all of the executive personnel of the Baghdad Vilayet, about fifty, half of them Turks, had gone.[53] Of those in Basra, just over a third remained.[54] In 1915 Hirtzel had concluded that on political and climatic grounds Indians were unlikely to integrate with the Arab population.[55]

However, the corollary of Indian personnel was Indian method and this association was fostered by successive viceroys, including Hardinge and Chelmsford, who argued for Government of India control in Mesopotamia.[56] By 1917 this urge had dissipated but both the Government of India and Cox still spoke in terms unnerving to officials imbued with an awareness of British commitments to the Arabs. Thus Cox demanded 'latitude' in terms of employing Indians and the Government of India repeated its warning of the 'legitimate' ill-feeling which a blanket ban on Indian immigration in the occupied territories would arouse.[57] There was, moreover, the sentimental argument, in itself controversial, on which Chamberlain spoke forcefully when the Mesopotamian Administration Committee discussed the issue on 8 May: that Indian blood had, largely, won Mesopotamia for Britain.[58]

The reluctance of Curzon, Hirtzel and the Foreign Office (Hardinge included) to contemplate Indian immigration into the Baghdad Vilayet on this occasion triumphed by default and, further, by virtue of Curzon's arrogance. Emphasising that a decision could only be reached when the views of the Government of India on land settlement and personnel requirements were known, Curzon had the passive assistance of Shuckburgh, Holderness and Sir Henry McMahon who were unwilling to endorse unrestricted immigration, the context in which Curzon chose to frame the discussion.[59]

Shuckburgh, though sympathetic to the arguments of the Government of India, nevertheless opposed Indian immigration because it raised false hopes.[60] Anticipating this, Hirtzel had repeatedly urged upon the Government of India that Basra might not eventually be governed from India. Opposing immigration in 1917, Hirtzel advanced a subtle argument, designed to conform to current expressions of self-determination and to deny Britain's Allies grounds for complaint when

Britain predominated in Baghdad, possibly after the collapse of Arab government:

> there is surely a serious risk that the administration will be begun on Indian lines . . . that it will reach a considerable pitch of efficiency, if the military occupation is prolonged; and that, *either* this efficiency will be made an argument for maintaining it after the war, *or* when an attempt is made to replace it by an Arab administration, chaos may supervene and our direct intervention even be required – which would be a very unfortunate beginning.[61]

It is not perhaps too fanciful to surmise that Hirtzel intended the new Mesopotamian administration to provide a degree of efficiency which would render an Arab administration undesirable or unsuccessful but which would not compromise Britain with Hussein or the French. Failing direct control there was another possibility to which Hirtzel alluded in February 1916: namely, that for reasons of expediency Britain and her Allies should actively support the pretence of Arab self-government embodied in a façade.[62]

'THE FAÇADE MUST BE ARAB'

The emergence of a strongly Arabophile British foreign policy from 1915 placed prominent India Office officials in the paradoxical position of having to support a policy with which they disagreed to varying degrees and which threatened to upset their control of policy in the Arab world.

Hirtzel's main concern lay in the initial expectation that McMahon had promised the establishment of a Moslem entity and that Britain might conceivably be expected to help in the creation of a new Caliphate. This would have the double disadvantage of being open to misinterpretation by Britain's Moslem subjects and the possibility that temporal ambitions, bolstered by injudicious pledges of support, would, as previously noted, create a large, possibly hostile, Moslem state on India's western flank. Gradually, however, several factors rendered an Arabophile policy more appealing to Hirtzel.

Firstly, it became clear that Hussein did not have the backing of many important Arab chiefs. Secondly, by the end of 1916 if not before, Britain had controlled Hussein's claims on the religious loyalties of other Moslems. He was, therefore, permitted to style himself 'King of the Hejaz', but not, as the French were willing to permit, 'King of the Holy

Places'.[63] The reluctance with which Hirtzel and Holderness agreed even to this was symptomatic not just of Britain's fears but of Hussein's vulnerability and of the weakness of the notion of the Arab State. Thirdly, Hirtzel became publicly more sympathetic to the Arab cause because of what Britain stood to gain, by virtue of the Sykes–Picot Agreement, if this weakness proved irremediable. This would explain why Hirtzel repeatedly pressed the Government of India to follow an actively pro-Arab policy. It might equally explain why, during the Rabegh crisis in the autumn of 1916, Hirtzel advised limited military action by Britain which would, above all else, avoid the impression that France rather than Britain had saved the Arab revolt.[64] Advising a more vigorous military effort in the autumn of 1916, Hirtzel quoted Curzon, who had 'expressed the opinion that it is useless any longer to pretend that we are not supporting the Shereef. We should come into the open, and do all we can for him.'[65]

Like Hirtzel, Curzon had been initially sceptical of the wisdom of supporting Arab claims. There were, to Curzon's mind, in April 1915, too many uncertainties, not least the military position at the Dardanelles, to justify a discussion of the future of the Caliphate. Britain had yet to reach Constantinople and even if the Caliph were replaced there was no guarantee that he would be accepted by the Moslem world. Curzon continued his explanation in a letter to Cromer:

> The Arabs are now opening their mouths very wide and appear to want a new Arabian State and Khalifate from the Persian Gulf to Egypt and from Egypt to Syria (which it is to include). What evidence have they shown of their capacity to organise or administer such a state? Where is the new man of the Koreish tribe whom they will accept? Where is to be his seat of Government? Is it to be at Baghdad, which is still in possession of the Turks and likely for a long time to remain so? Or is it to be at Sanaa, which the Yemen Arabs are so feeble that they have never been able to hold – or at Jerusalem – a pretty kettle of fish! How futile it would be to declare the formation of a new state without territory, without capital and without ruler!

Uncertainties apart, there were unpalatable implications inherent in this proposal. According to Curzon, if Britain supported the Arabs she would forfeit to them significant gains in the Middle East when they were 'at this moment fighting against us as hard as they can, and are known to be in the pay of the Germans'.

As Curzon continued, Britain must move towards establishing 'a possible new Khalifate in the future' by influencing important Arabs. He concluded: 'Should we not be in a very unfortunate position if we were now to give public pledges which we afterwards failed to redeem?'[66]

The Curzon–Cromer correspondence was sustained by letters written to Cromer from the Sudan and Cairo by Sir Reginald Wingate and by McMahon, in which they divulged plans for enlisting Arab support. Though sceptical in tone, Curzon's letters to Cromer, which were relayed to Cairo, reveal an underlying interest which increased with time:

> We ought to know more about this Sherif of Mecca. His family and position are impeccable. But what of the man? I am amused at the tacit assumption of all the Arab or Moslem writers that whoever the new Khalif is he will have to be bolstered up by us. This is rather dangerous, for if we subsidise him and make him our man, we shall, no doubt, be called upon to support him with our arms when his Khalifate begins to totter or crumble. It will be the old Afghan business, but worse.[67]

Curzon's preoccupation with other duties and Cromer's illness obscure the development of Curzon's thinking on the Arab question after the beginning of 1916. What is certain is that Curzon objected strongly to the Sykes–Picot Agreement of May 1916.

Curzon believed that French territorial ambitions in the Middle East overreached any realistic expectation of future physical control. In a letter to Grey in the first days of February, he observed:

> I am at a loss to understand why the French – apart from their Syrian ambitions – should want to push Eastwards to Diarbekir and the Persian Frontier.
>
> This would be folly for them – as they would soon find out when they presently had to deal with the Armenian and Kurdish questions and further . . . I regard it with some alarm for ourselves.[68]

More significantly, the ensuing strain or breach in Anglo-French relations would leave France not only with a promise of future retention of Cyprus, which, Curzon believed, would lead to its cession within twenty years; but, more importantly, with a 'huge Asiatic Protectorate – a substantial voice in determining the future of Persia and Mesopotamia and therefore of our Indian Empire'.

Moreover, Curzon objected to the proposed French control of the one rail link, via Alexandretta and Aleppo, which would ensure the commercial development of Northern Mesopotamia, Britain meanwhile having to content herself with a desert line from Haifa and Acre through Palestine – of strategic but not economic value.

Anglo-French relations would also suffer because of confusion over water rights, because it was not stated exactly how Jerusalem was to be governed and because there was no clear delineation of the border between the proposed internationalised Palestine and Egypt. There was also the question of where the Arab 'authority' should reside as Britain and France, Curzon noted, had 'gobbled up' most of the available towns.

However, early in 1916 Curzon doubted whether the scheme would ever be realised because, according to McMahon, Arab support could only be won and their defection prevented by implementing Kitchener's proposed landing at Ayas Bay, something rendered impossible by lack of troops. The strength of Curzon's opposition to the Agreement is explicable with reference to a much more fundamental aspect of it and one which provided much of the impetus for his subsequent thinking on the Middle East:

> This scheme emerged out of the discussions between the Arabs and ourselves as to the adjustment of our future relations arising out of our advance to Baghdad and the contemplated defeat and disappearance of the Turks.
>
> France played no part in the initial discussion . . .
>
> . . . the upshot of the whole thing is to be the creation of a great French Asiatic Protectorate, in countries where they have none but the most shadowy sentimental claim, while they have not landed a man or fired a shot.

In addition, Curzon's dislike of Sykes–Picot was due, increasingly, to the fact that although Russia was extremely weak, Britain could not capitalise on this fully by virtue of French gains in Syria, Cilicia and Mosul.

THE MEN ON THE SPOT

At the meeting of the Mesopotamian Administration Committee on 8 May, Austen Chamberlain expressed doubts about regenerating native government in the Baghdad Vilayet. The corollary of this, the assimilation of the two Vilayets, Curzon objected to on 'international' grounds. He argued, unconvincingly, that the Baghdad Vilayet might be used as a counter 'to effect the restoration of the Allied territory in Europe now in German hands'. Equally improbably he held that, in the event of a separate peace with Turkey, Baghdad might be the necessary price for Britain's retention of Palestine.[69] Curzon was content to dabble in hypothetical calculations with which he perhaps felt it necessary to be seen to associate himself when, in fact, like Hirtzel, he had no intention of agreeing to a peace of any kind, let alone a compromise peace, until all his imperial desiderata, including Baghdad and Palestine, had been secured. Writing in May 1917, Curzon noted in a memorandum:

> As to Turkey there appears to be no reason why she should wish to con-
> clude a separate peace at the present stage. She now knows that she will
> retain Constantinople, without in all probability having to pay any price
> for it. No argument would prevail but the restoration by ourselves of
> Mesopotamia, or at least of Baghdad, which we are not prepared to con-
> sider . . . Just as we are fighting in the West to reduce the military strength
> of Germany to a point at which she would be prepared to consider peace
> on reasonable terms, so we must continue to fight Turkey in the East if we
> desire to bring her to a similar state of mind.

Uncertainty about Turkish operations in Mesopotamia prevented the despatch of a commission to study local conditions, the necessary precursor to a decision on the nature of a future Arab administration. Curzon apparently continued to invest hope in this uncertainty and in the force of physical occupation. Writing about the peace movement in May 1917, he observed:

> it is very easy to engage not to annex what you have not already won and
> have no chance of winning – and . . . it will be necessary to bear very
> closely in mind in the approaching months the sharp distinction between
> the abandonment of impossible territorial ambitions, and the surrender of
> territories already in military occupation.[70]

In the morally charged political atmosphere of 1917, Hirtzel, in reiterating that Arab areas would not revert to Turkish control, wielded a more potent weapon than Curzon. To Hirtzel, especially, the flies in the ointment were the men on the spot with their alarming Indianising tendencies. These persisted despite repeated attempts by the Mesopotamian Administration Committee to reinforce the separation between the Vilayets and the need to avoid actions which might be seen to prejudice the establishment of an Arab government in Baghdad. This was precisely what Hirtzel feared might happen if Cox were granted the latitude with regard to personnel which he requested. Holderness and Chamberlain sympathised with Maude's view that 'Before any truly Arab façade can be applied to [the] edifice it seems essential that [a] foundation of law and order should be well and truly laid'.[71] Moreover, although not in favour of Indianisation, Holderness supported uniform laws and administration in the two Vilayets, and emphasised Cox and the Government of India having 'considerable freedom' in providing 'such temporary political and administrative staff as cannot at once be spared by Egypt and Sudan'.[72]

The continuing threat of a Turkish counter-offensive also disrupted communications between Cox and his superiors in London and triggered a lingering controversy over the status of Maude and Cox which preoccupied the Mesopotamian Administration Committee inter-mittently, well into the summer of 1917.

The question was first addressed by the Committee on 12 June, and from the outset Curzon's proposed solution was clear. He presented the controversy as 'a question of policy' and stated that the Committee's objective must be 'to decide which side they should take in this differ-ence of opinion – whether to stand by Cox, or whether they should give way to General Maude'.[73]

In a personal telegram to the India Office on 25 May Cox had suggested either that he be permitted to report direct to the India Office or that he be made High Commissioner.[74] Curzon favoured the second option, commenting on Cox: 'His position must be consolidated and, as time . . . [goes] on, his powers extended and there was danger of losing ground in this direction.'[75]

By implication, civil administration must proceed and be given time to take root regardless of the military situation. Neither the objection raised by Chamberlain, that this would contravene the Hague Convention, nor the possibility of upsetting the Russians, to which Robert Graham alluded, deterred Curzon who, noting the concurrence of Hardinge and McMahon, suggested that the views of the Government of India be sought on a change in Cox's status. Pending their reply, Curzon suggested that Cox's ideas be sought in greater detail.[76]

The Maude–Cox dispute had arisen in another context, that of river irrigation, on which the future exploitation of Mesopotamian wealth was seen to hinge. The Mesopotamian Administration Committee had proposed that control of irrigation in both Vilayets be placed under a single British administration and that this should be the case with navi-gation and river conservancy. In this the Committee had the approval of Cox and the Government of India, although the latter advised against any large-scale initiatives until the question of Indian immigration had been resolved.[77]

Cox knew that military interference with Arab water rights could seriously hinder civil administration. Conversely, local reports suggested that a scientific development of irrigation might quell tribal unrest. To avoid interference by the military, Cox requested that the proposed irrigation officer for Mesopotamia be placed under his orders.[78]

Shortly afterwards Curzon, who endorsed Cox's request, and Chamberlain met with Sir William Robertson, CIGS, and gained his approval for a telegram sent to the Government of India and Cox, whereby Cox was to have the rank of Civil Commissioner in Mesopotamia and with it the duty to report regularly to the India Office.[79] Obtaining War Office approval had delayed matters and exposed the disadvantages of there being no War Office representative on the Mesopotamian Administration Committee until the eighth meeting on 10 August.

The strengthening of Cox's hand reflected the drift towards providing for what, in Chamberlain's view, was more than a mere Arab façade.[80] However, Robertson had capitulated only on condition that Maude's position as 'the ultimate seat of authority' be clearly understood; and Maude objected strongly to his new status, adding that until the military situation was 'securely established', the 'development of civil administration' in the Baghdad Vilayet would have to wait.[81]

By appointing Ronald Storrs as Oriental Secretary to Cox, in default of General Clayton as Deputy High Commissioner, the Mesopotamian Administration Committee had increased Cox's authority.[82] In view of the nature of Maude's telegram, however, Shuckburgh and Holderness wished to drop the matter until the military situation cleared.[83] The War Office and Government of India concurred.[84]

Subsequent minutes of the Mesopotamian Administration Committee do not reveal with clarity who the activating figures were in reviving efforts to strengthen Cox's position. Hirtzel, certainly, while content that full-scale civil administration should lie in abeyance, pressed that Cox should be allowed to report freely.[85] His views were attributable, in part, to fears that military interference with Arab water rights would compromise Britain with the Arabs. In this he found an ally in Curzon to whom he sent a letter from Gertrude Bell claiming that Cox's correspondence was subject to military censorship and that Maude was both failing to execute orders and to communicate them to Cox. Hirtzel did not circulate the letter to the Mesopotamian Administration Committee fearing that it would 'give her away to the soldiers'.[86] The outcome of this manoeuvring and a further communication with Cox was that on 20 August Cox telegraphed that Maude had agreed to his appointment as Civil Commissioner and to his communicating direct with HMG so long as Maude was first shown this correspondence on the understanding that he could alter it.[87]

Maude feared, and Curzon may have intended, that this submission paved the way for a revival of civil administration.[88] Allying himself with Curzon, Hirtzel perceived sufficient restraints on Cox to preclude any new large schemes of civil administration but sufficient scope to guarantee a free channel of communication, the creation of order where before there was chaos and a regime which, blending efficiency and sensitivity to local opinion, would guarantee Britain's future in Mesopotamia.[89]

The Mesopotamian Administration Committee, like its successors the Middle East and Eastern Committees, suffered throughout its existence from conflicting departmental interests. It seems likely that departmental loyalties found expression in decentralising tendencies and that the area of conflict grew in proportion to the geographical scope of the Committee.

By July 1917 Sykes believed for various reasons that the scope must be enlarged:

> you may have noticed that the coming into being of the Mesopotamian Administration Committee has, under your Chairmanship, tended to act as a long felt want viz: a co-ordinating instrument. Both the Foreign Office and the India Office have referred to you for your decision matters which would not otherwise have been dealt with at all, or would have appeared and disappeared as did the 'Rabegh' question. The influence of the Committee under your guidance has been to speed up decisions and clear up situations, however . . . you may not have noticed that . . . the Committee is becoming a permanent factor in the conduct of our middle and near Eastern affairs. If this is to be continued (and it has been what both Clayton and I have long prayed for, namely that you should assume control of the whole of the middle Eastern problem), I think it will be advisable to give a new name for the Committee, to define its scope of work and fix on regular ordinary meeting days. There should also be some means devised for disposing of minor questions in order to avoid delay, as the agenda of the Committee is likely to become over charged.
>
> If the Committee resolved that you as Chairman should dispose of these lesser questions while keeping them informed of the action taken, one weekly meeting would suffice.[90]

This improbable enthusiasm for increasing Curzon's power was not sufficient to ensure that it gained the approval of the members of the Mesopotamian Administration Committee when the proposal was discussed on 21 July. It was instead decided that administrative matters rather than questions of policy, which required immediate action, would be referred to Curzon, Montagu and Balfour.[91] Further, the Committee subsequently recommended that the approval of the War Cabinet should be sought for a change in the Committee's name to the Middle Eastern Administration Committee.[92]

The Middle East Committee, as the Mesopotamian Administration Committee ultimately became, did not meet in its new composition until January 1918.[93] Well before that, however, Curzon had steered the Committee towards accepting a permanent British presence in the Basra and Baghdad Vilayets. As far as the retention of Basra went, there was Turkish aggression, the fact of British military control, historic trading links, the unpopularity of the Turkish 'interlopers' and, above all, the 'solemn promise' given to local chiefs and by the Viceroy publicly at Basra that the Basra Vilayet would not revert to the Turk.[94] Also there was the related moral responsibility: 'we have administered Basra and the Basra Vilayet for nearly three years and have made ourselves responsible for the welfare and good Government of the people. It is impossible that we should break with them and allow them to revert to their oppressors.'[95]

Impelled by strategic necessity Britain had, according to Curzon, occupied the Baghdad Vilayet. By 1917 even military defeat could not, for strategic reasons, justify the cession of the Basra Vilayet whilst, if victorious, there were, according to Curzon, many reasons against returning the Baghdad Vilayet to the Turks. If abandoned, Britain's Mesopotamian allies would be 'massacred to a man' and would, if spared, 'desert the British cause at such a flagrant exhibition of weakness and bad faith'. More broadly, Curzon argued, Hussein's fate would be sealed and the success of the Arab movement would be seriously jeopardised. Turkish prestige would revive at the cost of Britain's throughout the east. In this atmosphere retreat from Baghdad would 'restore to life the shattered German ambitions of a great Teutonised dominion stretching through Europe and Asia Minor as far as the Persian Gulf – which is the real dream of German world policy and is the weapon with which, in a future war, the British Empire is to be struck down'.

The underlying purpose of Curzon's involvement in Mesopotamian affairs was to maximise Britain's presence in the country. His belief in the benefits conferred by Britain on subject peoples was unflinching but in the context of the war was of small significance when compared with the vital fact of occupation. This would ensure and was already assured by the fact that German ambitions were 'shattered'. Subsequent memoranda place the Baghdad Vilayet in its proper context. It was, neither in 1917 nor in 1918, something to be bargained over. Rather it was a legitimate spoil of war, to be retained at all military costs and, when hostilities ceased, to reflect glory on the Empire. If Britain's defeat were unthinkable, the corollary was the defeat of Germany and Turkey and the need to prepare to face other potentially hostile powers. France, certainly, had economic and strategic ambitions in the country and this was reflected both in Sykes–Picot and in subsequent diplomatic developments. Yet for Curzon and Hardinge at least, the 'unpublicised motive' for the advance arose from a traditional conception of Anglo-Russian rivalry in which Britain had to capitalise on the weakness of her foe.

NOTES

1. See Appendix 1. With neither foresight nor imperial ambitions in the east to enhance his judgement, Sir William Robertson, CIGS, viewed the capture of Baghdad as setting the seal on British gains in the Middle East, provided, of course, that Russia was able to occupy Mosul: Robertson to Murray, 14 March 1917, War Office, Robertson–Murray Correspondence Add. Ms 52462, f. 65. Writing from Paris, where he was Counsellor at the British Embassy, George Grahame noted that 'the capture of Baghdad, coming on the top of our advance on the Western front, created an enormous impression'. Concerns about Russia and about internal politics merely served, in Grahame's opinion, to boost Britain's kudos in French eyes: Grahame to Drummond, 17 March 1917, Paris, confidential, FO 899/12. For Lord Esher, also in Paris, the fall of Baghdad provided an opportunity to gloat in the triumph of British arms and in the disparity between British and French attainments. Writing on 13 March Esher observed, in a manner which must have done much to cement Anglo-French relations,

   > This week has brought Baghdad to us, but the French *may* well have lost Alsace. As I have told some of these Frenchmen, *we* are a curiously lucky people. Everything hitherto has come our way. The Empire accrued by accident. Now we have Mesopotamia, and *all* the German Colonies. German expansion is at an end.

   Entry of 13 March 1917, Esher Papers and Diaries 2/18; see also entry of previous day. There was some evidence to suggest that Esher's final remark reflected sentiments in the German Chancery: Rumbold to Balfour, 3 April 1917, Berne, FO 371/3081, p. 121.
      By 16 March Esher's euphoria knew no limits. Britain, as he informed Robertson, was 'following our usual destiny' and would be the only power to emerge from the war with territorial gain. The Empire, Esher concluded, 'will be a very formidable organism': Esher to Robertson, 16 March 1917, Paris, Esher Papers and Diaries 2/18.
      This evidence would tend to contradict B.C. Busch's notion of the taking of Baghdad as being a 'hollow victory'. Even in the context of Anglo-Russian rivalry, Britain's possession of the city was a valuable asset in view of the possibility of a revival of Russian strength; see B.C. Busch, *Britain, India and the Arabs, 1914–21* (Berkeley, Los Angeles, London, 1971), p. 135.
2. This strong India Office contingent was buttressed by the presence of the Secretary of State for India and, on most occasions, by that of the Military Secretary, Sir H.V. Cox. Sir Henry McMahon attended regularly in an independent capacity and, once the War Office had begun its involvement with the Committee, it was represented either by Major-General Macdonogh or, in his absence, by Lt. Colonel Steel. Sir Ronald Graham, as the Assistant Under-Secretary with responsibility for eastern affairs, was the usual Foreign Office delegate and he was joined on a number of occasions by George Clerk, a Senior Clerk at the Foreign Office, by Lord

Hardinge, and by Foreign Secretary, A.J. Balfour. Lord Milner, who attended the first meetings, thereafter withdrew on account of pressure of work. Sir Mark Sykes was Secretary of the Committee and J.E. Shuckburgh of the India Office acted in this capacity in his absence.

3. On the outbreak of war with Turkey, Britain had issued a declaration to the Trucial Chiefs confirming them in their rights and in their special relations with the British Empire.
4. Minute by Hirtzel for E.G. Barrow, 24 February 1915, Barrow Collection E420/12, ff. 14–15.
5. Note by Hirtzel, n.d., (December) 1914, L/P+S/11/87 P342.
6. Ibid.
7. Ibid. For an assessment of the significance of Britain's relations with the Arabs in the inception of Britain's Mesopotamian campaign see S.A. Cohen, 'The Genesis of the British Campaign in Mesopotamia, 1914', *MES*, 12 (1976).
8. See Hardinge, *Old Diplomacy: Reminiscences of Lord Hardinge of Penshurst* (London, 1947), pp. 218–19, 243; D. Goold, *HJ*, p. 944.
9. Hardinge to Curzon, 10 February 1915, Viceregal Lodge, Curzon Papers F112/163.
10. See ch. 1, n.34.
11. See ch. 1, n.130; also at L/MIL/5/753; ibid., conclusions of a committee on question of advance on Baghdad, 16 October 1915, App. 8, p. 3. Besides Holderness, who chaired the Committee, the following attended: E.G. Barrow, D. Gamble, Louis Mallet, L. Oliphant, M.G. Talbot, S.S.W. Paddon. E.D. Swinton and S.K. Brown were, respectively, Secretary and Assistant Secretary.
12. See ch. 1, nn.135, 136.
13. Note by the Under-Secretary, India Office, 'The War With Turkey', 13 June 1916, L/P+S/18/B234, secret.
14. Maude to S/S, 6 March 1917, L/P+S/10/666, p. 183.
15. Ibid. S/S to Viceroy, draft, despatched 12 March 1917, p. 180.
16. Ibid. Political Officer, Basra, to Foreign Department, 8 March 1917, no. 1795, P1079/17, pp. 189–90; minute by Hirtzel, 9 March 1917, pp. 168ff.
17. Ibid. Minute by Hirtzel.
18. Ibid.
19. Ibid.
20. Ibid. Whilst Nevakivi, *Britain, France and the Arab Middle East*, p. 60, mentions that Sykes drafted a proclamation, he does not state that the proclamation, in its final form, was drawn up by 'a Whitehall Committee'; see H.V. Winstone, *The Illicit Adventure*, p. 329.
21. Attached in its final form as Appendix 2.
22. Ibid.
23. See n. 16, minute by Hirtzel.
24. Draft Proclamation 'To the People of Baghdad', secret, Curzon Papers F112/256, ff. 5–6; Minute by Chamberlain, 10 March 1917, G.T. 139, f. 4.
25. Ibid. Memorandum by Sykes, 10 March 1917, G.T. 142, ff. 8–10.
26. Ibid.
27. Minutes of the War Cabinet, 12 March 1917, CAB 23/1, secret.
28. GOC, Force 'D', to Foreign Department, 16 March 1917, X1309, L/P+S/10/666, p. 160.
29. Ibid. Minute by Chamberlain, n.d., on draft telegram S/S to Viceroy, despatched 17 March 1917, p. 158.
30. Ibid.
31. Ibid. Minutes by Hardinge, n.d., Curzon and Milner, 17 March 1917, p. 155.
32. Ibid. Minute by Hirtzel, 17 March 1917, p. 156.
33. Mesopotamian Administration Committee, provisional recommendations of the Committee, 21 March 1917, Mark Sykes, G.T. 230, CAB 27/22.
34. S/S to Viceroy, 29 March 1917, Foreign Secret, Mesopotamian Administration Committee, P1315, Curzon Papers F112/256, f. 66; see E. Kedourie, *England and the Middle East: The Destruction of the Ottoman Empire, 1914–1921* (London, 1987), p. 176; Cox to Foreign Department, 7 April 1917, T. 1049, ibid., f. 18ff.; Viceroy to S/S, 27 April 1917, secret, G.T. 614, ibid., ff. 23–4. The GOI did not reply in full to the telegram of 29 March until 25 May 1917; GOI to S/S, 25 May 1917, no. 44, secret, ibid., ff. 76–8.
35. Ibid. See also, tabulation of responses, G.T. 661, f. 28ff.
36. Minutes of a meeting of the War Committee, 6 July 1916, CAB 42/16; App. 1, memorandum by Sykes, 6 July 1916.

37. Ibid.
38. Ibid.
39. Ibid. See also, minutes of the War Committee of 11 July 1916.
40. See n.33.
41. Ibid. See also, n.36, minutes of the War Committee.
42. See n.33.
43. R. Adelson, *Mark Sykes, Portrait of an Amateur* (London, 1975), p. 224.
44. See n.34, S/S to Viceroy, 29 March 1917.
45. Mesopotamian Administration Committee, report of sub-committee appointed under paragraph 17 of the minutes of 21 March 1917, J. E. Shuckburgh, 27 March 1917. Also on the sub-committee were Holderness, Sykes, McMahon, Graham and Clerk. Curzon Papers F112/256, ff. 58–9, 60–1.
46. Ibid.
47. Ibid.
48. Note by Hirtzel on Chelmsford's letter of 30 December 1916, CAB 27/22; also at L/P+S/18/B246; quoted in H. Mejcher, 8, *JCH*, p. 84.
49. See n.45.
50. See n.34, Cox to Foreign Department, 7 April 1917.
51. Ibid. S/S to Viceroy, 29 March 1917.
52. See n.34, G.T. 614.
53. Cox to IO, 20 April 1917, L/P+S/10/516 P1661; see P. Sluglett, *Britain in Iraq, 1914–32* (London, 1976), p. 14.
54. See n.50.
55. See ch. 1, n.34.
56. Note by the Viceroy of India, Hardinge, 24 February 1915, App. 5, CAB 27/1; extract from a private letter from Lord Chelmsford, 18 October 1916, L/P+S/18/B246; for a broader perspective on the issue of Indianisation see Sluglett, op. cit., p. 14ff. Implicit in the question, as Sluglett suggests, was the matter of introducing into Mesopotamia a system which was in the process of reform in India. This factor had to be balanced with a need, accepted by many but not by Curzon, to find new territories for India's over-large population.
57. See n.34, Cox to Foreign Department, 7 April 1917, T. 1049; ibid. GOI to S/S, 25 May 1917, no. 44.
58. Minutes of the Mesopotamian Administration Committee, 8 May 1917, second meeting, secret, CAB 27/22.
59. Ibid.
60. Minute by Shuckburgh, 9 April 1917, L/P+S/10/666, pp. 123–5; minute by Shuckburgh, 23 April 1917, L/P+S/10/514, pt. 2 P1671.
61. Minute by Hirtzel, 11 April 1917, L/P+S/10/666, pp. 125–6.
62. This idea had occurred to A.S. Ryan, Acting First Dragoman, Constantinople, some time before; see S.A. Cohen, *MES*, 12, n. 96.
63. Minute by Hirtzel, (?5) December 1916, L/P+S/10/637 P5097. For a fresh and relatively recent perspective on this matter see E. Tauber, *The Arab Movement in World War I* (London, 1993), pp. 158–9.
64. Minute by Hirtzel, 10 December 1916, L/P+S/10/602 P5213. R. Bidwell provides a broader assessment of the Rabegh question in 'The Bremond Mission in the Hijaz, 1916–17: A Study in Inter-Allied Co-operation', in *Arabian and Islamic Studies*, ed. R. Bidwell and G.R. Smith (London, New York, 1983), pp. 184ff.
65. Minute by Hirtzel, 1 September 1916, L/P+S/10/600 P3528.
66. Curzon to Cromer, 22 April 1915, 1 Carlton House Terrace, Cromer Papers, FO 633, vol. 24, f. 77; see Kedourie, *The Chatham House Version*, pp. 14–15.
67. Ibid. Curzon to Cromer, 9 June 1915, 1 Carlton House Terrace, f. 115.
68. Curzon to Grey, 3 February 1916, 1 Carlton House Terrace, Grey Papers FO 800/106, f. 526. The remaining material in this section relates to this letter.
69. Minutes of the Mesopotamian Administration Committee, 8 May 1917, second meeting, secret, CAB 27/22.
70. Memorandum by Curzon, 'Policy in view of Russian Developments', 12 May 1917, secret, G.T. 705, drafted by Leo Amery and rewritten by Curzon.

71. GOC Basra to Foreign Department, 16 March 1917, X1310, L/P+S/10/666, p. 160.
72. Ibid. Minute by Holderness, 3 May 1917, pp. 120–1.
73. Minutes of the Mesopotamian Administration Committee, 12 June 1917, third meeting, secret, CAB 27/22.
74. Cox to S/S, 25 May 1917, personal, L/P+S/10/666, p. 105.
75. See n.73.
76. Ibid.
77. See n.35.
78. Cox to S/S, 6 June 1917, L/P+S/10/678 P2308.
79. Minutes of the Mesopotamian Administration Committee, 3 July 1917, fifth meeting, CAB 27/22; see appendix 1 of this meeting. For Robertson's feelings on the matter see Robertson to Monro, 1 August 1917, secret and personal, Monro Papers D783/2.
80. Minute by Chamberlain, 31 March 1917, L/P+S/10/617, p. 276.
81. See note eleven, Appendix 1: GOC Mesopotamia to C-in-C, India, 9 July 1917, no. x2782, secret, CAB 27/22.
82. Ibid. Fifth meeting of the Mesopotamian Administration Committee.
83. Minutes by Shuckburgh and Holderness, 1 August and 31 August 1917, L/P+S/10/666, pp. 67–8.
84. Robertson to Montagu, 1 August 1917, War Office, SW, enclosed in Shuckburgh to Bosworth Smith, 3 August 1917, Curzon Papers F 112/256, f. 113.
85. Ibid. Minute by Hirtzel, (?28) July 1917.
86. Ibid. Hirtzel to Curzon, 13 August 1917, India Office, Whitehall, SW, private, p. 124.
87. Cox to S/S, 20 August 1917, L/P+S/10/666, p. 53, no. 3321.
88. See Mejcher, *JCH*, 8, pp. 87–8.
89. Minute by Hirtzel, 27 August 1917, L/P+S/10/666, p. 42.
90. Sykes to Curzon, 2 July 1917, Offices of the War Cabinet, 2 Whitehall Gardens, London, SW1, Curzon Papers F112/272. Whilst the discussion of spheres of influence by the Mesopotamian Administration Committee entailed some examination of Southern Persia, it seems that the gradual extension of the Committee's remit to include Arabia and the Hejaz was triggered by Sykes's letter. Balfour agreed to the change possibly because of his awareness of the volume of work generated by international rivalries in those areas; Drummond to Hankey, 7 July 1917, CAB 21/60; see also, Mejcher, *JCH*, 8, p. 82.
91. Minutes of the Mesopotamian Administration Committee, 21 July 1917, seventh meeting, secret, CAB 27/22.
92. Ibid. Minutes of the ninth meeting, 22 August 1917.
93. Minutes of a meeting of the Middle East Committee, 19 January 1918, *MEC* 1, new series, CAB 27/23. The final meeting of the Mesopotamian Administration Committee, so called, took place on 22 August 1917. The Committee, in its original composition, subsequently sat on two further occasions, 13 September 1917 and 12 January 1918, under the name of the Middle East Committee.
94. Memorandum by Curzon, 21 September 1917, 'British Policy in Mesopotamia', secret, CAB 21/61. Curzon's memorandum was written in response to a claim by the Labour member of the War Cabinet, George Barnes, that the Labour Party wished to know what attitude the Government would adopt towards Mesopotamia after the war. Moreover the Labour Party, according to Barnes, suspected the Government of imperialist intentions and wondered why, if Britain won the war, Mesopotamia should not revert to Turkey. Although Curzon did not, as Rothwell implies, state that Britain had given a 'solemn pledge' to annex the Basra Vilayet, it was implicit in his memorandum on Mesopotamia; see Rothwell, *HJ*, 13, pp. 274–5. It is interesting to note, however, that Cyril Longhurst, Curzon's private secretary, when asked by Sylvester Ives of the War Cabinet Offices if any action was required on Curzon's memorandum, replied that it was 'on no account to be circulated to anybody unless Lord Curzon gives instructions'; minute by Longhurst, 22 September 1917, CAB 21/61. On Curzon's instructions, a copy of his note and of the proclamation issued on the capture of Baghdad were to be given to Barnes.
95. Ibid. Memorandum by Curzon. The remaining material in this section relates to Curzon's memorandum.

❀ 3 ❀

Arabian Matters

THE POLICY OF DRIFT

B Y ARTICLE TEN of the Sykes–Picot Agreement, Britain and France declared themselves to be co-protectors of the Arab State. The clause continued: 'they will not acquire and will not consent to a third Power acquiring territorial possessions in the Arabian Peninsula, nor consent to a third Power installing a naval base either on the east coast, or on the islands of the Red Sea'.[1]

Directly upon the divulging of this Agreement to the Italians on 18 May 1916, their inevitable cries of exclusion began to be heard. Previous efforts by Italy to encourage trade across the Red Sea, between her colony of Eritrea and the Yemen, had been frustrated by the British blockade.[2] In September 1916, writing to Hardinge from Rome where he was British Ambassador, Sir Rennell Rodd reported that the Italian Minister for the Colonies had, with the approval of the Italian Foreign Minister, Baron Sonnino, suggested that the moment was opportune for a joint Anglo-Italian declaration of policy regarding the Red Sea littoral.[3] Then, on 23 September, Rodd suggested that Italy might wish to be included alongside France and Britain as a protector of the Arab State. Rodd mistakenly assumed that the Arabian Peninsula lay within area 'B' of Sykes–Picot, thereby conferring on Britain priority of right of enterprise and of local loans. However, this notwithstanding, Rodd was sympathetic to Italian fears of economic exclusion:

> It is clear that with the long coastal possessions of the Italians on the western side of the Red Sea they must trade with the Eastern side and anything which menaced exclusion would be resented. A certain group here has long put forward the idea of priority of enterprise in the Yemen, and though I have not had a clear indication that the Government support such a proposal, they can hardly not be susceptible to the agitation which will be aroused on the subject in this country. When you look at their possessions on the western side of the Red Sea it is clear that they must feel an interest in what takes place on the other side.[4]

Hardinge's perception of the issue during 1915–16 reflected the unyielding stance of senior British officials to these and other Italian pretensions in subsequent years. In response to Rodd's letter of 9 September, Hardinge had spoken of the uniform suspicion with which Italian territorial designs on Western Arabia were viewed in London and Delhi. It was, Hardinge observed, ostensibly to pre-empt such acquisitive instincts that Britain had occupied islands in the Red Sea in 1915. Hardinge continued:

> We ourselves have no desire to extend our possessions in the Red Sea or to hold any more than a protected territory round Aden, but we have for a very long time – much longer than the Italians – had agreements and relations with the tribal Chiefs of the eastern coast of the Red Sea, and I am unable to say off hand whether it would suit us and the Government of India to subscribe to a Self-Denying Ordinance as to the future.[5]

Hardinge's irritation at Rodd's implication that Britain might be fettered by Italian interference was reflected in this and subsequent correspondence where Hardinge's tone reflected a strong consensus that the Italian claims were quite inadmissible.[6]

Rodd maintained that such an attitude would increase antipathy towards the French in Italy. Without colonies the large emigrant Italian population must settle in the predominantly French controlled North African seaboard and this, Rodd believed, might stimulate nationalist sentiment which questioned the wisdom of Italian loyalty to the Entente.[7]

At the India Office, the task of defining British interests in the Arabian Peninsula had fallen to Hirtzel in the Political and Secret Department, and to Barrow in the Military Department. It was a basic precept of British policy that what was then an exclusive British preserve should remain thus, lying as it did on the path of two main approaches to India. This was especially the case because, as Hirtzel noted, Britain could only maintain internal tranquillity in the Peninsula by sustaining her relationship with the tribal chiefs on its periphery.[8] The peculiar character of the tribes of Arabia rendered the population volatile and prone to unrest and enduring feuds. This was compounded by the survival of remnants of Turkish suzerainty in the Yemen and by Turkish manipulation of the Imam of Sanaa.[9]

The demarcation of the Yemen–Aden frontier by Britain had, according to Hirtzel, been an exercise in containment, aimed at curtailing the activities of the Imam who held claim to tribes east of Aden.[10]

This fragile arrangement was sustained by friendship with the Sultan of Shehr and Mokalla[11] and on the untamed section of the Aden frontier by the existence of the Rub al Khali desert.

Barrow assessed as follows the military implications of the injection of an element of foreign intrigue into the Peninsula:

> If some other European power gains a footing in either Yemen, Asir or Hejaz we shall be confronted with a new era of intrigue and tribal disturbance. We shall have warring factions on our borders, the arms trade will be intensified, the peaceful development of commerce will be arrested and the 'Haj' in which, on account of our Mahommedan subjects, we are so profoundly interested may be interrupted to our detriment.

The ensuing anti-Christian feelings would, in Barrow's opinion, necessitate a considerable increase of British troops at Aden and Perim. Worse still, active intervention in the Lahej hinterland and the permanent occupation of Sheikh Said and Camaran might be necessary. As Barrow concluded, the repercussions of this might stretch to several areas of the Middle East including Mesopotamia and Egypt: 'All Arabia and with it all adjacent Islamic countries may be unsettled, and we shall then have to increase our garrisons at Basra and elsewhere in Mesopotamia as well as in Egypt.'[12] Hirtzel agreed but in a memorandum of January 1917 directed his analysis specifically to the issue of Italian involvement in the Yemen.

In 1915 Britain had guaranteed the independence of the Idrisi[13] and, according to Hirtzel, there were other lesser tribal leaders in the region adjoining Aden whose independence Britain would hope to see maintained. There was, further, a risk of the diversion of the valuable land trade between Aden and the Yemen should a rival power be established in the Yemen.

The hostility between Islam and Italy arising from the Italo-Turkish war, was compounded in Hirtzel's view by 'Italian methods of colonial administration' and by 'national characteristics'. Should Italy attempt to foment conflict between the Imam and Idrisi then this would, in Hirtzel's opinion, affect the Aden frontier necessitating an active British response. Should the Imam acquiesce in Italian domination, then those claims most likely to be pressed with success would lie south of those areas claimed by the Idrisi, either within the Aden protectorate or in the neighbouring Hadramaut.[14]

Such developments were symptomatic of what might happen should Italy be admitted to the Arabian Peninsula on an equal footing with

Britain. It was for those reasons that, in September 1916, Hirtzel had argued so forcefully against such a move on the basis that to do this would be to repeat the mistake of the Anglo-Russian Convention on Tibet of 1907. As Hirtzel noted, the Convention failed to acknowledge that Britain, being limitrophe with Tibet, had far greater interests there than had Russia. Similarly, whilst Italian interests in the Arabian Peninsula lay mainly in trade across the Red Sea and, in particular, with the Yemen, Britain was already an established territorial power in the Peninsula. As Britain was limitrophe with the Yemen, and as political relations with 'its master' were therefore necessary, it was inconceivable that Britain should disregard developments there.[15]

Though sympathetic to Hirtzel's desire to deny Italy a foothold, Holderness felt that Britain could not aspire to achieve this by seeking to obtain a recognition of Britain's superior interests in the Yemen on the basis of being a limitrophe power.[16]

By January 1917 more general considerations influenced Hirtzel. Characteristically juxtaposing the cataclysmic with the prophetic, Hirtzel wrote that if Britain condoned Italian expansionism it would be regarded by Hussein and his followers 'as a breach of faith towards the so-called Arab State'. According to Hirtzel, 'the whole Moslem world', India included, would agree, perceiving a further instance of Britain's capacity for betrayal. In his view, Arab friendship was equivocal: 'The Arabs have made use of our support against the Turks, but they do not like us any the more; and when the Turkish danger is removed it is by no means certain that the brunt of their dislike will not in any case fall on us, and with redoubled force if it is thought that we have released them from the Turk (who is at least a Moslem) only to hand them over to the most hated of Christian nations.'[17]

More immediately, Italian control of the Yemen would effectively confer on Italy a predominating influence in the Hejaz; something entirely incompatible with the transfer of the Khalifate to Arabia and therefore with the entire direction of Anglo-French policy. As Barrow noted, 'If . . . we must throw her a bone to gnaw I would suggest rather that it should be in Somaliland and towards Abyssinia . . . [where] Mad Mullahs and Neguses and such like weird potentates would keep her as amply occupied as the Senoussi does in Cyrenaica, and we should hear no more of her Arabian pretensions for a long time to come.'[18]

Suitably impressed by this logic Hardinge recommended it to Rennell Rodd, in whom he detected the need for stiffening.[19] In fact, Barrow's suggestion had been considered earlier when, in consultation with Sir

Louis Mallet's territorial committee, the India Office had suggested that Italy might drop her Arabian claims if she were offered French Somali-land.[20]

The apparent consensus regarding the need to exclude Italy from the Yemen belied considerably diverging interpretations of British policy in South-Western Arabia during the first years of the war. Disagreement centred on the concern that British prestige was being undermined by the inactivity of her troops in that region. Hirtzel was the foremost critic of British policy and it was he who, on the outbreak of war, and along with various Foreign Office officials, was required to formulate a policy for that strategically important corner of Arabia.

At an interdepartmental meeting held in the Foreign Office in November 1914, it was decided to transmit to Delhi instructions for the occupation, in turn, of Sheikh Said, the Camaran and Farsan Islands, and Hodeidah.[21] This tallied with the importance attached by the GOI to the Farsan Islands in terms of possible oil exploration and as a coaling station, and to the Camaran in view of pilgrim traffic.

However, in view of a proclamation made by Britain on the outbreak of hostilities to all those chiefs with whom she enjoyed privileged relations and which precluded the extension of the Aden frontier, the GOI would not endorse the occupation of Sheikh Said and Hodeidah.[22] The latter fell within the territory of the Imam of Sanaa who, like the Idrisi and the Turkish Arabs of the region, had yet to reveal his intentions. The priority attached to Sheikh Said was at Hirtzel's instigation and was attributable to his fear that Britain, having regrettably with-drawn from the territory immediately upon her occupation of it in 1914, had invited a recurrence of French and Turkish claims to it.[23]

On 1 December 1914 the Resident at Aden reported that Sheikh Said had been occupied by Arab troops.[24] Whilst Hirtzel favoured their immediate eviction due to the proximity of Sheikh Said to Perim and Aden, he was overruled by Crewe who was unable to see any advantage in military operations of any nature.[25]

In the event a compromise was reached on the basis of a protective understanding between the British Government and the Sheikh of Mavia: a powerful chief whose territory lay outside the Aden Protectorate but athwart the main trade routes to the Yemen. Mavia had recently allied himself with Abdali, another important border chief, and it was intended by the GOI that, to secure their active hostility towards Turkey, Britain might initially provide them with money, arms and ammunition sufficient to pacify their own territories. Although, as

Hirtzel observed, this precluded an attack on Sheikh Said, such an arrangement would potentially 'bring within our sphere of influence, if not within our actual border, the triangle of territory (including Sheikh Said) which the Turkish Government had undertaken not to alienate'.[26]

Hirtzel's peace of mind was short-lived. In June 1915 reports reached London of the shelling of Perim from Sheikh Said. Hirtzel's request that troops be provided from Egypt lest British prestige again suffer was rejected by Chamberlain who, like Barrow, considered it a matter for the Navy.[27] Furthermore, early in 1915, it had emerged that the order to occupy the islands in the Red Sea had not been executed. These matters were compounded by a further development which, like Sheikh Said, was to prove a running sore in British policy.

On 8 February Hardinge communicated a report from the Resident at Aden that Turkish troops, in alliance with the Imam and another chief, Amir Nasir, had crossed the Aden frontier. The latter had been deposed by his followers who now requested arms and military assistance. Mavia, in turn, declared his willingness to oppose the Turks on Britain's behalf, contingent upon the provision of R75,000.

The risk of Mavia being compelled by Turkey to undertake hostile action against Aden and the scale of the Turkish incursion necessitated, in Hardinge's opinion, the despatch of British troops and artillery from Aden. These, he maintained, would act as a catalyst to tribes loyal to Britain who must not, if British prestige were to remain intact, be left alone to repel the Turks.[28]

Hirtzel strongly agreed and had this to say of British policy:

> With the advance of the Turks across the frontier the necessity will be forced upon our tribes to choose who they will serve. To these tribes we have distributed certain scraps of paper extending to them 'the gracious favour and protection of H.M. the King Emperor'. That they will not side with the party that betrays his weakness by not keeping his word is a reasonable conjecture; and if they join the Turk, it is certain that in a short time we will be shut up in Aden. The effect of that on the whole Arab question will be deplorable. There is therefore a crying need for reinforcements. For these the financing and arming of the Mavia Sheikh is no real substitute *at the present juncture*. It is – it is true – a method universally practised by the Turks in Arabia and to that extent would be understood by the Arab: but it is not what they expect from us.[29]

Two years later, with the Turkish incursion still unchallenged, the impetus for action had grown. The establishing of treaty relations with the Idrisi in January 1917 was due, in part, to the inability or unwillingness of the General Staff to sanction military measures in South-West Arabia on a scale necessary to redress the situation at Lahej.

Circumstances encouraged the hasty sanction of the terms negotiated by Lt. Colonel Jacob,[30] but within the Foreign and India Offices concern was expressed that, in securing the conditions regarding the Farsan Islands, Jacob had committed Britain too far. Moreover, Hirtzel disliked the fact that, notwithstanding previous correspondence which provided that Camaran should become a British possession, Jacob had limited Britain to a temporary occupation.[31] Early in 1917 a future revision of those terms seemed possible, but in certain quarters a strong distrust of the Idrisi persisted. It was in this context that Hirtzel sought a more vigorous policy in the Yemen during 1917.

Hirtzel's efforts were hampered by a feeling that in definitely siding with the Idrisi rather than the Imam Britain had backed the wrong horse. Furthermore, for some time after the fall of Lahej, the Imam emitted contradictory signals. In March 1917 Jacob reported that the Imam wished to break with the Turks.[32] During the following months Jacob produced a stream of memoranda advocating support for the Imam on the basis that, owing to his present position in the Yemen, he would remain Britain's most formidable friend or enemy in the region after the war.[33] On this basis and because he doubted if Britain was getting value for money from the Idrisi, Shuckburgh was sympathetic to Jacob's arguments; as indeed was Holderness, who described the Idrisi as 'shifty'.[34]

It seems unlikely that Hirtzel was in principle opposed to a reconciliation with the Imam. His increasing disenchantment with British policy owed much to the GOI and Jacob pressing their conviction that Britain was wrong to back the Idrisi to the extent of wrecking what, to Hirtzel, was the only feasible alternative to British military action from Aden.

The notion of an Arab Confederacy in South-West Arabia first emerged shortly after the Turkish capture of Lahej and amid efforts to generate enthusiasm among sympathetic tribes for offensive action by proxy. Hirtzel liked the idea partly because if British prestige were to remain intact, such action on the part of tribes must be undertaken with British co-operation. His only stipulation was that such co-operation should be such as to nullify Italian ambitions in the Yemen.[35]

Inexplicably, as late as May 1917, the GOI held that Italy would not attempt to interfere in the Yemen and that, in view of the possibility of alienating the Imam, a hands-off policy should be observed.[36] Like the GOI, Sir Reginald Wingate felt that the Idrisi aspired primarily to fulfil territorial aims at the expense of the Imam.[37] If, however, assurances that the movement was primarily anti-Turk were forth-coming, then he would provide necessary weapons and money. When referred to the Foreign Office, though gaining the support of Robert Cecil, the scheme was dropped at Hardinge's instigation and by virtue of his unwillingness to overrule Jacob.[38] The original India Office proposal had in any case involved only an expression of the sympathy of HMG towards the Confederacy and was unlikely to placate those to whom British policy appeared weak.

Though much in favour of Jacob's support for an attack from Aden, Hirtzel's affinity for the Confederacy was based partly on the assumption that no offensive action from Aden by British troops was likely before November 1917. Jacob, on the other hand, remained a persistent advocate of non-interference, in spite of the success of confederate tribes and notwithstanding a softening in the GOI's attitude, to the extent that arms and money might be provided for results obtained. As a result of an interdepartmental committee on 16 August, this formula of bare sub-sistence was adopted as policy, pending an expression by the General Staff of their views.[39]

INTER-ALLIED RIVALRY IN THE ARABIAN PENINSULA

International rivalry in the Arabian Peninsula persisted throughout the First World War. This was partly due to unremitting Italian efforts to obtain a share of the spoils in the Ottoman Empire as a whole. That these efforts did not observe the parameters of territory promised to her in the Treaty of London,[40] and that the methods used in remedying her perceived exclusion were devious, served to complicate matters.

Such was the impression derived by George Grahame writing to Bertie in September 1916 from the British Embassy in Rome where he was then Counsellor:

> Sonnino has been making a great fuss about having an equal share for Italy in the division of Asia Minor. He put his hand on his heart when speaking to Sir Rennell and said 'I feel it here', and that it was 'unfair' and so on. Imperiali told Lord Grey that Sonnino and all the Ambassadors concerned in the negotiations would be swept away if Italy did not get equivalent compensation, or something to that effect.

The difficulty, as Grahame continued, was that Grey, the Foreign

Secretary, seemed quite overcome by such theatrical displays. It was by virtue of such 'cunning' and 'artifice' that, according to Grahame, Italy aspired to control the coast from Smyrna to Alexandretta. To Grahame, and many others, this seemed unjust when the scale of prospective Italian gains around the Adriatic was considered. More unreasonable still was Italy's claim to equal treatment when seen in the context of her belated entry into the war.[41]

In the spring of 1915, in terms of territory extending eastwards from Adalia, Italy had claimed only Mersina and Konia, yet it was, according to Grahame, precisely by recourse to such tactics that, as a price for her co-operation with the Allies, Italy had extracted promises of extensive territorial reward, not only in southern Europe but in North Africa; where, as Grahame recalled, if the Allies increased 'their African colonial possessions at the expense of Germany' Italy would obtain 'some corresponding and equitable compensation, more particularly in the settlement in her favour of boundary questions affecting the Italian colonies of Erithrea, Somalia and Lybia'.[42]

By January 1917, although more sensitive to the delicacy of Sonnino's position and of the need to secure an agreement on Asia Minor, Grahame remained alert to Italian slipperiness, as he revealed when writing to Bertie. According to Grahame, Britain must not be 'bluffed' into making exaggerated concessions in Asia Minor, by the devious bargaining tactics of 'Southern peoples'.[43]

With the approach of an inter-Allied conference, and bombarded by the pleas of the Marquis Imperiali for equal treatment of Italy, Hardinge needed no encouragement, remarking that the Italians were 'a most grasping and unreasonable people'.[44]

Whereas the only explicit mention of Arabia in the Treaty of London related to the association of Italy with her Allies in their declaration that Arabia should be left under the authority of an independent Moslem power, as time passed there was in some quarters an increasing awareness of the interconnection between the Treaty of London and the Sykes–Picot Agreement; both, after all, related to the dismantling of the Ottoman Empire. Most importantly, this was reflected in article nine of the Treaty of London whereby, in the event of the partition of the Ottoman Empire, Italy was to receive just compensation in the eastern Mediterranean. This issue was to be of some importance in the Syrian negotiations of 1919 and in the broader question of the apportioning of mandates. As a region geographically contiguous with Syria, the Arabian Peninsula was an important element in the consideration by British officials of Britain's position in the Middle East as a whole in relation to that of her Allies, and this was as true in 1915–16 as in 1919.

Opinion at the Foreign Office was that the more extravagant Italian claims in Asia Minor should be denied, yet this blade had a double edge. A sympathetic treatment of Italian claims might induce more reason in Italy regarding British predominance in the Arabian Peninsula. Conversely it was in Asia Minor that any such concessions to Italy might be seen by France and Russia to affect their interests most closely, and too liberal an approach by Britain might encourage those powers to support Italian claims elsewhere.[45]

The nature of disquiet caused by these and other developments was reflected in February 1919 in a note written by Alwyn Parker[46] of the Foreign Office in which he suggested that, as alleged by the Italians in a note sent to Grey in November 1916, articles ten to twelve of Sykes–Picot were open to the interpretation that in El Katr, the Trucial Chiefdoms, Muscat, the Hadramaut and Sheikh Said, Britain's position was no longer one of predominance but was, instead, one of equality with France.[47]

Asked to explain this, Sykes's argument did not placate those who saw both France and Italy with a foot in the door and conniving to undermine Britain's position:

> The map signed by Picot and I [*sic*] is not coloured over Koweyt – But the map which the French use, and they have is. I saw it last night. This includes [indecipherable] and they agreed with Lord Grey to go by that map as it was the one used at Petrograd, and the one agreed to by the British War Committee of the War Cabinet.
>
> I don't think we need worry about the French in Muscat etc if we are [to] get Haifa and Baghdad. The agreement is not mine . . . I think the total result of the agreement has been to facilitate our military operations, and prevent friction arising out of them.
>
> The Arabs are occupying 5½ Turkish divisions and we have militarily a free hand in Syria. If we win we get as much influence as we want where we most want it. Tho' I always regretted Mosul.[48]

To compound matters, a declaration of disinterest in the Arabian Peninsula made by France in December 1916 was being openly transgressed. Specifically, at the end of January 1917, Wingate reported the acquisition by France of a large building in Mecca.[49] Balfour questioned the legitimacy of this in view of 'the French acknowledgement of our Arabian position'.[50] However, as Hardinge noted, even if as suspected by Sir Robert Graham, head of the Foreign Office Eastern Department, the building was destined to become a consulate, as co-protector of the Arab State France was acting within her rights.[51] Whilst it soon emerged that the building was to be a hostel for French pilgrims, concern arose because of a request by Hussein that France should send French Moslem doctors from North Africa to the Hejaz. When this was referred to the India Office for comment Hirtzel noted incisively that the logic which required Britain to respond in kind must undermine the grounds upon which her position rested:

> the only means by which a materially weak Power like the Arab State can hope to present the necessary appearance of independence is by rigidly maintaining the inaccessibility of the Hejaz to the influence of the Christian Powers. It was doubtless a consciousness of this fact that caused the Grand Sherif more than once to say that he desired to have no relations with any Power except Great Britain.[52]

Hirtzel therefore recommended, and in this the Foreign Office concurred, that France should be told and if necessary induced to desist from complying with Hussein's request.[53] This was, in Hirtzel's opinion, consistent with Cambon's note of 8 December whereby France had recognised Britain's preponderant influence in the Peninsula and, in Hirtzel's words, 'implicitly disclaimed the desire to play a leading role in that Country'.[54]

An uncompromising stance entailed the danger of provoking rather than eliminating intrigue. Drogheda expressed this fear towards the end of February 1917 when the Marquis Imperiali offered to contribute a force to serve with the Anglo-French Mission to the Hejaz.[55] Drogheda felt that the idea possibly originated in the mind of a Frenchman. This fear was only dispelled with the receipt of a letter from Cambon on 13 March which expressed French opposition to the proposal.[56] The task of formulating a reply which, though not wounding, would reflect the unanimous opposition to a discussion of the Arabian issue within the Foreign and India Offices, fell to Robert Graham. Sonnino was to be told that hitherto British and French help had been limited, that in future Hussein's operations must be conducted without foreign assistance, and, confidentially, that Britain was trying to secure the withdrawal of the French Military Mission.[57]

Notwithstanding increasing indications that Britain might have to abandon her traditional aloofness[58] in order to exclude foreign influence from the Peninsula, the means if not the will were often lacking. This was exacerbated by differences of approach to the problem in London,

Cairo and Delhi, and was compounded by a recurring debate about respective spheres of influence and control between those centres. Deeply opposed to any schemes for radically altering traditional spheres in the Persian Gulf and adjoining region, Curzon none the less perceived considerable scope for maximising British influence and thereby fulfilling aims which had eluded him when Viceroy. Important in this was the unquantifiable matter of foreign intrigue which, though it might not lead to open inter-Allied hostility, threatened to betray notions of disinterested support on their part for the Arab movement. This touched the heart of British policy in the Middle East and was a matter of considerable sensitivity and importance.

BRITISH POLICY IS REASSESSED

Against this backdrop of suspicion and intrigue efforts were being made to elucidate British territorial desiderata in the Arabian Peninsula and the Persian Gulf. In March 1917, in the third report of Sir Louis Mallet's sub-committee on territorial changes, it was advised that Britain should obtain the abrogation of the French claim to the territory of Sheikh Said.[59] This might possibly be achieved by means of a swap and was necessary for the security of Aden. The idea was strongly endorsed by Sir Rosslyn Wemyss, Naval Commander-in-Chief East Indies and Egypt, who pressed for a pre-emptive occupation, an idea which had been current among officers on the ground for some time.[60] Mallet's report also recommended that Britain should attempt to abrogate the Anglo-French Declaration on Muscat of 1862, partly in order to assist attempts to decrease gun-running but also in an attempt to remove French influence from the Gulf.[61]

The conclusions of Mallet's report were adopted by Curzon's Committee on Territorial Desiderata at its second meeting on 18 April 1917, and formed part of broader attempts to undermine French footing in the Middle East as a whole and on the eastern seaboard of Africa.[62] However, according to Austen Chamberlain, both the GOI and CIGS retained their previous opposition to deploying troops in Aden to rectify the frontier there because other spheres had priority.[63]

In its report, however, the Territorial Committee gave a rather different analysis of British rights and aims in the Arabian Peninsula. Having reiterated the conviction of the Committee that Sheikh Said should be occupied, the report continued:

It is highly desirable that no foreign Power other than Great Britain should exercise political influence in Arabia, and that the experiment of an Arab State or congeries of States under the protection of Great Britain should receive every encouragement. No restoration of Turkish sovereignty or suzerainty should be permitted in these regions. The ultimate connection by railroad of Egypt, Palestine, Mesopotamia and the Persian Gulf is an object to be kept steadily in view.[64]

Curzon subsequently wrote that the report was based largely upon the desiderata of the Dominion representatives.[65] Mention of territorial continuity suggests Amery's hand and it was indeed Amery who, as Secretary of the Territorial Committee, initially wrote the report before submitting it to Curzon.[66] However, Curzon and Amery were not alone in proposing a revision of existing arrangements with regard to Arabia. During subsequent months Sir Reginald Wingate became a forceful exponent of this policy.

Writing on 27 April, Wingate held that the behaviour of Colonel Brémond[67] at Jeddah had, amongst other things, convinced him that the provisions of Sykes–Picot were open to misinterpretation. Whereas, in Wingate's opinion, the spirit of the Agreement implied British paramountcy over the Peninsula, when read in conjunction the map and text of the Agreement were misleading. Moreover, in view of negotiations between Sykes and Picot relating to a joint advance into Palestine, Wingate wanted a more definite acknowledgement of Britain's traditional preponderance in the Arabian Peninsula outside the Hejaz than was provided for in article two of Sykes–Picot. This, he maintained, would strengthen Britain's position should difficulties arise with Italian intrigues with the Idrisi or those of France with Sheikh Said.[68] Wingate believed that British interests in the Hejaz would be adequately safeguarded if the French Government accepted Picot's advice that France should declare her disinterest in the Hejaz.

This trend towards a more explicit acknowledgement of Britain's position was generally welcomed at the Foreign Office. The temptation was to use Picot's initiative to confront the Arabian issue in its entirety with France and Italy. Robert Graham, anxious to preserve Allied unity in anticipation of the summer campaign in Palestine, felt it unwise to broach the matter. Whilst previous rebuffs should, in Graham's view, be sufficient to cool Italian ardour, French policy as expressed in recent initiatives by Picot, who besides advocating a renewed statement of French disinterest in the Hejaz had also recommended the ultimate withdrawal of Brémond's mission, must be allowed to mature.[69]

Hardinge agreed that the moment was not propitious yet the issue was irrepressible. On 11 May the Marquis Imperiali communicated a memorandum in which he claimed for Italy a position of equality with Britain and France in the Arabian Peninsula.[70] Simultaneously, debate resumed about Britain's blockade of the Red Sea, from which French and Italian participation was debarred and which stimulated clandestine trade by those powers. France at least might be asked to adhere to the blockade, but there was some risk of her interpreting this as an invitation to equal participation in the Red Sea.[71] A subsequent Italian request to co-operate in enforcing the blockade again threatened to raise the issue of Italian rights in the Peninsula as a whole, unless a suitable reply could be framed on the basis of the desirability of maintaining control of the blockade under a British officer. There was a further point – that the extent of the blockade had apparently been increased to the further detriment of Italian trade.

Robert Cecil, to whom the matter was referred, firmly opposed any such 'try-ons' by Italy.[72] Hardinge agreed, but the question also involved France and the broader issue of British predominance at a time when Britain hoped to gain her support for an advance into Palestine and a reduction of the French Military Mission in the Hejaz.

A reply to Italy's request to participate in the blockade remained unanswered pending a suitable opportunity to gain an acknowledgement by France of Britain's predominance in the Arabian Peninsula. Notwithstanding continuing suspicion of Italian political designs in the Yemen, by October 1917, in order to avoid lasting grievances, some Italian trade was permitted. However, not until well into 1919 did the issue come close to resolution.

The desire of the Foreign Office to define a stiff policy and to avoid discussion of the Arabian issue found an outlet in the resolution of a further difficulty which arose by virtue of the talks at St Jean de Maurienne on 19 April 1917. By article seven of that Agreement,[73] Italy obtained a position of equality with Britain and France in the Arabian Peninsula.[74]

In spite of general disbelief that Lloyd George had conceded so much to Italy, Robert Cecil was willing to milk the contingent clauses of the arrangement to prevent either a reopening of the London Conference or, more broadly, the conferring on Italy of a position of equality in those areas covered by Sykes–Picot. On the other hand, Cecil was prepared, in his words, to 'devise some formula which would be sufficient to satisfy Italian public opinion and yet one which would not antagonise the Russians'. Recalling a meeting with the Marquis Imperiali on the subject, Cecil wrote:

> I suggested that we might say something to the effect that the Russian, Italian, and British Governments were agreed in principle as to the Asia Minor question, but that for the moment it was impossible to conclude a definite Agreement. I asked the Ambassador to suggest to Baron Sonnino that he might draft some formula of that kind. I would try to draft one myself.

Having established the parameters of the debate, Cecil played his trump:

> I then hinted to the Ambassador that I thought it quite possible that all the international agreements would have to be revised. This was a great shock to the Ambassador. He jumped to the conclusion that I meant that none of the advantages secured to Italy would be insisted on. I told him that was not what I had intended, but that I thought it quite possible that we should have to reconsider all the questions involved, or at any rate express our readiness to reconsider them. He seemed very much disturbed at this intimation, but promised to convey it to Baron Sonnino.[75]

In fact, Cecil was on firm ground and had only to allow events to take their natural course to derail Italian ambitions. The 'formula' communicated to George Buchanan, Britain's Ambassador in St Petersburg, spoke of 'a provisional agreement as to the extent of their interests in Asia Minor' which 'recognises the principle of equality'.[76] No mention was made of Arabia and, in any case, the Russian Foreign Minister rejected the suggested wording, substituting for 'the principle of equality' the idea of 'equal treatment for all interested parties',[77] an equally vague ordinance which preserved a free hand for Russia but also for Britain. As to an official resumption of the London Conference, the precariousness of the position of the Russian Government was such that Cambon also considered such a move unwise.[78]

ANGLO-FRENCH RIVALRY IN THE ARABIAN PENINSULA

From the spring of 1917 debate about the revision of arrangements regarding the Arabian Peninsula intensified. This was due in part to Italian and French activities in the Red Sea and to the possible withdrawal or reduction of the French Military Mission in the Hejaz. However, neither issue presented the opportunity of addressing the Arabian problem as a whole. That opportunity arose in the context of a possible reply to a note[79] communicated by Cambon on 16 May 1917.

In this note Cambon stated that his government proposed to send to the Hejaz an envoy, a Monsieur Cherchali, in order both to take in hand matters relating to the Haj, the annual pilgrimage to Mecca, as they affected French pilgrims, and to conduct talks on certain matters with King Hussein.

Specifically, Cherchali might attempt to remove misunderstanding regarding the political future of Syria. However, he would neither divulge the content of agreements between France and the Arabs nor would he convey more than a general outline of Sykes–Picot. Should discussion of the future of Syria arise with Hussein, then Cherchali would first refer to his government for instructions. The memorandum stated, moreover, that among other matters the question of the establishing at Jeddah of an Anglo-French bank might be discussed; this idea had apparently been raised by Brémond.[80]

The issue of French banking interests at Jeddah was highly contentious and had aroused considerable disquiet when raised in November 1916. Several officials, including Shuckburgh, C.E. Wilson, British Resident in Jeddah and agent of the Sudan Government, Wingate, and even Mark Sykes had forcefully opposed the move.[81] Their reasoning was captured in a letter written by George Lloyd[82] to Wingate in which he argued that the bank would assist French trade and prejudice Britain's Indian trade by minting coinage in decimal equivalents. Furthermore, Lloyd anticipated that Hussein's borrowing requirements would rapidly increase the bank's influence in the Hejaz:

> Much as the Shereef might dislike the idea of a French bank at first, the temptation of loans given at first upon favourable terms would be great and . . . facile descensus Averni. This is obviously one of the points where economics becomes politics and where by methods of trade political hold may be, and constantly is acquired.

According to Lloyd, that the French knew their proposal lay outside the confines of the Anglo-French Mission was evidenced by their attempt to prompt the Sherif in the matter. Lloyd therefore advised that Hussein be told that Britain saw no advantage in the proposal; and France, in turn, might be informed that while hostilities persisted the scheme was not feasible. Lloyd then concluded: 'After some small delay we could get to work ourselves.'[83] The same desiderata militated against a favourable response to the proposal in May 1917, notwithstanding the fact that France now envisaged a joint Anglo-French venture.

The real significance of Cambon's note of 16 May was that the language in which Cherchali's instructions were embodied amounted, in the opinion of Foreign Office officials, to a reversal of the explicit acknowledgement by France of British predominance in the Arabian Peninsula. In addition, the presence of Cherchali's Mission might negate the effect of the withdrawal of the French Military Mission from the Hejaz.

At the very least, it was clear that France intended to relegate Britain's position in the Peninsula as a whole to one of commercial rather than political predominance. As regards the question of banking, Robert Cecil referred Cambon to a note communicated to France by Grey in November 1916 in which it was stated that the situation in the Hejaz was not sufficiently secure to warrant the establishing of a foreign bank. In present conditions, Cecil continued, HMG was not inclined to alter its position. This was especially so given that the 'antecedents and relations' of the Imperial Ottoman Bank were such, in Cecil's view, as to render it 'an object of suspicion' and to preclude British support for its claim.[84] Officials at the India Office agreed and whilst a more detailed study of the French note was undertaken, the views of Wingate were solicited.

THE ARAB LEGION

Discussions on Mesopotamian issues by the Mesopotamian Administration Committee led inexorably to a redefinition of the remit of that body to reflect the contiguity of Mesopotamia with other areas of the Middle East covered by treaty arrangements. Pending this, Curzon's involvement in matters of vital interest to himself, such as French activity in the Hejaz and in the Middle East as a whole, was discretionary.

One illuminating episode is revealed in the minutes of a conference on 3 April 1917, held to brief Sykes on his impending mission to the Egyptian Expeditionary Force,[85] to which Picot was to be attached as the force entered Palestine. Curzon, Lloyd George, Sykes and Hankey attended. Sykes proposed to raise the Arab tribes and employ them in guerrilla raids against Turkish communications in the van of the British advance. At the conference Lloyd George and Curzon emphasised the need to avoid committing Britain

> to any agreement with the tribes which would be prejudicial to British interests. They impressed on Sir Mark Sykes the difficulty of our relations with the French in this region and the importance of not prejudicing

the zionist movement and the possibility of its development under British auspices. The attachment of a French Commissioner and of two French Battalions to General Sir Archibald Murray's Force was a clear indication that the French wished to have a considerable voice in the disposal of the conquered territories, and the recent negotiations of Colonel Brémond with the King of the Hedjaz showed how pertinacious they were in these matters.

Curzon perceived great scope for French intrigue and, before departing, Sykes was berated by him for the provisions of the Anglo-French Agreement – not because of promises made to the Arabs, but because of the cession of important territories to France.[86]

The fears of Curzon and others were vindicated when it emerged that Sykes had found fresh scope for his Francophile tendencies in his new appointment. Sykes wished to overcome previous difficulties in recruiting Arab prisoners to the Sherifian cause in view of the anticipated renewal of the enemy offensive against Egypt. Initially enthusiastic, Wingate envisaged well-trained active units of Arab volunteers and mercenaries employed as an 'ADJUNCT [*sic*]' to Hashemite forces or in 'general operations in Arab countries'.[87] The drawback was that Sykes had enlisted the support of Picot who, on behalf of his government, had offered to supply half of the necessary capital. Robert Cecil considered it 'a very hazardous proposal . . . [and] a direct invitation to the French to take further part in the Arabian operations after they have put in a claim for political partnership there'.[88] Though recognising the merits of the scheme, like Cecil and several figures associated with the Arab Bureau, both Curzon and Graham wished to avoid French involvement.[89]

On 10 June, however, Wingate reported that he now deprecated the dual control of the Legion.[90] Possibly for this reason and because Wingate reported Sykes as having said that the Legion would be used primarily in the Hejaz, the matter was referred to a sub-committee of the Mesopotamian Administration Committee. When that Committee met on 5 July it decided to proceed with the Legion but it was to Curzon that Balfour turned to reply to Wingate.[91] Curzon wrote:

> while it is most desirable to defend [the Hejaz], . . . and while we would gladly raise troops for that purpose, the existence of a force, partially recruited from and largely officered by Arabs from the French sphere, with French sympathies, and in part trained by the French, will both encourage French pretensions in the Hedjaz, and give them claim to employ force elsewhere in furtherance of French ambitions in Palestine or Syria . . . In

these circumstances I should have preferred a force raised and trained by ourselves and confined to service under the King in the Hedjaz.[92]

According to Sykes, at a further conference on 20 July Curzon had a decision on the future of the Legion deferred to a forthcoming conference in Paris. Curzon's stalling tactics provoked the following outburst from Sykes which, he requested, should be shown to Balfour:

> Now for two years I have given the best work I could to these middle Eastern affairs. I have only had one object in view and that has been the better prosecution of the war, I have refused office and decorations, I have backed up whatever Government there was, and I have done my best to keep the Entente together in trumpery questions, and I have endeavoured to work up every available political asset on the Entente side . . . I have tried to work on war lines and not pre-war lines viz: Nationality, Co-operation, and Alliance, instead of Imperialism, isolated action and special individual war aims. Hitherto the work has been fairly successful, but I have had to contend as you know with many difficulties, the prejudices of the past both British and French, the mutual suspicions and susceptibilities of out-of-date minds, the anti-British policy of Brémond, the anti-French attitude of Lawrence and Newcombe, and the Fashoda memories of the British functionaries in Cairo. The immense difficulties of dealing with the Indian Government you will also remember.
>
> . . . in spite of all this somehow Picot and I managed to pull things along, Picot having the same difficulties in Paris and Egypt as I have had in London and Egypt. Picot is accused in Paris of having given away everything to England just as Curzon never ceases twitting me with having given everything to France.

As Sykes continued, by having delayed consideration of the Arab Legion for over a month, Curzon had rejected the findings of a unanimous committee, the opinion of Wingate and of himself, and Sykes now believed that if the issue were raised at Paris, Picot's standing would be irrevocably undermined. As Sykes lamented, Curzon 'and his French prototype Senateur Flandin will have matters all their own way'. Furthermore, the Arab cause would 'collapse', and the Entente would 'get another shake'.

If, however, he were given some latitude, then Sykes felt that he might manipulate the Arabian movement 'as a political-military asset'. Coupled with a 'sane and sound policy' towards France, Britain might obtain her objectives in the Middle East and, in Sykes's opinion, thereby contribute substantially to Allied victory. As Sykes continued, important in this was the immediate sanctioning of the Arab Legion, a rare symbol of Anglo-French co-operation in the Middle East which might help to avert disasters should Britain adhere to pre-war policies.[93]

Sykes felt strongly on the matter not least because of the attitude of Curzon or, as Sykes called him, 'Alabaster'.[94] Hogarth's perception of the Arabian issue and of Sykes–Picot as a whole was equally inflexible. For this reason he had, in Sykes's words, been 'trounced' by the Foreign Office for producing a memorandum on the Sykes–Picot Report[95] without consulting them.[96] As Hogarth observed, Sykes viewed the Arabian issue as a single though not unimportant element in the well-being of Anglo-French relations as embodied in the Sykes–Picot Agreement.[97] Writing to Clayton on 11 July 1917, Hogarth recalled that he had circulated his memorandum direct to members of the Mesopotamian Administration Committee but that in retrospect he felt that it might have been fairer to Sykes (the Committee secretary) to have acted through him so that he might then have circulated a note of his own. Hogarth continued:

> Not on that account, but about the effect which he says, gives the *coup de grace* to the Sykes–Picot Agreement (I doubt this very much). Mark Sykes is very angry and I had a stormy interview with him this evening. Finally he challenged me to produce an alternative draft, and, in my haste, I said I would. But, on reflection, I have gone back on that undertaking: for the situation is just this: either the Western Front situation demands encouragement of the French at any cost, in which case this Agreement must stand, or far better to denounce this and have no 'bear skin' agreements at all till the Russian and Turkish situations have developed. I'd rather have the latter. Mark Sykes admits that Curzon's rejection of 'co-operation' in the Arab Legion, had already queered his pitch. My note came on top of that, and 'Alabaster' will get it all his own way. But so far I have found no one who takes the Sykes–Picot Agreement seriously and approves it – except Mark Sykes himself. The DMI and DID both declare they were always dead against it. I have not yet seen the biggest wigs, – Milner, Curzon etc – but many of the lesser. Mark Sykes now threatens the Italians at Kamaran, the French at Muscat, the Turco-Bosch in Syria and everlasting 'pin-pricking'. Well, as for pin-pricking, I reply that it is always going on as it is, and the rest is as it may be.[98]

Meanwhile, on 3 June and in the first of several telegrams on the subject during that month, Wingate reiterated his views on Britain's position in the Arabian Peninsula. At this stage it seems that Wingate had not yet attempted to deal specifically with the redefinition of French rights as contained in Cherchali's instructions. To Wingate the Foreign

Office must obtain from France formal recognition of Britain's pre-dominance in the Peninsula. This was a matter of tradition, as Britain had long established treaty relations with many chiefs on the Peninsula, and, with the Hejaz lying 'on the road to India and [the] Persian Gulf', one of geography. As Wingate suggested, only by Britain's efforts had France made contact with Hussein and without British inspiration and continued financial and military support the Arab movement would never have occurred. The importance of this connection was reflected in clause two of Sykes–Picot and it seemed to Wingate that France forgot that, for the realisation of her aims in the Middle East, she was dependent upon Britain. This was true by virtue of British influence in the region as a whole but, more specifically, because of her influence with the Hashemite dynasty, with whom France would have to establish some understanding if she were to realise her ambitions on the Syrian littoral. Consideration of this interdependence led Wingate, as it did others before him, to reflect that Britain should capitalise on this position to obtain from France 'recognition of our special political rights in the region of Arabia South of area "B" . . .', wherein, according to Wingate, Britain should be established in a position similar to that of France in area 'A'.[99]

This was clearly a most uncompromising stance, particularly so given that Wingate believed the French Government would not formally accept British predominance and that he regarded as necessary 'a vigorous and sustained advance into Palestine and Syria', something which would involve French co-operation or good will.[100]

Wingate's determination to exclude France from the Middle East was primed by the activities of Mark Sykes. In conjunction with Picot, Sykes had produced a report in which he outlined plans for introducing similar administrative methods in Syria and Mesopotamia. Sykes had also recorded his views on Arabia: namely, that the Allies must defeat the Turk and assist the regeneration of the Arab peoples by supporting King Hussein, the chosen instrument of that policy.

Both aims required, in Sykes's opinion, the discouraging of intrigue by outside powers. In the case of the Hejaz, France might therefore be asked to recognise British commercial and financial predominance. Regarding the Yemen and Asir, the Italians might be asked for a similar admission. This, in turn, presupposed the recovery of Lahej and the eviction of any Turks remaining on the western littoral of the Red Sea. Only thus could Britain maximise the potential enmity between Arab forces and the Turk. As Sykes continued, the special conditions of the

Hejaz necessitated the effective creation and support of a native army and this might best be achieved by employing the Arab Legion. More broadly, Sykes wished to have other Arab chiefs regard Hussein 'as titular leader and premier among the Arabs'.[101]

On 10 June Wingate rejected Sykes's suggestion that, instead of seeking to obtain French recognition of Britain's political supremacy south of area 'A', Britain should aspire to have recognised her commercial and financial influence in the Hejaz.[102]

On the following day Wingate resumed the attack, arguing that, as a matter of strategy,

> we should deny to any other European Power the possibility of acquiring political control or influence on the Eastern littoral of the Red Sea. Our position here must be unassailable or we run the risk of creating a 'Baghdad Railway' question in the Red Sea, the development of which may gravely impair our relations with France and Italy and even menace the security of our Imperial system.[103]

The disagreement between Wingate and Sykes arising on the completion of the Sykes–Picot report was considerably broader than the issue of British predominance in the Arabian Peninsula. It arose partly from a differing perception of the permanence of the Sykes–Picot Agreement. For Sykes, that Agreement formed the keystone of a strongly Francophile policy to which he continued to adhere. It was, conversely, precisely towards the revision of that Agreement that Wingate hoped to steer British policy: firstly because it did not permit of sufficiently close British control in Arabia; secondly because, if it stood, it would prevent Britain obtaining Syria after the war. There was, moreover, the incompatibility between the 'Arab' policy embodied in the McMahon correspondence and Sykes–Picot Agreement – and the role of disinterested supporter of this which Britain was supposed to play – with the need not to be outdone in the acquisitive atmosphere of 1917. It was no coincidence that on 10 June Wingate had stated almost in the same breath that it was premature to try to 'fill in the framework of the Sykes–Picot Agreement' but that the 'critical moment' had arrived in the east and that a 'vigorous and sustained advance into Palestine and Syria now promises decisive results'.[104]

This was necessary, Wingate continued, if Britain and France were to realise their respective aims:

> delay bids fair considerably to impair our military prestige, to render doubtful the attainment of our ultimate objectives and even to risk the loss

of what we have already gained. In my opinion, a swift decision followed by a prompt military action in Palestine or Syria is required to secure the cards we should hold at the final Peace Conference, if we are to fulfil our promises to Arab peoples and to acquire undisputed political control over territories which command vital lines of communication with our Eastern Empire.[105]

Wingate developed these views on 11 June. Having reiterated the obligations imposed on Britain by virtue of Imperial necessity or in respect of relations with her Allies, Wingate stated that, with every vestige of Ottoman suzerainty gone, the Allies must obtain the consent of the populations to the form of government which they sought to prescribe. He continued: 'This desideratum presents less difficulties of achievement in the Arabian Peninsula, with the majority of the Chiefs in which we have already concluded agreements, and in Mesopotamia where the majorities appear willing to accept the logic of events, than in Syria.'[106]

This logic dictated that whilst by virtue of agreements already concluded the solution of the Syrian question had been entrusted to France, Britain, as Wingate continued, was similarly bound to the Arabs, 'to assist in arriving at a solution satisfactory both to the future administration of the country (i.e. the French) and to its inhabitants'.[107]

Assurances conveyed to Hussein by Picot that the French position in the Syrian littoral would be analogous to that of Britain at Baghdad, implying the future possibility of closer Arab union, were therefore to be welcomed.[108] 'At the same time', Wingate conceded, 'it is very necessary to make a clear distinction between practical politics and propaganda or ideals: and I consider that, at the present juncture, schemes of unification or federation must be regarded as amongst the latter and, as such, hardly worth of mention in international agreements or documents of to-day.'[109]

Sykes's response to this might be illustrated with reference to his criticisms of a telegram despatched by Wingate on 10 June. According to Sykes the changed international climate of 1917 rendered impossible the continuation of pre-war Imperial methods which entailed unremitting internal strife. He observed:

> If we are to work towards annexation then I am certain that our plans will sink in chaos and failure; if on the other hand the two Governments resolve to work hand in hand to revive and re-establish a great people and assist in the development of a new civilization, and will protect these things

in a dictionary and not a diplomatic sense, then I feel we have before us the prospects of great success, and an opportunity of obtaining for the democracies of England and France the full economic reward which they require.[110]

Regarding the Hejaz, both Wingate and Sykes were predictably scrupulous in distancing Britain from any action likely to compromise the sanctity and independence of Islam and of Hussein. Yet Wingate perceived greater scope for a more flexible interpretation of what might be necessary and possible. Thus he wrote:

> in view of the fact that we have created, directed and financed the Arab revolt I see no difficulty in obtaining from [Hussein] by treaty, all the terms of which need not be made public, such guarantees of preferential treatment as will prevent other European Powers, under guise of their Pilgrims' interests, from acquiring concessions to buy land, create banks, build a railway, etc., in the Hedjaz. To this end it is obvious that any claims by France or other Power to most favoured nation treatment by the Sherifial Government must be strenuously and successfully resisted.[111]

Sykes was prepared to endorse attempts to obtain such a treaty with Hussein provided they did not imply any 'disguised suzerainty' over the latter.[112] However, the thrust of Sykes's activities was directed towards placing the Arab movement on 'business like lines' and avoiding the collapse to which many, including Wingate, looked to create conditions in which Britain might abandon the fetters of Sykes–Picot.[113]

Such thoughts prevailed among influential observers in Cairo. Clayton, when commenting on the Sykes–Picot report, purposely confined himself to generalities on the main question of federation, concluding, not surprisingly, that until the general outlook became clearer even the broadest lines of policy could not be defined without risk of entailing unwanted commitments:

> Many of the areas concerned, and all those in which French interest predominates, are still in the hands of the enemy and it has not been possible to ascertain the wishes and tendencies of the inhabitants. The outstanding point is the vital necessity of insisting immediately that the whole of the Arabian Peninsula should fall within the terms of the agreement as applied to Area B. Until this is done, friction will arise at every turn and if a settlement on broad lines is delayed, an extremely difficult situation may arise as between England and France.

Clayton was certain on one point – that 'predominance' was in itself a vague notion:

> Recognition of *political* predominance is essential – commercial and finan-
> cial predominance are not sufficient. Moreover, the term 'predominance' is
> a loose one and capable of being evaded. It would be infinitely preferable
> to take the Sykes–Picot Agreement as a basis and to insist that the whole
> of the Arabian Peninsula, south of the southern boundary line of Area B,
> should be recognised as coming under exactly the same conditions as Area
> B, it being of course recognised that the status which Great Britain has
> guaranteed to the Hejaz holds good.[114]

Like Wingate, Hogarth believed that total exclusion of French influence
might be ensured only by embodying the recognition of British political
predominance in a treaty. Moreover, Hogarth maintained that Britain
should obtain complete control of Hussein's revenues.[115]

According to George Lloyd this treaty would remain private and
would take the form of a refusal on the part of Hussein to alienate
territory, grant concessions to a third power, or negotiate with other
foreign powers without British foreknowledge. Only thus, Lloyd held,
could Britain deny France the ability to pursue national interests under
the guise of provisions for the Haj.[116]

By this time, however, the Foreign Office had received another telegram from Wingate who, having now read the Cherchali note, believed
that any settlement with France over the Arabian Peninsula would
depend upon the revision of Sykes–Picot. Failing an extension of those
conditions pertaining to Area 'B' to the rest of the Peninsula then,
Wingate held, Britain's entire position in the east would be jeopardised.
Whilst, as regards arrangements with the Arabs, Sykes–Picot held good,
the relative inactivity of French arms in the Middle East coupled with
the increasing unpopularity of France in Syria rendered its revision
necessary.[117]

At the Foreign Office a general disinclination to raise the Syrian issue
with France prevailed, but the general debate on the Arabian Peninsula
provided a suitable opportunity to frame a reply to the Cherchali note.

On the basis of conversations with Picot and Cambon, Graham
believed that France would recognise British predominance in the
Peninsula as a whole. However, Graham neither desired nor thought
that France would make such a declaration regarding the Hejaz. Such a
declaration would compromise Hussein's position and might lead to
undesirable commitments for Britain.[118] Both Graham and Hardinge
were content to deny such a position to other powers and felt that, by
virtue of the proximity of Egypt, the predominantly British pilgrim
traffic, existing financial and political support, and Britain's 'special

position' with Hussein would be secure without a public declaration to this effect.[119]

The limited remit of the Mesopotamian Administration Committee precluded discussion of matters relating to the Arabian Peninsula at its meetings. Wingate's telegram of 11 June (no. 127) had been referred to it, but, pending further clarification of the Committee's functions, its consideration was deferred.[120] However, Curzon's close interest in these matters was evidenced by a memorandum written by him which strongly criticised a draft reply to the Cherchali note prepared by Balfour.[121]

Curzon agreed with Balfour's observation that, when read in conjunction, the French claims and statements about the involvement of European governments either in the Hejaz, or the rest of the Peninsula or the Middle East as a whole, tended to 'magnify and safeguard the future French role in Arabia while restricting and minimising that of Great Britain'.[122]

Whilst the French claimed that 'No European Power shall exercise a dominant or even preponderant influence in the Holy Places of Islam' and that 'we are resolved not to interfere at all in the political questions of the Arabian Peninsula', according to Curzon's memorandum, quoted with its original emphasis, the French note proceeded to state:

(3) (a) 'No European Government should acquire *any new establishments'* (whatever that may mean) 'in Arabia' (without qualification).
(b) 'No Power should acquire fresh territory or political prestige in Arabia' (again without qualification).

As to existing British rights, quoting the French note, Curzon continued, '. . . "the proximity of the Egyptian shores on the one side and of the Persian Gulf on the other, create a situation in favour of the commercial interests of Great Britain, which Monsieur Cherchali must take into account" '.

Lastly, regarding the position of France in the Middle East as a whole, Curzon observed: 'France, meanwhile, is to exercise exclusive political control in Syria, and the Arabian provinces or territories extending eastwards as far as Mosul, creating Amirates, with French political advisers or counsellors.' Curzon was concerned that the Foreign Office would be duped into imposing on Britain a more restricted role in the Hejaz than was justifiable either on the basis of her traditional preponderance in the Arabian Peninsula or on that of strategic requirements.

Whilst Curzon accepted Balfour's approval of the French statement regarding the Holy Places, as Curzon observed, the Foreign Secretary's draft had proceeded to state: '. . . "it is undesirable that the Arab Power in possession of the Holy Places should, *as regards its internal affairs*, be under European influence at all".' Curzon objected to the explanation of this provided in Balfour's memorandum that whilst Britain had, by virtue of her military and financial support of the rising, been placed in a very special position in the Hejaz, '. . . "there is no reason known to His Majesty's Government why this exceptional condition of things should continue when the war is over, at which date it is the intention of His Majesty's Government that the status of the Hejaz should revert to the condition of complete internal independence" '.

As Curzon noted, the example used to illustrate internal interference was inappropriate. Moreover, irrespective of Hussein's success in relation to his dynastic ambitions, Curzon predicted that, in terms of a subsidy and arms, Hussein would be dependent upon Britain for many years. It seemed senseless to Curzon that, whereas in Balfour's draft a tradition of British predominance in the Arabian Peninsula was assumed, the memorandum then precluded continued British support for Hussein, which was unavoidable, unless he were to be allowed to collapse, and which was the most obvious illustration of that British pre-dominance. Curzon continued:

> The analogy of Afghanistan seems to be the one that we ought to bear in mind. The Amir is in closer political relations with ourselves than with any other Power; he accepts our money; he to a large extent looks to us for advice. But his internal independence is quite unqualified, and the Russians, who after all are contiguous to his dominions, which the French are not to the Hejaz, occupy in relation to him much the sort of position in which the French wish to stand to King Hussein.
>
> I hope therefore that while stating our intention not to interfere with the internal administration of the King, and our interest in the internal inde-pendence of his Kingdom, we shall not tie our hands by disclaimers which will probably be a source of much trouble in the future.

Curzon expressed a more fundamental objection to Balfour's draft. Having detailed the justifications of her preponderance in the Arabian Peninsula, something which had the explicit acknowledgement of France, the draft then proceeded, by implication, voluntarily to disclaim such preponderance in the Hejaz. Stressing the need for a strict delineation of spheres of influence, Balfour's draft continued: 'it seems evident that, if this policy is to be carried out in Arabia, it is to Great

Britain that Arabian factions should be taught to look as the advocate of internal peace and the supporter of Arabian independence.'[123]

It was, however, in Curzon's view, precisely to the Hejaz 'that the French geographical admissions about the contiguity of Egypt apply, and it is to Arabia without qualification, i.e. Arabia including the Hejaz, that the French admission of a "preponderant interest" and "a peculiar situation in favour of Great Britain" extends'. Curzon therefore recommended that Britain align herself with France in a policy of non-interference in the Holy Places, beyond matters pertaining to the safe conduct of the Haj, and respecting the complete internal independence of the Hejaz. He continued: 'But our historical connections, our geographical position, and our political interests in Arabia, render it inevitable and indeed essential, as is admitted by the French, that a preponderant political influence should be exercised by Great Britain throughout the Arabian peninsula.'

On 29 August 1917, the British Government replied to Cambon's note of 18 May.[124] The manner of its preparation renders difficult any precise assessment of Curzon's part in this. Moreover, the nature of this preparation suggests that Curzon and the India Office were misled by the Foreign Office.

Curzon had written his memorandum in response to a memorandum which he claimed had been produced by Balfour and which, in Curzon's opinion, failed to secure for Britain the necessary degree of control in the Hejaz. According to a minute by Hirtzel, dated 1 September, the memorandum which Curzon criticised had been approved by the India Office, and Montagu referred to it as being 'our draft'.[125] By the time that Hirtzel wrote, a reply to Cambon's note had already been sent to France. According to Hirtzel, the reply approved by the India Office had been 'discarded' and another, which had been prepared by Curzon, had been sent instead.[126] Moreover, the Foreign Office had failed to consult the India Office and when asked later in September for a copy of the original draft replied that it had disappeared.[127]

In July 1917 several attempts had been made within the Foreign Office to produce a reply to the French note. These drafts all claimed for Britain recognition of her predominance in the Arabian Peninsula. None of them claimed, and one explicitly disclaimed, such a position for Britain in the Hejaz.[128] On Oliphant's[129] recommendation the question was referred to the Mesopotamian Administration Committee which, on 21 July, postponed it pending further discussion.[130] In August, Harold Nicolson prepared a further draft which, it was claimed, incorporated

Curzon's memorandum on Balfour's draft.[131] In its final form the text was not resubmitted to Curzon because, Hardinge claimed, Curzon had already seen it. As G.R. Clerk noted regarding the final version, the French admissions applied to Arabia, including the Hejaz, but this was not assumed in the final draft, the important section of which read:

> His Majesty's Government are convinced that the avoidance of internal strife in Arabia can only be secured through the retention by Great Britain of the influence which this country has for so long held throughout the Peninsula as the European Power most closely concerned with the internal peace and external politics of Arabia.[132]

The issue of spheres of influence in the Arabian Peninsula remained unresolved, notwithstanding the receipt of a note from the Quai d'Orsay in reply to Britain's response to the Cherchali note, in which it was suggested that Sykes might travel to France and there negotiate a settlement.[133] Detecting ambiguity in the French note, Graham none the less perceived a suitable opportunity for an agreement, and in this conclusion Montagu concurred.[134] Curzon, however, felt obliged to explore this ambiguity before sanctioning Sykes's mission.

Having associated the French Government with Britain's desire to avoid foreign interference in the Arabian Peninsula, the French note continued: 'Il est donc en principe d'accord avec lui sur l'entier désintéressement que les Alliés doivent pratiquer à l'égard des Etats du Malek Housseine et sur les abstentions de toute intervention dans son administration.'[135]

Curzon detected two areas for 'suspicion'. Firstly, that the phrase 'Etats du Malek' might have a wider definition than simply the Holy Places alone.[136] Consequently, Britain's declarations of non-interference with the Holy Places, of the internal independence of the Hejaz, and of a preponderating interest in the rest of the Peninsula might restrict the latter sphere. Secondly, Curzon wished to avoid Britain being debarred from providing the Hejaz with assistance after the war by virtue of the phrase 'intervention dans son administration'.[137]

The French note continued: 'Il (le Gouvernement de la Republique) reconnait que dans les autres parties de la péninsule, il n'a aucun intérêt à mettre en regard de celui du Gouvernement britannique à voir regner l'ordre dans les régions avoisinant le Golfe persique.'[138] As Curzon observed, this was a 'curious limitation' which failed to acknowledge Britain's position in the Aden hinterland, the Hadramaut and the interior.[139]

Regarding the first point, the Quai d'Orsay was merely responding with suitable ambiguity to a matter which Curzon and Nicolson had perhaps intentionally left vague. As Montagu noted, the physical area in which Britain had abstained from interference required geographical definition.[140] In his opinion this area would represent the Hejaz, and it is unsurprising therefore that Curzon did not attempt such a definition himself.[141]

Curzon felt comfortable with the Arabian issue anchored in rougher seas where he could circle at leisure awaiting an opportunity to dislodge France and Italy. The question was, however, drifting into calmer water, hastened by those like Montagu who felt indisposed to raise contentious matters.

Curzon's role in the preparation of Sykes's instructions and his reaction to the draft agreement[142] with France do not emerge with clarity. Given the nature of these instructions, the draft agreement submitted by France and the Foreign Office minutes on these, it seems possible that Curzon was forced to capitulate on at least one matter of importance: namely, his insistence on the inclusion of the Hejaz, minus the Holy Places, in the area of acknowledged British supremacy. More likely still is that, amid continuing debate about the functions of the Mesopotamian Administration Committee, Curzon's views were deliberately misinterpreted to allow the Foreign Office position to prevail.

In article two of Sykes's instructions it stated:

> it is essential to obtain explicit recognition by France of British political supremacy in Arabia as a whole with the exception of the Hedjaz.
> b. That the limits of the Hedjaz shall be defined.
> c. That within those limits the Hedjaz shall be recognised as a sovereign, independent State but that the existing arrangements for dealing with King Hussein and the Arabs shall hold good for the duration of the war.[143]

On this George Clerk minuted correctly that Curzon's objection to the French acknowledgement of British predominance only in those 'regions adjoining the Persian Gulf' had been covered. As to Curzon's point that the 'Etats du Malek' might be open to wider interpretation than the Holy Places alone, Clerk said that this had been covered by the definition of the Hejaz.[144] Further, as to the provision of assistance, again either disingenuously or mistakenly, Clerk assumed that Curzon proposed only to provide assistance to Hussein until hostilities ended.[145]

The draft agreement achieved what the Foreign Office had wanted all along – explicit recognition of British political predominance in the Arabian Peninsula outside the Hejaz. By confirming existing arrangements for the support of the Sherif, the draft agreement ensured that no other Power would dislodge Britain. Furthermore, as Clerk noted, the draft was so worded as decisively to prevent France from gaining a foothold in Zone 'B' of the Sykes–Picot Agreement and to prevent Britain's exclusion from obtaining concessions in the Blue area of that agreement – neither of which had been provided for in Sykes's instructions.[146]

As the price to be paid for these concessions, opinion at the Foreign Office was that French claims to equal commercial and navigational rights within the Peninsula could not well be denied even though this would inevitably lead to Italian demands for equal treatment.

Regarding Curzon's objections, Foreign Office officials sought to dissuade him from pressing his point on the basis of references made by them to the likely reaction of other nations to British claims for a privileged economic position in the Hejaz. The discussion arose in the context of clause two of the draft agreement which read:

> Au cas où des concessions de tout nature seraient offertes à un particulier, à un groupement ou à une société ressortissant à l'une des deux Puissances contractentes, le Gouvernement français et le Gouvernement britannique s'engagement respectivement à ne pas donner leur agrément à l'enterprise envisagée avant d'avoir prévenu l'autre partie et s'être assurée qu'une coopération des ressortissants des deux pays n'est pas réalisable.[147]

Graham interpreted this as a French bid for the joint economic exploitation of the Hejaz alongside Britain, something which would probably entail the establishing of a joint banking enterprise and a division of contracts. To Graham it seemed that Britain had several options: either she might 'insist upon a supreme commercial position in the Hedjaz' for herself or share commercial supremacy with France. Other options were the sterilisation of the Hejaz, temporary or permanent, by 'refusing to allow British or French enterprises and discouraging all others', or, as Graham concluded, opening 'the trade of the Hedjaz to the world on conditions of equality'.[148]

As Graham noted, the first proposition had influential proponents in George Lloyd and Wingate. Yet, for the very reason which Lloyd used to endorse his argument, Graham rejected it. To Graham it seemed impossible that the French would agree to this when 'the border line between political and commercial supremacy in such a country is so thin as scarcely to exist'. Moreover, as Graham added:

The same may be said of all of the other Powers who have Moslem subjects attending the annual pilgrimages – the Italians, Dutch, Russians, and
even Japanese. No minister of a State with Moslem subjects could admit in
his Chamber that he had consented to place political or commercial
supremacy in the Holy Places in the hands of any one Power. We should
find all of them united against us on this question.

Graham compounded this feebleness in rejecting the second possibility.
Italy, he maintained, would immediately demand to be on an equal footing, on the basis of 'equality for all Powers with Moslem subjects in the
Holy Places'. Rejecting a hands-off policy as impossible, in view of
anticipated economic development in the Hejaz, Graham believed an
open-door policy to be inevitable.[149] Further, as both Graham and
Hardinge observed, given Britain's position in Egypt, Aden and
Mesopotamia, and in view both of her relations with the Hashemite
dynasty and her influence in the Haj, her political and commercial preponderance in the Hejaz would in time be assured.[150]

When this was sent to the India Office for comment, Shuckburgh
raised the general point that any agreement with France would not
necessarily exclude a third power.[151] Besides German intrigues, the India
Office had for some time been concerned about Japanese commercial
penetration in the Persian Gulf and, whilst regarding an open-door
policy as unavoidable, Shuckburgh sought to give advance warning of
this.

There was, certainly, evidence to suggest that Italy would be
tenacious in advancing her claims to equality of treatment. In conversation with Robert Cecil, Sonnino had pressed for Italy's admission
to a self-denying ordinance alongside Britain and France. He had, moreover, proposed a secret clause to Italian claims defined at St Jean de
Maurienne whereby, in the event of Russia's failure to consent to these
claims before a Turkish peace, those claims would none the less stand.[152]

Curzon's views on this issue were perceived by the Foreign Office as
obstructing the conclusion of an agreement with France and, more
broadly, as implied by Bidwell and Nevakivi, Curzon was seen to be
actively undermining the policy of Anglo-French co-operation which the
Foreign Office aspired to maintain throughout 1917.[153] This was
compounded by a perception of the Middle East Committee as cum-
bersome, and there was a general reluctance within the Foreign and
India Offices to convene it when matters might be decided informally.
According to a minute by Lancelot Oliphant, the final draft prepared by
Nicolson in response to the Cherchali note and dated 29 August was

circulated to the Middle East Committee on 10 September, yet there is in the minutes no record of either having been considered by the Committee.[154]

As if to confirm this interpretation of Curzon's role, on 28 August Mark Sykes had received a letter from Picot, which he then sent to Robert Graham, and which read as follows:

> Si la guerre se poursuit encore pendant deux années, il me semble qu'aucune affaire ne pourra plus aboutir, à voir le lenteurs croissants de l'administration. Lord Curzon a enfin remis son memorandum sur la note Cherchali; il fait cinquante observations diverses. La note doit maintenant être rédigée à nouveau et faire une de plus le tour des Comités et des Ministères intéressés. Dans ces conditions, je désespère de voire le terme de l'adventure – et je rentre en France. J'espère y faire oeuvre plus utile qu'ici, en m'efforcant de dissiper les suspicions que justifient tant des lenteurs à résoudre une question si simple.[155]

Commenting on this to Graham, Sykes noted:

> I would point out that it is very ridiculous to adopt a 1960 A.D. [*sic*] policy in India and an 1887 A.D. policy in the Red Sea. We certainly do not require any rights in the Hejaz over and above those to be enjoyed by our allies. The Hejaz must be a completely independent State if we are to defeat the Turks. It will never be independent if we have a special position there, and the Sherif will always be our dependent and therefore out of running for the Caliphate, which is contrary to our interest because it fastens the Caliphate for good and all onto the Turks.[156]

With policy directed by one with such percipience, it therefore seemed to Hardinge unnecessary to change the response to the Cherchali note drafted by Nicolson in the Foreign Office. Yet, though unwilling to go as far as Curzon, Hardinge did not entirely dissociate himself from the views of George Clerk[157] who at this stage, at the end of August 1917, sympathised both with Curzon's advocacy of a special position for Britain in the Hejaz and with his opposition to a self-denying ordinance. Should the latter contingency arise then, like Curzon, Clerk viewed as inevitable the extension of French influence from Syria to the Arabs of the Hejaz. Clerk had one further objection to Sykes's letter and it was one to which Curzon would have readily subscribed:

> Throughout these Asia Minor and Arabian negotiations it has seemed to me that Sir Mark Sykes, while quite rightly endeavouring to reach an understanding with the French which shall be free from all suspicion and

misunderstanding, has gone to work on the wrong principle. He appears to think that the way to get rid of suspicion is always to recognise what the other party claims and to give up, when asked, our claims.[158]

However, the Foreign Office continued to rely upon Sykes to contrive an agreement with the French. Towards the end of 1917 an impression had emerged within the Foreign Office that France was widely regarded with 'dissatisfaction and mistrust' by the peoples who inhabited areas covered by agreements in which France was a contracting power.[159] This was due partly to French persistence in efforts to stimulate banking in the Hejaz and to her demands to participate in the administration of Palestine. When he returned to Paris in December 1917 Sykes was required to reiterate Britain's opposition to banking in the Hejaz before the cessation of hostilities, and to insist that the administration of Palestine must remain in the hands of military authorities.[160] This second point reflected the view within the Foreign Office that Sykes–Picot did not provide for any such immediate dual administration, nor would it be possible even if it were desirable, in view of inevitable Italian opposition. An improvement in the co-ordination of Allied policy in the Middle East by removing ambiguity in French policy was the main object of Sykes's mission and it was as a subsidiary matter that he was to raise the question of the Arabian Peninsula.[161]

A further discussion of this issue was necessary owing to events towards the end of October when Picot crossed the Channel to attend a conference at the Foreign Office. The conference had been convened to settle outstanding difficulties surrounding the Projet d'arrangement and, apparently, met on 25 and 26 October at the Foreign Office. Although the conference tackled the Arabian issue in its entirety it has proved impossible to locate material providing details of its deliberations.[162] Balfour chaired the conference and Curzon attended at least part of the proceedings. Since the Projet was altered, it was taken back to Paris by Picot to obtain the sanction of his government.[163] The conference also decided that the question of Muscat and Sheikh Said should be raised in conjunction with the Egypt–Morocco negotiations.[164] This question had been raised partly in connection with arms traffic, and Lord Islington, Under-Secretary of State for India, had attended the conference in this connection. In spite of this, other senior India Office officials remained ignorant of what passed at the meetings.[165] Besides the discussion of Sheikh Said and Muscat, the only indication of the business of the conference was a proposed preamble to the Projet d'arrangement. By

virtue of this, Britain and France were to co-operate to the fullest extent
in maintaining the independence of the Hejaz and preventing the mono-
polisation of commercial, financial and industrial concessions in the
Hejaz by any one power.[166]

During 1917 there was an ongoing clash of interests between Sykes
and Curzon regarding British affairs in the Arabian Peninsula. The
nature of this friction does not emerge with precision, yet much of the
criticism of Curzon's policies clearly stemmed from a perception of these
policies as being outdated and at variance with the conditions of 1917.
The 'Fashodaism' of which Sykes complained was often more widespread than he was willing to believe and much of the debate about
Britain's position *vis-à-vis* the Peninsula centred on the means by which
British predominance might be assured rather than the end result.

It was all too easy, however, in view of the didactic tones in which
Curzon addressed the Mesopotamian Administration Committee, to
detect the younger man in viceregal splendour presiding over the
Durbar at Shargah in 1903, and to which he had stated:

> We were here before any other Power, in modern times, had shown its
> face in these waters. We found chaos and we have created order . . . We
> saved you from extinction at the hands of your neighbours. We opened
> these seas to the ships of all nations, and enabled their flags to fly in peace.
> We have not seized or held your territory. We have not destroyed your
> independence, but have preserved it. We are not now going to throw away
> this century of costly and triumphant enterprise; we shall not wipe out the
> most unselfish page in history.[167]

The concern which had troubled the Cabinet on the eve of Curzon's
mooted Gulf tour of 1901 – that Curzon might engineer fresh commitments for Britain – continued to worry his colleagues in 1917.[168] In
the years after the Durbar, Curzon originated a distinct conception of
British interests in the Gulf, something which was commented upon at
the time and which represented a landmark in British involvement in
the region.[169] Whilst by 1917 the threat of a Russian port in the Persian
Gulf had temporarily receded, French and Italian pretensions in the
adjoining Peninsula had grown and the effects of German economic
penetration endured. It therefore seemed reasonable to Curzon to continue the policies which he favoured in the previous decade, including
a closer relationship with Koweit and Muscat. What was unreasonable,
as Hogarth observed in the summer of 1917, was the assumption
implicit in the Sykes–Picot Agreement that the 'pin-pricking' which had

3. Sir Ronald Storrs

Source: Illustrated London News

4. Sir George Clerk

Source: Illustrated London News

5. Sir Ronald W. Graham

Source: Illustrated London News

6. Viscount Milner

Source: Illustrated London News

characterised pre-war international relations in the region might one day cease.[170]

The Foreign Office believed that Curzon, Hogarth and others were, in their support of a privileged position for Britain in the Hejaz, undermining the foundations of British policy and their interference was therefore resented. In addition, the strength of feeling aroused by the Arabian issue among senior figures threatened to expose the hypocrisy of the Foreign Office in its attempt to forfeit important British desiderata to benefit inter-Allied relations. Further, the very fact that such views were being expressed on the ground confirmed that Sykes–Picot had done little to alter the imperial mind-set of senior figures in the Middle East. Unfettered British predominance throughout the Peninsula accorded with the notion of a British Viceroyalty in the Middle East championed by Storrs back in 1914–15. Writing in February 1915, Storrs observed:

> Syria is not only a goal per se but also a necessity both with regard to Irak and the Arabian peninsula. If, as would seem the ideal solution, we could make this latter into a sort of Afghanistan uncontrolled and independent within, but carrying on its foreign relations through us we would be giving a maximum of satisfaction and assuming a minimum of responsibility; but the plan is not feasible unless we hold Syria.

This arrangement, Storrs continued, would be underpinned by the Caliphate reverting to Mecca and by Britain supporting the Sherif as a 'hereditary spiritual Pope' with no temporal power, and maintained by means of a subsidy and the proceeds of the Haj:

> guaranteed against foreign and especially Turkish aggression, but not defended against himself or an occasional internecine turn up with a powerful neighbour . . . this I say is by far the most favourable atmosphere we have any right or hope to expect of Arabia for the better part of this century, and it is to this ideal that we should shape our course.[171]

By the summer of 1917 Storrs's brainchild was far from dead. On the contrary, ambitious operations were afoot in Palestine, a landing at Alexandretta was being mooted at the highest levels, and concerted efforts to undo Sykes–Picot were being made by Cairo officials.

The assumption of Storrs and those officials was that Anglo-French co-existence in the Middle East was impossible. This directly contradicted the policy evolving at the Foreign Office. Moreover, implicit in the reasoning of those critics of the Sykes–Picot report was a highly cynical assessment of the Arab movement and one which was perhaps most neatly summarised by Sir George Macdonogh, Director of Military Intelligence, in 1917. In allying with Hussein and lesser chiefs, Britain's principal objectives, according to Macdonogh, were to occupy Turkish troops in a minor theatre and prevent Germany landing on the coast of the Arabian Peninsula: 'The Arab movement should therefore by regarded as a means to an end in itself, but at the same time it is necessary to disguise such a policy by sympathetic treatment of Arab aspirations and to keep in view our relations with the Arabs after the war.'[172]

This opinion found sympathy among senior India Office officials, but those officials were prepared to criticise Curzon's support for a closer relationship with the Hejaz, because it might provoke rather than eliminate difficulties with Britain's Allies.

Yet the common factor in the reasoning of British officials in general, even if it were seldom explicitly stated, was the immense strategic significance to Britain of a paramount position in the Arabian Peninsula as a whole. This importance resurfaced most frequently in departmental minutes which stressed the importance of denying to Britain's Allies a footing on the Peninsula. However, George Lloyd, writing to Wingate in July 1917 on the subject of increasing French economic ambitions in the Hejaz, gave a true assessment of the significance of British interests in the Arabian Peninsula:

> I sometimes fear that you may think that I see these Red Sea matters out of proportion. I do not think it is so for I am certain that if we lose grip of our Red Sea and Persian Gulf communications there is practically no gain in this war that could compensate us for them. Certainly no land communications via the Middle East could do so, though this latter idea is very prevalent in Mark Sykes's mind. Those that doubt need only read Vasco da Gama or Mahan.[173]

Possibly Curzon agreed with prominent Foreign Office officials who believed that, in the general context of Middle Eastern affairs, Lloyd overstated the issue. Yet if Curzon did hold such views he did not communicate them to senior colleagues. Moreover, it seems at odds with his previous involvement in Arabian matters to suggest that he would have capitulated on the issue of British predominance in the Hejaz without dissent. The Foreign Office was clearly determined to muzzle Curzon, not least by attempting to smother the Middle East Committee.[174] This interpretation is enforced by evidence surrounding Sykes's visit to Paris in December 1917.

Neither in Sykes's report of his trip to Paris, nor in the text of speeches made by him and Monsieur Gout during his visit, is there any mention of Arabia. Early in 1918, however, Sykes found himself reiterating his opposition to a 'singular' position for Britain in the Hejaz; something for which Wingate continued to evince enthusiasm.

As wider discussions developed and as Curzon was drawn into the debate, the nature of his involvement emerged. In March 1918, minuting angrily that he was unable to find copies of these speeches, Curzon observed:

> It seems to me a very extraordinary thing that though I happen to be the Chairman of the Middle East Committee I was neither informed of Sir Mark Sykes's visit to Paris, nor was ever shown his report upon it, nor even heard of his speech until it was long over.
>
> This must be an accident: for it is of course impossible for a War Cabinet Committee to do its duty when even its chairman does not get vital papers.[175]

NOTES

1. See Appendix 1.
2. For a detailed account of the blockade, see a memorandum by Capt. George Lloyd, 'Franco-Italian Trade from Jibouti and Eritrea to [the] Arabian Coast', June 1917; also memorandum by Maj. W. M. P. Wood, First Assistant Resident, Aden, 6 September 1917, both at FO 882/15, ff. 394ff., 404ff.

   According to Wood, in November 1915, and as a result of an attack on a British ship at Khoka, all traffic with Arabian ports south of Medi had been suspended. This was the main element of the blockade which permitted a restricted dhow traffic with Medi. In March 1916, Medi was replaced by Jaizan due to fears that the former permitted intrigue with the Idrisi (see n.13). Thereafter, alterations in the severity of the blockade reflected the fear among British officials that this intrigue persisted.
3. Rodd to Hardinge, 9 September 1916, British Embassy, Rome, private, Hardinge Papers /25, f. 65.
4. Ibid. Rodd to Hardinge, 23 September 1916, British Embassy, Rome, private, f. 230.
5. Ibid. Hardinge to Rodd, 13 September 1916, Foreign Office, private, f. 115.
6. For example, see ibid., Hardinge to Rodd, 27 September 1916, private, f. 27.
7. Ibid. Rodd to Hardinge, 7 October 1916, British Embassy, Rome, private, /26, f. 118.
8. Memorandum by Hirtzel, 'British Interests in Arabia', 20 January 1917, B247, FO 371/3054/117173, p. 512. On this policy and the instability of Bedouin society see, for example, D. Holden and R. Johns, *The House of Saud: The Rise and Fall of the Most Powerful Dynasty in the Arab World* (New York, 1981), pp. 11ff.
9. Imam Yahya, religious leader of the Zaydi Shi'ah sect in the Yemeni highlands, concluded an agreement with the Porte in 1911. The Imam was vested with limited religious and legal autonomy but remained in tributary relationship with the Sultan, whose suzerainty he recognised. Loyal to the Porte in World War I, Yahya asserted his independence immediately after the Mudros Armistice. He occupied in 1919 certain districts in the Aden hinterland belonging to Shaykhs in protectorate relations with Britain and later refused to surrender the districts, claiming that historically they formed part of his patrimony. J. C. Hurewitz, *The Middle East and North Africa in World Politics: A Documentary Record* (Yale, 1979).
10. See n. 8, Memorandum by Hirtzel. Besides a brief article by J. Baldry in *Arabian Studies*, ed.

R.B. Sergeant and R. Bidwell (Cambridge, 1990), secondary literature on the Yemen and British policy in South-West Arabia during World War I is scant.

11. By a treaty of 1888 Britain exercised a protectorate over the Sultan's territories.

12. See n. 8, Memorandum by Hirtzel. Memorandum by Sir Edmund Barrow, 'Italy and Arabia', 22 January 1917, ibid., pp. 528–30.

13. 'Idrisi Sayyid of Sabya: Gt. Grandson of Ahmad bin Idris, Moroccan-born founder of religious movement that sponsored the Sanusiyya brotherhood in Cyrenaica. The Idris . . . had wrested autonomy from the Porte in 1906 . . . and in the Tripolitanian war of 1911–12 accepted arms from Italy without seeking or receiving formal Italian recognition. In the unratified British–Ottoman instrument on the Arabian Peninsula in 1913–14 . . . it was implicitly acknowledged that the amirate fell under Ottoman sovereignty. Soon after the outbreak of war . . . Lt. Jacob, the British Indian Assistant political resident at Aden, proposed "an offer of protection and friendship and a distinct adjudication of his claims against [the] Imam; we could also make over to him Farsan, which was his property once". After the British declaration of war against the Ottoman Empire the Viceroy and the India Office still hoping to reach an agreement with Imam Yahya, approved Jacob's proposal except for the projected clause on relations with Yemen . . . negotiations were started at the end of January 1915.' Hurewitz, op. cit., pp. 24–5.

14. See n. 8.

15. Minute by Hirtzel, 17 September 1916, L/P+S/10/527 P3777, pp. 153ff.

16. Ibid. Minute by Holderness, 18 July 1916.

17. See n. 8.

18. See n. 12.

19. Hardinge to Rodd, 27 September 1916, private, enclosing note by Shuckburgh written on the basis of minutes by Hirtzel of 17 and 20 September 1916, in L/P+S/10/527 P3777, 22 September 1916, Hardinge Papers /25, f. 270ff.

20. See n. 15.

21. Minute by G. R. Clerk, 16 November 1914, L/P+S/10/558 P4502.

22. Ibid. Viceroy to S/S, 29 November 1914, P4666.

23. See note by Sir Robert Graham on 'proposed Anglo-French Agreement Regarding Arabia', 25 October 1917, at FO 371/3056/239988. In this note Graham observed: 'The French have certain shadowy claims on Cheik Said since 1734, when Admiral La Bourdonnais obtained a cession of the Cape from the local Sultan. The French have since made various attempts to take over Cheik Said by purchase, occupation or other means, but have never been able to do so, and a Turkish garrison has been maintained on the spot. Cheik Said is an important place in so far as the command of the Red Sea is concerned, and it is desirable that the French should abandon their claims however shadowy they may be.'

24. Viceroy to S/S, 1 December 1914, L/P+S/10/558 P865.

25. Ibid. Minute by Crewe, 1 December 1914 P4666.

26. Ibid. IO to FO, 26 December 1914 (drafted by Hirtzel), P4959.

27. Minute by Chamberlain, 16 June 1915, L/P+S/10/559 P2153, p. 105.

28. Ibid. Viceroy to S/S, 8 February 1915, P522, p. 215.

29. Ibid. Minute by Hirtzel, c. 9 February 1915, p. 213.

30. First Assistant Resident, JP and Acting Resident, Aden, 1910–17, Chief Political Officer, Aden Field Force, 1914–17. Adviser to High Commissioner, Egypt, on SW Arabia, 1917–20.

31. IO to FO, 28 February 1917 (drafted by Hirtzel), L/P+S/10/562 P748.

32. Précis of Relations Between Aden Residency and Tribesmen of Hashid and Bakil, secret, in J.M. Stewart to Chamberlain, 28 March 1917, Aden Residency, no. C–221, secret, L/P+S/10/683 P1925.

33. See, for example, note by Jacob, 25 May 1917, Willingdon, Sussex, ibid., pp. 231ff.

34. Minutes by Holderness, 24 February 1917, L/P+S/10/562 P748; c. 18 January 1917, L/P+S/10/638 P184.

35. Minute by Hirtzel, 17 May 1917, L/P+S/10/683, p. 250.

36. Ibid. Viceroy to S/S, 17 May 1917, p. 238.

37. Ibid. Wingate to FO, 18 May 1917, no. 532, P2073, p. 242.

38. Ibid. A meeting to consider the question had taken place at the Foreign Office on 29 May 1917, P2144; minute by Shuckburgh, 29 May 1917, P2144.

39. Minute by H.G. Nicolson, 27 August 1917, FO 371/3056.
40. See appendix 3.
41. Grahame to Bertie, 29 September 1916, Bertie Papers Add. Ms 63043, f. 220 (British Library).
42. Ibid. As Grahame observed with reference to Italian artifice and her territorial gains in Europe:

> By this means, he [Sonnino] got the Allies to promise the Italians the Trent region, Cis-Alpine Tyrol, territory North East and East of the Isonzo, Trieste, Istria, including Pola, Dalmatia, a quantity of Islands in the Adriatic and territory round Valona. Also a confirmation of the possession of the Dodecanese Islands by Italy; a promise of a 'proper share of the provinces washed by the Mediterranean contiguous to the zone of Adalia'.

43. Ibid. Grahame to Bertie, 6 January 1917, British Embassy, Rome, Add. Ms 63045, f. 37.
44. Ibid. Hardinge to Bertie, 17 January 1917, Foreign Office, private, f. 55.
45. Memorandum by Lord Drogheda, 'Italy and the Partition of the Turkish Empire', 15 January 1917, FO 371/3043/12848, pp. 231–6.
46. Assistant Clerk and, later, Foreign Office Librarian.
47. Minute by Parker, 9 February 1917, FO 371/3043/33231, p. 322.
48. Ibid. Minute by Sykes, n.d., p. 323.
49. Wingate to FO, 29 January 1917, no. 79, FO 371/3048/22836.
50. Ibid. Minute by Balfour, n.d.
51. Ibid. Minutes by Graham and Hardinge, n.d.
52. IO to FO, 15 February 1917, FO 371/3049/36361.
53. Ibid. Hirtzel also suggested that Britain might build a bigger hostel herself; see R. Bidwell, in Bidwell and Smith, p. 190.
54. Ibid.
55. Note communicated by the Italian Ambassador, 28 February 1917, FO 371/3050/46706; ibid., Minute by Drogheda, 3 March 1917. As part of the arrangements surrounding the Arab revolt, Britain and France sent a military contingent to the Hejaz.
56. Ibid. Note communicated by the French Embassy, London, 13 March 1917, 56205.
57. Ibid. FO to Rodd, 23 June 1917, confidential, no. 1209, and minutes by Graham, 20 June 1917, and Hardinge, n.d., 125480.
58. See J. B. Kelly, 'The Legal and Historical Basis of the British Position in the Persian Gulf', St Antony's Papers, no. 4, *Middle Eastern Affairs,* no. 1 (London, 1958).
59. Third Report of Sir Louis Mallet's Sub-Committee on Territorial Changes, 28 March 1917, CAB 24/3. Besides Mallet, the following signed the report: W. Tyrrell, G.R. Clerk, H. McMahon, H.J. Read, H.C.M. Lambert, C. Strachey, T.W. Holderness, Islington, Macdonogh, F. Maurice, A.K. Wilson, W.F. Nicholson, H. Llewellyn Smith, H. Fountain, P. Ashley.
60. Copy of a report by Vice-Admiral Wemyss, Naval C-in-C, East Indies and Egypt, no. 423/1171, 3 April 1917, CAB 21/77, G.T. 563; for opinion on the ground see Memorandum by H. Pirie-Gordon in Pirie-Gordon to Maj. O'Sullivan, HMS *Exmouth,* 21 February 1916, FO 882/15, RS/16/3, f. 329; note by G.F. Clayton, 9 March 1916, FO 882/15, RS/16/14, f. 326.
61. See n. 59.
62. Minutes of the Committee of the Imperial War Cabinet on Territorial Desiderata in the Terms of Peace, second meeting, 18 April 1917, CAB 21/77. Besides Curzon, who chaired the meetings, the following were present: Robert Cecil, W. Long, A. Chamberlain, Hazen, Massey, Smuts, Sir E. Morris, Sinha, A.K. Wilson, H.C.M. Lambert. L.S. Amery and Maj. L. Storrs acted as secretaries. Besides the reasons suggested by V.H. Rothwell for the preponderance of non-Middle Eastern matters over those pertaining to that region in the business of the Committee must be added the important point that Curzon and Amery would deprecate the interference of the Dominion leaders in such matters; see Rothwell, *HJ,* 13, n. 45.
63. Ibid., minutes of the Imperial War Cabinet.
64. Ibid. Imperial War Cabinet, Report of Committee on Terms of Peace, Territorial Desiderata, 28 April 1917, P16; see J. S. Galbraith, *JICH,* 3, p. 31.
65. Curzon to Balfour, 29 June 1917, 1 Carlton House Terrace, SW, Balfour Papers FO 800/199, f. 80 (PRO); see Galbraith, op cit., n. 40.

66. See Barnes and Nicholson, *The Leo Amery Diaries*, vol. 1, entries of 26 April and 2 May 1917, pp. 151ff.
67. Brémond co-ordinated French military and political operations in the Hejaz.
68. Wingate to FO, 27 April 1917, FO 371/3054/87288, p. 497. For a detailed assessment of Brémond's role see R. Bidwell, in Bidwell and Smith. Bidwell emphasises that Brémond had strict instructions to co-operate with his British counterpart. Whilst, as Bidwell alleges, Sir Henry McMahon was initially extremely suspicious of Brémond, these suspicions were not shared, from the outset, by Clayton. Bidwell plausibly attributes the deterioration in Anglo-French relations in the Hejaz to the persistence of pre-Entente sentiments in the minds of Brémond, C.E. Wilson, Resident at Jedda, and other officers in the Hejaz. As Tanenbaum demonstrates, such feelings were displayed in higher circles in France: Tanenbaum, *TAPS*, 68, p. 19.
69. Ibid. Minute by Graham, 30 April 1917. According to Bidwell, op. cit., p. 191, it was Briand who first suggested the idea in February 1917.
70. Memorandum by the Marquis Imperiali, 11 May 1917, FO 371/3044/95567, p. 18.
71. Minutes by Hardinge, n.d. and L. Oliphant, 14 May 1917, FO 371/3055/94223.
72. Ibid. Minute by Cecil, n.d., 170005.
73. See appendix 4.
74. As Nevakivi states, this was in direct contradiction to the findings of Curzon's Territorial Committee: Nevakivi, *Britain, France and the Arab Middle East*, p. 47.
75. FO to Rodd, draft, 19 May, no. 112, FO 371/3044/102248, pp. 40–1.
76. Ibid. FO to Buchanan, 21 May 1917, no. 1028, p. 42.
77. Ibid. Buchanan to FO, 23 May 1917, no. 756, 104290, p. 46.
78. Ibid. Cecil to Bertie, 19 May 1917, no. 330, 102249, p. 44.
79. Hereafter referred to as the Cherchali note. Appendix 5.
80. Note communicated by Monsieur Cambon, 16 May 1917, confidential, Curzon Papers F112/277.
81. Wingate to FO (Sirdar), Khartoum, 16 November 1916, no. 25, secret, L/P+S/10/530 P4831; ibid., Wingate to FO, 25 November 1916, no. 38, P4948; ibid., extract from Mark Sykes's Appreciation of Arabian Reports, no. xix (New Series), 29 November 1916, P5000; ibid., Minute by Shuckburgh, n.d.
82. Hon. Attaché Constantinople; Special Commissioner for HMG to inquire into and report upon the future of British trade in Turkey, Mesopotamia and Persian Gulf, 1908. During 1914–18 he served in Egypt, Gallipoli, Mesopotamia and the Hejaz.
83. Extract from a Private letter dated 24 October 1916, from Capt. George Lloyd to H/E the Governor General, L/P+S/10/530; see Tanenbaum, op cit., p. 19.
84. Cecil to Cambon, 7 June 1917, FO 371/3056/111433.
85. Hereafter EEF.
86. Notes of a conference held at 10 Downing Street, 3 April 1917, secret, copy, CAB 24/9, G.T. 372.
87. GHQ EEF-WO, 25 May 1917, FO 371/3043/109892, p. 90.
88. Ibid. Minute by Cecil, n.d., p. 96. According to Tauber, *The Arab Movement*, pp. 117ff, Clayton perceived the Legion as 'a symbol of Arab nationalism'. Regarded with suspicion not only by many British officials, but by King Hussein, by the French – who regarded its Arab recruits as would-be creators of an Arab kingdom – and by Arabs in the Hejaz, the Legion was doomed to failure.
89. Ibid. Minute by Graham, n.d., p. 114, and draft telegram by Curzon, no. 717, 115283, p. 121.
90. Ibid. Wingate to FO, 10 June 1917, no. 606, p. 115.
91. Interdepartmental Committee on the Arabian Legion, attended by Graham, Hirtzel, Shuckburgh, Macdonogh, F. Maurice and Sykes. The issue had been referred to the Mesopotamian Administration Committee on the advice of the Foreign Office. According to a minute signed by Balfour, Hardinge and Cecil, the Foreign Office had changed its mind on the issue and subject to clarification by Sykes on the proposed nature of French involvement, was willing to endorse the scheme; see memorandum by Sykes, 'The Arab Legion', secret, and appended Foreign Office minute, n.d., CAB 24/18, G.T. 1229.
92. Draft telegram by Curzon, no. 717, FO 371/3043/115283, p. 126.
93. Sykes to Drummond, 20 July 1917, Offices of the War Cabinet, 2 Whitehall Gardens,

London, SW, Sykes Papers DS.42.1, f. 68 (St Antony's College, Oxford).

94. Ibid. Sykes to Clayton, 22 July 1917, 1 Whitehall Gardens, London, SW, DS 42.1, f. 69.

95. See pp. 86–7

96. See n. 94.

97. Memorandum by D.G. Hogarth, 7 June 1917, FO 882/3, AP/17/6, ff. 18–19.

98. Hogarth to Clayton, 11 July 1917, Hogarth Papers.

99. Wingate to FO, 3 June 1917, Cairo, no. 583, FO 371/3056/110589. The strategic and political interdependence of Syria and the Hejaz had been commented upon by Storrs back in February 1915. Two years later, though transposed into a different context by virtue of the Arab revolt, the connection remained strong. One Cairo official, probably A.C. Parker, Kitchener's nephew, the first Director of the Arab Bureau and, later, Director of Military Intelligence in the Arab revolt, observed: 'The Sykes Picot Agreement was roughly to the effect that the Hejaz is our pigeon and Syria that of the French.'?(A.C. Parker) to ?(Wingate), 10 February 1917, Cairo, secret, FO 882/16, ff. 47–50. The fact that little was made of this connection in diplomatic terms by Britain might be explained with reference to the more significant parallels which emerged between Syria and Mesopotamia by virtue of the activities of Sykes and Picot in May 1917. Moreover, as Bidwell argues, Brémond was keenly aware of this interconnection fearing, somewhat improbably, that if the Arabs took Medina they might continue their advance into Syria and stage a revolt there; see Bidwell, in Bidwell and Smith, p. 11ff.

100. Wingate to FO, 10 June 1917, no. 605, FO 371/3054/115281, pp. 503–4.

101. Note by Sir Mark Sykes, 'Observations on Arabian Policy as a result of visit to Red Sea Ports, Jeddah, Yembo, Wejh, Kamaran and Aden', 5 June 1917, with joint recommendations drafted by Sykes for Picot, ?(3) June 1917, Curzon Papers F112/277; also at FO 882/3 AP/17/5; see Nevakivi, *Britain, France and the Arab Middle East*, pp. 60–1.

102. See n. 100.

103. Wingate to FO, 11 June 1917, The Residency, Ramleh, confidential, no. 127, FO 371/3054/125564.

104. See n. 100; also Kedourie, *The Chatham House Version*, p. 21.

105. Ibid.

106. See n. 103.

107. Ibid.

108. Ibid. On the meeting at Jeddah see Kedourie, op cit., p. 26; Tanenbaum, *TAPS*, 68, pp. 17–18.

109. Ibid. Wingate to FO, 10 June 1917, no. 609, FO 371/3054/115603; note on this by Sykes, 22 June 1917, G.T. 1146, CAB 24/17.

110. Ibid. Note by Sykes.

111. See n. 103.

112. See n. 110.

113. Ibid.

114. Memorandum by Clayton, 'Notes on Draft Report of Sykes–Picot Mission, as submitted to H.E. the High Commissioner', Observations on Arab Policy, FO 882/3, f. 40ff.

115. Ibid. Memorandum by Hogarth, 7 June 1917, AP/17/6, ff. 18–19.

116. Ibid. Memorandum by George Lloyd, ?(7) June 1917, AP/17/7, ff. 20–4.

117. Wingate to FO, 3 July 1917, Cairo, no. 696, FO 371/3056/131922.

118. Ibid. Minute by Graham, 5 July 1917.

119. Ibid. Also minute by Hardinge, n.d.

120. Minutes of the Mesopotamian Administration Committee, fifth meeting, secret, CAB 27/22.

121. Note by Curzon, 'British and French positions in Arabia', 23 August 1917, Curzon Papers F112/277. Ibid., draft reply to French Ambassador, Foreign Office, July 1917, marked in Curzon's hand 'AJB's draft reply to which I objected'.

122. The remaining material on pp. 91–3 relates to Curzon's memorandum unless otherwise indicated.

123. See n. 121. Draft reply to French Ambassador.

124. Cecil to Cambon, 29 August 1917, Foreign Office, no. 165801/W/44, Curzon Papers F112/277.

125. Minute by Hirtzel, 1 September 1917, L/P+S/10/616 P3487; ibid., Minute by Montagu, 3 September 1917, p. 109.

126. Ibid. Minute by Hirtzel.
127. Ibid. Minute by Hirtzel, 17 September 1917, p. 109.
128. FO 371/3056/132784.
129. Assistant Clerk at the Foreign Office.
130. Minutes of the Mesopotamian Administration Committee, 21 July 1917, seventh meeting, secret, CAB 27/22; minute by Oliphant, n.d., FO 371/3056/165801.
131. FO 371/3056/132784.
132. See n. 124.
133. Note communicated by the French Embassy, London, 18 September 1917, FO 371/3056/181851.
134. Ibid. Minutes by Graham, 20 September 1917, and Shuckburgh, 24 September 1917.
135. See n. 133.
136. Ibid.
137. Ibid. See also minute by Curzon, 22 September 1917.
138. Ibid. Note from French Embassy.
139. Ibid. Curzon's minute.
140. Ibid. Minute by Shuckburgh (for Montagu), 24 September 1917.
141. Ibid.
142. See Appendix 6. The draft agreement was called and is hereafter referred to as the 'Projet d'arrangement'.
143. FO to Bertie, 26 September 1917, no. 2387, FO 371/3056/181851.
144. Ibid. Minute by Sir George Clerk, 8 October 1917, 191542.
145. Ibid. Admittedly, in his comments on the French note of 18 September, Curzon did not make explicit his view that he envisaged a continuation of British support to the Hejaz after the war. From a note written by Graham a week later it is clear that Graham was well aware of Curzon's views but that he was not inclined to translate Curzon's points into an order if they were communicated to Sykes in Paris; minute by Graham, 24 September 1917, FO 371/3056/181851.
146. Ibid. Minute by Clerk, 8 October 1917, 191542.
147. See Appendix 6.
148. Minute by Graham, 9 October 1917, FO 371/3056/191542.
149. Ibid.
150. Ibid. Also minute by Hardinge, n.d.
151. Ibid. Minute by Shuckburgh, 11 October 1917.
152. Note by Lord Robert Cecil for Balfour, 31 July 1917, FO 371/3044/153074, pp. 120–1.
153. See Bidwell, in Bidwell and Smith, p. 195; Nevakivi, *Britain, France and the Arab Middle East*, p. 63.
154. Minutes of the Middle East Committee, CAB 27/22. Of course it is quite possible and even probable that Nicolson's draft was circulated to the Committee without a formal sitting of that body. In an undated addition to Oliphant's minute it was stated that the draft had been circulated to the Committee on 10 September. However, the Middle East Committee was not convened until 13 September. It seems unlikely that Curzon would have passed up the opportunity provided by a meeting of his Committee to tackle the issue yet there is no evidence of him having attempted to capitalise on this.
155. Picot to Sykes, 23 August 1917, Ambassade de France à Londres, copy, enclosed in Sykes to Graham, Sledmere, Malton, in Egerton-Beck to Graham, 27 August 1917, Offices of the War Cabinet, 2 Whitehall Gardens, London, SW, FO 371/3044/168691, p. 299.
156. Ibid. Sykes to Graham.
157. Senior Clerk at the Foreign Office.
158. See n. 155. Minute by Sir George Clerk, 28 August 1917, p. 298.
159. Explanatory note on instructions to Sir Mark Sykes, n.d., FO 371/3056/239988.
160. Ibid.
161. Ibid.
162. Available evidence surrounding the conference held on October 25/26 is difficult to interpret. At the Eastern Committee on 8 August 1918, Curzon made reference to negotiations with the French 'about six months ago' to reach an agreement on the entire Arabian issue. As Curzon continued, 'The French, taking advantage of our reluctance to proclaim a protectorate then,

had tried to claim absolute equality with us in the Hedjaz, where our interests were necessarily predominant. The War Cabinet had, at the time, asked the Secretary of State for Foreign Affairs and Lord Curzon, on behalf of his Majesty's Government, to meet a French Minister and Monsieur Picot at the Foreign Office, with a view to arriving at an agreement. A form of words had been drawn up for submission to the French Government, but he had heard nothing of it since.'

Only after an exhaustive search of War Cabinet minutes and the Foreign Office card index failed to verify Curzon's recollection of events was it discovered that a conference had, in fact, been held in October 1917. Again, only after subsequent searches was it revealed that Curzon had attended the conference. In addition, there is an interesting gap in the chronologically arranged Hejaz section of the Foreign Office card index. In view of the arrangement of these cards it seems possible that the missing cards refer to the October conference. A possible explanation of this is provided by a minute of the Eastern Department of 12 September 1919, in which it was stated that as Lord Milner (who was by then entrusted with the Arabian negotiations) had no record if certain papers which dealt with French policy in Arabia and Syria had been taken to Paris by the British Delegation the originals were being sent. The assumption is that the papers referred to, and which cannot now be traced in the appropriate FO 371 files, were not returned and the corresponding cards in the Foreign Office index were removed. Minutes of the Eastern Committee, 8 August 1918, *EC* 23, secret, CAB 27/24; FO 371/3056/131922.

163. See n. 159.
164. Minute by J.E.H. for Sir Robert Graham, 23 December 1918, FO 371/3056/208697.
165. Minute by Shuckburgh, 12 January 1918, L/P+S/10/616 P74, p. 54.
166. Text submitted for discussion with France, marked by Hardinge 'Text Under Discussion, October 25th, final form'. Enclosed in a minute by Hardinge for Balfour, 26 October 1917, FO 371/3056/208697.
167. Address by Lord Curzon, Viceroy and Governor-General of India, to the Trucial chiefs of the Arab coast, at a Public Durbar held at Shargah on 21 November 1903. India Foreign and Political Department, Treaties and Engagements, including a speech by Curzon, I.S 158/2 (British Library).
168. See Ronaldshay, *The Life of Lord Curzon,* vol. 2, p. 313.
169. See David Roberts, 'The Consequences of the Exclusive Treaties: A British View', in *The Arab Gulf and the West,* ed., B.R. Pridham (London, Sydney, 1985).
170. Hogarth to Clayton, 11 July 1917, Hogarth Papers.
171. Storrs to his parents, 22 February 1915, The Residency, Cairo, private, Storrs Papers II.3.
172. Mesopotamian Administration Committee, Observations by the Director of Military Intelligence on Sir R. Wingate's dispatch, no. 127 (of 11 June), 6 July 1917, secret, War Office, CAB 27/22.
173. Lloyd to Wingate, 17 August 1917, Lloyd Papers 9/13. It was also appreciated by Georges Picot who, attempting to restrain Ribot, the French premier, in his resolve to deny Britain a privileged position in the Hejaz, observed in June 1917: 'in this question of Hejaz, as formerly in that of Fashoda, we are clashing with a vital interest of the British Empire, which feels that it can give up nothing in Arabia that it needs in order to be assured of complete possession of the route of the Indies and exclusive control of the Persian Gulf.' See Tanenbaum, op cit., p. 19.
174. There is strong evidence to suggest that the Foreign Office, and in particular Lord Robert Cecil, wished to prevent the Middle East Committee from meeting; see ch. 4, nn. 1, 16. Regarding Curzon's apparent climb-down at the October conference, there are two obvious interpretations. It is possible that on his return to Paris after the conference Picot took with him a different version of the Projet d'arrangement than the one apparently approved by Curzon. In the note written for Balfour explaining Sykes's instructions for his trip to Paris in December 1917, reference is made to the Projet '*as amended* [*sic*]' having been taken to Paris by Picot for the approval of his Government. There were, of course, broader grounds than the Arabian issue alone for discouraging Curzon's interference in the matter. To develop this interpretation, it is interesting to speculate that the gaps in the Foreign Office card index and FO 371 Turkey series were, perhaps, the work of a Foreign Office official in 1919, anxious lest Curzon's proclivity for archival searches penetrate what may, in this case, have

amounted to a concerted attempt by Foreign Office officials to exclude him. Assuming the foregoing treatment of available material is correct, it can only be supposed that the official concerned did not approach his task with sufficient vigour.

Another possibility, scarcely less fanciful given the year and Curzon's temperament, is that in response to the excesses of Curzon and his French counterparts, Sykes might have pressed for a stronger Arab policy in Syria and the Hejaz and that Curzon might then have capitulated. Senior officials were mindful of the fact that British policy in the Hejaz would influence the degree of latitude afforded to France in Syria. Sykes, of course, had the ear of some senior figures whereas the disinclination of the India and Foreign Offices to summon the Middle East Committee effectively reduced Curzon to the position of a Cabinet Minister without portfolio. Faced with this combination it may be that Curzon vested hope in the preamble of the Projet whereby Britain might still hope to establish her influence in the Hejaz by means of concession hunting.

175. Minute by Curzon, 12 March 1918, FO 371/3380/38817.

∞ 4 ∞

Britain, Mesopotamia and the Middle East, 1918

THE FORWARD IMPULSE

F AILURE BY THE War Cabinet to endorse a more vigorous military policy in Palestine and Mesopotamia left Curzon a very frustrated man by the end of 1917. Equally infuriating was the tendency of departments to deal with matters of policy which might properly have been referred to the Middle East Committee. Curzon unleashed those feelings in the following letter, written to Robert Cecil early in 1918:

> There is or was a Middle East Committee of the Cabinet of which I am or was Chairman and of which Sykes is or was secretary. We used to have frequent meetings and all the earlier Mesopotamian and Hejaz policy was formulated by us.
>
> The Foreign Secretary was of course present whenever he desired. Now I observe that no questions are referred to us. We have not been summoned for some 2 months & the Foreign Office policy as regards these countries is formulated and published without any reference to us at all.
>
> For instance on the occasion you suggested an American Protectorate over Palestine – quite a new idea. Today I read . . . an entirely new statement of Arab and Palestine policy.
>
> This morning I read an astonishing telegram to Buchanan . . . suggesting that we should stir up the Russian Moslems by laying stress on *female suffrage* (Good God!) and progressive self-Government for Oriental peoples!
>
> Who in your office is doing all these things I cannot imagine. I am quite willing to give up being Chairman of the Middle East Committee which was created by the Cabinet to promote coordination between Foreign Office and War Cabinet.
>
> But as long as we exist I do not think we ought to be given the complete go by and I am sure that is the very last thing that you yourself would desire.

> Both in Palestine and Arabia and Central Asia we ought to be very
> circumspect and there are considerable advantages in the consultation of
> men who know.[1]

Many currents conspired to produce this letter, not least, real or
imagined differences of approach to questions of policy between Curzon
and Cecil. Certainly, it was symptomatic of the frustration and sense of
futility to which departmental bickering led. Further, such disagree-
ments emphasised the vulnerability of Curzon's position as a Cabinet
Minister without a department, chairing an increasingly redundant, yet
potentially very powerful, Cabinet Committee.

Curzon's impatience resurfaced soon afterwards at the first meeting
of the newly constituted Middle East Committee in January 1918 when
he raised the question of an advance up the Euphrates to Hit. In
response, Major-General Macdonogh advised against such a move
because of military uncertainties.[2]

Within a week, however, Curzon had his way. Evacuation of Hit by
the Turks enabled General Marshall, GOC Mesopotamia, to march to
its outskirts. Curzon informed the Cabinet that he had recommended
such an advance some weeks before 'on account of the oil wells'.[3]

Feelings in Baghdad reflected Curzon's impatience. Such, at least,
was the unmistakable message conveyed in a memorandum by A.T.
Wilson, Deputy Civil Commissioner, forwarded by his superior Sir
Percy Cox:

> It may here be noted that for strategical purposes it would probably be con-
> venient to hold the gorge at Fatha and in any future discussion on frontiers
> this point should not be lost sight of. The next point at which we have
> definite information of the boundary between Mosul and Baghdad
> Wilayets is between Abu Kemal and El Qaim, on the Euphrates. It may be
> assumed that the boundary runs in a straight line between the Tigris and
> Euphrates.
>
>   . . . El Qaim forms a very definite jumping off point for Syria in view of
> possible railway developments, the distance in a straight line from El Qaim
> to Homs being a little over 250 miles, the distance to Damascus less than
> 300. It would seem desirable therefore in view of possible developments
> that the northern boundary of the Baghdad Wilayat should be pushed as
> far north as possible.[4]

Wilson's was a fascinating character; he was a meteor in the war-time
sky of the Middle East, whose cultivated anonymity, in part, perhaps
denied him the future public recognition accorded to others who exhibited the same combination of personality, drive and talent. There

was, however, sufficient of the Younghusband in him, with perhaps an added dash of real administrative ability, to render him mutually acceptable as the executor of their policy to men like Curzon and Hirtzel – and, by the age of 34, in an area stretching from the Indian Frontier to Syria.

In fact, it seems that Hirtzel had seen enough of Wilson to leave him with the impression of a man of intelligence who could be trusted to safeguard British interests. In June 1915 Wilson wrote to his mother:

> There is very little now to stop us from going to Baghdad, if we wish to do so. The arguments for and against going there (considered apart from the question of staying there) are very interesting.
>
> The moral effect would be great, and the strain on Persia due to Turkish action near Karmanshah would be relieved. There are many considerations, but I think generally speaking that in such cases the only sound thing is to go on as far as one possibly can and not to try to look too far ahead.[5]

To Wilson, advance was not simply a matter of prestige; to Britain and to the Mesopotamian Arabs, British occupation was of strategic value. Moreover, there were economic considerations for Britain and for the rest of Europe. An earlier incident, for which Wilson was strongly censured, provides a more penetrating insight.

In a letter to a Colonel Yate, MP, written towards the end of November 1914, Wilson had expressed himself openly on his vision of the future Mesopotamia:

> I should like to see it announced that Mesopotamia was to be annexed to India as a colony for India and Indians, that the Government of India would administer it, and gradually bring under cultivation its vast unpopulated desert plains, peopling them with martial races from the Punjab . . .
>
> Mohammedan India would feel that it was getting in this manner a quid pro quo for its action in this war, and it would be an inspiring thought to them to be able to reflect that India, which had a greater population than any Mohammedan country in the world, will have its 'place in the sun' in the future.[6]

As Wilson continued, irrigation in India was unlikely to expand further, while Mesopotamia's oil wells would permit the irrigation of 'millions of acres' hitherto neglected.

In Wilson's view this scheme had the added merit that it would enable the British Government to avoid Indian settlement in the Colonies. Unfortunately, however, Wilson had failed to mark his letter private and personal, and, as a result, when its contents were leaked a suspicion lingered of attempts to influence decision-making by encouraging Parliamentary pressure. Hirtzel, on the other hand, found the letter 'interesting . . . but obviously not the fruit of mature reflection'.[7] In spite of, or perhaps because of, this 'excess of zeal', it was in the execution of British policy in Mesopotamia that Wilson's superiors sought to employ his talents, both as a distinguished junior officer in the field and, later, regularly working an eighteen-hour day in the administration of the country.

However, there was an aspect of Wilson's character, a curious blend of egotism and single-mindedness, which Hirtzel possibly did not fully appreciate, and which his private correspondence with Wilson did little to diminish. Lamenting Kut in June 1916, Hirtzel confided: 'The important thing is to ginger up HMG into seeing that the situation must be retrieved.'[8]

At the time Hirtzel's fondness for providing slower mortals with ideas which resurfaced in Whitehall in the text of telegrams or memoranda did not particularly matter. It began to matter when the ideas and methods which Hirtzel had cultivated in others were no longer compatible with wider political conditions. Certainly, in May 1917, Hirtzel had intimated to Wilson a feeling that these conditions might change: 'The future is, of course, still obscure: we have not won the war yet, and no one knows exactly where the talk about "no annexations" may lead, or what the effect of the new Russian policy may be on the Anglo-Russo-French agreement about the Arab State.' But then, in the next breath, and when expressing the hope that Wilson would stay on until the administration was in place, Hirtzel recorded his disappointment with the failure of the Mesopotamian authorities to establish contacts with Sheikhs in northern Mesopotamia and in the Syrian desert. In Hirtzel's view the situation in Palestine and the dismal handling of the Kurds by Russia meant that Britain should try to contact the Yezidis and the Milli.[9]

Hirtzel was no more inherently acquisitive than Wilson but confidences such as these from a senior official, for whom Wilson evidently had considerable respect, were unwise. This was especially so given Wilson's workaholicism, the centralising which this involved, and, periodically, indications that the burden was too great. Hirtzel did not fully understand the nature of the man whom he sought to influence and, partly for this reason, the need to influence became a need to harness, to check and, eventually, to restrain.

The forward impulse to which Curzon and Wilson gave expression was in keeping with Hirtzel's instincts, yet, as he himself had foreseen, developments in international conditions rendered it imperative that Britain should not be seen to be land-grabbing. Not only would Britain have to be circumspect about further acquisitions of territory, but the fact of occupation would alone no longer suffice to justify land taken since 1914. He expressed this view in a note of 11 January 1918 for the Middle East Committee.[10]

Hirtzel was acutely aware of the delicacy of Britain's position in Mesopotamia. Speculation about serious and imminent peace moves coincided with speeches by Lloyd George and President Wilson which implied that national self-determination might well be applied in the former Ottoman Empire with more vigour than had been anticipated.

Hirtzel's response was essentially to apply previous methods, although, as the stakes were now higher, it became increasingly important to guide more closely the thoughts of those whose unfettered enthusiasm for naked imperialism might jeopardise Britain's future in Mesopotamia. This he sought to do by setting down unequivocally the new conditions within which Mesopotamia must now be considered, and the steps necessary to secure British control: 'Annexation (e.g. of Basra) is presumably now out of the question, or even the veiled annexation contemplated in the Anglo-French agreement. The Arab façade of which the Committee[11] talked must be something more than a façade.'[12] If indigenous administration were to be established, it was vital, as Hirtzel implied, that Britain's association with it should be as close as possible. The safest means of achieving this, with regard to prying and puritanical allies, was to deal with the matter locally. Therefore, Hirtzel recommended, firstly, that Sir Percy Cox be asked his opinion of what, in view of changed conditions, might be achieved. Secondly, Hirtzel advised the abandonment of a proposed investigatory commission to Mesopotamia. Furthermore, and as a continuation of earlier plans, he advised 'that all possible immediate action be taken on the Mesopotamian Trade Commission's report to get ourselves started commercially so as to be ahead of competitors whom it may be impossible to exclude after the war'.[13]

Reiterating these views in a memorandum produced with Shuckburgh at the end of the month, Hirtzel wrote:

> our position towards Mesopotamia is, or may become, not that of a ruler towards his subjects, but that of a candidate towards his constituents. We shall want their votes; and unless we nurse the constituency in advance, we

may not get them. Is it possible so to handle the local population, or the elements in it that count, as to ensure that, if and when the moment for 'self-determination' arrives, they will pronounce decisively in favour of continuing the British connection? That seems to be the immediate question we have to ask ourselves; and it is one to which the local authorities are alone competent to furnish us with a reply. They alone can say what elements in the population it is desirable to strengthen and encourage, what materials exist for setting up a local administration of a suitable character, what leaders if any can be found who are likely to command general acceptance, and by what means these leaders can be brought to identify themselves with British interests.[14]

To some extent Hirtzel was preaching to the converted. Early in 1918 communications from several parties suggested a broad and now articulated consensus that, as far as possible, Britain must maximise her presence in Mesopotamia even in defiance of the McMahon pledges and Sykes–Picot Agreement.[15]

Equally, with Britain's position in Basra now threatened, a greater, though still fragile, consensus was emerging in favour of Hirtzel's approach as the best means of attaining British control. Where differences persisted they tended to result from differing perceptions as to the immediacy of the dangers posed by peace and American ideology, though, naturally, discussion about the purpose of British policy continued.

The delicacy of the situation was deemed sufficient to merit a discussion with Cox in person, either in Cairo or in London, and the agenda and other arrangements for this meeting were delegated to the India Office.

PEGGING OUT CLAIMS

Curzon's suspicions that he was being excluded from discussions on British policy in the Middle East were well founded. In retrospect it may seem that the Foreign and India Offices had much to gain from an overall co-ordination of policy. However, even assuming that only matters of policy were to be referred to Curzon for his decision, it seems likely that, given the nature of his involvement to date, his presence would be discouraged.

Evidently reeling from Curzon's indignant letter of 6 January, Robert Cecil confessed his despair to Balfour:

The existence of the Persia Committee seems to add a rather unnecessary

entanglement to any possibility of action; but George holds strongly to it
as he does to another body called the Middle East Committee: the function
of which seems mainly to be to enable George Curzon and Mark Sykes to
explain to each other how very little they know about the subject. An
attempt by me to smother decorously both Committees was detected by
George, and had to be abandoned. They are now to meet regularly on
Saturday mornings: a time fixed with the hope that it may ultimately prove
discouraging to their existence.[16]

Cecil also bemoaned the birth of another body, the Russia Committee,
and to the extent that he insisted that it be denied any urgent matters for
its decision, it seems that he disapproved of committees vested with
executive powers framing and executing foreign policy. However, unlike the Middle East Committee and the Persia Committee, the Russia
Committee was a Foreign Office Committee and, although Cecil initially declined to sit on it himself, he did concede that it might be useful.
In the case of the Middle East Committee, however, this tussle between
Curzon and Cecil had, by the autumn of 1918, flared into what was considerably more than a debate about the delegation of executive powers.

From the perspective of the India Office and more especially from
that of Hirtzel, whose thinking continued to predominate, there were
even stronger reasons for discouraging Curzon's interference.[17] The
matter was not so much of policy but of method.

As we have seen, Hirtzel had long considered it possible, if not likely,
that international politics would make it necessary for Britain to be able
to justify her retention of a predominant position in Mesopotamia other
than on a basis of military occupation. To the extent that Curzon had
been an enthusiastic and influential advocate of military advance, had
preached the necessity of British control of Mesopotamia, and was
receptive, generally, to any possibility of further gain, he had played an
important part in Hirtzel's calculations. However, as 1917 progressed,
Hirtzel was increasingly aware that political conditions were changing
and that this necessitated a definite change of emphasis, giving decided-
ly more weight to the policy of gradual development of Mesopotamian
civil administration under British auspices.

This trend is much in evidence in the internal debates within the India
Office during the autumn and winter of 1917. Hirtzel's urgency on
the subject is reflected in a letter written by him to Sir William
Clark, Comptroller-General of the Department of Commercial Intelligence, at the end of 1917. Referring to the Holland–Wilson Report on
commercial prospects in Mesopotamia, Hirtzel strongly believed that

Britain should act on its findings. However, although the Turkish military threat to Mesopotamia had receded, a more potent danger had replaced it. To Hirtzel it rendered action on the report urgent:

> we must at least consider the possibility of a peace which will not give us the absolute political control over Mesopotamia which we should like to have, and which may throw us back again on Commerce, in competition with other Powers (Germany included), for the maintenance of our political position. If that is a real possibility – as I think it is – then the next few months are all-important to us to enable us to get a start of our rivals.[18]

Concern about the possibility of France gaining a foothold in Mesopotamia was long-standing. Writing to Sir Percy Cox in Baghdad on 20 July 1917, Wingate had requested information about the alleged appointment of a Monsieur Roux as French Consul at Baghdad, adding that 'any decision of a kind regarding Mesopotamia would presumably affect Jeddah and other Red Sea Ports where up to the present we have succeeded in avoiding [the] appointment of foreign consuls'.[19]

This was, as Holderness wrote, 'a very awkward move', with a 'political motive' and one which, because of Russia's concession to France of a consulate at Trebizond, was difficult to challenge purely on the grounds of military uncertainty.[20]

It was none the less on this basis, and the possibility of 'misunderstanding' with Britain's other allies, that France was deterred.[21] In September, Cambon again raised the issue, complaining, as Shuckburgh anticipated, about other consuls at Baghdad, namely those of Persia and America.[22] In response, Balfour reiterated the possibility of enemy military activity and the probable clamour of appeals for equal treatment should France's claim be accepted. Further, he added that the American and Persian Consuls were not executing official duties but were merely 'treated with consideration as the heads of their respective communities'. If Roux wished to go to Baghdad in a similar capacity then, Balfour added, he would not object. On Hirtzel's insistence, however, even this concession was dropped.[23]

Further tension arose in November because of concern within the Political Department that the French Dragoman at Baghdad had commercial motives, and this unease persisted into 1918 owing to understandable French worries that they were being unfairly excluded from economic competition and the predictable India Office view of this as trouble-making.[24]

There was, similarly, in the case of banking in Mesopotamia and the

Middle East in general, a suggestion of acceleration to deter overtaking by rivals. Hirtzel possibly exaggerated the threat posed by foreign competitors, but concern about this by the end of 1917 was deeply imbued in the thinking of many officials in any case.

As early as February 1915, Hirtzel had emphasised the need to deny French capital a foothold in Basra in the form of the Imperial Ottoman Bank.[25] The Foreign Office agreed albeit more, apparently, on the basis of the bank's Turkish origins.

In the course of a letter to Sir William Clark at the end of 1917, Hirtzel mentioned banking as one area in which Britain really would have to get a move on:

> One step has been taken locally which is of some importance viz the formation of an irrigation Department. Two other things seem to be equally urgent – navigation and banking. If Mesopotamia is to be developed a lot of capital will be wanted, and the Treasury will give no help. It has been suggested that a really powerful British or Anglo-Indian banking syndicate should be formed, consisting of some of the leading London banks, and possibly Insurance Companies and acting in close association with Indian banks able and willing to finance irrigation and other agricultural projects on a very large scale . . . Lord Inchcape . . . is prepared to go in for something of the kind. But the first thing, it seems to me, is to get trade moving on the rivers, and for that purpose to get a British Company afloat. Lynch has already been plaguing us: but we don't love Lynch *per se*. The Inchcape–Lynch combine is, however, a different proposition, and I should be in favour of setting them on the rivers at once.

However, as Hirtzel concluded, opposition to this had already emerged from Sir Percy Cox, who objected to the creation of monopolies:

> It seems to me that he is wrong . . . A monopoly is not an amiable thing, and if Mesopotamia were going to be a British possession, we should, naturally not think of one. But it isn't; and it is more than likely that the only way in which we shall be able to keep e.g. the Japanese out will be by presenting the *fait accompli* of a monopoly.[26]

What Inchcape proposed, and what Hirtzel recommended, was the fulfilling of an arrangement reached but not ratified on the eve of war between Inchcape, the Turkish Government and the Foreign Office, whereby Inchcape and Lynch should operate steamers on the Tigris under the management of Mackay, Lynch & Co. Anticipating that peace was not far distant, Inchcape wished to establish a house in Baghdad without delay, suggesting that this might act as a catalyst for other busi-

ness and finance. Further, to pre-empt similar moves by rivals, Inchcape
spoke of eventually creating 'a powerful banking Syndicate in which
possibly Indian and Australian interests as well as British might be associated'. All this, Inchcape insisted, could safely be justified on the basis
of pre-war arrangements, and would not therefore provoke other
similar claims.[27]

Shuckburgh, as head of the Political and Secret Department, was
required to give a somewhat longer assessment of Inchcape's proposition and of the Commissioners' report as a whole. Like Hirtzel, he
wished to establish the Inchcape–Lynch concession, but, though in
favour of 'pegging out claims', was more conscious than Hirtzel that
provision for civil administration was necessarily dependent upon military conditions. Moreover, Shuckburgh was disinclined to recommend
an agriculture department because of its association with the question of
irrigation and the need for a more settled international climate.[28]
Holderness agreed, and his reaction to this proposal and to the
Holland–Wilson Report as a whole revealed the extent to which Hirtzel
was pushing ahead:

> It is a storehouse of information, which will be permanently useful if the
> conditions of the peace-settlement leave the destinies of Mesopotamia in
> any degree in British keeping. But a good deal of the writing is coloured by
> assumptions as to the completeness of the domination which England will
> exercise in this region that are far removed from anything that is likely to
> happen.

Regarding the creation of an Agriculture Department, Holderness felt it
inexpedient. According to Holderness, there were practical difficulties to
be considered. More broadly the idea seemed inconceivable 'until war
is over and the future of the country has been settled'.[29]

Lord Islington was more in tune with Hirtzel's thinking and with
reality. Writing to Chelmsford in March 1918, and referring to the proposed visit of Sir Percy Cox to London, Islington observed that, in her
efforts to retain Mesopotamia, Britain must adhere to the principles of
no annexation and self-determination:

> It is therefore of the utmost importance that we should have established
> ourselves through the country in such a way that we shall have become as
> far as possible both indispensable to, and acceptable by, the native com-
> munity. This can best be done by discreetly developing our trade and agri-
> cultural position in the country and on such lines as will be recognised by
> the native community as to their advantage.[30]

Islington had already spelled out the same message to Curzon, in clear terms, when recommending the consideration of the Holland–Wilson Report by the Middle East Committee:

> I think we are all agreed that it must be our policy so to fortify our position in Mesopotamia it will remain proof against any theoretic cessions to the doctrine of local self-determination or to the claims of the Arab Kingdom that we may be obliged to make. From this point of view it seems to me all-important that we should set about the task of consolidating our commercial interests in the country.[31]

The methods of Islington and Hirtzel represented a flexible and far-sighted response to changing conditions and, in addition, as a logical continuation of earlier methods, had much to commend them.

POLICY IS CAMOUFLAGED

At the meeting of the Middle East Committee on 18 February, when the question of the commercial and civil development of Mesopotamia was discussed, there was a tangible air of restraint among those anxious to move more quickly in these matters.[32] Of these there were several at the meeting, including Alwyn Parker, George Lloyd, Sir William Clark and the Lords Islington and Hardinge. Moreover, although Hirtzel did not attend the meeting, Shuckburgh, when preparing a note on the Holland–Wilson Report for the Middle East Committee, was less equivocal than in departmental minutes. In his note he urged immediate action on several points, including an agricultural department, and strongly favoured the Inchcape–Lynch concession.

Anticipating opposition, Shuckburgh had composed his case with great care. There was, he suggested, a close resemblance between the proposals made by Inchcape and the specifications of the Trade Commissioners for British control of navigation. Moreover, notwithstanding Sir Percy Cox's views, as Shuckburgh noted, the 1913 'concession' had never been ratified and would not come into effect until after the cessation of hostilities. 'In the meantime', Shuckburgh continued, 'Lord Inchcape is willing to open business at Baghdad at once, apparently without asking for definite pledges as to the future; and there would seem to be strong grounds for encouraging him to do so, without prejudice to the ultimate decision on the question of monopoly.'[33]

Had Curzon been more closely in touch with the prevailing trends of policy then he might well have seen in this a convenient loophole.

Instead, however, the context in which he introduced the question and the tenor of the discussion suggest that he was out of touch. According to Curzon, the concession was a monopoly pure and simple. Further, the India Office supported it and the granting of banking facilities at Baghdad, firstly, 'to anticipate the creation of German and Japanese interests', and, secondly, on the basis of the near completion of the agreement on the pre-war concession.[34] The minutes continue:

> On the other hand, he [Curzon] felt bound to point out to the Committee that the proposed concession raised a question of high policy, viz, 'Was it either possible or desirable that His Majesty's Government should take any immediate step which assumed continued British occupation of Baghdad after the War?' The fact that the future of Mesopotamia lay on the lap of the Peace Conference rendered it hardly possible, even if desirable, that His Majesty's Government should give monopoly rights to a British firm now. Further, in the event of questions arising in Parliament, it would be difficult to reconcile the proposed action with the war aims of the Allies as stated by the Prime Minister and President Wilson. The view might be expressed that we were prosecuting the war for British capitalistic expansion.[35]

Curzon did not take well to camouflage. Nor did he take to Alwyn Parker's suggestion that 50 per cent of the original share capital which, under the terms of the original concession, was to go to Turkey, should now go to whatever government was established in Mesopotamia. Such a monopoly, Parker contended, was the only effective means of deterring foreign competition.[36]

However, even among those anxious to make progress in Mesopotamia, there were genuine concerns about the advisability of vesting such an important section of British trade and, in effect, political control in the hands of the Lynch–Inchcape group. Balfour and George Lloyd were strongly against conceding control of river conservation to any private concern.[37] Both Lloyd and Macdonogh felt disinclined to support a monopoly when, before the war, monopolistic control had enabled Inchcape's British India Company to operate with such inefficiency that it actually stimulated German competition.[38]

There were, therefore, substantial areas of debate among the well informed besides Curzon's rather facile points and, pending further investigation and until Sir Percy Cox had pronounced on these matters, decision was deferred. Meanwhile, at the India Office, plans were being devised for the discussion with Cox.

The India Office had intended to communicate to Cox roughly the same interpretation of world events as portrayed by Hirtzel in his note of 11 January 1918. The draft telegram, after reiterating the recent speeches of Lloyd George and President Wilson, proceeded to state that annexation was now impossible and posed the following questions:

> Can a large majority of voices be secured in favour of British assistance and if so how far can request for actual British administration at all events for a period of years be counted upon, or what can be done to prepare the way for it? To what extent will such assistance or administration require maintenance of British or Indian troops or police in Mesopotamia? Again, what form of Arab Government is practicable? Is it conceivable that Member of Shereefial family would be accepted as sovereign under Shereef's suzerainty? If not, is there any other individual? And if not, what body or bodies are practicable and what powers could be entrusted to them?[39]

Before this could be circulated to the Middle East Committee, however, according to Shuckburgh, Curzon had 'taken strong objection' to it, and vetoed its circulation until the matter had first been discussed by the Committee.[40]

An added difficulty caused by Curzon's meddling on this occasion and at the meeting of the Middle East Committee of 18 February was that it led to a rather unlikely alliance between Curzon and Mark Sykes. Like Curzon, Sykes had previously been of considerable value to Hirtzel. Both men were disinclined to see France deprived of what might rightfully be regarded as her fair share of territory in the Middle East. Further, the continued support of Arab nationalism was regarded as important by Sykes and Hirtzel, albeit for rather different reasons. Precisely because of this, differences arose.

Certainly in January 1917 Sykes had expressed regret that Mosul had been promised to France, and by the autumn of 1917 he spoke of establishing political control in Mosul as being a British interest.[41] However, with regard to 'world interests' he wrote that 'we should do all in our power to foster and revive Arab civilization and promote Arab unity with a view of preparing them for ultimate independence'.

Notwithstanding this objective and the fact that Sykes, unlike Curzon, anticipated an immediate cessation of hostilities, there was to some extent a strong similarity with Curzon's misguided optimism:

> Our position in Mesopotamia if judged by pre-war standards is sound.

> Our armed forces are quite able to hold the ground. The population is tranquil. Our rule is popular. Our relations with the surrounding tribes are exceedingly friendly.

However, as Sykes continued,

> If America had not come into the war, if the Russian Revolution had not taken place, if the idea of no annexations had not taken root, if the world spirit of this time was the world spirit of 1887, there would be no reason why we should take any steps to consolidate our position against a peace conference, it would be good enough.
>
> However, we have to look at the problem through entirely new spectacles. Imperialism, annexation, military triumph, prestige, White men's burdens, have been expunged from the popular political vocabulary, consequently, Protectorates, spheres of interest or influence, annexations, bases, etc. have to be consigned to the Diplomatic lumber-room.

As Sykes concluded, if Britain were to run Mesopotamia, she must find 'up to date reasons for . . . doing so and up to date formulae for them to work the country on'. This was necessary to convince the British public and other peoples of the world.

The lumber-room, thus described, was too cluttered for Hirtzel's liking, but to an extent their thinking was compatible. It was when considering the purpose of British occupation that Sykes went badly astray: 'Mesopotamia is one of the potential store-houses of fuel and food for the world. If it is properly developed the workers of the world will be better fed and warmer than if it is not.'

To conform to the opinion of the 'modern democrat', Sykes continued, 'its development should not be for the benefit of Capitalist groups . . . should not add to the military power of those who run it' and 'should not impede the political liberty of the inhabitants'. Furthermore, 'if any one or all three of these desiderata cannot be secured then Anarchy and no development is preferable'.

The danger of what Sykes proposed was that, although his preferred methods for inducing the population to opt for British rule were similar to those of Hirtzel, it was to be 'provisional rule' and the 'fore-runner of actual independence'. In fact, Sykes recommended that Britain should have the United States propose a 25-year provisional British government answerable to any 'international authority' which might evolve, to which Britain would hand the country after 25 years.[42]

Hirtzel menacingly conveyed his rejection of this to Islington. Rather than relying on further 'schemes evolved from the inner consciousness of Sykes', policy must originate with Sir Percy Cox at the local level, once the latter had been acquainted with the wider perspective.[43] Islington agreed, although it now seemed that not only had Curzon to be satisfied but Sykes also.

Illness prevented Hirtzel from playing an active role in the inevitable disagreement which arose in connection with the discussion with Cox on his impending visit. Shuckburgh's memorandum on the subject conformed to the general principles of recent discussions on the future of Mesopotamia within the India Office and at the Middle East Committee.

Whilst anxious to stress that the policy of March 1917 would not be fundamentally altered, Shuckburgh noted that the Allies might 'have to content themselves with a peace by negotiation based on some principle such as that of no annexations'.[44] Further, in the event of negotiation with the enemy on the basis of 'mutual relinquishment of conquests', Britain's retention even of Basra, on humanitarian grounds, might well be challenged, especially, as Islington had observed, because Britain alone of the Allies occupied enemy territory; whereas of the enemy, Germany, Austria–Hungary and Bulgaria were in the same position.[45] Shuckburgh stated, 'It must be assumed that, in the event of a peace by negotiation, Mesopotamia will have to take its chance in the general settlement.'[46]

Shuckburgh elaborated on the continuation of British control of Mesopotamia other than on a basis of right of conquest. Besides a general discussion about commercial and administrative development and the coaching of elements likely to pronounce in favour of Britain, there were two specific issues:

(1) Is the administrative system now being built up adapted to the contingency of the cessation of direct British control?

(2) What further means, if any, can be devised locally to secure that, whatever form the ultimate settlement may take, the main object desiderated by His Majesty's Government, viz., a Mesopotamia under British influence, shall be secured to the utmost extent circumstances permit?[47]

Implicit in this, but something which Shuckburgh was less keenly aware of than Hirtzel or less inclined to articulate, was that by the time peace talks took place the structure of Mesopotamian administration and commerce must be entirely dependent upon Britain. Though Islington agreed, Holderness dissented, referring to a speech by Asquith in which he had stated that he and his adherents looked to an international decision on the future of the territories in occupation at the end of hostilities. Holderness continued:

> I believe that His Majesty's Government will have to accept this principle. We should not therefore pitch our hopes too high or expect that our views of the marvelous effect which British occupation has already produced in these regions will be necessarily regarded as conclusive to our claim to continue to control and guide their development.[48]

Shuckburgh's memorandum reflected the trend at the India Office towards a more pragmatic approach *vis-à-vis* Britain's future in Mesopotamia and was strongly criticised by Curzon. The disagreement rested, as Curzon observed, on the extent to which the maximising of British influence in Mesopotamia might be affected by the doctrine of self-determination. In Curzon's view, ' "self-determination" as a principle of international settlement at the Peace Conference' had been discredited by German acquisitiveness in the Ukraine. Given that Germany would not relinquish this territory, Curzon believed that 'for the Allie[s] . . . to preach or still more to practice self-determination, if it be contrary to their own interests will be ridiculous'.

Curzon viewed the restoration of occupied enemy territory as inconceivable. Furthermore, Britain was 'pledged' to institute native government in Mesopotamia. He continued:

> I do not agree therefore that 'in the event of negotiations Mesopotamia will have to take its chance in the general settlement'. I think that we should be in a position to convert that chance into a certainty and that we ought not to contemplate 'the cessation of direct British control' (all turns on what is meant by 'direct').[49]

As Islington suggested, both Curzon and the India Office were hoping to obtain a settlement in Mesopotamia which reflected the decisions of March 1917. Any difference rested principally on the degree to which they were, respectively, prepared to modify the methods by which this might be achieved.[50]

Curzon's cavalry charge was quite unsuited to the delicacy required in the formulation of policy at this juncture. As a result the India Office especially sought to minimise his contribution. The extent to which this had occurred is evidenced in the conclusion of Curzon's comments criticising Shuckburgh's memorandum.

According to Curzon, Shuckburgh had failed to consider the extent to which Indian administration had been established in Mesopotamia and what would happen if it were 'sharply modified or withdrawn'. From the very outset of British involvement in Mesopotamia in the autumn of 1914 the India Office had consistently opposed 'Indianisation' of the country and the institution of civil government had thereafter been directed with this in mind. Curzon wished to know the compatibility of that administration with Arab ideas and local opinion and whether it resembled Turkish administration. Also, the question arose of whether the system could be administered other than by Indian agents, and if British officials might be required.[51]

Whether or not the contingency planning of the India Office would be necessary was a matter which could only be settled by the outcome of the war. However, Hirtzel especially anticipated that to make British retention of Mesopotamia the certainty which Curzon desired, required that the formulation of British policy for Mesopotamia be undertaken on the assumption that self-determination was to be a fixture in international relations. This was certainly a matter of policy and one on which Curzon, as Chairman of the Middle East and Eastern Committees, might have been expected to pronounce. Yet this re-emphasis originated in the late summer and autumn of 1917 when the Middle East Committee had been in limbo and when the formulation of policy *per se* had been in the hands of Sir Arthur Hirtzel.

The upshot of Sir Percy Cox's visit was simply to strengthen Curzon in his belief that America would not insist on complete self-determination in Mesopotamia. His confidence was reflected in Cox's view that by her actions in Russia, Germany had largely discredited the idea. None the less, President Wilson might see things differently. Assuming Britain was in a strong position at the war's end, Cox believed that Britain would still aspire to annex the Basra Vilayet and to 'exercise a veiled protectorate over the Baghdad Vilayet'. In connection with annexation, Cox anticipated difficulties with President Wilson when the Peace Conference met and suggested that Britain's original proposals must therefore 'be regarded as a counsel of perfection, and we must be prepared to accept something less'. However, Cox continued in a more positive tone, suggesting that both on the basis of previous assurances to the Mesopotamian populace and investment in the port at Basra, Britain had strong claims to annex the Basra Vilayet and a small territorial enclave.

Regarding other parts of Mesopotamia under British occupation, Cox believed that the elimination of Turkish sovereignty was the main object, although in the unlikely event of a compromise peace, the retention of nominal Turkish sovereignty over Mesopotamia would not, in his opinion, necessarily hamper its development.[52]

Naturally Cox wanted considerably more than the denial of Turkish sovereignty in the Iraq province and, writing to Curzon in this sense in February, he had observed: 'Everything depends on full practical British control of the administration for many years to come.'[53]

By the time of his visit to Britain in April, Cox had refined his thoughts and spoke of 'protective British supervision' as the context best suited to the development of the country:

> How is this supervision to be achieved? The most satisfactory solution would seem to be government by a High Commissioner assisted by a Council, formed partly of the Heads of the most important Departments of state, and partly of representative non-official members from among the inhabitants. But the foreign relations of such a government must surely lie in British hands, and it would thus be practically a British protectorate.

Should such an arrangement prove impossible, Cox predicted a need for a titular native ruler.[54]

The combination of British military successes, pledges given to the native population and, not least of all, the considerable success of British administration to date rendered Cox as reluctant as Curzon to dilute British control. It was partly for this reason that Cox strongly opposed the nomination of a Hashemite ruler of Mesopotamia. He had, according to his memorandum, 'always ventured to deplore the fact that the discussion of the future of Iraq with the Sherif, as one of the pawns in the negotiations with him, was ever permitted'.[55]

Mark Sykes wished at least to obtain King Hussein's concurrence to the proposed constitution by means of a fixed subsidy from Mesopotamian revenues.[56] While agreeing to a subsidy, if essential, Cox deprecated moves which might be interpreted by Hussein as increasing his authority beyond those sovereign powers pertaining to the Kingdom of the Hejaz.[57] In recommending the Naqib of Baghdad for this function, Cox claimed to be promoting a dynasty 'which would carry the necessary moral sanction, in the Baghdad Vilayet undoubtedly, and, in my opinion, in Iraq as a whole'. As Cox continued, the prestige and influence of the Naqib would render his selection acceptable throughout Mohammedan India.[58]

The issue was not simply that of local allegiances. Importantly, the Naqib's family 'could be brought to identify themselves with British interests'.[59] British interests in Mesopotamia, as perceived by those who had been closely associated with its occupation and the institution of civil government, were broadly seen to lie in the exclusion of Hashemite influence.[60] This trend originated in the scepticism of the Government of India, its political agents and senior India Office officials about the Arab policy pursued in Cairo. This in turn was based partly on differing strategic perceptions of the Middle East and on the traditional friendship between Delhi and Ibn Saud.

By the end of 1918 Allenby had, admittedly, made striking military advances in Syria, but these were belated moves, across a quicksand of local and international political difficulties and were moves which, ultimately, failed to fulfil the hope, cherished by many Cairene officials, of the annexation of Syria. The Hashemite dynasty was identified by many in Mesopotamia as opportunistic and acquisitive, feelings which were strengthened subsequently by Hashemite military activity on the Euphrates River.

However, in the spring of 1918, the compatibility of the Arab façade with the exclusion of a dynasty which was seen, increasingly, to be complicating and compromising British efforts in the Syrian theatre, remained an academic problem. More worrying to Curzon, according to Cox, there was not the material among the population at either a local or a higher level from which to draw the manpower necessary for a purely native administration. Nor, indeed, was there any foreseeable prospect of this, and Cox therefore predicted the need for 'extensive and close supervision by British officers'.[61]

Curzon was content to see the development of irrigation and education as being, in Cox's opinion, the best means of popularising British administration, but it was not the urgent matter which it seemed to Hirtzel. Quite simply, unlike Hirtzel, Curzon did not anticipate a serious challenge to British retention of the country.

For one thing, Cox was wary of a plebiscite. Intelligent Iraqis were not, in his view, sufficiently confident of British success in the field and at the Peace Conference to pronounce in favour of Britain without fear of retribution. Other substantial sections of the population were 'inarticulate' and it was unclear exactly who should be consulted.[62]

Moreover, like Curzon, Cox probably underestimated the extent to which international opinion might limit British ambitions in Mesopotamia. Holderness attempted to raise the possibility of demands for international control of Mesopotamia when the Eastern Committee discussed the future of that country on 24 April. However, the tenor of this meeting precluded the discussion of such remote contingencies.

r one, failed to see any inconsistency between self-determina-
the Arab façade. The minutes record:

> r. Balfour expressed the belief that President Wilson did not seriously
> mean to apply his formula outside Europe. He meant that no 'civilised'
> communities should remain under the heel of other 'civilised' communi-
> ties: as to politically inarticulate peoples, he would probably not say more
> than that their true interests should prevail as against exploitation by con-
> querors. If so, an Arab State under British protection would satisfy him
> (and with him the American public, though less enlightened), if it were
> shown that the Arabs could not stand alone. Doubtless the Arabs, if offered
> the choice, would choose what we wished.

Accordingly, Cox's memorandum was approved and he was instructed
to develop the Mesopotamian administration on the lines contained
therein.[63]

Events during the summer and autumn of 1918 did little to diminish
the sensitivity of British policy-makers, and, in particular, of India Office
officials, to American opinion. The alarm bells began to ring in June
1918, particularly in response to a letter sent by G.L. Beer, an influential American historian, to Lionel Curtis. The letter focused on a scheme
of the Aga Khan's for the settlement of Indians in East Africa and was
sent to Sir Malcolm Seton,[64] who in turn brought it to the attention of
the Political Department.[65] Shuckburgh's fears that the discussion would
expand to include Indian immigration into Mesopotamia, something to
which he was now firmly opposed, were vindicated by subsequent
correspondence between Beer and Curtis.[66] By the end of July, Curtis
had circulated proposals for a discussion on Indian settlement in
Mesopotamia and American opinion with regard to this.

According to Shuckburgh, Beer wished to camouflage Britain's acquisition of Mesopotamia to make it acceptable to American opinion.
Shuckburgh continued:

> The suggestion is that Americans will acquiesce in annexation in the
> interest of a 'down trodden' race, which they would not tolerate if the
> beneficiary were to be the 'imperialistic' Britisher. If this is so, it will be no
> answer to say that we are satisfying Indian aspirations elsewhere. On the
> other hand, it is an answer (of a sort) to say that we are taking over the
> country for the benefit not of ourselves, but of the indigenous Arab: and
> this is, as I understand it the line that H.M.G. do actually intend to take if
> challenged to justify themselves on Wilsonian principles.[67]

To Hirtzel, Beer's activities appeared 'extremely dangerous', not least because of the American's enthusiasm for his country to share the burden in the Middle East.[68]

Concerns about American opinion recurred in October in response to the proposed passage of an American humanitarian mission to Persia via Baghdad. A.T. Wilson referred to it as a 'unique' opportunity and Shuckburgh agreed.[69] A year before this Shuckburgh had expressed equal enthusiasm for a journalist of the *New York Evening Post* being allowed to visit Mesopotamia, commenting that 'it might in certain circumstances be of the very greatest advantage to us to have American opinion profoundly "educated" about the work we have done in Mesopotamia, and the crime that would be committed against civilization if our work were wasted and the country allowed to relapse into Ottoman darkness'.[70]

By October 1918, the matter was urgent and, as Shuckburgh wrote, 'every effort should be made to fortify these influential Americans in their conviction that "you British must stay here". Our fate lies in President Wilson's hands, and the opportunity of influencing him in a favourable direction ought not to be lost.'[71] The Foreign Office agreed.[72] The prospect of imminent peace moves intensified the fear of international opposition to British predominance in Mesopotamia and provided an added incentive to cultivate American friendship.

THE COMMISSION

On 27 September, A.T. Wilson requested an investigatory commission for Mesopotamia. The proposal had been deferred on 27 August 1917, because of military uncertainties, but on this occasion it had the support of Sir William Marshall, GOC, Mesopotamia, and of Sir Percy Cox. Wilson suggested that a commission composed of about three members might convene in November or December and sit for three months.

The issues on which the Commission might pronounce were, in Wilson's words, 'a large class of political and administrative questions not covered by the decisions of His Majesty's Government, which will inevitably call for settlement immediately on peace'.[73] Included in this were matters directly or indirectly connected with demobilisation, such as the nature of the garrisons, and the facilities to be provided for it and for aviation. Wilson then strayed on to more controversial territory, mentioning the transfer to civil administration of railways, military works, plant and telegraph services, as being legitimate areas for the Commission. Further, the formation of a civil department of transportation and the question of civil medical organisation might be considered. The Commission might also investigate matters of a general nature including the organisation of civil administration, banking, commercial policy, navigation rights, irrigation, agricultural policy and immigration.

The increase of centralisation implied by these measures was not an entirely novel step on Wilson's part. Earlier, on 15 September, he had suggested that 'the time has come for development and improvement of our administrative organisation on uniform lines throughout [the] occupied territories'. Also, and with the assent of General Marshall and Cox, Wilson reported his intention to run both the Baghdad and Basra Vilayets from Baghdad.[74]

The sense of immediacy presented by the prospect of peace and international criticism of British gains crystallised previous differences. International conditions in October 1918 appeared, at the India and Foreign Offices, to necessitate a revision of the basis on which British policy in Mesopotamia had rested since Cox's visit in April 1918. According to Cox, the original policy of creating a veiled protectorate over the Baghdad Vilayet and of annexing something approximating to the Basra Vilayet might prove possible.[75]

Shuckburgh contended that Wilson's proposal for unifying administrative control in the Baghdad and Basra Vilayets and the appointing of an investigatory commission, rather than conflicting with wider international considerations, might in fact strengthen the position of Britain in relation to them.[76]

Holderness strongly disagreed, commenting:

> The practical advantages of such an investigation, as facilitating and expediting the establishment of civil institutions on lines familiar to British administrators, are obvious. But it starts and must start from the assumption that the two vilayets will come, in deed though not in name, under British control: and whether that would be consistent with the principle which, I believe, is now accepted by the Entente powers under the guidance of the U.S., that until the general peace settlement separate [?dispositions] of territory and populations should not be made is open to question – If Turkey were to submit tomorrow, she would apparently be told that no decision as to any part of the Turkish Empire (including of course Mesopotamia) would be taken until the general peace. Whether such an announcement would be consistent with what is proposed to be done to lay down the permanent administrative system of Baghdad and Basra seems to me doubtful.[77]

For his part, Robert Cecil wished to be shown by a commission not the possible workings of a future British administration in all its detail, but the broad lines upon which British policy might be executed. To Cecil that policy would be, in his words, to establish 'an Arab Government or Governments advised and supported by British officials, the object being to confer on the Arab administration the greatest amount of power consistent with the good government and development of the country'.[78]

However, Holderness defied Cecil's attempts to forge a compromise. Whilst unwilling totally to dismiss the value of 'a preliminary survey of the ground', in terms mainly of political and diplomatic matters, Holderness remained sceptical of the value of a commission when many questions would have eventually to be submitted to an international conference.[79] Included were matters such as the respective economic and financial rights pertaining to various nations.[80]

The revival of the idea of a commission by A.T. Wilson was a logical expression of the feeling that Britain should be establishing the ground-work for a future British administration of Mesopotamia. It was, further, a logical progression from the implementation of the policy of administrative unification of the Basra and Baghdad Vilayets as sanctioned by the Eastern Committee.

On the other hand, when officials involved with the administration of Mesopotamia attempted to give practical expression to what exactly the Commission might investigate, serious discrepancies emerged in their interpretation of the impact of international events on British aims. By October 1918, both Cecil and Montagu believed that the annexation of Basra was inconceivable and Cecil found it necessary sharply to modify Shuckburgh's language in his draft instructions for the Commission.[81] Had this draft remained unaltered, then Britain would still have aspired to the 'protective supervision' envisaged by Cox.

The meeting of the Eastern Committee on 29 October, at which discussion of the Commission took place, occurred only a day before the signing of the Armistice of Mudros. It also provided the setting for the dénouement between Curzon and Cecil with regard to the functions of the Committee.

The draft instructions for the Commission, as corrected by Cecil, had been circulated to the Committee on Montagu's instructions, and he and Cecil spoke strongly in its favour. Given the probable difficulty in establishing an Arab regime in Mesopotamia, Cecil argued that the advice of an 'authoritative' commission with first-hand knowledge would be invaluable. In response to Smuts, who endorsed the view of the GOI that the Commission was premature, Cecil held that the lines of policy on which the Commission would base its findings would, by the time it got to work, be considerably clearer.[82] In his view this would not, in any case, be for another three to four months.

Smuts and Curzon criticised the proposal on the grounds that a good deal depended upon future arrangements made with Hussein and his sons.[83] Discussion about the acceptability of the Hashemite dynasty in Mesopotamia between the departments concerned had been minimal. For some time A.T. Wilson had been emphasising the desirability of administering the Mosul Vilayet from Baghdad and this was one matter which was to have been referred to the Commission.[84] The desirability of predominant British influence in Northern Mesopotamia received a veiled endorsement from T.E. Lawrence at the Eastern Committee on 29 October. However, he added that it would be necessary to create a separate administrative entity there, possibly under the control of Zeid, Hussein's son. It was precisely because of this uncertainty that, according to Montagu, information about Mosul was required. As Cecil added, a commission of some nature would ultimately be necessary if the decisions taken with regard to Mesopotamia were to be well informed and, in view of Arab apprehensions, the present was a propitious moment.[85]

The note of finality in Curzon's response to this is unmistakable, yet these were conclusions with which Smuts agreed. As the minutes record:

> The Chairman said that at present he saw serious objections to the proposal. If the Commission were sent out, the fact would become public, questions would be asked in Parliament, and our Allies would say 'you propose, at the Peace Conference, to confront us with a *fait accompli*'. He did not agree with Mr. Montagu that the Indian Government were more opposed to the choice of subjects than to the scheme itself. That Government had raised many other objections. What the Committee had just heard from Colonel Lawrence showed that the orientation of Middle East affairs had recently entirely changed. He, himself, thought that the proposed instructions to the Commission went much too far, and he believed that a Commission of this kind would only prejudice our case at the Peace Conference; it would hamper and not help us.[86]

Curzon was relying on the possibility of international accusations of prejudging matters in Mesopotamia to disguise his conviction that the instructions to the Commission, if implemented, would not lead to a sufficient degree of British control. His claim that these instructions went too far belied his real concern that British forces had yet to gain control of areas which might fall under scrutiny should the existence of the Commission be publicised. In any case it had never been proposed that the Commission should do anything more than advise, yet the criticisms of Curzon and Smuts apparently assumed that its findings would be implemented. Failing the despatch of a commission, failing the continuation of discreet agricultural and commercial development under British auspices, the only course left, as Lloyd George stated in January 1918, was to let Mesopotamia take its chance at the Peace Conference. There, presumably, Curzon planned to defend British retention of the country with reference to her military efforts and the wishes of the population.

The gulf which existed between the methods of Curzon and, in particular, Hirtzel was sufficient to encourage various officials and ministers who attended or were members of the Eastern Committee to adopt a more flexible interpretation of what might properly be regarded as a matter of policy and of what might be shown to Curzon. The thoughts of Hirtzel, Islington and, albeit more gradually, of Shuckburgh, were increasingly channelled towards the creation of the body behind the mask of the Arab façade and this by means which were heavily disguised.

As for Cecil, the Eastern Committee minutes mention only his dissent from the decision to veto the Commission.[87] They omit any reference to his sudden outburst, the nature of which Curzon recorded in characteristic detail for Cecil's benefit:

> Your attitude this afternoon placed me in a very difficult position. I endeavour to conduct the affairs of the Eastern Committee – to which I was appointed, not at my own request, but by the wish of the War Cabinet – as well as I can and till recently I was allowed to conduct them without friction.
>
> But if my principal colleague is to proclaim before the assembled Committee that the Eastern Committee is hated by all the Departments (as it evidently is by himself) and that he would like to move for a return of all the recommendations that it has postponed . . . I confess that I feel very little temptation to go on.
>
> Surely it is open to me as a minister and as Chairman to differ from you on a matter concerning which I am at least as justified to pronounce without provoking the explosion to which the Committee and its Chairman had to listen this afternoon.

> I daresay you personally regard the Committee as a great nuisance. But I think you are apt to forget that it was appointed for a specific object, that it is not altogether destitute of authority or experience, and that for two years its predecessors and it have spared the Foreign Office a single reference to the War Cabinet which might not have proved to be either so discriminative or so patient a judge.[88]

Though apologetic, Cecil stood his ground. In his view, Curzon's handling of the Commission proposal suggested that he had already decided to reject it but that he was not prepared openly to articulate his reasons for so doing. As Cecil observed, the Foreign and India Offices had given much thought to the idea:

> I hope you will forgive me for adding that the incident appears to me to illustrate the difficulty of the present position. I have never been able to believe that a Committee however admirably constituted can discharge the functions properly belonging to an executive department of government.
>
> In my view the Eastern Committee should confine itself to the same class of duties as those performed by the Cabinet where it would fulfil a very useful and much needed function. That is to say it ought to decide questions of policy and disputes between departments. If it tries to go further than that I cannot but believe that it will prove a hindrance and not a help to the public service.[89]

Curzon, denying the charge of prejudging the matter of the Commission, reiterated his previous objections. Firstly, there was the opinion of the GOI. Secondly, as Curzon wrote, it was his 'conviction that if we acted prematurely we should not be helping but hindering our case at the Peace Conference, and giving a handle to the Pacifists, Idealists, anti-Imperialists and Incompetents at large, who will be against British occupation in any form'. Lastly, it was his belief that the 'main structural outlines of the future government' would only be determined by negotiation with Hussein and his sons, irrespective of an investigatory commission.[90]

Curzon then gave his interpretation of the intended function of the Eastern Committee, which was, if unpalatable to Cecil, considerably more accurate than Cecil's view and blunted his criticisms:

> In my view the Eastern Committee was not set up with the restricted sphere of duty which you prescribe. It was intended to take the place of the War Cabinet for the discussion of Eastern affairs, and to save the Foreign Office the trouble of referring to the War Cabinet upon them. Consequently just as the War Cabinet every day deals with Foreign Affairs

in general and is far from confining its actions to 'questions of policy and dispute between departments', so the War Cabinet Committee for the East is empowered and expected to deal, in precisely the same way with the affairs of the East.[91]

Meanwhile, developments in the administration of Mesopotamia continued. During the summer of 1918 the War Office had proposed sending a commission of its own, under Sir John Hewitt, to examine the military administration of the country. Lack of interdepartmental consultation led to India Office complaints that the Commission as proposed would trespass on matters pertaining to the office of the Civil Commissioner. Among those were the control of irrigation and agriculture, both of which Hirtzel was desperately anxious to have transferred to civil control to avoid the effects of Curzon's stultifying methods.

For a time it was considered possible that some expansion of the scope of Hewitt's Commission might meet Wilson's renewed demand of 2 November for an investigatory commission. However, there were widespread doubts about the scope, nature and timing of the Commission as it stood. Hewitt's suitability had been questioned because of his background in Indian administration. His appointment to chair a civil commission might substantiate accusations of Indianising, especially as he had been mentioned in connection with the future governorship of Mesopotamia.

A.T. Wilson shared these concerns yet in the matter of the original Commission he remained equivocal. Writing to Hirtzel on 20 November he stated that he would not object if it were deferred until after the peace settlement. In the next breath, however, reporting that the transfer of agriculture and irrigation to civil control was a matter mainly of finance, he also dwelt on the obstructive attitude of senior military personnel with regard to irrigation and civil medical work.[92] Then, on 23 November, Wilson requested the cancellation of the Commission.[93]

According to Wilson the context of British policy in Mesopotamia had been entirely changed by the publication on 7 November of the Anglo-French Declaration.[94] In a telegram of 17 November he wrote of the Declaration: 'unless [the] latter is superseded or modified by a pronouncement of the Peace Conference, I anticipate that in years to come we shall be faced with alternatives of evading the spirit whilst perhaps keeping within [the] letter of this Declaration, or of setting up [a] form of government which will negative orderly progress and will gravely embarrass efforts of European Powers to introduce stable institutions into the Middle East.' Wilson then continued:

> I can confidently declare the country as a whole neither expects nor desires any such sweeping scheme of independence as is adumbrated if not clearly denoted in [the] Anglo-French Declaration.
>
> [The] Arabs are content with our occupation; [the] non Mahometan element clings to it as the tardy fulfillment of hopes of many generations; [the] world at large recognises that it is our duty and our privilege to establish an effective protectorate, and to introduce a form of government which shall make possible [the] development of this country, which in spite of centuries of neglect is still the ganglion of the Middle East. If we allow ourselves to be diverted from this path by political catchwords, our soldiers will have fought and died in vain, and [the] treasure we have lavished on this country will in the eyes of the world and of [the] peoples of the Middle East have been wasted.
>
> I think, therefore, that our best course is to declare Mesopotamia to be [a] British Protectorate, under which all races and classes will be given forthwith [the] maximum possible degree of liberty and self-rule that is compatible with the good and safe government to which all nations aspire, but so few now enjoy.[95]

The GOC, Mesopotamia, Sir William Marshall, agreed but as the country was effectively under British protection because of the military occupation, the time-scale for the transfer to national administration envisaged by the Declaration would have to be reconsidered. Moreover, though objecting to the unnerving effect of the Declaration on the native population of Mesopotamia, he denied that its terms precluded a British protectorate proper.[96] Shuckburgh agreed, suggesting that the effect of the Declaration was to place the onus on Britain to have the Mesopotamian population declare in favour of a British protectorate.[97] The despatch of a commission, whose purpose would be to implement the wishes of the native population would in this sense, but for that reason alone, be premature. A considered response to A.T. Wilson's concerns would, however, have to await the next meeting of the Eastern Committee.

The uncertain international position and the protracted debate about the desirability of sending a commission to Mesopotamia seriously hindered the policy of gradual commercial development championed by Hirtzel and Islington. In April and again in August 1917, Sir Percy Cox had requested that, subject to certain conditions, companies might once more be permitted to trade with Baghdad.[98] On both occasions permission was refused because of the Trading with the Enemy (Occupied Territory) Proclamation of 1915 whereby Baghdad had first to be considered under 'effective military occupation' before trade could be resumed.[99] What amounted effectively to a blanket ban on British enterprise north of Basra remained until 2 October 1918, when both vilayets were declared to be under friendly occupation.[100]

The lifting of this veto was not to have the effect for which Hirtzel had hoped. In June 1918, Lord Farringdon of the British Trade Corporation had requested that a small mission might visit the Persian Gulf and Mesopotamia to investigate the possibility of establishing English merchant houses, or, failing this, 'to introduce a leaven of English blood into some of the existing firms'.[101] Hirtzel considered the proposal 'most desirable'.[102] The scheme lapsed, however, and by October 1918 A.T. Wilson and Shuckburgh were both disinclined to sanction the mission until the investigatory Commission had first conducted its investigation.[103]

Islington warned against being 'hyper-sensitive', predicting that the 'British association with the future administration of the country will be predominant'.[104] Commenting on proposals by A.T. Wilson to improve banking facilities, Islington wrote in a similar vein:

> I am strongly of [the] opinion that we should not further delay in making, at least, preparations for the establishing of Banking and Commercial facilities in Irak. The stage the war has now reached makes the case for *preparation* overwhelmingly strong.
>
> I think that we must assume that whatever happens at the Peace Conference in regard to the various disposals of territories that must come under revision, Mesopotamia above and before all others must be so disposed of as to leave Great Britain with a large and dominant share in its future administration and development. If we leave all these *essential* foundations, or rather the preliminaries and preparations of them, until the Peace Conference has concluded we shall have lost a great deal of invaluable ground – whilst it may be pretty certain that other Powers will not be idle in this respect.[105]

Holderness strongly disagreed, emphasising that such preparations would merely stimulate counter-claims on the part of Britain's Allies. Moreover, Britain, he held, would be taking 'improper advantage of the purely provisional occupation', adding that, in the event of Mesopotamia falling to another power, Britain might burden herself with an obligation to protect those banks.[106]

Another inevitable side effect of the revival of the Commission by Wilson was to give colour to suspicions that he was rather volatile and involved in traversing a difficult path in Britain's climb to ascendancy in the east.

With the departure of Sir Percy Cox for Teheran in the summer of 1918, Wilson assumed control of Mesopotamian administration. With the bit firmly between his teeth, the war in the east was far from over. Writing to his mother early in May Wilson lauded the aeroplane, which had, 'enabled me to "take hold" of things in distant districts as nothing else could have done'.[107] Later that month, Wilson explained to Hirtzel the nature of these trips:

> The Kurdistan situation is very interesting: I am just back from a trip to Kirkuk, Tuz, Kifri, and Khanikin by plane: I saw two Divisional Commanders and their Staffs, and all the A.P.O.'s on this line . . . within 24 hours, and got a move on in a single direction with I hope some result. Anyway I have convinced all concerned I hope that it is worth while to try to stay at Kirkuk even if at the risk of being pushed out.
>
> But for Dunsterville[108] and his force we would be in Altun Keupri and Sulaimaniyah.[109]

It was, in fact, precisely because of the drain placed upon the resources of the Mesopotamian force by operations in Persia that Marshall insisted on the withdrawal from Kirkuk to Tuz.[110] Yet Wilson's letter was indicative of the direction and nature of his regime, nourished at least partly by Hirtzel's prompting. In the autumn of 1918 it remained unclear to what extent such forward thinking might be reconciled with international opinion to ensure British predominance in Mesopotamia.

THE ARMISTICE

The need to prevent the penetration of Persia by enemy agents had been one factor in the military advance into, and occupation of, territory north of the Basra Vilayet. By the end of 1917, as British strategists assessed the implication of Russia's collapse, military advance again seemed appealing. The reorientation of Turco-German military ambitions entailed an increasing British involvement in the Caucasus itself, but British resources in Mesopotamia played an important part in the initial moves to create a barrier against German advance.

From this time Leo Amery championed a much more vigorous policy in Mesopotamia and one which rested upon British military advances and on the arming of Caucasian native elements hostile to Germany. As Amery wrote in December 1917:

> If . . . a really considerable Armenian Force could be organised it would not only effectively help the position of Mesopotamia by occupying the Turk on the Armenian frontier and keep them out of Transcaucasia, but it might also later on be in a position to spare detachments to hold the Western Persian Frontier north of Baghdad, or better still to push forward through Diarbekir, thus threatening the Turkish communications to Mosul, and enabling us to advance in that direction and so join hands with the Armenians on the line from Diarbekir to westwards of Mosul.[111]

Amery's strategy also involved further advances in Syria and the possibility of landings at Alexandretta. His concept of an eastern front, evolved in response to *Drang nach Osten*, was considerably broader than the ideas of those preoccupied with the slenderness of British resources. Mesopotamia was a vital link in this unified shield of forward defence stretching from the Mediterranean to the Caspian.

The scale of the eastern offensive deemed necessary by Amery increased in proportion to the success of enemy activity in the Caucasus. In March 1918 he recommended a march to the Aleppo–Mosul–Baghdad line.[112] By May 1918, the complete loss of the Black Sea to the enemy sharply increased the Allies' mobilisation requirements and he now spoke of an advance to a front from Alexandretta through Mosul and into the Caucasus.[113]

Amery had long been pressing on Sir Henry Wilson, CIGS, his deep dissatisfaction with the lack of co-ordination in eastern theatres.[114] Towards the end of May he wrote to Wilson complaining of the lacklustre strategies of Marshall and Allenby and the need for Wilson to impress on them the need to advance:

> Make Allenby feel that he has got to get beyond Aleppo to the line of the Taurus, and Marshall that he has got to make his left flank join Allenby and his right flank the Black Sea or at least the Caucasus range, and they will both work in a very different spirit. They both need a new sense of space and time and you can give it them.[115]

Wilson acted swiftly on Amery's letter, writing to Allenby a few days later: 'I want to see Aleppo joined to Mosul joined to Baku joined to the Urals joined to the Japanese army; and from that base an advance against the Boches.'[116] Amery's strategies were a counsel of perfection. They rested on a highly optimistic assessment of the war, and it was evident that *Drang nach Osten* and the moves necessary to counter it presented opportunities as well as hazards. In his letter to Wilson of 25 May, Amery had pressed for an eastern offensive 'as soon as we are over our anxiety in the West' and 'because there is less time before peace, and therefore we must push faster in order to make sure of the Alexandretta–Mosul–Caucasus (or Caspian) line before the Peace Conference begins'.[117]

The sudden possibility of peace with Turkey arising on the completion of the Bulgarian Armistice provided the backdrop to the discussions about the future of Mesopotamia in the autumn of 1918. Like Amery, Curzon had long pressed for a resumption of offensive operations against Turkey in both the Syrian and Mesopotamian theatres. This was partly based on his desire to increase the amount of territory under British occupation before the conclusion of hostilities with Turkey. His involvement in the discussions before the signing of the Armistice reflects his concerns that it was premature, and that the retention of territory under British occupation might be jeopardised by incautious diplomacy.

Curzon was not alone in these beliefs. At the War Cabinet on 3 October Lloyd George raised the possibility of concluding a peace treaty rather than an armistice to avoid the inconvenience of negotiating the future of Mesopotamia. Responding to Curzon, who recalled the speech made by Lloyd George on 5 January in which the latter said that Mesopotamia would be dealt with at the Peace Conference, Lloyd George suggested that if, by virtue of a peace treaty with Turkey, Britain obtained Mesopotamia, then it would be for Britain to dispose of it.[118]

However, there was more to Lloyd George's apprehension than fear of 'political catchwords' at the peace conference. When Balfour raised the possibility of inducing America to declare war on Turkey, Lloyd George objected

> that the President might claim that it was his threat and not the British arms that had brought Turkey to terms, and this would give him a voice in the Turkish settlement to which he was not really entitled. He said that from the point of view of British prestige there was a good deal to be said in favour of preserving our claim to have a predominant voice in theatres where the position of the Allies was due to British arms.[119]

Though methods differed, most politicians wished, like Curzon, to preserve intact British military gains in the Middle East. In August 1918 Beaverbrook had written to Balfour asking for an outline of the terms for Turkey which had been suggested by Balfour in February.[120] In reply, Balfour reiterated the main British desiderata, namely, the opening of the Straits, the independence of Armenia, Arabia and Mesopotamia, and the complete autonomy of Palestine and Syria. Moreover, although, as Balfour mentioned, in the spring of 1917 the Turks had been offered the retention of nominal suzerainty in Mesopotamia as an inducement to an immediate peace, by September 1918 Balfour held to the original terms.[121]

With peace looming there was no shortage of those anxious to keep Balfour up to the mark. Forwarding a copy of his memorandum entitled 'War Aims and Military Policy' in July 1918, Amery warned in characteristic language of the perils of a premature peace:

> What remains of Russia is in complete anarchy and at the mercy of any Power that is prepared to step in and recognise it. Farther south the conquest of the Caucasus by Turks and Germans is imminent and, for the moment, cannot be prevented. Persia and Turkestan are directly menaced, and with them once in their possession the Germans hope not only to expel us from Mesopotamia and Palestine, but to threaten our whole position in India. A territorial suzerainty and control extending from Antwerp to the Pamir – possibly even to the Pacific – and from the Varanjer Fjord to the Red Sea and the Persian Gulf, with a great tropical Empire across Africa from the Atlantic to the Indian Ocean extorted as the price of evacuation of France and Belgium, – an Empire combining and, indeed far transcending Germany's former Central European and Colonial ambitions, such is the prospect of a 'German Peace'.[122]

Balfour may have been influenced by the importance of oil in considering the broad desiderata of a possible armistice. On 1 August Hankey had urged this factor on him, commending as vitally important a memorandum by Admiral Slade[123] on the petroleum situation in the British Empire. Hankey suggested that in 'the next war' oil would have at least the importance of coal in the present conflict. Of major supplies, Britain could only aspire to control Persian and Mesopotamian resources and, as Hankey advised, their control represented 'a first class war aim'. As an ex-First Lord of the Admiralty about to address the Imperial War Cabinet on the subject of war aims, Balfour seemed well placed, in Hankey's words, 'to rub this in'. There was also the possibility of further unclaimed deposits in Mesopotamia which, according to Hankey, 'might have an important influence on future military operations'.[124]

Exactly what Hankey contemplated was articulated in a long letter written to Balfour on the eve of his speech to the Imperial War Cabinet.

Since his letter of 1 August Hankey had discussed with Balfour the question of acquiring oil reserves as a major British war aim; something to which Balfour had referred as being 'purely imperialist'.[125] Hankey was prepared to agree but, whilst admitting that this might shock 'President Wilson and some of our Allies', he none the less felt that even from the perspective of the idealist 'it is almost unavoidable that we should acquire the Northern regions of Mesopotamia'. As Hankey continued, it was generally accepted, even by President Wilson, that Mesopotamia would not revert to Turkish control: 'If these regions are not to be under the control of the Turk, under whose control are they to be? I submit there is only one possible answer, and that is that, in some form or another, they will come under British control.'[126]

According to Hankey, there was another vital matter which should not be overlooked in any stampede for peace. By virtue of Sykes–Picot, Britain was to have a guarantee of a given supply of water from the Tigris and Euphrates. Hankey expressed concern that should Mesopotamia relapse to Turkish rule, British-sponsored navigation and irrigation might be denied sufficient water.[127] By advancing at least to the Lesser Zab, Hankey maintained, both oil and water might be secured. The Foreign Office was sufficiently interested in the matter to delegate it to George Lloyd for his comment.

Like Hankey, Lloyd firmly believed in the desirability of securing the Mesopotamian oil fields. However, he was unwilling to pronounce on the efficacy of a military advance to achieve this, and further suggested that Britain might better establish her position in Mesopotamia and induce peace moves from Turkey by advancing in Palestine. Regarding water supplies, Lloyd's views were more expansive than those of Hankey and, by implication, he was considerably more questioning of the status quo.

Lloyd believed that any Middle Eastern settlement based upon the Sykes–Picot Agreement would not last. His objection rested on the widespread hostility to French control and the incompatibility between the British policy of reconstruction and the discontent to which French control would lead. Also, as Lloyd continued, 'from a British strategical and political point of view a settlement which allowed a great power to establish an eastern empire right athwart of us in middle Asia would immensely add to our anxieties, to our military commitments and to our difficulties in administering Arab and local nationality'.

Instead, statesmanship demanded that Britain frustrate the Oriental in his pastime of 'intriguing between two protecting and neighbouring powers'. This was traditional strategic thinking in which French aspirations in the Middle East were portrayed as an attempt to obtain bargaining power. Clearly, Britain's duty was to tether the French to safer pastures in West Africa, whilst Britain arranged Middle Eastern matters to her own satisfaction. As Lloyd suggested:

> if Mesopotamia is to control its own water supply it must have administrative control of all that lies south of a line Biredjik on the Euphrates to Rowanduz on the Eastern frontier. Mesopotamia, however, as its name implies, properly comprises all that area that lies between the two great rivers plus that area which contains the main tributaries of the Tigris. So described, the confines of Mesopotamia can be carried down to the foot-hills of the Kurdistan Mountains from Jerablus on the river to a line Urfa–Mardin Jezire Ibn Omar–Amadia – giving ample control for all water questions.
>
> Mesopotamia so defined can be justified historically, economically and administratively. Mesopotamia otherwise defined cannot be defended except as a piece of political patchwork similar to that which, in the Balkans and elsewhere, caused feuds and bitterness between the Chanceries of Europe for so long. In this respect also, the Sykes–Picot Agreement is capable of criticism; for it drives a wedge, economically unnatural and politically unsound from Syria through the northern plains of Mesopotamia to the Persian frontier. The reasons for this cannot be found in the welfare of the peoples concerned nor in economic necessity. It was an expedient devised solely to satisfy France's ambitions for the acquisition of a corridor from her potential possessions in Syria right through to Central Persia and for the construction of a French mid-eastern empire.[128]

Such thinking appealed, increasingly, to many senior politicians and it appealed not simply, or even primarily, because of oil but because of the strategic ideas developed several years before, by Kitchener, Hirtzel and others, whereby Britain might aspire to control Mosul. With *Drang nach Osten* in its initial death throes, statesmen already looked to the post-war world in which a resuscitated Russia loomed large. At any rate, on 3 October the Cabinet began to consider the more immediate matter of the apparent inconsistencies between Sykes–Picot and the logical development of the British military occupation.[129]

Curzon informed the Cabinet that he and Smuts found themselves strongly opposed to the conclusions of a Foreign Office conference summoned to consider the nature of French involvement in the administration of Syria.[130] These conclusions assumed the continued existence of Sykes–Picot which, according to Curzon, had withstood recent efforts to reconsider its clauses. Curzon's explanation for this was that 'the French had received far more out of this Agreement than they had ever hoped for'.[131]

With the prospect of an imminent peace Lloyd George revealed his hand:

> The Prime Minister said he had been refreshing his memory about the Sykes–Picot Agreement, and had come to the conclusion that it was quite inapplicable to the present circumstances and was altogether a most undesirable agreement from the British point of view. Having been concluded more than two years ago, it entirely overlooked the fact that our position in Turkey had been won by very large British forces, whereas our Allies had contributed but little to the result. As an objection of detail he pointed out that if General Marshall were to advance to Mosul this place would be treated as though it were part of Syria and in the French sphere. He thought that the whole question ought to have been discussed at the War Cabinet before the Conference took place at the Foreign Office.

By virtue of Sykes–Picot, Britain had provided for substantial territorial gains in the Middle East. The collapse of Russia strengthened the arguments of those who, like Curzon, regarded these gains as insufficient and who opposed an agreement which left France coterminous with the Russian sphere and in possession of Syria and Mosul. It was, in fact, on the basis that Russia could no longer 'fulfil her share' of Sykes–Picot that Curzon raised the possibility of its revision. Lloyd George, who only a year previously had been open to a separate peace with Turkey, now employed the cynical argument that Britain could not fight on 'simply because the French wanted Syria or Armenia or the Italians wanted Adalia'.[132]

In spite of his growing enthusiasm for British retention of Mosul, Balfour was extremely reluctant to raise the revision of Sykes–Picot; something which the acceptance of Lloyd George's idea of a peace treaty with Turkey would entail. Further, and with the concurrence of Bonar Law, Balfour mentioned that the Allies had agreed that any territories occupied by them would not be considered as belonging to the occupying power.[133]

However, the fact of military occupation remained of considerable importance to several ministers. The inter-Allied Conference in Paris summoned to draft the terms of an armistice had decided that the Allies might occupy territories the possession of which was deemed necessary to secure their position. Britain was left with territories already occupied and with no real restraint on future operations.[134] By 21 October, when the Cabinet met to discuss terms proposed by Turkey, the area under British occupation was expanding as rapidly as the resources available to General Marshall and Field Marshal Allenby would permit.[135]

The Turkish proposals were, however, peace proposals and envisaged the retention of Turkish sovereignty over areas in Allied occupation and the immediate cessation of hostilities by Britain.[136] As such these terms were uniformly unacceptable and widely regarded as bluffing.

None the less, there was an equally widespread feeling that Turkey should not be deterred from splitting with Germany by an ungenerous or too inflexible approach on the part of the Allies. At the Cabinet on 21 October Curzon was almost alone in wishing rigidly to adhere to the armistice terms agreed on in Paris. Balfour, Bonar Law, Milner, Lloyd George and Henry Wilson viewed free access through the Straits and into the Black Sea as the essential and only indispensable basis of any deal. Balfour was also prepared to consider guarantees as to the future possession of Constantinople by Turkey. Smuts was more guarded and tended to see such desiderata as a preliminary and as a sign of good faith on the part of Turkey.[137]

The narrowness of the desiderata agreed upon by the Cabinet was partly due to the prospect of Britain having to undertake to rid Constantinople of up to 20,000 German troops, in order to induce the Turks to treat for peace. The troops under General Milne, at present in Salonica, might take up to six weeks to reach the area, by which time the German contingent might be stronger and more securely entrenched. Greater haste was encouraged by French behaviour. Not only did she insist that a French Admiral should command the fleet which first passed the Dardanelles but, more crucially, she insisted that General Franchet d'Esperey conduct the negotiations with Turkey on behalf of the Allies.[138]

Curzon challenged his colleagues on the basis, firstly, that in view of the crushing defeat inflicted on Turkey, Britain could not disregard the armistice terms agreed on with France. His second objection stemmed from the fear that Britain would not cut a sufficiently strong military presence unless a military officer was there to oversee this part of the Armistice. Henry Wilson was not convinced and said that much would depend on Turkish military activity. Lloyd George pointed out that if a military officer was to be selected it would be difficult to overlook d'Esperey.[139]

Curzon was deeply unnerved by the potential disruption of British gains. Not only was Balfour contemplating action in response to peace terms rather than armistice conditions, but he was not averse to leaving Turkey in possession of Constantinople. There were still many uncertainties in the Caucasus and Curzon did not wish to foreclose on the possibility of British military activity of an unforeseeable nature in that region.

Most importantly, Curzon felt the entire discussion to be premature. Austen Chamberlain had to an extent shared this concern, advising that Admiral Calthorpe, the Allied representative selected by Britain for the Armistice negotiations, be instructed to obtain possession of Aleppo and Mosul in the final settlement.[140]

This interpretation of Curzon's views is borne out by a long letter written by him to Lloyd George on 23 October, which is worth quoting from at length:

> I have not felt at all happy since we were, as I think, stampeded by Milner and others, into jettisoning practically the whole of our terms vis a vis of Turkey for the sake of getting through the Dardanelles and up to Constantinople.
>
> In the case of Turkey we are dealing, far more than in those of Bulgaria or Germany, with a beaten and discredited foe. She is in the last stage of exhaustion. She has no claim upon our consideration or mercy. The whole East is looking to see how we shall treat her. The Indian soldiers who have beaten her to the ground will look anxiously for the results of victory that they have won for us. Arabia will claim the complete [?vindication] of her independence and fulfillment of our promises. This is [the] moment at which in the, as I think, headlong desire to get her out of the war, we propose to forego the greater part of our military clauses, and further, if the French agree, to [?assure] her in the retention of Constantinople, and of her Bulgarian frontier.
>
> I say nothing however at this moment as to these conditions. What concerns me is the dropping of the remainder.
>
> We contemplate the cessation of war, even the conclusion of peace with her, before we have got Mosul or Aleppo, before we have turned her out of Lahej, before we have recovered the whole of Syria or reached Alexandretta, while she is still in the Caucasus, and at Baku and Batum, before any attempt has been made to settle the Armenian question. I am not surprised that the French should be annoyed.
>
> But I am more concerned with the feelings of the Turk assuming that he has decided to break with the German (only because he believes the latter to be beaten). Conceive his delight when he realises that no more is required of him than that he should admit his new friends (us, of all the

people in the world!) to his capital, and that nothing more for the moment is demanded of him.

True that we do not propose to give him back Mesopotamia, Syria, Palestine, etc. But when once he has been promoted to the role of a friend it will not be with ease that you will get him out of any position or territory of which you are not already in military occupation. You will find him a first rate and astute bargainer. He will flatter you all the while with his assurances of conversion. And all the while he will be laughing behind our backs at his skill in escaping the penalty of his misdeeds and getting the better of the stupid Englishman.

I venture to put these views before you from the point of view of one who knows the Turk and the East, and who fears that a great chance of settling all these affairs may be jeopardised in our eagerness to grasp the plum which in any case must soon fall from the tree.[141]

Towards the end of 1918 several informed onlookers offered cogent reasons for British advances in order to control Mosul. Yet Curzon remained the foremost spokesman of the inflexible school, which sought to justify retention of Mesopotamia, Syria and other areas largely on the basis of British military efforts. Certainly, both Lloyd George and Balfour at times employed similar arguments, but these were part of wider diplomatic efforts designed to evade unfortunate agreements with Allies.

Repeating his warning to Lloyd George on 25 October, Curzon forwarded the views of D.G. Hogarth who shared Curzon's conviction that not even a shadow of Turkish sovereignty, let alone one Turkish soldier, must be left in Arab territories. As Hogarth stated, unless Britain acted immediately to 'secure . . . the practical fulfilment of our pledges to the Arabs', then she would never do so. If Britain accepted 'anything short of fulfilment', her prestige would be severely affected and she might be obliged to use force against the Arabs. As Hogarth concluded, unless Turkish authority was 'completely excluded', 'the problem of the Arabs' would remain unresolved.

Endorsing this, Curzon concluded with a final warning: 'If we do not clear them out now the clearance will be a matter of negotiation which means paying a price.'[142]

Curzon had not been mollified by the Cabinet decision of the previous day to instruct Allenby and Marshall to complete the occupation of Aleppo and Mosul *poste haste*. This was partly owing to Balfour's insistence that, to assist the negotiations, the Porte might be assured of the retention of an independent Turkish monarchy in Asia Minor and of the continued possession of Constantinople.[143]

Again, at the War Cabinet of 25 October, Curzon questioned the wisdom of concluding an armistice primarily on the basis of the opening of the Straits and in disregard of the other terms agreed on in Paris. The minutes record:

> He [Curzon] pointed out that the bulk of the fighting against Turkey had been undertaken by the Indian forces. It was not altogether without difficulty that these had been arranged for. India, however, looked to complete victory as the result of this fighting. He reminded the War Cabinet also of our obligations to King Hussein. The establishment of continuing peace in the East depended largely on our ability to carry out this undertaking. If, however, the Turks accepted the reduced terms of an armistice, . . . [what] would be the military position? Our troops probably would not be at Mosul or Alexandretta, and perhaps not at Aleppo. The Turks would still be at Batoum, Baku and in North-West Persia. The conclusion of an armistice would mean that operations would cease. When we demanded the Turks should retire from Syria, from Mesopotamia, and from the Caucasus there would be months of bargaining. The Turks would dispute every point. They would allege that Alexandretta was not in Syria, and make difficulties of this kind at every point.

However, Curzon's persistence failed to pay off. As Wilson and Lloyd George suggested, Curzon's perspective was slightly blinkered. Access to the Black Sea was seen to be important primarily because it exposed the enemies southern flank, and even Chamberlain, who had misgivings about the Armistice, felt that having been agreed upon with France, it could not now easily be altered.[144] In his despair Curzon could only protest that Calthorpe's instructions remained unaltered.

The case for British retention of Alexandretta, Aleppo and Mosul had been expressed by several well-informed officials at various points during the war. To the extent that Britain's chances of success in this endeavour might be enhanced by their occupation when negotiations began, Curzon's persistence was admirable. Towards the end of October, however, there seemed little doubt that Aleppo and Mosul would not be occupied. Curzon's dissatisfaction stemmed from his desire for a much more explicit avowal of Britain's legitimacy as an occupying power.

The anxiety of Curzon's colleagues to preserve British gains in the Middle East was reflected in their support for the early occupation of Mosul and Aleppo and free access to the Black Sea. These were minimum desiderata, but as Curzon had been told repeatedly they had, if only by implication, been agreed upon with Britain's Allies. To obtain explicit recognition from France of Britain's right to occupy Mosul and Aleppo would again open discussions on Sykes–Picot. This was precisely what Curzon wanted and what his colleagues wished to avoid.

In the flush of victory, with Mosul, Aleppo, Alexandretta and Constantinople under British occupation, Curzon believed that Britain's position would be unassailable. Further, with a sizeable British military contingent on the Black Sea co-operating with General Dunsterville's troops, expansion into the Caucasus became a possibility.

However, Lloyd George was alive to Curzon's motives. Replying to Curzon's view that Turkish evacuation of the Caucasus must be enforced in the interests of Armenia, Lloyd George stated that the Turkish presence prevented German exploitation of the region.[145] In any case, as he added, the presence of the Allies in Constantinople afforded them complete freedom of action with regard to Armenia. The only genuine hazard was, as Balfour noted, the possible Turkish massacre of Armenians.

Possession of Constantinople would not, in Curzon's view, amount to the stranglehold necessary to ensure the departure of the Turks from the Caucasus, Persia, Syria, Mosul and Arab territories such as Lahej, without recourse to negotiations. In addition, he persisted in his belief that the Turks might accept an armistice on the basis of the opening of the Straits and then exploit their friendship with Britain to avoid compliance with any further terms.

The last days of October 1918 were punctuated by the Armistice negotiations aboard HMS *Agamemnon*, by a meeting on 30 October at the Quai d'Orsay of Allied Prime Ministers and Foreign Ministers, and, for Curzon, by a brief visit to the British Embassy in Paris.

The conclusion of the Armistice on 30 October came as a relief to Curzon and to the Cabinet as a whole. For one thing, Britain was being charged with duplicity for having resolved secretly to accept the first four terms of the draft agreed upon in Paris as a basis for negotiation. By the terms of this Armistice the possibility of further British territorial gain was assured. Clause 7, to which Curzon had previously attached so much importance, enabled the Allies to occupy any strategic points should events there threaten their security. Furthermore, the Allies were to occupy the Taurus Tunnel system and, in the event of disorder, the Armenian Vilayets.

Elsewhere in the Caucasus, the Allies were to occupy Batum and

Baku and the evacuation of North-West Persia by Turkey was to be enforced. In addition it was to be decided whether, on investigation, the remainder of Trans-Caucasia should also be evacuated.

Curzon's delight was scarcely surprising. Certainly, hostilities had officially ended, yet there was every reason to be hopeful, in the dawn of peace, that Britain might find the embers of further gain on the turbulent fringes of her new frontiers. That, however, was a matter for the future.

NOTES

1. Curzon to Cecil, 6 January 1918, 1 Carlton House Terrace, private, Cecil Papers FO 800/198, f. 186 (PRO).
2. Minutes of a meeting of the Middle Eastern Committee, 19 January 1918 (New Series) *MEC* 1, secret, CAB 27/23.
3. Minutes of a meeting of the War Cabinet, 25 February 1918, WC 353, secret, CAB 23/5.
4. Cox to S/S, 22 January 1918, Offices of the Civil Commissioner, Baghdad, L/P+S/10/666 P1499.
5. Wilson to his mother, 15 June 1915, Amara, Mesopotamia, Wilson Papers, vol. 2 (London Library).
6. Wilson to Col. Yate, 28 November 1914, P & O, S.N. Company, S.S. *Multan*, L/P+S/11/88 P4717.
7. Ibid. Minute by Hirtzel, (?11) February 1915, P552.
8. Hirtzel to Wilson, 4 June 1916, Polzeath, Cornwall, private, Wilson Papers, vol. 2, f. 37 (London Library).
9. Hirtzel to Wilson, 23 May 1917, India Office, private, Wilson Papers Add. Ms 52455c (British Library).
10. Note by Hirtzel, 'Future of Mesopotamia', 11 January 1918, secret, *MEC* 24, CAB 27/23.
11. The Mesopotamian Administration Committee. It will be remembered that the phrase was Hirtzel's.
12. See n. 10.
13. Ibid.
14. Ibid. Memorandum prepared by the India Office, 'The Future of Mesopotamia', 31 January 1918, secret, *MEC* 68.
15. Ibid. See discussion of Wingate's telegram of 22 January 1918, and comments thereon by Sir Percy Cox and GOI in minutes of the Middle East Committee, *MEC* 3 (New Series). This discussion might also be followed in Memorandum by Political Department, India Office (Shuckburgh), 30 January 1918, *MEC* 60.
16. Cecil to Balfour, 8 January 1918, Foreign Office, private, Balfour Papers Add. Ms 49738, ff. 200–2 (British Library).
17. It seems that Curzon may have got off to a bad start with the India Office when, on the outbreak of hostilities with Turkey, he bombarded the India Office with advice on various matters. To Hirtzel, at least, this was too much to bear; commenting, on 9 November, on a particularly irritating letter from Curzon, that the latter 'seems to think we were born yesterday'. Minute by Hirtzel, 9 November 1914, Crewe Papers I/19/3.
18. Hirtzel to Clark, 31 December 1917, India Office, private, L/P+S/10/367, pt. 3; see Sluglett, *Britain in Iraq*, p. 18.
19. Wingate to Cox, 20 July 1917, no. 765, L/P+S/10/693 P3000.
20. Ibid. Minute by Holderness, 24 July 1917.
21. Ibid. Graham to Cambon, 15 August 1917, Foreign Office, no. 152411/W44, P3396.
22. Ibid. De Bunsen to US/S India Office, 8 September 1917, P3645.
23. Ibid. Draft Hirtzel to US/S Foreign Office, 13 September 1917.
24. Ibid. L/P+S/10/693, passim.

25. Minute by Hirtzel, (?19) February 1915, L/P+S/10/528 P653.
26. See n. 18.
27. Inchcape to Hardinge, 30 October 1917, 122 Leadenhall Street, private, L/P+S/10/367, pt. 3 P4511; also at CAB 27/23, f. 119.
28. Ibid. Minute by Shuckburgh, 4 January 1918, P5192.
29. Ibid. Minute by Holderness, (?26) January 1918.
30. Islington to Chelmsford, 15 March 1918, Chelmsford Collection E264/4, f. 36.
31. Islington to Curzon, 4 February 1918, India Office, L/P+S/10/367, pt. 3, P537/18.
32. Minutes of the Middle East Committee, 18 February 1918, secret, *MEC* 4, CAB 27/23.
33. Ibid. Note prepared by the India Office (Shuckburgh), 'Mesopotamia Trade', 6 February 1918, *MEC* 72.
34. See n. 32.
35. Ibid.
36. Ibid.
37. Ibid.
38. Ibid. See H. Mejcher, *Imperial Quest for Oil, Iraq 1910–28* (London, 1976), p. 35.
39. Draft telegram S/S to Civil Commissioner, Baghdad, very secret, L/P+S/10/686, pp. 145–6.
40. Shuckburgh to Sykes, 29 January 1918, Sykes Papers FO 800/221, f. 211 (PRO).
41. Sykes to Cecil, 13 October 1917, in S. Leslie, *Mark Sykes: His Life and Letters* (London, 1923), pp. 272ff.
42. Copy of a draft memorandum by Sykes, sent to Hirtzel, 16 January 1918, Sykes Papers FO 800/221; see Mejcher, op cit., pp. 52–4.
43. Minute by Hirtzel, 22 January 1918, L/P+S/10/686, p. 144; see Mejcher, op cit., p. 54.
44. Ibid. Note by Political Department, India Office (Shuckburgh), on points for Discussion with Sir Percy Cox, 3 April 1918, pp. 125–7; also at CAB 27/25, pp. 101ff.
45. Ibid. See also minute by Islington, n.d., p. 128.
46. Ibid. Note by Shuckburgh.
47. Ibid.
48. Ibid. Minute by Holderness, 30 March 1918, p. 130.
49. Ibid. Note by Curzon for Eastern Committee, 3 April 1918, pp. 122–4.
50. Ibid. Minute by Islington for Curzon, n.d., pp. 120–1.
51. See n. 49.
52. Note by Sir Percy Cox, 22 April 1918, EC 173, CAB 27/25; also at L/P+S/18/B284; for an assessment of Cox's visit see Sluglett, *Britain in Iraq*, pp. 20–1.
53. Cox to Curzon, 9 February 1918, Camp, Mesopotamia, Curzon Papers F112/121a, f. 136.
54. See n. 52.
55. Ibid.
56. Minutes of the Eastern Committee, 24 April 1918, *EC* 5, secret, CAB 27/24.
57. Ibid.
58. See n. 52.
59. Ibid.
60. See, for example, n. 10.
61. See n. 51.
62. Ibid.
63. See n. 56.
64. Secretary of the Judicial and Public Department at the India Office.
65. Curtis to Seton, 7 June 1918, enclosing Beer to Curtis, 13 May 1918, L/P+S/10/686, pp. 79–80.
66. Ibid. Note by Shuckburgh for Seton, 8 June 1918, pp. 76–7.
67. Ibid. Minute by Shuckburgh, 5 August 1918, p. 68.
68. Ibid. Minute by Hirtzel, 8 August 1918, p. 65; for a longer assessment of the Beer episode see Mejcher, *Imperial Quest for Oil*, pp. 56–8.
69. Minute by Shuckburgh, 14 October 1918, L/P+S/11/137 P3320 4483.
70. Minute by Shuckburgh, 11 October 1917, L/P+S/11/146 P4039.
71. See n. 69.
72. Graham to US/S India Office, 18 October 1918, Foreign Office, no. 172694/W/44, L/P+S/11/137 P3320 4648.

73. Pol. Baghdad to S/S, 27 September 1918, no. 8075, L/P+S/10/686 P4252, p. 60; also at EC 1735 CAB 27/33.
74. Ibid. Pol. Baghdad to S/S, 15 September 1918, no. 7725 P4150, p. 62; also at EC 1593 CAB 27/32.
75. See n. 52.
76. Note by Political Department, India Office, 'Administration of Mesopotamia', 21 October 1918, EC 2030 CAB 27/35.
77. Minute by Holderness, 2 October 1918, L/P+S/10/686 P4252, p. 56.
78. Ibid. Minute by Cecil, n.d., P4424, p. 50.
79. Ibid. Minute by Holderness, 23 October 1918, pp. 34–5.
80. Ibid.
81. Ibid. Minute by Montagu, 2 October 1918, P4252, p. 55.
82. Minutes of the Eastern Committee, 29 October 1918, *EC* 37, CAB 27/24.
83. Ibid.
84. See n. 74.
85. See n. 82.
86. Ibid.
87. Ibid.
88. Curzon to Cecil, (?30) October 1918, 1 Carlton House Terrace, private and confidential, Chelwood Papers Add. Ms 51077 (British Library).
89. Ibid. Cecil to Curzon, 30 October 1918, Foreign Office.
90. Ibid. Curzon to Cecil, 31 October 1918, 1 Carlton House Terrace, SW.
91. Ibid.
92. Wilson to Hirtzel, 20 November 1918, Baghdad, Wilson Papers, vol. 2, f. 63 (London Library).
93. Pol. Baghdad to S/S, 23 November 1918, EC 2470 CAB 27/37.
94. See Appendix 7.
95. Pol. Baghdad to S/S, 17 November 1918, no. 9926, L/P+S/10/755 P5104; see also Sluglett, *Britain in Iraq*, p. 28.
96. Ibid. GOC Mesopotamia to WO, 19 November 1918, X3016, p. 85.
97. Minutes by Shuckburgh, 20 November 1918, L/P+S/10/755; 26 November 1918, L/P+S/10/686.
98. Cox to S/S, 2 August 1917, no. 2903, L/P+S/10/569 P3140.
99. Ibid. Minute by Shuckburgh, 3 October 1917, P3933.
100. Ibid. L/P+S/10/572 P4382.
101. Farringdon to Foreign Office, 28 May 1918, British Trade Corporation, 13 Austin Friars, London, EC2, copy, L/P+S/10/368 P2582.
102. Ibid. Minute by Hirtzel, 18 June 1918, p. 258.
103. Ibid. Pol. Baghdad to S/S, 10 October 1918, no. 8566, p. 243; minute by Shuckburgh, 12 October 1918, P4471, p. 242.
104. Ibid. Minute by Islington, 17 October 1918, P4451, p. 235.
105. Minute by Islington, 17 October 1918 L/P+S/10/531, pt. 5, P4469.
106. Ibid. Minute by Holderness, 11 October 1918.
107. Wilson to his mother, 5 May 1918, Baghdad, Wilson Papers, vol. 2, f. 56a (London Library).
108. Major-General L.C. Dunsterville led the British Mission to the Caucasus formed at the beginning of 1918. The Mission was despatched to Enzeli and later to Baku ostensibly to prevent enemy penetration into Persia and access to the Caspian.
109. Wilson to Hirtzel, 22 May 1918, Office of the Civil Commissioner, Baghdad, secret, Wilson Papers Add. Ms 52455c (British Library).
110. Marshall to Wilson, 25 May 1918, GHQ, Mesopotamian Expeditionary Force, secret, Papers of Field Marshal Sir Henry Wilson 2/21 (Imperial War Museum).
111. Supreme War Council, 'Note on Military Situation in Armenia', by L.S. Amery, 3 December 1917, SWC 1, CAB 25.
112. Ibid. Note by Amery, 'Germany and the Middle East', 12 March 1918, SWC 113.
113. Amery to Wilson, 25 May 1918, 9 Embankment Gardens, Chelsea, SW, enclosing memorandum by Amery, 'Future Military Policy', 22 May 1918, Papers of Field Marshal Sir Henry Wilson 2/8.

114. Ibid. Note by Amery for CIGS, 'Unity of Operations in the East', 20 March 1918.
115. See n. 113.
116. Wilson to Allenby, 29 May 1918, War Office, Papers of Field Marshal Sir Henry Wilson 2/33a.
117. See n. 113.
118. Minutes of the War Cabinet, 3 October 1918, WC 482a, CAB 23/14.
119. Ibid.
120. Beaverbrook to Balfour, 6 August 1918, MOI, Norfolk Street, Strand, London, WC2, private, Balfour Papers FO 800/206, f. 335 (PRO).
121. Ibid. Balfour to Beaverbrook, 9 August 1918, Foreign Office, ff. 336–8.
122. Ibid. Amery to Balfour, 19 June 1918, enclosing memorandum by Amery, 'War Aims and Military Policy', FO 800/207, f. 190.
123. Slade had a fairly distinguished service record and this included various secondments in connection with oil fuel supply; see Gilbert, *The Challenge of War*, p. 215, n. 1.
124. Hankey to Balfour, 1 August 1918, secret, enclosing memorandum by Admiral Slade, 'Petroleum situation in the British empire', GT 5267, FO 800/204; Lovat Fraser of *The Times* attributed Balfour's enthusiasm for the advance on Baghdad towards the end of 1915 to Slade's influence: Fraser to Curzon, 7 December 1915, White House, Slough, Curzon Papers F112/110, f. 174. There can be no doubt as to Hankey's motive in introducing the issue of oil and it may be that in assessing Hankey's letter to Balfour, and his letter to Lloyd George of the same date, Mejcher neglects the extent to which, on this occasion as on others, oil was a pretext for an advance which was deemed desirable on broader grounds; see Mejcher, *JCH*, 8, pp. 39ff.
125. Hankey to Balfour, 12 August 1918, Offices of the War Cabinet, 2 Whitehall Gardens, SW, personal and secret, Chelwood Papers Add. Ms 51094; see Rothwell, *HJ*, xiii, p. 290.
126. Ibid.
127. Ibid.
128. Ibid. Note by George Lloyd for Lord Robert Cecil, n.d.
129. Minutes of the War Cabinet, 3 October 1918, WC 482a, CAB 23/14.
130. Ibid. See also, *EC* 34 App. 'A', EC 1769 CAB 27/24.
131. Ibid. Minutes of the War Cabinet.
132. Ibid.
133. Ibid.
134. Ibid. Appendix. It has proved impossible to locate a copy of the terms agreed upon in Paris and the appendix appears to represent those proposed by Britain.
135. Ibid. Minutes of the War Cabinet, 21 October 1918, WC 489a.
136. Ibid. Appendix 1.
137. Ibid. Cabinet minutes.
138. See D. Fromkin, *A Peace to End All Peace*, pp. 366, 371.
139. See n. 135.
140. Ibid.
141. Curzon to Lloyd George, 23 October 1918, 1 Carlton House Terrace, SW1, Lloyd George Papers F/11/9/19; See B.C. Busch, *Mudros to Lausanne: Britain's Frontier in West Asia 1918–23* (New York, 1976), pp. 16–17.
142. Ibid. Curzon to Lloyd George, 25 October 1918, 1 Carlton House Terrace, private, enclosing Hogarth to Curzon, 23 October 1918, Atheneum, private, F/11/9/20.
143. Minutes of the War Cabinet, 24 October 1918, WC 490a CAB 23/14.
144. Ibid. Minutes of the War Cabinet, 25 October 1918, WC 491a.
145. Ibid. Minutes of the War Cabinet, 26 October 1918, WC 491b. The remaining material in this section relates to the minutes of this meeting.

∞ 5 ∞

The War for Mastery of Asia

THE PROPHET OF IMPERIALISM

To MANY British imperialists the implications of Russo-German rapprochement towards the end of 1917 rapidly assumed the dimensions of a global threat, and one in relation to which events on the Western Front in 1918 were to appear a mere 'side show'.[1]

The most prolific of those imperialists was Leo Amery who, early in December 1917, began to grapple with the problem. Attached to the Supreme War Council as head of the Political Section of the British Staff, as the personal representative of Milner and Lloyd George, and as liaison officer with the War Cabinet, Amery was in a position to influence many senior figures.

According to Amery, the failure of Turkey to prosecute with vigour her pan-Turanian schemes in the face of disintegrating Russian opposition had been due to military weakness and poor communications.[2] However, Amery considered that Falkenhayn's military preparations against Baghdad might be intended for another purpose and that, in the event of further Russian desertions, the Turks would advance through the Southern Caucasus, Northern Persia and possibly into Central Asia to obtain new sources of manpower.[3] The lynchpin in this advance was Armenia, and it was by kindling national resistance among Armenians in the Russian Army and among Armenian volunteer forces in the Caucasus that Amery proposed to frustrate Turkish designs. With sufficient funds the Armenians might purchase from the Russian Army munitions which might otherwise, in Amery's words, 'pass into the hands of Kurds and Tartars and be used either for massacring Armenians, or for arming pro-German bands of brigands in Persia'.[4]

In fact, Amery envisaged a broader role for Britain than simply the financing of such resistance. In addition to Armenian officers released from service in the Russian Army, Amery envisaged British military representatives in the Caucasus and officers serving with the forces in Mesopotamia and Persia assisting in the organisation of the movement. Moreover, amenable Georgian and Tartar elements might be enlisted either as passive or active elements in these preventative measures. According to Amery, the purpose of British involvement in the Caucasus was to prevent Turkish military and territorial gain. If successful, this involvement might justify greater efforts in the Palestinian and Mesopotamian theatres to create an offensive line from Alexandretta to the Caucasus, 'in order to drive the Turks out of the whole of the Arab and Armenian regions, and to bring about a collapse of their forces and a demand for peace'.[5]

Amery was anticipating the parameters of the response to the Russian problem advanced by many forward-thinking observers. Throughout the first half of 1918, he lobbied indefatigably on behalf of this response, repeating his thoughts to several senior figures.[6]

Discussion of the Russian question by the Supreme War Council towards the end of 1917 suggested that it was a multi-faceted problem and one that would necessitate a broad and immediate Allied response. In fact, Amery and others like him seemed to offer an antidote to the stifling westernism of Robertson and Haig. It was in the context of Robertson's increasingly marginalised role as CIGS, and amid unanimous support for a knock-out blow in the east among Milner, Smuts, Lloyd George, Amery and other senior figures, that Lloyd George had referred the matter to Versailles. Amery had keenly supported this move, impressing upon Hankey on 26 December that 'in view of the Russian question as well as on general grounds the whole question of co-ordinating our military efforts in the East, viz., Armenia, Mesopotamia, Palestine, a possible French landing on the Syrian Coast, etc., should be referred to Versailles to produce a co-ordinated scheme'. In Amery's view Britain's overall eastern strategy required definition. Given the position of Russia and Turkey, he recommended that 'we ought to do everything in our power to knock out the Turk without a moment's delay'.[7]

As Amery noted, Milner intended to impress the same idea on Lloyd George.[8] In Amery's view it was not necessarily a question of the need for large-scale troop deployments but, rather, of a more generous allocation of aeroplanes, the more efficient use of rail-track, and the development of the port of Haifa by the Admiralty.[9] Responding to a memorandum by Robertson about Palestinian operations, Amery developed these points in a memorandum for Lloyd George.[10] Almost in tones of desperation, Amery had reiterated these arguments at length in a letter to Lloyd George on 29 December, adding 'I am so profoundly convinced that we have in Turkey at this moment the one chance of turning the scales in this war and altering the whole political future there and in Russia'.[11]

According to Amery, Turkish power was ebbing rapidly. Turkish troops had greatly diminished in number and their communications were weak and vulnerable to further attacks. Morale among the Turkish population was poor, especially now, shorn as it was with the collapse of Russia of any real purpose. A co-ordinated offensive in Mesopotamia, Palestine, on the Syrian coast and with Armenian guerrillas, with the possibility of a single connecting front line, was the solution which Amery recommended. This must be accompanied by the creation of a new body which would oversee British insurgency in Turkey.[12]

The urgency of Amery's tone was partly attributable to his assessment of the forces at play in Southern Russia where, he believed, Germany would not be alone in assisting Turkish schemes:

> If the Bolsheviks gain control of Odessa and the Black Sea coast, and the provisions of the armistice are carried out, it will be possible to ship grain at once to Constantinople, and relieve the food situation in Turkey, which is if anything more critical than in Germany itself. The even more serious crisis in Turkey in regard to fuel and petrol might be solved from the same source. The control of South Russia is in fact for the Germans the only condition on which they can put Turkey on its legs again, check our advance, and carry out their scheme for linking up the Turks of Asia Minor with the Turkish populations of the Eastern Caucasus, North-Western Persia, Turkestan in a Pan-Turanian combination which could be a most serious threat to our whole position in the East.

Again, as Amery continued, the implications of the Russo-German rapprochement had to be considered:

> it is vital to make all the progress we can in Turkey, and if possible knock her out altogether, before all resistance to the Bolsheviks collapses in Southern Russia. And, indeed, there is always the hope that if we can eliminate Turkey quickly, and get into touch with South Russia through the Dardanelles, we can keep our friends in Russia going permanently and turn the tables upon the Germans in that part of the world.[13]

There was more to Amery's proselytising than a dispassionate calculation of 'Allied' interests. Attached to the Supreme War Council in Paris, he was acutely aware of the basis on which such interests were formulated. Writing to Lloyd George on 29 December, with reference to a decision of the previous week to divide Southern Russia into areas of British and French activity, Amery commented upon the speed with which Foch had acted to implement that decision as it affected French deployments in the Ukraine.[14] Amery recommended that Britain should immediately send several hundred officers into Armenia and South-East Russia. Moreover, as possible Naval activity on the Black Sea had not been discussed on 23 December, Amery advised that Britain might send Naval officers into the Black Sea to 'organise the Ukrainian Navy, and establish a submarine base either at Odessa or Novo Rossiisk or Batoum, in order to interfere with enemy traffic in the Black Sea'.[15]

Amery had also mentioned French enthusiasm to Robert Cecil and it was of interest to both men that General Berthelot had, according to Amery, been instructed 'to get possession without delay of Odessa and the coast ports'. In this context of unusual gusto on the part of France, Amery pressed for the despatch of British officers to Armenia, adding that according to local intelligence, 'shipping in the Eastern Black Sea is in a great muddle, and that no improvement will be possible until the Black Sea fleet is controlled by some Foreign Authority'. Amery wondered if Britain might 'take over Naval Affairs in the Black Sea', by sending immediately a Naval Detachment either through Russia or by submarine through the Dardanelles, or by Mesopotamia.[16]

To a considerable extent Amery was preaching to the converted. Writing to Lloyd George on 23 December, Milner recorded that he and Robert Cecil were at one on the question of Russia. Further, he drew the attention of Lloyd George to a point to which Sir Henry Wilson attached importance and which was at risk of being neglected: namely, that by the terms of Brest-Litovsk, Germany would have the co-operation of Russia in shipping foodstuffs across the Black Sea. At least, this would be the case once Odessa and Batoum were under Bolshevik control. As Milner continued:

> It therefore becomes of particular importance to us, even if we cannot ulti-mately prevent, *to delay as long as possible* the establishment of an authority favourable to trade with the Central Powers *in the ports of Southern Russia.* Civil War, or even the mere continuation of chaos and disorder, would be an advantage to us from this point of view.[17]

The precise method of defeating German–Turkish designs outlined by Milner may have diverged slightly from Amery's advice, yet as Sir Henry Wilson recorded in his diary on the eve of 1918, the consensus was for action: 'He [Milner] agrees with me that we ought to push about like the devil in the Caucasus and if possible push on in Palestine . . . Also we must try to get command of the Black Sea.'[18]

Though entrusted to the Supreme War Council in its wider aspects, routine analysis of developments in the Caucasus and Southern Russia remained in the hands of various officials at the Foreign Office.[19] Their handling of the enemies' eastward advance was sufficiently sluggish to earn a rebuke from those anxious to respond more swiftly.[20] There was in fact a considerable discrepancy between the views of Amery and the action sanctioned by the Russia Committee. To an extent this was understandable; unlike the members of that body, Amery was not exposed to a flow of confusing local information from the region.[21] Moreover, during the first months of 1918, debate persisted about the means by which *Drang nach Osten* might best be arrested.

Amery's view was more detached and more optimistic. His positive language arose from a detailed assessment of the war-making capabilities of Germany and Turkey. By mid-January 1918 his ideas had crystallised. The cardinal aim, Amery wrote, was

> that Germany should not, after the war, dominate Russia and Turkey in a political, economic or military sense. The domination of Russia will make her all powerful economically, while the domination of Turkey, especially of those great parts of Turkey-in-Asia which lie beyond Asia Minor properly speaking, would not only add greatly to her economic strength but would put her in a geographico-strategic position between Asia and Africa which would make her, in effect, Mistress of both these Continents.[22]

It followed from the assumption implicit in this about the Russo-German Armistice that, in attempting to resuscitate 'a new federal Russia' from the elements in Southern Russia, this organisation might begin among 'the existing elements of resistance to the Bolsheviks'.[23]

Yet Amery's assessment of German and Turkish military power suggests that there was, potentially, rather more in this nucleus of anti-Bolshevism than met the eye. Likewise, when pressing on Sir Henry Wilson the need to amalgamate the various committees which dealt with eastern affairs to reflect a single eastern front, Milner's thoughts revealed a similar reading of events: 'I am seriously worried about the Eastern Front. Russia has gone and we must set up a barrier somewhere to stop the Bolshevist flood, carrying German influence with it, or paving the way for it, from sweeping right over Asia.'[24]

According to Amery, it required only the frustration of the pan-Turanian scheme to render Turkey a broken reed and receptive to peace overtures. Battle casualties, disease, famine and successive and symbolic defeats in battle were compounded by the 'wasting away' of the Turkish army as a whole. Communications with Germany were unlikely to sustain a pace necessary to replenish losses suffered in the event of a major Allied offensive. It was, moreover, an army unable to concentrate, due in part to poor communications, but also to the need to protect the Turkish coastline between the Dardanelles and Haifa. For this reason, and in Amery's opinion because of the superiority of the Allies in 'quality, organisation, artillery and equipment of all kinds', the limited Allied superiority in troop numbers mattered little.[25]

These advantages were being consolidated by rail developments in areas under Allied control and by the possible use of naval and air operations in support of the main advance. If these resources were properly co-ordinated in a massive and rapid offensive, then Amery envisaged that the Allies might 'annihilate' the Turk. At least they might be driven to the Taurus, whereupon a peace would be arranged, giving access to the Black Sea and, presumably, leaving Armenia in the hands of those officers detailed to organise Armenian resistance. This would also leave Britain, and most probably Britain alone, in possession of Syria and Mosul.[26] Paradoxically for an Easterner, and for one to whom *Drang nach Osten* portended the cataclysmic, Amery was in no hurry to hasten the departure of German forces from Southern Russia.

If, Amery observed, the Allies prevented the passage of wheat and oil to Germany from Southern Russia and forestalled the enemy advance, then Germany would have to maintain troops in that region. Similarly, if operations were undertaken in Turkey in accordance with Amery's advice, then Germany would have to deploy forces there which might otherwise be used in the west.[27]

Besides the conflict then raging in the west, Amery had in mind the Eleven Day War and the spur which would be given to Bolshevik ambitions by a German withdrawal. During the following months the impetus of Amery's thoughts was maintained by the failure of Allied efforts to stem the Turco-German advance. In addition, the full implications of Brest-Litovsk had now to be considered as they emerged.

According to Amery, in detaching the area from the Baltic to the Ukraine, Germany had in view 'not an indefinite desire for extension of territory Eastward in Russia', but rather the consolidation and economic exploitation of this area. Amery continued:

Given this policy, Germany is not likely to make any attempt to push further forward into Russia with any organised force. The object will be to try and get, as soon as possible, a friendly Russia which she can exploit economically. In so far as her agents, officers, prisoners at large etc. can promote this by bringing about a change of government, she may interfere unofficially. But generally speaking her activities in Russia will be confined to those of agents, bagmen and concessionaires, and not extend to the action of German military forces. The idea of German forces pushing on across a demoralised Russia into Siberia, and penetrating the Far East, may be safely ruled out.[28]

Sir Henry Wilson entirely agreed.[29] To both men, however, the limited nature of territorial expansion in Russia proper served merely to highlight the extent of German ambitions in the belt of Moslem states stretching east to Turkestan.[30] There was, moreover, the accretion to Germany of sources of supply and markets should Caucasia and Trans-Caspia fall into her clutches; something which Amery believed might be averted if Britain were to 'detach the whole, or at any rake the bulk, of Arab regions from the enemy', and establish an Allied front from the Mediterranean to the Caspian.[31]

In a note for Sir Henry Wilson of March 1918, Amery portrayed the position in more desperate terms, observing: 'Unless we can get Dunsterville and his crowd through in the next few weeks, the German landing at Batum will have put themselves in possession of the whole of the Caucasus, and will have control of the Caspian as well and get through to Turkestan.'[32]

As Amery continued, Persia was doing little to facilitate this expedition and had little incentive to be more helpful. Rather than vague assurances of sympathy for the idea of 'Persia for the Persians', Britain might sever the protruding tongue of Turco-German influence with a policy of 'More Persia for the Persians', by encouraging the union of Eastern Trans-Caucasia with Persia. As Amery argued in a note for Lloyd George and Sir Henry Wilson, this had strong historical and religious roots and would permit Britain to form a nucleus of opposition to the Turco-German advance either in Western and Central Caucasia or among Armenians in Eastern Caucasia retreating before the enemy. Failing efforts to secure Trans-Caucasia itself, Amery recommended a frontier from Lake Urumiya to the Caspian, with a small cavalry force at Meshed ready to destroy the Trans-Caspian Railway should the Germans cross the Caspian.[33]

Such expansive measures of forward defence were bound to find favour in a climate of apprehension created by tangible German gains and a corresponding failure on the part of the Allies to prevent these. There was, moreover, an irresistible logic in the measures which Amery advanced. This was clearly reflected on any map of the region, which revealed communications which might permit a rapid enemy advance from west to east by means of the Batum–Baku Railway. By March 1918, Amery was thus already advising measures to prevent German control of the Caspian and measures which were bound to lead to some degree of direct British involvement, possibly control, in the Caucasus.

The breathless pace at which Amery attempted to anticipate enemy advances and the consequent need perpetually to change the position of the Allied forward line of defence render difficult any precise assessment of the interplay in his mind of strategic defence and acquisitiveness. Amery had pressed for more expansive measures in the east from 1915 but these became considerably broader after the Russian Revolution. In any case, such precision as was necessary to justify defensive measures was provided by the enemy and by what, in March 1918, Amery regarded as a blue-print for the invasion of India:

> The German plan of campaign is, in its main outlines, obvious enough. By seizing, first Trans-Caucasia, and then North-Western Persia, they hope on the one hand to get in touch with Turkestan and Afghanistan, and if possible provoke an Afghan invasion of India; on the other, by controlling Persia and stirring up the Bakhtiaris in combination with a revival of the attack on Baghdad, to make our whole position in Mesopotamia impossible. After that they no doubt consider that troops can be effectively concentrated against Allenby, and Syria and Palestine recovered. It is all in fact, one great plan of campaign.[34]

It was partly in view of the extent of German ambitions – because Amery foresaw the continuation of these ambitions after the cessation of hostilities – and in anticipation of an increase in the influence of powers such as the United States that in August 1918 Amery suggested to Lloyd George

> that what the world wants, before it can get to an effective League of Nations, is something in the nature of a series of Monroe doctrines, of which the specifically British one would cover the region lying around the coasts of the Indian Ocean i.e. Eastern Africa, the southern border of Asia, and Australasia.

Asking not to be seen 'as a mere land grabber', Amery defended this extension of British territory on the basis of minimising dangerous frontiers and points of friction.[35]

THE PENDULUM OF WAR

Towards the end of June 1918 Curzon had evolved an equally expansive interpretation of the challenge posed by German ambitions. These, he maintained in a speech to the Imperial War Cabinet, were channelled in two directions:

> The first is from the Black Sea, through the Caucasus to the Caspian Sea, then crossing the Caspian Sea through Trans-Caspia by the Trans-Caspian Railway, built by the Russians, through Turkestan and Central Asia, to the borders of Chinese Turkestan, the very heart of Central Asia, from which point the Chinese Empire stretches far away to the Pacific Ocean. That is the northern line of movement and advance. The southern line, upon which we and our enemies are equally moving, is the line that runs from the eastern coast of the Mediterranean, through Palestine, through Arabia, through Persia, through Afghanistan to the borders of the Indian Empire. It is the countries comprised within these two lines that constitute the Middle-East problem.[36]

It was indeed fitting that Curzon should address his thoughts to the Imperial War Cabinet; a body whose members represented peoples in all corners of the earth, and to whom the German ambitions were presented as being a deadly peril. 'The whole of this great area', Curzon continued, 'is a theatre either of actual war or of probable war. That alone indicates the world-character of the problem with which we are confronted.'

Just as in the first years of the war, when British military advances in Mesopotamia had shielded Persia from enemy incursions, so in 1918 a similar panorama unfolded before the assembled statesmen:

> Had that campaign not been undertaken it is pretty certain that the enemy would have swept over Persia. He is endeavouring, indeed, to do so now. If you admit the enemy into Persia, Afghanistan is no longer secure. If Afghanistan is aroused the frontiers of your Indian Empire are in danger, and you are faced with a grave peril . . . the pendulum of war, swinging so fiercely in the West, is also swinging and, I think, swinging increasingly towards the East; and should the prospect be realised in which the Western armies of the enemy are held up on the coasts of France and Flanders, it may very well be that he will devote very much greater effort to the East, and that even greater responsibility and risks will have to be incurred by us in that theatre.

This was Curzon at his best, juxtaposing a threat to the very life-blood of the Empire with the mechanism which might be employed to defeat it. It was, Curzon observed, only by virtue of vigilance at the decisive moment that the Baghdad Railway had been terminated.

In Curzon's view, the collapse of Russia and the signature of Brest-Litovsk at once broadened the scope of potential German gains and rendered more immediate the threat to India. This was reflected in the terms of the Russo-German Armistice and of Brest-Litovsk whereby the evacuation, independence and integrity of Persia had been assured, and the political and economic independence and territorial integrity of both Persia and Afghanistan had been recognised.

Otherwise, Curzon's assessment of the development of *Drang nach Osten* closely resembled Amery's views. Besides Romanian oil revenues and the potential for wheat production in the Ukraine, the Caucasus, so Curzon argued, was an immensely rich area, yet one in which the native political elements were either unable or unwilling to oppose Germany's advance:

> We must look at the Caucasus as one of the greatest sources of supply of materials essential to Germany that exists in the world. It is a country of great economic value. The natural product of cereals is very great; there is an immense amount of threshed corn . . . there are mines of silver, lead, copper and manganese, capable of being developed to a greater extent than anything previously attained. On the eastern shores of the Black Sea tea is already cultivated and is capable of much wider development . . . I believe 20 per cent of the production of petroleum in the world comes from . . . oil wells at Baku and Grozny, and you can well conceive that if Germany possessed of these resources, as she is on the verge of doing, she will be absolutely independent of the American supply for the future.

For many observers, the brandishing of the fiery cross in this fashion represented a suitable means of forward defence.[37] Curzon, in stating to the Imperial War Cabinet that Britain could not accept the Brest-Litovsk treaty, was, as V.H. Rothwell has argued, anticipating the widespread fear of a powerful and acquisitive Russia radicalised by German power which might be tempted to expand in a southerly direction and towards the frontiers of India.[38]

> Germany . . . can afford to give up everything she has won in Western parts, in France and Flanders, if only this door in the East remains open to her . . . She could afford to give up the whole of [this] . . . and provided she were left to retain the string of subject-States she has created for herself on the western borders of Russia, she would still have the illimitable range of future ambition and opportunity which I have been describing this morning. Let us . . . realise fully that Germany is out in this war to destroy

the British Empire. That is the first and foremost of her objects, and one of the methods of destroying . . . [it] is by rendering her [Britain's] position in the East insecure. She sees that the power of Great Britain is built upon her overseas strength. I am not dealing for the moment with the Dominions, but the core and centre of the British Power in the Eastern world is India, and it is at India along these lines of advance I have been describing that Germany is striking. And observe that if she is unsuccessful now, if she does not push her forces right forward, as she is trying to do, or if she is held up by our efforts, the object will not be abandoned, but the attempt will be renewed; and just as India for the last three-quarters of a century has been in a state of feverish anxiety, and has consequently had to maintain large armies, and to tax her people, all for the fear of what might happen from a Russian invasion from the north-west, so that danger may be reproduced in what appears to me likely to be a much more sinister and ominous form if the place of Russia in Central Asia is taken by Germany.[39]

What is in retrospect particularly interesting about the first eight months of 1918 is not so much the preoccupation of senior figures with the Turco-German threat. Given the fact that it had previously been valuable in justifying British occupation and retention of various regions in the Middle East this was not surprising. Rather, the striking aspect of this period has been its portrayal by at least one historian[40] as a time of almost unqualified panic among senior British officials; as if, confronted by an apparently novel threat to the Empire, the fine calculation and cynicism which underpinned British War Imperialism in the Middle East was swept along on a tide of hysteria. Amery, among others, antici-pated hostilities enduring into 1920 and, accordingly, Britain finding herself repelling German advances for some time to come. Publicly, men such as Curzon and Hirtzel agreed, portraying German greed as the animating force in post-war international affairs where before it had been Tsarist Russia.

A precise and entirely convincing analysis of British motives in becoming involved militarily in the Caucasus and Trans-Caspian regions has eluded most authors. The consensus would appear to reflect C.H. Ellis's contention that these operations were undertaken 'primarily' with the German–Turkish ambitions in mind; although, as Stanwood argues, the initial motives for involvement were often obscure.[41] That officials were prepared to exaggerate the likelihood of those ambitions being realised and, equally, of the associated threat of German-sponsored pan-Islamic unrest has obfuscated the picture.

Periodically, this view was put forward by India Office officials, by the Goverment of India – when resisting forward moves by Marling – or, most cogently, by the Political Intelligence Department (PID) of the Foreign Office. As Stanwood has written:

> The P.I.D. disagreed with speculation which saw enemy plans as elaborate and grandiose. Instead it found enemy intentions vague. There was little doubt, in their view, that the Russian Revolution had given Germany and Turkey a good opportunity for stirring up trouble in Asia. But, in fact, their objectives seemed to be rather limited, appearing to be directed at securing command of the Black and Caspian Seas. In any event, it seemed to the P.I.D. that the Central Powers were only prepared to use propaganda and would not use force in Northern Persia, Russian Central Asia, and Afghanistan. This less than martial enterprise, it was suggested, was based on the calculation that a successful propaganda effort would produce sufficient dislocation to have important effects in India and China.[42]

Certainly, as Stanwood observes, fluctuations in the military balance tended periodically to highlight the seriousness of German–Turkish ambitions. Yet as events after the retreat from Baku revealed, *Drang nach Osten* was a hollow threat. This was equally true of the danger of pan-Islamism igniting the nationalist tensions of Afghanistan and India. Stanwood's preoccupation with Asian nationalism as the engine of British Imperial policy is misleading.[43] Naturally, the Government of India and British officials who encountered the Indian perspective were instinctively wary of any developments which might tend to radicalise and unify Moslem populations within the Empire. It is, however, questionable whether it is possible to say without qualification, as Schwarz does, that 'the British feared and believed that a small number of German and Turkish agents could spread calamitous political disorder in Persia, Afghanistan and India'.[44] Implicit in Curzon's speech to the Imperial War Cabinet was that *Drang nach Osten* was in the process of maturation and had yet to overcome those obstacles which Britain had placed in its path.[45] There was, moreover, no irrefutable evidence that Afghanistan had abandoned her neutrality or that counter-insurgency measures in India were entirely unsuccessful.

The nationalist question provided, in Mesopotamia especially, a means of reconciling imperialism with Wilsonian ideology in the form of mandatory control. Far from revealing any irremediable flaw in imperial thinking, as Stanwood has claimed,[46] the circumstances of 1917–19 nourished advanced imperial thinking among several officials. There were casualties in some cases – Curzon among them, with regard to Mesopotamia – but by the end of 1918 British Imperialism was not a redundant force in the Middle East; rather, in the case of some officials, circumstances had refined it and rendered it more flexible. The possible 'explosion' of nationalist feeling to which Stanwood refers did not occur precisely because of the success of this adaptation, as witnessed by the desire of large sections of the populations of Mesopotamia, Syria and Palestine, the Caucasus, Turkestan and the Arabian Peninsula to continue the British connection.[47]

In November 1918, attempting to secure lasting British influence in Mesopotamia, Hirtzel had exposed the interaction of the imperialist mind with *Drang nach Osten*. Minuting in response to certain amendments which Shuckburgh proposed to introduce to an important memoran-dum,[48] which would have toned down the acquisitive aspect of a passage relating to Mesopotamia, Hirtzel observed:

> It is true that the downfall of Germany is more complete than we had expected, and that there are now signs of disintegration. But personally I doubt whether democratic Germany will be, eventually, much less 'imperialist' than the old regime. The urgent necessity for raw materials will drive her into the old paths. The danger which threatened us in Mesopotamia was not immediately military: it was a potential military danger which might be exploited for political or other ends. If we were to leave a vacuum there history might, and probably would, repeat itself, and it would be folly to expose ourselves to the risk by letting the game pass out of our hands now.[49]

Vested with less foresight than Hirtzel and less forthright in ex-pressing imperialistic views, neither T.W. Holderness nor H.V. Cox accepted this analysis. To both men a resuscitated and imperialist Germany seemed far-fetched.[50] Similarly, to Cox, an aggressive and unified Russia seemed at worst a distant prospect, whilst French ambi-tions in Mesopotamia might be frustrated by encouraging American influence in Persia and, alongside Britain, in Northern Mesopotamia.[51] Holderness, who in 1917 had acted to rein in his imperialistic deputy, was more direct, observing of the memorandum only 'that it is inclined to portray the possible dangers that may beset us in Meso-potamia in excessively lurid colours as an argument for securing the maximum possible security for British supremacy'.[52] This was precisely the mentality which Hirtzel had struggled against for several years, an obstacle which certainly sharpened his prophetic powers, for the simple reason that, as Cox volunteered, it led directly to the conclusion that in presenting Indian desiderata in Mesopotamia to the Peace Conference, Britain must emphasise maintaining her grip on Basra.[53]

Drang nach Osten strengthened War Imperialism by fostering a pre-occupation with the eastern theatres of war among politicians whose gaze was ordinarily focused on the west.[54] However, the mental processes of those who favoured advance in the east differed. For some the pendulum of war had always been in the east. Writing to Wingate in the Autumn of 1915, Lord Cromer observed:

> The whole Arab question has now come to a head . . . The attitude of the Bulgarians and the defection of Greece has, for the time being, entirely altered the character of the war. It is no longer a European war. The European side has, for the moment, fallen into the background and the war has become one for supremacy in the East.[55]

For Crewe, towards the end of 1914, the east appeared as a field of conquest.[56] Thus it appeared to Amery in December 1917 and thus it remained in 1918, by which time, as Curzon noted in his speech to the Imperial War Cabinet, Britain had liberated much of the region from Ottoman dominion.[57] The parameters of areas designated for future conquest corresponded to the vast area in which, according to Curzon, German ambitions were rapidly maturing.[58] It was the interplay between political idealism, fear of a premature peace and the constant manipulation of threats posed by the enemy, by Britain's allies or by unruly subjects, to the Empire or to areas under British occupation, which had nourished Curzon's imperialism. To this extent, *Drang nach Osten* did not materially affect Curzon's aims. It did, however, present added opportunity for imperial gain in the Middle East. In addition, it elevated to the status of War Imperialists men such as Amery and Milner who, though easterners at heart, had prioritised rather limited gains in the Middle East before Brest-Litovsk. Certainly, those gains were for the duration of the war predicated upon perceived defensive requirements. From the end of 1917, however, they were formulated publicly as a response to *Drang nach Osten*; and in this game of shadow boxing, with apparently so much at stake and with the Foreign Office in such a lamentable state of torpor, it was not for Curzon to throw in the towel.

Curzon's was by no means a 'bleak' view, as Schwarz argues.[59] There was in German ambitions an inherent interdependence between events in the east and the west which could only favour moves designed to achieve perceived strategic security by those who genuinely feared the

MAP 3. TRANS-SIBERIAN RAILWAY

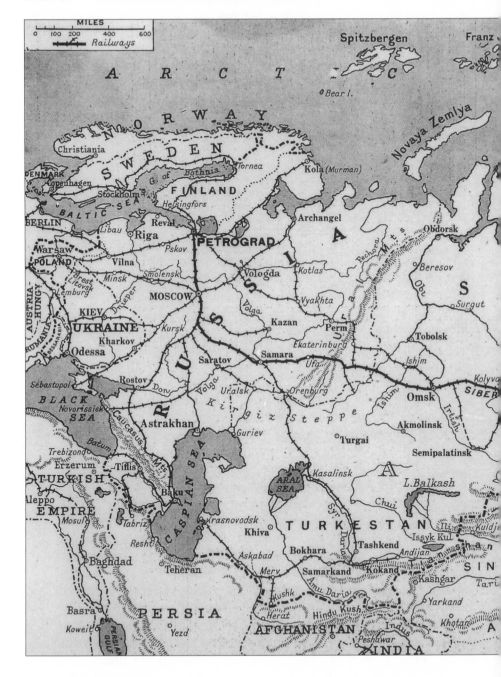

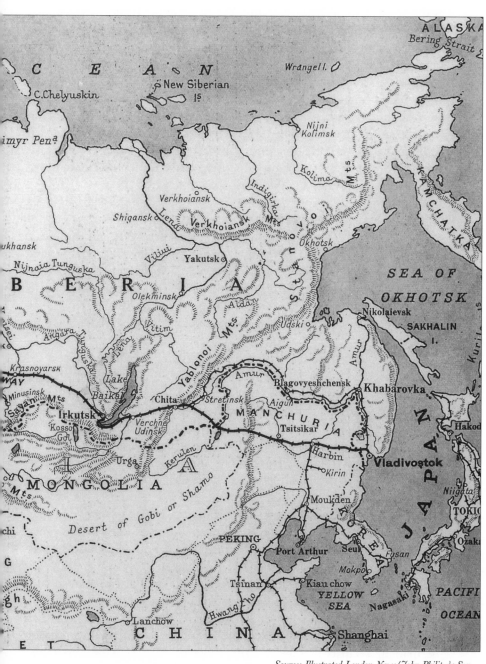

Source: *Illustrated London News/John Philip & Son*

collapse of the British Empire. Publicly, Curzon portrayed the situation in the west in suitably dark terms. Yet his true optimism was revealed by his efforts during the height of the German western offensive to prevent the acceptance by Britain of a compromise peace in the west; something which was, for those who regarded *Drang nach Osten* as an imminent and deadly threat to the Empire, the natural corollary of this view. Similarly, in June 1918, Curzon was willing to conceive of a lull in the west if this might encourage greater efforts in the east.[60] That Curzon was more circumspect than Amery in envisaging possible territorial additions to the Empire was due to his desire to maintain a consensus among senior politicians for the expansive measures which, unbeknown to them, would render such additions possible.

Tactically it remained important not to facilitate the eastward advance of Turco-German forces and for this reason in the summer of 1918 it seemed unwise to develop railways in the Mosul Vilayet and those east of the Caspian. However, at no time was it proposed to forgo a permanent British presence in Mosul, something which would have been essential if German–Turkish forces presented too strong an opponent, if they were other than a transitory phenomenon, and if, as Sir Henry Wilson stated, Britain was to avoid 'unlimited liability for defence' in this region.

British policy in the Caucasus during the first eight months of 1918 was chiefly, and in so far as it could be said to relate to any single threat, intended as a response to *Drang nach Osten*. To the extent that German and Turkish ambitions were seen as inimical to British interests there was a broad consensus among senior figures in the analysis of eastern matters. That in formulating his acquisitive desiderata Curzon's mental processes differed from other imperialists did not matter in theory. Rather, those who might loosely be termed the War Imperialists resembled confluent streams which merged for a time to produce a broad theoretical consensus. Such differences as existed between Curzon and his colleagues were increased by a fairly widespread antipathy towards the committees he chaired and which dealt with eastern affairs.[61]

Defining with precision the various elements of War Imperialism and the origins of this phenomenon is problematic. However, J.S. Galbraith has helpfully exposed that underlying vein of 'peace with victory' which in the east was articulated in support for schemes designed to provide 'permanent security'.[62] Clearly, the roots of such schemes pre-dated 1914 and lay in the psychology of individuals. Those factors which provided an outlet for and which gave impetus to this predisposition to favour advance are more easily discernible. In terms of the Middle East, as previously stated, there was from the autumn of 1914 the broad consensus of War Cabinet members that Britain's possessions in the region must be extended. Failure to realise Kitchener's ideas, failure to have accepted the partition scheme of the De Bunsen Committee and failure to take Baghdad were compounded by the perceived limitations of Sykes–Picot. As Galbraith implies, the discrepancy between the expectations engendered by the discussions on the Middle East of 1915 and the stagnant reality of British policy there in the following months encouraged a determination to resist a compromise peace.[63] Amery and others harnessed this spirit by portraying German dreams of *Mitteleuropa* and *Drang nach Osten* as being interconnected.[64]

It would seem that, in time, War Imperialism, the pursuit of territories, the possession of which was for any number of reasons inherently desirable, itself became a 'war aim' for Britain in the Middle East.[65] Certainly it must have appeared thus to Montagu in his efforts in December 1918 to combat 'the mania for territorial gain'.[66] War Imperialism emerged in schemes for closer British control in the Arabian Peninsula and in Mesopotamia, in support for British control of Palestine and Syria and for the undoing of Sykes–Picot. It found expression both in the disparity between inter-Allied rivalries and measures taken to exclude competitors and in the *Drang nach Osten* scare.

If such were the origins and manifestations of War Imperialism, what then were its physical limits? Whilst opportunity existed to secure territorial gain as Russia withered, less than a year after the October Revolution German reverses on the Western Front cast doubt on the continuation of Germany's eastern expansion. Although it remained impossible to predict what might happen in Russia, by mid-August Leo Amery, who had done so much to fuel imperialism with his thoughts on *Drang nach Osten*, had perhaps unconsciously begun to define future Russian and Anglo-Russian boundaries in Asia.[67]

DEBATE ON INTERVENTION

As 1918 progressed, Bolshevism exerted an increasing influence on the minds of Western politicians. This was so, firstly, because, as time passed, it seemed the most likely factor to unify Russia as a potentially hostile force in the east. Secondly, although this might present only a long-term military threat, there was, from December 1917, considerable ambiguity about the extent to which Bolshevik leaders might facilitate German aims in the east.

The ambiguity of Bolshevik intentions clouded over and compounded the difficulties inherent in the strategy devised to contain *Drang nach Osten*. This ambiguity was in turn reflected in the fact that the Allies, in providing assistance to nationalist elements in Southern Russia, supported those elements which were, by the end of 1917, hostile to the Bolsheviks.

The question of Japanese intervention attracted considerable interest during 1918.[68] In January, the Russia Committee prepared a memorandum which argued that if the Japanese were to capture and advance along the Trans-Siberian Railway then effective help might be given to nationalist elements in Southern Russia.[69] The proposal attracted growing if inconsistent support among several senior figures during the following months. Critics pointed to the immense difficulties involved in holding and maintaining such a vast extent of track. Even Hardinge, a voluble if wavering proponent of such an undertaking, as late as June 1918 was to express doubts on this point.[70] In January, Balfour had recorded similar concerns although his misgivings apparently related to political as well as military factors.[71]

British relations with the Bolsheviks as a whole and, more particularly, in attempting to gain their co-operation in repelling German advances were closely connected with the intervention proposal. On the one hand, there were those who, like the Ambassador in Petrograd Sir George Buchanan, viewed with equanimity the prospect of a breach with the Bolsheviks, largely on the basis of his conviction in the efficacy of American–Japanese intervention in Siberia.[72] Moreover, evidence suggested that British support for southern nationalist elements was being undermined by her unwillingness to break with the Bolshevik leadership. At the other extreme, Lockhart[73] remained for a time a vociferous opponent of intervention in Siberia, arguing that Russia would not necessarily succumb to Germany and that any action such as intervention which in his view would throw Bolshevik Russia into the German embrace must be avoided.[74]

The interrelationship between British policy in the Caucasus and the intervention proposal was complicated. Whilst Japan at times appeared willing to go into Siberia as a mandatory power of the Allies, suspicion of her motives persisted well into 1918. In addition, the nature of Bolshevik actions could not be ignored. In December 1917 they had, as Curzon recalled in his speech to the Imperial War Cabinet, joined with

Germany in what was evidently an attempt to entice Afghanistan from the British sphere.[75] By February 1918, the Bolsheviks had effective political control in Siberia. Further west, by this time, centres of Cossack resistance at Orenburg and in the Don had been dispersed. Within a month the Bolsheviks had control of the Kuban. Equally, by this time Kiev had fallen and the collapse of Romania seemed imminent. Such developments provided an indication of a fundamental incompatibility between Bolshevik policy and that of Britain. Confirmation of this was evidenced in the terms of Brest-Litovsk.

As the protracted debate about Japanese intervention revealed, the ability of the Allies to take effective action on the periphery of Russia was extremely limited. The implication of this for British policy in the Caucasus was that Britain had necessarily to aspire to maintain that degree of co-operation which she had periodically enjoyed with the Bolsheviks prior to Brest-Litovsk. This co-operation Balfour described as 'one of calculation not of love'.[76] However, in the aftermath of Brest-Litovsk and amid the tense atmosphere created by Lockhart's increasingly shrill telegrams, Balfour defined a more realistic appraisal of Bolshevism. As Balfour observed, in response to Lockhart's protest that Britain should not preclude the possibility of an understanding with the Bolsheviks, it was impossible to avoid the conclusion that the Bolshevik leadership was co-operating with German aims. Balfour continued:

> The Bolshevists have destroyed every force which was capable of resisting the enemy: The Russian Army, the Roumanian Army, and the Trans-Caucasian Levies. The equipment with which the Allies supplied them has not even been destroyed: it has been surrendered without a blow. According to our reports, Bolshevists have aided the Turks in blocking Dunsterville's way to assist the Armenians and Georgians. German officers are said to swarm in Petrograd. Only one Bank in Moscow is permitted to carry on business: we are informed it is a German bank. The press, which is completely under Bolshevist control, has been systematically anti-British. Though of all the Allies we are the ones who without the least hope of material gain have made the greatest sacrifices for Russia, and without the smallest wish to interfere in its internal affairs, have shown more desire to work with it's [*sic*] revolutionary Governments we are, under Bolshevist inspiration, systematically described as selfish and imperialistic.[77]

The only instance of Bolshevik antipathy towards Germany that Balfour could remember was the refusal to conclude the negotiations at Brest; something which, as Balfour added, had merely detached from Russia great territories on her European and Caucasian flanks, ensured

the early demise of Romania, and given Armenia to the Turks.[78]
Moreover, Balfour added, neither had the Bolsheviks done anything to
help themselves nor apparently would they permit the Allies to do so by
means either of a landing in Northern Russia or a Japanese landing in
Siberia.

> You ask us to 'play with the Bolshevists', and to 'adopt a more elastic
> attitude towards them, even to the extent of promising more than we can
> perform'. At the present, however, they refuse to accept even what we
> can perform; and you give no hint of suggestion as to the kind of promise
> they would like us to make.[79]

Within the Russian Department of the Foreign Office L.H. Lyons
had, from the beginning of 1918, presented an equally lucid assessment
of the Russian question. Lyons believed a breach with Bolshevism to be
extremely undesirable. However, this might prove unavoidable if
Britain continued to support those elements which actively opposed the
Bolshevik regime.[80] Moreover, Lyons, unlike Milner, was deeply and
persistently suspicious of Japanese intentions. Commenting on a
suggestion by the French Foreign Minister that an Allied expedition
might start from Tientsin with the aim of cutting the Trans-Siberian
Railway and of securing raw materials, he noted:

> In the first place, as the British, French and American contingents in North
> China could not spare more than 1500 men at the outside the expedition
> would be in the main Japanese. To suggest this move would be to give the
> Japanese the very opportunity they want. They would probably jump at
> it, refuse the help of Allied contingents and regard the suggestion as a
> mandate for the invasion of Siberia. Such action would appear certain to
> lead to a combination of all factors in Siberia against allied interests.[81]

Nor did Lyons share Hardinge's belief that if Japan went into Siberia as
a mandatory power of the Allies, and if local measures were taken to
ease her path, the problem would disappear.[82] Indeed, even if 'incon-
testable guarantees' were given and 'clear declarations' were made, as
France wished, then Lyons believed the Allies would be asking the
Japanese to undertake not to seize any Russian territory when ordinarily
they could do so freely. To Lyons the idea appeared not only 'unprac-
tical' and 'useless' but, risking as it did the formation of an anti-Allied
movement in Russia, 'dangerous'. He would only support Japanese
intervention in Siberia if the Allies obtained a definite and public
agreement defining Japan's military role and if Japan were to agree to

withdraw within a certain time; whereupon she would be given compensation elsewhere.[83]

However, events in the first months of 1918 strengthened the hand of those who proposed with enthusiasm the immediate despatch of Japanese troops to Vladivostock. Lyons vested hope in the possibility of Bolshevik opposition to German advances. He had, moreover, detected the futility of attempting to assist the South-Eastern Federation[84] because it apparently did not wish to be rescued.[85] However, a feeling that Britain's sponsorship of nationalist elements was a gamble which had not paid off tended to dissipate in view of fresh developments.

The imminent prospect of German political control of Russia in the spring of 1918 enforced arguments for vigorous action. In addition, by this time there was evidence both that native reaction to Japanese landings in Siberia would be less extreme than previously anticipated, and that the Bolshevik leadership might no longer have the ability openly to take such measures as might minimise the gains made by Germany in her advance.

With so many variables in play it was not surprising that widely diverging interpretations existed of what might be expected in the way of co-operation with the Bolsheviks. Policy formulation was also rendered more difficult by the nature of the information provided by British representatives abroad. In Lockhart's case this was seen as being unduly pro-Bolshevik; and in the case of Marling in Tehran, frequent accusations of inconsistency were made. During March and April 1918 there were, admittedly, indications that Bolshevik Russia wished to co-operate with the Allies in repelling German forces. In the wider context, however, the only possible interpretation of developments was one which reflected continuing unease about Bolshevik intentions.

This feeling was put forward most succinctly by Curzon in a note for the War Cabinet dated 26 March 1918.[86] During many of the debates on the Russian situation Curzon had remained ominously silent, but the implication of this note would suggest that Curzon deeply distrusted the Bolshevik leadership, to the extent that he was prepared to risk serious disagreement, if nothing worse, with them.

The issue of intervention tended increasingly to be seen less through the prism of *Drang nach Osten* than through that of the fortunes of Bolshevism. This was partly owing to continuing faith in Britain's abilty to persuade the Japanese to advance to the Urals, notwithstanding the fact that in military terms there were more obstacles in the way. Such was Hardinge's opinion by mid-June.[87] Sir Henry Wilson had spoken similarly prior to this implying that, conversely, the prospect of German troops marching into Eastern Siberia had never been a realistic possibility.[88] Intervention, in Wilson's view, might be undertaken to prevent Germany obtaining access to India by means of a northerly route through Western Siberia and Turkestan.[89] Milner had conveyed this idea to Curzon in February 1918. Curzon, a vigorous supporter of intervention, alluded to it in his concluding remarks to the Imperial War Cabinet on 25 June:

> does not all that I have been saying point to the supreme and crowning importance of getting in Japan from the Far East? There is another great area of possible advance north of the tract with which I have been dealing, namely the regions of South Siberia and Northern Turkestan, which are well supplied with railways from Russia, and along which it is perfectly certain that Germany will push her advance, and where the only means of holding her up is by Allied intervention from the East. If there is one conclusion more than another that I would impress upon you it is this: That the policy we are not pursuing to-day because of the opposition of the American President is the right policy, and the sooner we can throw our Allied forces in as large numbers as may be possible into the heart of Central Asia from that side, the more shall we facilitate the movements which our inferior forces are making in the South, and the better will be the chances of saving Asia from the German clutch.[90]

Precisely what Curzon had in mind regarding the necessary conditions to be attached to Japanese involvement is unclear. When in the autumn of 1917 he had, controversially, proposed the use of Japanese troops in Mesopotamia to press the attack, Curzon had not specified any conditions for their use. Clearly, however, he did not want a Japanese enclave in the Middle East. What in the above quoted passage began as 'getting in Japan from the Far East', became 'throw[ing] our Allied forces in as large numbers as may be possible into the heart of Central Asia'.

In any case, Cecil doubted if the Bolsheviks could be relied on to oppose Germany.[91] Yet, in view of the creation of this power vacuum, Lloyd George feared that such action as Curzon proposed might act as a catalyst for forces in Russia which were potentially hostile to the Allies.[92]

Largely as a result of the failure of Britain and her Allies either to secure Japanese intervention or successfully to prevent the prosecution of German aims by measures taken from the Mesopotamian and Persian railheads, by May 1918 the Eastern Committee had to revise its policy of maintaining a defensive cordon across North-West Persia and sanction the despatch of British troops into the Caucasus. Predictably, when addressing the Imperial War Cabinet, Curzon attached a suitable degree of importance to the move in respect of frustrating German ambitions, commenting:

> It means in all probability that unless we can destroy it in advance, the seizure of the Caspian Fleet . . . by the enemy is almost certain. The possession of the Caspian Fleet is valuable for three reasons, firstly, because it gives the Germans, if they obtain it, the control of the mouths of the Volga at Astrakhan; secondly, because it gives them the means of transport across the Caspian Sea to the eastern side, where you will see Krasnovodsk as the starting point of a new advance; thirdly, it gives them an opportunity of conveying their forces, if so required, to the northern shores of Persia.

Such an advance, Curzon added, might utilise the Trans-Caspian Railway and, should it progress to Tashkent, around 40,000 Austrian and German prisoners.[93] The implication was that, as had happened with the Black Sea Fleet, the Bolsheviks would present little opposition to German control of its counterpart on the Caspian. Such was the reading of events to which Curzon alluded, retrospectively, in June 1918, by which time British forces had entered Baku. A more detailed examination of the move suggests a rather different possibility.

'A GIGANTIC GAMBLE': THE ADVANCE TO BAKU

The possibility of despatching British troops to Baku was first discussed by the Eastern Committee on 28 May 1918. To the assembled officials Curzon reported that

> General Dunsterville telegraphed on the 24th May . . . the surprising news that Bicharakof[94] was moving North to the Caspian and that General Dunsterville proposed to accompany him in order to try and carry out his own plans in the Caucasus. Sir Charles Marling[95] had pointed out what a dislocation of our general policy this departure involved. The Chairman said that, after consultation with Lord Hardinge and General Macdonogh, he had authorised the latter to draw Marshall's[96] attention to the fact that this new departure meant a complete reversal of our policy.[97]

As Curzon continued, Marshall defended the move on the grounds that the mission was to be small and on the basis of instructions given to him at the end of March which stated that he should not neglect the possibilities of the Caucasus. Curzon went on to state that

Since then, the situation had changed and, naturally, former suggestions
had gone by the board. The chairman assumed that the Committee still
adhered to their policy of concentrating all our energies on the line
Kerman–Hamadan–Kasvin. He confessed his surprise at the proposal that
Bicharakof should be allowed to go and leave the line from Kerman open
and to let General Dunsterville – the only man who could possibly fill the
gap – go with him.

Macdonogh agreed, reporting that only recently he had acted to veto a
proposed mission to Baku by Dunsterville.

The changed situation to which Curzon referred related partly to the
growing need in the face of a more imminent threat from German–
Turkish forces to avoid any dissipation in the strength of the cordon in
North-West Persia. This potential threat was sufficient, in the opinion of
the Committee, to necessitate a mobile column for the cordon, which
would provide a more effective force. The intention to afford the
cordon offensive capabilities was confirmed at the next meeting of the
Committee. However, that fear of German–Turkish penetration was
only partly responsible for Curzon's opposition to the Baku Mission.[98]

The more significant change in the Caucasus since the end of March
was that, along with Armenian forces, Bolshevik troops now occupied
Baku. Hardinge, among others, viewed this as an opportunity for co-
operation with the Bolsheviks.[99] Macdonogh was more cautious, and for
this reason he had, at a meeting of the Eastern Committee on 3 May,
vetoed a favourable response to a request from Armenians at Baku that
Dunsterville should proceed there with two armoured cars.[100]

Curzon shared this fear of being ensnared in the political jungle of the
Caucasus. It was no coincidence that, having discussed and vetoed
Dunsterville's Caucasian Mission on 28 May, Curzon then directed the
attention of the Eastern Committee to the Jangali movement:

> The Chairman said that the Committee had previously regarded the
> Jangalis as a troublesome but not too formidable people. They were now
> rumoured to be moving to the southeast corner of the Caspian towards
> Astrabad and the Turkoman country, Gumesh Tepe & c. – They were
> further reported to be on friendly terms with the Bolsheviks. Probably the
> Germans were behind this. Unfortunately, we could take no measures to
> stop this movement, which marked, however, an ominous development of
> the situation. Some of the Jangalis were said to be at Damgan, and their
> intention was apparently to cut the main route between Meshed and
> Teheran.
> General Macdonogh pointed out that there were a number of Hazaras

in North-East Persia, and he wondered whether it would be possible to organise them against the Jangalis.

The Chairman thought that when our Mission reached Meshed they might find plenty to do in Persia itself, without attempting to penetrate into Central Asia.[101]

A reconsideration of the position previously adopted by the Eastern Committee was prompted by other developments. The refusal of the Eastern Committee to sanction Dunsterville's Mission at its meeting on 28 May had taken account only of proposals for a mission of limited size. However, Dunsterville had also suggested a more ambitious scheme.[102] For this he required a brigade of artillery and aimed to secure the co-operation of the Caspian Fleet. Confusion as to what Dunsterville intended was compounded by other factors. Firstly, the British Vice-Consul at Baku had urged the necessity of at least one British officer going to Baku to rally friendly elements. Secondly, in two telegrams, Marling had entirely altered his position and now seemed if anything to support the more ambitious proposal.[103]

As Curzon recalled, in a telegram of 28 May, Marling

> stated that all his information went to show that Dunsterville was anxiously awaited at Baku, and it was only by his going there that the Caspian fleet could be secured; that there was also a prospect that we might be able to gain over the Jangalis, in which case Dunsterville's retreat from Baku would be assured; and further, that in view of securing the fleet and destroying the oilfields, he hoped that the position might be re-examined.

As if to confuse matters further, on the following day Marling had despatched a telegram in which he requested clarification on the immediate aims of Britain in North-West Persia. Curzon continued:

> early in March he [Marling] understood that a sufficient force was to be despatched to North-West Persia with a view to stabilising the situation there and prevent the ingress of enemy agents, but later also for the purpose of keeping open the road to the Caucasus. He [Marling] now learned that Dunsterville's Mission was countermanded just at the moment when, so far as the former's information went, he had a better chance of achieving something than ever before, and when it seemed most necessary to take any risk in order to make things safe at Baku.[104]

Amid this confusion the ensuing discussion at the Eastern Committee developed into a debate about Bolshevik intentions.

By the end of May the basic minimum of British policy was to prevent collusion between the Bolsheviks, who controlled the Caspian

Fleet, and the Germans, enabling the latter to cross the Caspian Sea. The simplest way to achieve this, as the War Office advised, was to get the fleet away from Baku. Anything done from Baku itself would also deny its oil supplies to the Germans. Turkish preparations for offensive operations outside Baku pointed to the second option but was not the deciding factor. Conversely, nor was Curzon's opposition to the mission based entirely on what, with reference to Marling's proposal of 28 May, he termed 'a considerable expansion of the original Dunsterville programme'. Smuts hit the nail on the head whilst attempting to make sense of this proposal, as the minutes of the Eastern Committee record:

> General Smuts regarded it [Marling's telegram no. 473 of 29 May 1918] as an attempt to review the whole situation. In March we had adopted a certain policy. Now, however, when conditions had changed, and there was a favourable opportunity of General Dunsterville doing good at Baku, we had prevented his going there, although it seemed that the Bolsheviks were friendly.[105]

In his telegram of 26 May, Macdonell[106] had indeed stated that the Bolsheviks were friendly and that they intended to send three hundred infantry to Enzeli to release Dunsterville for Baku.[107] This fact rendered the operation possible.

At the meeting of the Eastern Committee on 31 May, somewhat predictably, Robert Cecil emerged as the champion of the Baku Mission. From the very outset he had been a vigorous proponent of forward defensive measures designed to impede the path of *Drang nach Osten*. It was unsurprising therefore that, in support of the mission and according to the minutes of the Eastern Committee, Cecil 'pointed out that Baku was really part of our cordon, otherwise the Caspian would be handed over to our enemies'.[108] Moreover, Cecil did not view with alarm the prospect of Japanese involvement in support of the South Eastern Federation.[109] Similarly, he saw no inherent contradiction between British actions in support of nationalist elements in Southern Russia and continuing relations with St Petersburg, provided, of course, that those elements were directed at the Central Powers and not at Bolshevik strongholds.[110] More broadly, in the spring and summer of 1918, Cecil was relatively sanguine about the extent of possible Anglo-Bolshevik co-operation.[111]

Hardinge was developing precisely opposite views at this time, just as he was beginning to question the feasibility of Japanese action along the Trans-Siberian Railway.[112] Lloyd George agreed with Hardinge fearing, as we have noted, that such action might jell elements hostile to the Allies under the Bolsheviks.[113] Lloyd George's thinking on the Caucasus at this time was interesting. While attention appeared to be riveted on the Turco-German advance, and while Curzon spoke in ambiguous terms of an Allied advance into the heart of Central Asia to forestall this movement, rather different thoughts were evolving in the mind of the Prime Minister, as the minutes of the War Cabinet of 20 June 1918 reveal: 'Mr Lloyd George expressed the opinion that it would be better for us for the Turks to hold Baku, as it was not probable they would ever be dangerous to our interests in the East, whilst, on the other hand, Russia, if in the future she became regenerated, might be so.'[114]

Towards the end of May 1918 Curzon was aware both of Bolshevik actions against centres of resistance to their authority and of their apparent duplicity in opening the door to German ambitions across the Black Sea. Such duplicity was, in Curzon's view, the best that might be expected from the proposal to send a force of any size to Baku. That this 'gigantic gamble' might depend for its success on '300 doubtful Bolsheviks' who, assisted by comrades further east or by Jangalis, were charged with holding the gate at Enzeli, seemed utter folly.[115]

Precisely what might be expected of the Bolsheviks at Baku and elsewhere in Central Asia was unclear for much of 1918. The Treaty of Brest-Litovsk provided an obvious context in which British officials attempted to rationalise events in the region, but in retrospect it was too restricting a model. In their public utterances Curzon, Milner and others identified the German–Russian alliance as incompatible with the future well-being of the Empire. Many authors, including Guinn, Rothwell and Ellis, have portrayed Bolshevism simply in the terms in which it was regarded by the War Office in 1918, namely as the 'hand maiden of German Imperialism'.[116] However, this analysis is too restricting. From the inception of the Malleson Mission[117] there was a perceptible incompatibility between Bolshevik aims – whether directed from the centre or not – and British imperial interests. This was clearly indicated by British support for the Askabad Government in its efforts to forestall Bolshevik ambitions. Certainly, British planning in Trans-Caspia reflected a concern at the highest levels with the German–Turkish advance. However, the reality of Malmiss, as the Malleson Mission came to be known, and later of Etherton's[118] activities at Kashgar – in the absence of the defection of Afghanistan, the penetration to Trans-Caspia by German–Turkish forces and an explosion of nationalism – was a growing preoccupation with Bolshevik aims.

Ellis's failure to acknowledge this is simply due to his distorted presentation of Anglo-Russian relations after 1907 and, in turn, his desire at all costs to refute Soviet allegations of British imperialistic aims in the region.[119] That these aims were not to find full expression, in the Caucasus at least, until the Bolshevik threat had matured further, was again symptomatic of the limitations of *Drang nach Osten* and pan-Islamic and nationalistic creeds in the imperialist mind. Naturally, Ellis disregards the enthusiasm evinced by Curzon and Churchill – admittedly at a later date – for a permanent British presence in Trans-Caspia.[120] That amid the confusion it seemed difficult to envisage a militarily hostile Soviet Union, at least when Bolshevik troops were not engaged in suppressing nationalist opposition, must be seen in the broader context of decades of Anglo-Russian rivalry in which Curzon had been a pre-eminent forward thinker. A more accurate reflection of the impact of Bolshevism might be to suggest, as Stanwood does, that it exerted an increasing influence on the thinking of British officials, even if they seldom made the effort to divorce it from the threat of *Drang nach Osten*.[121]

To varying degrees Curzon's doubts about the Baku Mission were shared by other members of the Eastern Committee. Montagu, whilst willing to sanction the despatch to Baku of a limited mission, was also aware that recent improvements in relations with the Jangalis might prove transitory and that, in the event of Dunsterville encountering difficulties in Baku, a retreat might be blocked by Bolshevik–Jangali forces.[122]

In spite of these reservations, however, the Eastern Committee gave its approval to a limited mission. This was partly owing to the importance vested by Cecil and Smuts in local opinion, and it was to the veracity of the judgement of those on the ground that Cecil appealed to have the measure sanctioned. Moreover, consideration was given to the feeling that the cordon should not be so depleted by the needs of the mission as to impair its efficiency and safety.[123]

CROSSING THE RUBICON

In the course of the negotiations relating to the Armistice of Mudros of 30 October 1918,[124] Curzon mounted a vigorous campaign to prevent the cessation of hostilities before British desiderata had been met in full. In relation to the Caucasus there were three essential points. Firstly, and in accordance with the views of other senior figures, Curzon wished to secure the free navigation of the Dardanelles and the ability to send ship-

ping into the Black Sea. Secondly, Curzon pressed for the acceptance of
the clause whereby Britain should be permitted to occupy such strategic
points as would render her position secure. Thirdly, and following on
from these points, Curzon desired that the German–Turkish presence in
the Caucasus should be eliminated. As we have seen, Lloyd George
knew that in taking measures to execute the last point Curzon was
capitalising on the dramatically changing strategic picture in the
Caucasus to lay the foundations of an imperial future for Britain in the
region.

Curzon had a keen interest in Bolshevik Russia and in the possibility
of a resuscitated, unified Russia which might threaten the British
Empire. With the Armistice of Mudros the opportunity arose of taking
pre-emptive measures to anticipate this eventuality, something which
had hitherto been impossible because of German–Turkish successes and
Bolshevik complicity in them.

Yet, until the very end of 1918 and beyond, the notion of *Drang nach
Osten* remained in common currency among those who formulated
British policy in the Caucasus. This was partly related to a perception
of the Turco-German combination as being a permanent factor in international affairs, even if by late September its potency seemed sharply
diminished. It was in this context that British policy towards Persia was
discussed by the Eastern Committee on 26 September – with Curzon
and Balfour implying that such was the incompatibility between British
and German–Turkish aims that defensive measures previously taken by
Britain in the form of the eastern and north-western cordons must
remain.[125]

By virtue of article 7 of the Turkish Armistice, whereby Britain was
to be free to occupy territories the possession of which was deemed
necessary to secure her position, Curzon pressed for measures which he
portrayed as sufficient in scope to render certain the complete elimination of German–Turkish ambitions in the east. However, it remained
of considerable importance to Curzon, if the opportunities presented by
that article were to be realised, that *Drang nach Osten* should be kept alive.
It must therefore have given him some satisfaction to preside over the
War Cabinet on 1 November when it was informed that, because of
reports that German troops were en route to Baku, General Marshall
had been ordered to reoccupy it.[126]

In fact, Curzon was not alone in keeping alive the embers of *Drang
nach Osten*. Well into December at discussions of the Eastern Committee,
when the future of the Caucasus was raised, their nightmarish impli-

cations were invoked. As late as 23 December, exactly a year since
Britain and France had defined areas in which they might act to oppose
Drang nach Osten, the Imperial War Cabinet again edged along the same
path, concluding 'that the British forces should not be withdrawn from
the Caucasus until after the Turkish and German forces have been withdrawn'.[127]

Implicit in Curzon's desiderata at the time of the Turkish Armistice
was that Britain should prepare herself to encounter the threat to her
position which was maturing to the north of the Caucasus range. That
Curzon failed to make more explicit his cognizance of the effect upon
Anglo-Bolshevik relations of the Turkish Armistice was probably inten-
tional, and certainly was not, as Stanwood claims, because the antennae
of the imperialists had yet to detect a hostile intent in Bolshevik
actions.[128] Given the nature of Anglo-Bolshevik relations in the autumn
of 1918, it is scarcely surprising that efforts were made to sustain the
pace of Imperial gain by recourse to those threats which were by that
time entirely illusory: namely, pan-Islam, nationalism and *Drang nach
Osten*. The note of caution sounded by the Imperial War Cabinet in its
decision of 23 December reflected the equivocal policy of Britain
towards Bolshevik Russia since the Turkish Armistice. At a conference
held at the Foreign Office on 13 November, and on the following day at
the War Cabinet, several senior figures had pronounced emphatically
on the need to avoid what might be perceived as a crusade against
Bolshevism.[129] Admittedly, the Cabinet was prepared to support governments which, like that of Trans-Caspia, were opposed to Bolshevism
and which were in close physical proximity to British interests.
However, it remained unclear whether the implication of this would
amount to an acceptance of Milner's view that 'considerations both of
honour and of interest demanded that we should keep Bolshevism from
the regions East of the Black Sea, i.e. the Caucasus, the Don
country, and Turkestan'.[130] Certainly, Milner spoke in terms of limited
military objectives, and the sanction by the War Cabinet to secure the
Baku–Batum Railway and to supply General Denikin[131] was the most
explicit expression of a policy which was best described by Robert Cecil
when addressing the War Cabinet on 14 November:

> he [Cecil] shared the view of the Foreign Secretary, that it would be fatal
> to let it be thought that we were committed to an anti-Bolshevik crusade.
> He doubted very much whether it was part of our duty to protect Esthonia
> and the Baltic States against Russian Bolshevism *but* we ought to do what
> we could to prevent the rich countries of Southern and South-Eastern

Russia from drifting into anarchy, and we ought to protect the people we have from time to time incited to help us in the war. We had induced General Denikin to continue fighting against Germans and to maintain a separate Government in those districts which were not Bolshevik. We should assist these people, not because they were anti-Bolshevik, but because they had during the war been pro-Ally. In the Ukraine there was a pro-German Government, and it was no part of our duty to support it.[132]

Cecil's circumspection was partly due to the scale of the anti-Bolshevik measures advocated by agents on the ground who, contrary to Stanwood's contention that Bolshevism became a threat at this time by default, regarded Bolshevism as an immediate peril.[133] Broadly, their reasoning assumed that the withdrawal of German forces left an open field for Bolshevik penetration and exploitation. On 10 October Sir Mansfeldt De Cardonnel Findlay,[134] reporting from Christiana, stated that the Russian Legation was insistent that Allied landings must be undertaken at Baltic and Black Sea ports to prevent Bolshevik excesses.[135] In addition, the French Government and her envoys had been pressing for active measures by Britain from the Persian and Mesopotamian railheads either to establish contact with Denikin or to draw Bolshevik troops away from the beleaguered Czech forces in Siberia by means of action in Turkestan.[136]

In the event, it was to Denikin that Britain would devote her efforts. This had the advantage of harnessing interventionist urges within the Foreign Office which might otherwise lead to unmanageable commitments. Such urges were articulated by E.H. Carr[137] who, though perceiving Allied landings at Baltic and Black Sea ports as 'fantastic', held that, in the event of an Allied landing in South Russia, an advance in a north-easterly direction to 'effect a junction' with the Czechs might be possible.[138] The force might then 'advance on Moscow in order to smash the Bolsheviks'.[139]

Strong action also appealed to Reginald Leeper of the Political Intelligence Department. Should the war continue, he argued, Bolshevism might easily spread to the borders of Russia and threaten Europe. If peace were to intervene, then, in the ensuing efforts to extinguish Bolshevism, Germany might regain her ascendancy in Russia. He wrote:

All this points to the urgency of an immediate settlement of the Russian problem by the Allies before the general peace settlement. The longer Bolshevism is left the more dangerous it becomes. If it is dealt with now a comparatively small army from the Urals might advance on Moscow and put it down by force, whereas if decisive action is postponed it may spread further West and the task will become much more difficult and will require a large army.[140]

An anonymous, more sceptical, colleague noted that on the reckoning of Lockhart a force of 200,000 and an occupation of two years might suffice for the purpose.[141] Amid the confusion created by such expansive proposals and as far as Bolshevist expansion affected those regions with which Britain had established contacts in the south, some officials were less restrained than Curzon in their anticipation of events. Within the Political Intelligence Department, an anonymous author assessed the position thus:

> In view of the collapse of German aspirations beyond the Danube, it looks as if the keystone of British policy with regard to the Farther East may need to be the assumption of a protectorate over these three Trans-Caucasian elements [Georgia, Armenia, Azerbaijan], or at least the furnishing of them with assistance towards their development as political unities on ethnographical lines. From this point of view it is therefore a serious question whether it may not be better to discourage Russian advances beyond Cis-Caucasia, that is to say, confine her to the northern side of the Caucasus, thus making Trans-Caucasia a barrier to any future Russian aspirations towards the south-east. This policy may also be stimulated by the pressure of immigration from Northern Russia, unless this can be diverted regularly towards Siberia; but, on the other hand, the attraction of the warmer south and its waters will always be irresistible. With an internationalised Dardanelles, Russian aggressive movement beyond the Caucasus could only be predatory in purpose, and the difficulty of restoring Baku to Russia lies in the fact that if she is given any footing in Trans-Caucasia she will inevitably attempt to recover all her former possessions. With the oil-fields of Grozny and Maikop and the ports of Derbent and Petrovsk she will not suffer essential loss or means of direct communication with her Trans-Caspian possessions.[142]

The absence of clear parameters for British involvement in Southern Russia likewise compelled Cecil to press for a limited and well-focused British contribution. The War Office wished to adhere to the division of interests agreed upon with France in December 1917, but as late as 22 November 1918, G.R. Clerk of the Foreign Office argued that Admiral Calthorpe should despatch a representative and, if possible, a ship to discover what attitude the Ukrainian Government proposed to adopt towards the Allies.[143] Balfour doubted the willingness of the Cabinet to sanction British activity there, but even with this option debarred there was, as Sir Henry Wilson recorded in his diary with reference to the views of himself and Milner, considerable scope for British activity: 'We are entirely agreed to keep out of Austria, Hungary, Poland, Roumania, Ukraine and north of the Black Sea except in so far as is necessary to beat the Boches, but on the other hand from the left bank of the Don to India is our interest and preserve.'[144]

Wilson's colleague, Major-General Radcliffe, Director of Military Operations, held that Britain should obtain from France a recognition of British paramountcy in the Caucasus.[145] Such intentions were not, as Stanwood claims, due to imperial 'paranoia' but rather to excessive French interest in British movements in the region.[146] It was also felt that, having mismanaged the section of territory apportioned to her to counter Turco-German forces, France might claim equal treatment on the basis of that division.[147]

Ironically, by October 1918, Cecil found himself recommending a more cautious policy precisely because the consequences of antagonising the Bolsheviks had grown. Unlike many of his Foreign Office colleagues, Cecil retained hope that it might be possible to treat with Bolshevism. As he observed in a departmental minute written in October 1918, although it was unpalatable to have to do so, the only alternative was that Britain or the Allies must suppress Bolshevism by force. As this was impracticable, Cecil argued, and as Allied efforts to resuscitate Russia appeared to have failed, Britain must not 'reject all idea of an arrangement with the Bolsheviks, if only because that may yet prove the best chance of preventing the spread of Bolshevik theories in their most exaggerated form, and of saving the existence of anti-Bolshevik Russia'.[148]

That Curzon remained silent during this debate on British policy towards the Bolsheviks was scarcely surprising. The indications were that British policy would tend to drift into more open conflict with Moscow. In addition, as Curzon defined British policy in the Caucasus, Britain and her rivals had already begun to jostle for position in the region. These developments were of considerable value to Curzon in the crucial weeks before the anticipated peace when, as Chairman of the Eastern Committee, he had an opportunity to breathe life into the dreams of imperialists.

NOTES

1. Amery to Lloyd George, 8 June 1918, Offices of the War Cabinet, 2 Whitehall Gardens, Lloyd George Papers F/2/1/24.
2. Note on Military Situation in Armenia by L.S. Amery, 3 December 1917, SWC 1, Supreme War Council, CAB 25/120.

3. Ibid. Amery was certainly under the impression that he was influencing events; see Barnes and Nicholson, *The Leo Amery Diaries*, vol. 1, entry of 1 February 1918, p. 204.
4. Ibid. SWC 1.
5. Ibid.
6. In particular, Amery targeted Milner, Sir Henry Wilson and Lloyd George. There is considerable evidence to suggest a wide measure of co-operation between Amery, Milner, Wilson and, to a lesser degree, Cecil, Hankey and Smuts, in pressing for the execution of a broadly similar policy in the east. This was certainly true with regard to key appointments in the Lloyd George administration; see Barnes and Nicholson, op. cit., entries for 2, 24 January, 4 March, 14 April, 7 June 1918. See also Amery to Lloyd George, 14 April 1918, Offices of the War Cabinet, 2 Whitehall Gardens, Lloyd George Papers F/2/1/17; ibid. Amery to Lloyd George, 8 June 1918, Offices of the War Cabinet, 2 Whitehall Gardens, SW, F/2/1/24.
7. Amery to Hankey, 26 December 1917, Supreme War Council, British Section, Versailles, CAB 21/4. Milner apparently shared this conviction; entry of 26 December 1917, Diaries of Field Marshal Sir Henry Wilson, reel 7.
8. Ibid. Amery to Hankey.
9. Ibid.
10. Amery to Lloyd George, 30 December 1917, Supreme War Council, British Section, Versailles, enclosing Note on Sir William Robertson's Memorandum of 26 December 1917, G.T. 3112, 'Future Operations in Palestine' by Amery, 30 December 1917, Lloyd George Papers F/2/1/10.
11. Ibid. Amery to Lloyd George, 29 December 1917, Supreme War Council, British Section, Versailles, F/2/1/9.
12. Ibid.
13. Ibid.
14. Ibid. On 23 December 1917, Amery had written with much frankness and foresight: 'The War is going East with a vengeance and we shall find ourselves fighting for the rest of it to decide where the Anglo-German boundary shall run across Asia. The French, as usual, have pushed into the first place and are going to run Rumania, Ukraine and the Poles. But their show may collapse and will never anyhow be under permanent French control, while we poor meek British will probably find our non-aggressive little Empire at the end of the war including Turkestan, Persia and the Caucasus!' Barnes and Nicholson, op. cit., entry of 23 December 1917, p. 188.
15. Ibid. Amery to Lloyd George, 29 December 1917.
16. Amery to Cecil, 27 December 1917, Supreme War Council, British Section, Versailles, FO 371/3296, pp. 225–6.
17. Milner to Lloyd George, 23 December 1917, personal, Hotel de Crillon, Place de la Concorde, Lloyd George Papers F/38/2/27.
18. Entry of 31 December 1917, Diaries of Field Marshal Sir Henry Wilson, reel 7.
19. Two committees dealt with matters relating to Southern Russia and the Caucasus, namely the Russia and Caucasus Committees, both of which sat at the Foreign Office. The Russia Committee consisted of representatives of the Foreign Office, War Office and Treasury and either Sir Ronald Graham, Lord Robert Cecil or Sir George Clerk attended as senior official. At its 22nd meeting on 29 January 1918, it was decided to limit meetings of the Committee to three a week and this was subsequently reduced to one weekly prearranged meeting. At the 41st meeting of the Committee on 4 April 1918, the following division of labour was outlined with the Eastern Committee: 'The Committee considered their position in relation to the newly formed Eastern Committee, and it was decided to suggest that in so far as the details of operations and undertakings in North-West Persia are concerned, it might be left to the Russia Committee to deal with inter-departmental questions connected with such matters: any question involving a fresh decision as to policy would be referred to the Eastern Committee.' The Russia Committee did continue to meet; see, for example, FO 371/3334, p. 303; FO 371/3341, p. 95. A very incomplete collection of the minutes of the Russia Committee may be found at FO 95/802, and a more complete one at WO 106/1560.

Information about the Caucasus Committee is scarce. Like the Russia Committee its permanent members consisted of Foreign and War Office officials. Sir Ronald Graham chaired the Committee and Sir George Clerk was a member. It may be that India Office representation was requested when necessary. In a memorandum written by Gleichen, head of the Intelligence Bureau at the Ministry of Information, in January 1918, it was alleged that Major-General Macdonogh, DMI, had requested that A.J. Toynbee and Professor Simpson of the Ministry of Information should not be allowed to attend meetings of the Caucasus Committee as their views were too pro-Armenian; note by Gleichen, 18 January 1918, Milner Papers /369, f. 59 (Bodleian Library, Oxford).

20. Minute by Cecil, n.d., FO 371/3283, pp. 103–4. Cecil had been extremely reluctant to sanction the creation of the Russia Committee – which, it seems likely, was formed in response to the Inter-Allied Conference of 23 December 1917 – confiding to Balfour on 8 January 1918: 'Unfortunately, I have had to agree to another Committee, called the Russia Committee, as the only means of unifying our action with that of the War Office in those parts. This Committee meets, I believe, every day; but I have declined to be a member of it, and I insist that no urgent decisions are to await its consideration. On the whole, it does not seem to be doing much harm at present; and so far as it has spurred on the Treasury to make real exertions to find money for all these people, it may have done some good.' Cecil to Balfour, 8 January 1918, Foreign Office, private, Balfour Papers, Add. Ms 49738 (British Library). It may be that the lethargy which Cecil detected in the deliberations of the Committee encouraged him to take a closer interest in its activities.

Ullman (*Anglo-Soviet Relations, 1917–1921*, Princeton, NJ, 1961–72) attributes the above quoted evidence regarding the Caucasus and Russia Committees to the diverging interpretations of the Foreign and War Offices of how best to approach policy formulation in Southern Russia. Ullman may have a point but he fails to acknowledge that early in 1918 British policy aspired to the creation of an independent Armenia as a means of forestalling *Drang nach Osten*. Also, if, as Ullman alleges, the War Office resented Foreign Office interference, then Macdonogh's desire that Toynbee and Simpson be prevented from attending meetings of the Caucasus Committee was based upon the misapprehension that, as employees of the Ministry of Information, both men were under Foreign Office direction; see M.L. Sanders and P.M. Taylor, *British Propaganda During the First World War* (London, 1982), p. 80.

21. It seems that Milner, who Amery represented personally at Versailles, regarded this as an advantage. Writing to Sir Henry Wilson, then chief British military delegate at Versailles, on 12 December 1917, in the context of on-going debate about the position of Sir William Robertson, Milner observed: 'You, at Versailles may sometimes feel rather out of it. But that situation has its strong points as well as its weak ones. You *can* stand back from the picture, and with a cool, unrattled brain see things as a whole, and distinguish the really important from the immediately clamorous. Don't throw away that advantage.' Milner to Wilson, 12 December 1917, 17 Great College Street, confidential, Milner Papers /354 (Bodleian Library, Oxford).

22. Amery to Lloyd George, 12 January 1918, Offices of the War Cabinet, 2 Whitehall Gardens, enclosing memorandum by Amery, 'The Turkish and South Russia Problem', Lloyd George Papers F/2/1/11.

23. Ibid.

24. Milner to Wilson, 5 March 1918, confidential, Papers of Field Marshal Sir Henry Wilson 2/11.

25. See n. 22.

26. Ibid.

27. Ibid.

28. Memorandum by L.S. Amery, 12 March 1918, 'Germany and the Middle East', Versailles, SWC 113, Supreme War Council, CAB 25/120.

29. Note by General Staff, War Office, 11 March 1918, secret, on Memorandum T. 21169 of 7 March 1918, circulated by Secretary of State for Foreign Affairs, WO 106/314.

30. Ibid., and n. 28.

31. Ibid.

32. Note for Wilson by Amery, 15 March 1918, Offices of the War Cabinet, 2 Whitehall Gardens, Papers of Field Marshal Sir Henry Wilson 2/8.

33. Ibid., and enclosure, memorandum by Amery, 'Policy on Persia and Trans-Caucasia', 14 March 1918; also at Amery to Lloyd George, 15 March 1918, Offices of the War Cabinet, 2 Whitehall Gardens, Lloyd George Papers F/2/1/16.

34. Note for CIGS by Amery, 'Unity of Operations in the East', 20 March 1918, Papers of Field Marshal Sir Henry Wilson 2/8.
35. Amery to Lloyd George, 16 August 1918, Offices of the War Cabinet, Lloyd George Papers F/2/1/29.
36. IWC 20, 25 June 1918, Imperial War Cabinet, CAB 23/43. Unless otherwise stated the material on pp. 164–6 relates to Curzon's speech.
37. Writing to General Marshall, GOC Mesopotamia, two days before Curzon's speech to the Imperial War Cabinet, Milner had spoken in terms which closely resembled those of Curzon: 'If the Germans make themselves masters of Trans-Caucasia, as I fear is inevitable, they are sure to give us trouble in Northern Persia, and probably also in Turkestan. The war, in fact, is spreading to the Far East, and if the campaign on the West this summer results in a deadlock – the best we can hope for – the Eastern side may become the most important portion of the struggle during the coming winter.' Milner to Marshall, 23 June 1918, Milner Papers /355, f. 98 (Bodleian Library, Oxford).

    To Hankey, Curzon's speech was 'admirable' and Montagu, though possibly not uninfluenced by Hirtzel's promptings, when sending a copy of Curzon's speech to Chelmsford, referred to it as 'the view that we take at home of the Eastern menace'. Montagu also noted that it had been a 'great success with the Cabinet'. Entry of 25 June 1918, Hankey Diaries 1/3 (Churchill College, Cambridge); Montagu to Chelmsford, 3 July 1918, private, Montagu Papers D523 (OIOC). Lord Robert Cecil had been thinking along very similar lines to Curzon; Cecil to Lloyd George, 7 June 1918, confidential, Lloyd George Papers F/6/5/28. Amery had expressed his opinion on the matter earlier than most; see n. 14.
38. See V.H. Rothwell, *British War Aims and Peace Diplomacy 1914–1918* (London, 1971), p. 196.
39. See n. 36.
40. B. Schwarz, 'Divided Attention: Britain's Perception of a German Threat to Her Eastern Position in 1918', *JCH*, 28, 1993, p. 108.
41. C.H. Ellis, *The Transcaspian Episode: 1918–1919* (London, 1963), p. 12; F. Stanwood, *War Revolution and British Imperialism in Central Asia* (London, 1983), p. 39.
42. Stanwood, ibid., pp. 123–4.
43. Ibid., pp. 197, 237–8, passim.
44. See B. Schwarz, *JCH*, 28, p. 108.
45. Writing to Lloyd George in May 1918 on the subject of rearrangements in the military hierarchy, Curzon observed that it would be 'invaluable' to have a strong and respected Commander in Chief for what would be a difficult task, 'should there be trouble in India, and should the Germano-Turanian scheme of aggression materialise'; Curzon to Lloyd George, 22 May 1918, 1 Carlton House Terrace, Curzon Papers F112/122a, f. 24. Popplewell's assessment of the true scale of the Turco-German military threat is accurate; Popplewell, *Intelligence and Imperial Defence*, p. 165.
46. Stanwood, op. cit., p. 249.
47. Ibid., p. 49.
48. Indian Desiderata for the Peace Conference, EC 2599.
49. Minute by Sir Arthur Hirtzel, 12 November 1918, L/P+S/11/142 P5421.
50. Ibid. Minutes by Sir Thomas Holderness, n.d., and Sir H.V. Cox, 29 November 1918.
51. Ibid. Minute by Cox.
52. Ibid. Minute by Holderness, 16 November 1918.
53. Ibid. Minute by Cox.
54. Perhaps the most notable convert to a position of sympathy with measures taken to defeat *Drang nach Osten* was Sir Douglas Haig who had served as Chief of Staff to the Commander in Chief in India before the War. At the Persia Committee on 22 March 1918, Haig was reported by Macdonogh, DMI, to have recommended the occupation of every town in Persia, 'failing which', Macdonogh continued, 'we must be prepared for the whole defence of the Khyber to be jeopardised, with the subsequent loss of India'. Minutes of the Persia Committee of 23 March 1918, Curzon Papers F112/271; also Milner to Lloyd George, 20 March 1918, 17 Great College Street, very confidential, Lloyd George Papers F/38/3/20.
55. Cromer to Wingate, 22 October 1915, Cromer Papers, FO 633/24, f. 344.
56. Crewe to Curzon, 4 December 1914, Crewe Papers I/20.
57. See nn. 2, 36.

58. Ibid. Curzon's speech to the Imperial War Cabinet.
59. B. Schwarz, *JCH*, 28, p. 115; J.S. Galbraith is more accurate: *JICH*, 13, pp. 37–8.
60. See n. 36.
61. See, for example, Cecil to Balfour, 8 January 1918, Foreign Office, private, Balfour Papers Add. Ms 49738 (British Library); Milner to Wilson, 5 March 1918, 17 Great College Street, SW, Papers of Field Marshal Sir Henry Wilson 2/11 no. 9. Although presented to the War Cabinet by Wilson on 11 March 1918, the idea of amalgamating the Committees which dealt with Asian affairs seems to have originated with Milner; Stanwood, op. cit., pp. 100, 104, is incorrect on this. Milner repeated this argument in a letter to Lloyd George of 20 March 1918: Lloyd George Papers F/38/3/20. Whereas Milner suggested that Curzon might sit on the unified body, he favoured Smuts as the co-ordinating figure; conveying the idea that, like Balfour, Curzon's methods were too dilatory. The need for greater co-ordination in eastern affairs, and particularly under Smuts, had been pressed for some time by Amery. Though in favour of greater co-ordination, Sir Henry Wilson regarded as impracticable the notion of a 'generalissimo' as championed by Amery. Entry of 16 January 1918, Diaries of Field Marshal Sir Henry Wilson, reel 8. However, Wilson was perhaps to regret his decision, bemoaning on 22 March 1918 the usual irresolution of the Persia Committee on a matter to which he attached importance. Also, on 8 July 1918, Wilson made reference to the 'wretched Eastern Committee of which Curzon is chairman'. By 26 August, with the Eastern Committee still under sustained bombardment, Wilson noted in his diary that he proposed to assist Cecil in the latter's efforts to create a 'ministry of the Central East'. Ibid. Entries for 22 March, 8 July, 26 August 1918.
   On the eve of the storm, on 17 June 1918, Amery recorded in his diary the events of that afternoon at an 'X' meeting of the War Cabinet, summoned to discuss the question of the control of forces in the Middle East: 'Montagu who has evidently been suffering under the cumbrousness of Curzon and his Eastern Committee, urged either that the whole business should be put under one member of the Cabinet (he mentioned Curzon because to have mentioned anyone else would have been offensive, though I am by no means convinced that he meant Curzon). His other alternative was a Commander-in-Chief in the East. Balfour of course pointed out in his best manner that he really couldn't expect anything else but a muddle in view of the weakness of our military position and that the defects in our machinery didn't really matter. It is rather interesting finding them coming back to the need to put the matter under a single command, or to my other suggestion of substituting Smuts alone for the whole Eastern Committee.' Barnes and Nicholson, *The Leo Amery Diaries*, vol. 1, entry for 17 June 1918, pp. 223–4.
62. J.S. Galbraith, *JICH*, 13, p. 26.
63. Ibid., p. 28.
64. Ibid., p. 30.
65. Marian Kent overlooks this in her assessment of the consequences of war for Britain in the Middle East: M. Kent, in Hinsley, p. 436.
66. See Galbraith, op. cit., p. 25.
67. Ibid., pp. 38–9.
68. According to Ullman, early in 1917 Balfour had encouraged Russia and Japan to engage in serious negotiations on a possible advance by Japan to the Carpathians in order to reinforce the Eastern Front. In December 1917 Foch argued for the despatch of Japanese troops along the Trans-Siberian Railway to European Russia as a 'security measure' and in order to transport supplies to Romania. Ullman, *Anglo-Soviet Relations 1917–21*, vol. 1 (Princeton, NJ, 1963), pp. 85–6.
69. Foreign Office Minutes on S.E. Russia, etc., GT 3243, CAB 24/38.
70. Minute by Lord Hardinge, c. 17 June 1918, FO 371/3319, p. 246.
71. Balfour to Milner, 19 January 1918, Foreign Office, private, Milner Papers /46 (Bodleian Library, Oxford).
72. Minutes of a meeting of the War Cabinet, 21 January 1918, WC 327, CAB 23/5.
73. Acting Consul-General, Moscow, 1914–17, employed in Foreign Office from November 1917.
74. See, for example, Lockhart to Foreign Office, 8 March 1918, FO 371/3285, no. 13, pp. 68ff.
75. Ibid. See n. 36.
76. Foreign Office to Lindley, 21 February 1918 (draft), FO 371/3299, no. 287, p. 38.

77. Foreign Office to Lockhart, 13 March 1918, FO 371/3285, no. 12, pp. 78–80.
78. Ibid.
79. Ibid.
80. Minute by Lyons, 25 January 1918, FO 371/3298/16373.
81. Minute by Lyons, 8 January 1918, FO 371/3288, p. 399. Conversely, Robert Cecil supported Japanese intervention precisely because it would distract her from imperial ambitions in India and the South Pacific. See Galbraith, *JICH*, 13.
82. Minutes by Hardinge and Lyons, FO 371/3289, pp. 20, 285, 290ff. In fact, Hardinge had doubts about many aspects of the intervention proposal but appeared to view the move as a necessary gamble in desperate times; see Hardinge to Bertie, 5 March 1918, Foreign Office, personal, Bertie Papers Add. Ms 63049 (British Library).
83. Ibid. Minute by Lyons, 19 February 1918, pp. 290ff.
84. The Federation was formed in November 1917 and was composed of the Cossacks of Southern Russia. For a time Britain sought to use it as a nucleus of opposition to Bolshevism. See Ullman, vol. 1, p. 44.
85. Minute by Lyons, 16 January 1918, on Note by Russia Committee on Question of Trans-Siberian Railway, FO 371/3289, pp. 81ff.
86. See Appendix 8.
87. See n. 70.
88. Minutes of the War Cabinet, 21 March 1918, CAB 23/5.
89. Ibid.
90. Milner to Curzon, 26 February 1918, Curzon Papers F112/122a; see also n. 36.
91. Memorandum by Lord Robert Cecil, 'The Russian Situation', 1 April 1918, FO 371/3285/58693, f. 234ff.
92. 'X' minutes of the War Cabinet, 19 June 1918, X-15, CAB 23/17.
93. See n. 36.
94. Leader of anti-Bolshevik forces in the Caucasus with whom Denikin co-operated.
95. Envoy Extraordinary and Minister Plenipotentiary at Tehran, and Consul General in Persia.
96. GOC-in-C Mesopotamia.
97. Minutes of the Eastern Committee, 28 May 1918, *EC* 10, secret, CAB 27/24. Unless otherwise stated, the material in this section relates to this meeting.
98. Ibid. *EC* 11, 31 May 1918.
99. Minute by Hardinge, c. 2 April 1918, FO 371/3300, pp. 582–3.
100. Minutes of the Eastern Committee, 3 May 1918, *EC* 6, secret, CAB 27/24.
101. See n. 97.
102. Ibid. See also, *EC* 11, 31 May 1918.
103. Ibid. *EC* 11.
104. Ibid.
105. Ibid.
106. Vice-Consul, Baku, from 29 April 1907, on special service at Tiflis from December 1917.
107. GOC-in-C, Mesopotamia, to DMI, 28 May 1918, no. X9121, EC 436, CAB 27/27.
108. See n. 98.
109. Memorandum by Cecil for Balfour, 1 April 1918 (circulated to King and War Cabinet), FO 371/3285/58693; see also Cecil in *The Times*, 11 March 1918; quoted in Ullman, vol. 1, p. 126.
110. Minutes of meetings of the War Cabinet, 24 January 1918, WC 330; 8 February, 1918, CAB 23/5.
111. Minutes of a meeting of the War Cabinet, 12 April 1918, WC 390, CAB 23/6.
112. Minute by Hardinge, 17 June 1918, FO 371/3319, pp. 245ff.
113. See n. 92.
114. Minutes of a meeting of the War Cabinet, 20 June 1918, WC 435, CAB 23/6.
115. See n. 98.
116. Stanwood, *War, Revolution*, p. 113.
117. Major-General Malleson of the Military Intelligence Branch of the Indian Army had been despatched to Meshed in July 1918 with a small group of officers to monitor enemy movements east of the Caspian.
118. Etherton was posted to Kashgar as Consul General early in 1918.
119. Ellis, *Transcaspian Episode*, pp. 31 and 133. Ullman tries hard, but without success, to refute the

idea of a growing incompatibility between British and Bolshevik aims in the Caucasus, attributing the Moscow directive, communicated via the Baku Soviet early in June, which forbade any British forces from entering Russian territory, not to the growing Bolshevik suspicions of British intentions in the region, but to Lockhart's protest about the disarming of the Czech forces in Siberia; Ullman, vol. 2, pp. 306–7. Hopkirk's recent study provides a more balanced assessment: P. Hopkirk, *On Secret Service East of Constantinople* (London, 1994); see n. 128.

Irrespective of the reasons for the withdrawal of Malmiss, there was, as Ullman acknowledges, a common interest between Britain and the Askabad Government in preventing the spread of Bolshevism to Turkestan; something which was explicitly stated in the Agreement between Britain and that body in the accompanying protocol written by Malleson; Ullman, op. cit., pp. 319ff.

120. Minutes of a meeting of the War Cabinet, 4 March 1919, WC 541, CAB 23/15.
121. Stanwood, op. cit., pp. 74 and 238.
122. See n. 98.
123. Ibid.
124. See pp. 140–52.
125. Minutes of the Eastern Committee, 26 September 1918, *EC* 33, secret, CAB 27/24.
126. Minutes of a meeting of the War Cabinet, 1 November 1918, WC 495, CAB 23/8.
127. Minutes of the Imperial War Cabinet, 23 December 1918, IWC 5, CAB 23/42. It is notable, however, that, as Ullman has observed, by the terms of the Armistice of Mudros and owing to the fear of Bolshevik atrocities on the departure of German troops from the Crimea, Ukraine and Black Sea Coast, the Allies did not envisage the immediate departure of German troops from those regions; Ullman, vol. 2, p. 44.
128. Stanwood, op. cit., p. 197. Whilst, as Ullman argues, during 1918 the relative geographical isolation of Caucasia and Trans-Caspia may have rendered more remote the connection between British intervention there and British relations with the Bolsheviks than her intervention elsewhere in Russia, British policy in both areas had for some time been contributing to the deterioration in Anglo-Bolshevik relations. Whilst recent research supports the contention that for much of 1918 British officials found it difficult to conceive of a militarily powerful and hostile Bolshevik Russia, British policy in those regions was from the end of 1917 influenced by this possibility; see Hopkirk, op. cit., pp. 259, 263. By July 1918, as Hopkirk observes, the possibility seemed more immediate with Stalin's directive ordering the arrest of all Allied missions and businessmen in the Caucasus. Also, the experiences of British officers on the ground suggested an increasingly overt anti-Bolshevik emphasis in Allied policy. Ibid., pp. 279, 311.
129. Minutes of a meeting of the War Cabinet, 14 November 1918, and appendix, WC 502, CAB 23/8. Curzon did not attend the Conference, at which the following were present: Balfour, Milner, Cecil, Hardinge, Clerk, DNI, DMI, DMO.
130. Ibid. Foreign Office Conference.
131. Commander-in-Chief of the anti-Bolshevik forces of Southern Russia during 1918–19.
132. Minutes of a meeting of the War Cabinet, 14 November 1918, WC 502, CAB 23/8. My italics.
133. Stanwood op. cit., p. 237.
134. Envoy Extraordinary and Minister Plenipotentiary, Christiana, 1 February 1911.
135. Findlay to Foreign Office, 10 October 1918, Christiana, no. 3616, FO 371/3344, p. 9.
136. See, for example, Alston to Foreign Office, 6 November 1918, no. 214, FO 371/3342, pp. 56–7.
137. Carr worked in the Russia Section of the War Department at the Foreign Office.
138. Minutes by Carr, 2 November 1918, FO 371/3342; 11 October 1918, FO 371/3344, p. 8.
139. Ibid. Minute of 2 November 1918.
140. Minute by Leeper, 14 October 1918, submitted to War Cabinet as (confidential) PID Memorandum, 'The Growing Danger of Bolshevism in Russia', 25 October 1918, FO 371/3344, pp. 37–40.
141. Ibid. Note on p. 39 of Leeper's minute of 14 October 1918.
142. PID Memorandum, 1 November 1918, 'The Future of Trans-Caucasia with Special Regard to British Interests' (Special 005), FO 371/3301, pp. 251ff.
143. Minutes by Clerk, 22 November 1918 and Balfour, n.d., FO 371/3344, p. 434.
144. Entry of 5 November 1918, Diaries of Field Marshal Sir Henry Wilson, reel 8.

145. Minute by Radcliffe, 13 November 1918, WO 106/315.
146. Stanwood, op. cit., p. 142; see n. 136.
147. Ibid. See Stanwood, p. 229, on Smuts, who had expressed this fear at the Eastern Committee of 5 December 1918.
148. Minute by Cecil, c. 21 October 1918, FO 371/3344, p. 54.

ᏇᎾ 6 ᏇᎾ

From the Turkish Armistice to the Foreign Office: 'All the Pieces on the Table'

SHADOWS IN THE PICTURE

IN THE FIRST days of 1919 there was a tangible note of optimism in the minds of several senior figures. To Sir Percy Cox, who had done so much to lay the edifice of British imperialism in the Middle East, the question of Persia loomed large. Writing to Curzon on 13 January, Cox expressed the hope that in Persia Britain would 'take a serious line, with a definite objective'. It was, Cox added, 'a clear duty to civilisation that she should be taken in hand'. In Cox's view, Britain was the only power fitted to the task. To Cox, surveying the region as a whole, the Pax Britannica emerged triumphant from the conflict:

> They had a splendid finish in Mesopotamia and I was very sorry to have missed it: we hardly hoped to be able to dispose of the Mosul Vilayet too when I was at home – it is a grand sphere now and I hope we shall be left in peace there by the Conference. It is glorious to feel in such a strong position everywhere, with a strong Government and the nation solid behind it. How one must rejoice to have lived in this generation.[1]

Robert Cecil, ever mindful of American opinion, was equally sanguine when reporting to Curzon, several days before Cox, a meeting with a Professor Judson, an American, recently returned from the Middle East. In the case of Mesopotamia, Cecil noted, Judson

> said it would be a crime against civilisation for British control to be removed for many years. The natural resources of the country were incredibly rich, and it would become one of the granaries of the world. The work accomplished by the British since their occupation was excellent in all respects. The populations were free and happy, justice was administered, life and property were secure. There were no shadows in his picture.[2]

Having been in close contact with Cox in Tehran, Judson was whole-heartedly behind Cox and, as Cecil remarked, the proposals of the Eastern Committee in favouring a strong British presence. This would be reflected in the appointing of British 'administrators' to all the principal Persian offices and the creation of a uniform force under British control; pending which, British troops should be maintained. Perplexed by the unstable position in the Caucasus, Judson had praised highly the Commander of British troops in the region, General Thompson, regarding the British presence at Baku as 'the only thing that kept the various sections of the population from flying at one another's throats'. Moreover, as Cecil added, Judson appeared to support British control of the Batum–Baku Railway 'with the right to intervene in case of disorder'.[3]

This was music to Curzon's ears. Newly installed at the Foreign Office where, according to Lloyd George, he 'beamed all over at being in charge', such reports tied in exactly with the conception of British involvement in the region evolved by Curzon in previous months.[4] Presented in such terms the crucial question of international opinion seemed scarcely to impinge upon Curzon's ambitious imperial formulae. An examination of the development of this theme in the minds of prominent statesmen suggests that Curzon's jubilation at the outset of 1919 was misplaced and that, in broader terms, it was a false dawn.

For some time before Curzon's Acting Foreign Secretaryship, debate had occurred at the highest levels about the nature of American co-operation with the Allies and the probable effect of this upon British imperial policies. At the height of the *Drang nach Osten* scare Milner wrote to Lloyd George impressing upon him the possibility of France and Italy being subdued by German arms: 'In that case', Milner warned, 'the German-Austro-Turko-Bulgar bloc will be master of all Europe and Northern and Central Asia up to the point at which Japan steps in to bar the way, if she does step in and has not been choked off by the more than disastrous diplomacy of the Allies.'[5]

As we have seen, such thoughts reflected the feelings of many senior figures on the issue. Milner differed from most in taking the nature of the perceived threat one stage further. It was, in Milner's view, a struggle for control of 'the whole world'. Naturally, Milner perceived earlier than most the need for an antidote on a corresponding scale, envisaging the knitting together, 'in the closest conceivable alliance', and readiness 'for the maximum of sacrifice' of Britain, America and the Dominions. With the Dominion leaders in London it seemed essential to Milner that Lloyd George should impress upon them the need for greater contributions in the way of resources if they were to see it through. Such contributions would be vital to sustain Allied fortunes if, as Milner feared, hostilities persisted into 1919. It was precisely with the requirements of a 'New War' in mind that Milner emphasised the need to have President Wilson drop '*co-belligerency*' or 'whatever half way house he loves to shelter himself in'. Otherwise, Milner observed, the anti-German forces would lack 'sufficient cohesion and inner strength'.[6]

Writing to Lloyd George a week later, Leo Amery reinforced Milner's message but had evidently considered the matter more deeply. A 'natural obstinacy' and unwillingness to accept 'an unsatisfactory peace' might, in Amery's view, ensure continued American efforts on behalf of the Allies in the event of a collapse on the Western Front. It appeared to Amery that, if skilfully organised, American policy might be influenced to the advantage of the Allies by the speeches of British and Dominion leaders. As Amery added, ever with an eye to British gains, a programme of complete re-education would be unnecessary:

> While not particularly sympathetic to the idea of our retaining the German Colonies she has learnt, or should be made to learn enough to make her object strongly to their restoration to Germany. She certainly also has a very healthy prejudice against restoring any territory to Turkish misrule. Nor, in view of her interests in China and the East, is she likely to be willing to see an immense German Empire extending to the frontiers of China, with its naval bases on the Indian Ocean and in the Pacific.

Moreover, according to Amery, it might in certain circumstances be desirable to draw America into a supervisory capacity on a temporary basis in the Belgian Congo.[7] It is an interesting commentary on Amery's thinking that, while the fate of the world hung in the balance, his vision should be fixed along this lateral plain. Milner, though sharing Amery's ideas on forward defence was, as we shall see, less inclined to lower his sights from a conception of a post-war order rooted in the mandatory principle and a perception of this order as imposing responsibilities on, rather than offering opportunities to, free nations working in common cause.

Aware of the limitations of idealism, Amery instead proceeded to devote his energies to the salvation of the world; a predominantly British world in which, notwithstanding the alleged immediacy of German domination, American support would be enlisted on terms. Precisely what those terms might be and what, in accordance with the

views of Sir Robert Borden, the Canadian Premier, America might herself obtain in the way of territorial gains, was a matter on which Amery
elaborated in the following months. Simply stated, Amery wished to
'educate' the American people about the nature of the British Empire.
Of primary importance, however, was Amery's strong aversion to the
introduction of American influence into any region such as East Africa
or the Middle East. Installed in either region, America would find free
scope for her own imperial ambitions and, most likely, this would
impinge upon the 'All-Red' route to India.[8] As Amery observed in a
letter to Smuts of 1 November 1918, there were other factors involved,
not least the puzzling issue of why Britain and not France should forfeit
territory:

> France is to get Alsace-Lorraine, which in present value is much more than
> any colonial territory; she is to get practically as much in Africa, and fully
> as much, if not more, in Turkey, whereas we, who stand not only for the
> United Kingdom, but for the Dominions as well, are supposed to be
> offending the conscience of humanity if we get anything. It all comes from
> the wrong conception of the British Empire as the property of the United
> Kingdom. If we regard it as what it really is – a group of nations – it seems
> absurd that those nations should not each be entitled to put forward their
> legitimate claims for their security, and should be regarded as collectively
> less entitled to anything than a single country like France.[9]

The important point, as Amery had written earlier, was to have the
American population 'sound in its general attitude towards the British
Commonwealth and towards East Africa and Eastern questions in
particular, before we get to grips in any Allied or international Con-
ference'.[10] As Amery argued, this might best be achieved by sending
Smuts to Canada and America.[11] Above all, as Amery told Curzon and
Lloyd George on 19 October, Britain must not accept a 'bad settlement'
in order to avoid offending America.[12]

It was partly in view of the mercurial activities of Lloyd George that
Amery had hoped to invest the issue with some immediacy. Though
characteristically evasive, it seems that Lloyd George was more sceptical
than most about the chances of America assuming mandatory functions.
Moreover, although he paid lip-service to visions of Anglo-American
friendship as the single most important outcome of the conflict, he was in
these deliberations ever the tactician and ruthless in abandoning any
doctrines which did not suit his immediate purposes. As far as Amery
was aware, Lloyd George's waywardness extended only to his willing-

ness to see America installed in East Africa.[13] However, early in October 1918 in an after-dinner conversation with Cecil, Bonar Law and Hankey, Lloyd George had revealed his hand. According to Hankey, Lloyd George had expressed a desire to reverse Sykes–Picot so as to obtain Palestine and Mosul and to keep France out of Syria. As Hankey proceeded:

> He also had some subtle dodge for asking America to take Palestine and Syria, in order to render the French more anxious to give us Palestine, so that they might have an excuse of keeping Syria. He was also very contemptuous of President Wilson and anxious to arrange the division of Turkey between France, Italy and Great Britain before speaking to America. He also thought it would attract less attention to our enormous gains in this war, if we swallowed our share of Turkey now, and the German Colonies later.[14]

Predictably, as Hankey recorded, Cecil's views on Sykes–Picot led him to a rather different conclusion: that Britain should stick to America 'at all costs' and that the Americans should be brought 'into the controversy at once'.[15] While reflecting on the nature of French and Italian claims contained in Sykes–Picot and on the probable tenacity of the French in pursuit of these, Smuts encapsulated the views of several statesmen on Anglo-American relations:

> In this matter America alone can help us. The Sykes–Picot agreement is in flagrant contradiction to all our openly professed ideal war aims, and it is a direct negation of the policy which President Wilson stands for. President Wilson must veto it and the similar bargains made with Italy.
>
> This means that we must from the very start of the Conference cooperate with America, and encourage and support President Wilson as far as is consistent with our own interests. In doing so, we are only following the line of our true policy for the future which will no doubt link the two great democratic Commonwealths in a common destiny.[16]

The extent to which any conception of Anglo-Saxon kinship might underpin the future of the British Empire was revealed at meetings of the Imperial War Cabinet later in December, when the issue was discussed in its wider aspects. The context in which the question arose on 20 December was the future of the German Colonies and this setting clearly did not provide Lloyd George with an opportunity to break cover as he had done in conclave with select colleagues. Though emphatic that the former German Colonies captured by Dominion troops must be retained by the Dominion concerned, in other respects

Lloyd George was obliged to be circumspect. Borden agreed with this argument but he effectively nipped in the bud any purely imperialistic digressions from the essential point of securing close Anglo-American relations by suggesting that as far as the other conquered territories were concerned, these should be entrusted to mandatory powers under the League of Nations.[17]

Having hinted at the possibility of drawing America into East Africa and taking his cue from a remark by Curzon that America might not accept such responsibilities but might have to accept them in Constantinople, Lloyd George dropped his guard. Responding to what Curzon intended as the literal meaning of his remark, that America probably would not accept any mandate, Lloyd George suggested that if Britain at least offered something to America then she would be absolved from any suggestion of 'land-grabbing'. Deftly removing the other prop of those preoccupied with American influence, Lloyd George observed:

> It was not a question of annexation, but of assuming a responsibility. These territories could not be left to be exploited by Arabs or by European capitalists without a strong Government to control them. He did not consider that we could postpone this matter till the League of Nations was actually set up. President Wilson was now inclined to keep Germany out of the League of Nations in the near future, so that the League of Nations for the present would, in fact, be nothing more than the existing Allied Conference. We could hardly put off the question till the League of Nations was completed. British and Dominion public opinion would not tolerate our giving back territories after we had held them for nine or ten years, whereas it might accept a transfer of some of the captured territory as part of the general settlement.[18]

What a pity, then, that the Dominion leaders might not leave directly and permit Lloyd George, Curzon and others to proceed with the real business of dividing the spoils. That this was the object of the assembled statesmen was revealed by the ensuing ruck in which the territorial claims of British and Dominion leaders were thoroughly aired. Anticipating this scramble, Milner suggested that it would be wise first to dwell upon the mandatory principle and, if this was accepted, 'we could then invite the United States, in a general way, to become one of the mandatories and share in the "white man's burden," before beginning to discuss in detail the particular region in which she has to exercise her mandate'.[19]

A brief reflection on the nature of mandatory control failed to subdue the acquisitive appetites of those present; the tenor of the discussion being reflected in Montagu's remark that 'it would be very satisfactory if we could find some convincing argument for not annexing all the territories in the world'.[20] It was also reflected in the fact that the only allusion to self-determination was made by Curzon and, predictably, in the context of Palestine where, if that doctrine were applied, Britain would find herself in charge. Milner alone articulated a broader concept of international affairs as he surveyed his colleagues picking the carcass:

> Lord Milner said that he wished to get America in any case. He considered the future peace of the world depended on a good understanding between us, and regarded this policy of a mandate by the League of Nations, not as a mere cloak for annexation, but as a bond of union leading to better working between the United States and ourselves. The essential thing was that we should survey the whole field from that point of view.[21]

Curzon simply was not prepared to be constrained by such considerations, notwithstanding indications that President Wilson attached paramount importance to the establishing of the League as the first action of the Peace Conference. In fact, such was Curzon's optimism that when, at a further meeting of the Imperial War Cabinet on 30 December, Lloyd George and Balfour divulged this, Curzon reinforced it by stating that Wilson had previously advised this course because the apportioning of mandates could not occur until the League had been created.[22]

Curzon's optimism lay in Wilson's apparent ambiguity as to what powers might actually pertain to the League. More importantly, when recalling that Balfour had suggested to Wilson that the Eastern Committee had favoured America assuming a mandate in Constantinople, Lloyd George commented:

> With regard to this, President Wilson had pointed out that the United States were extremely proud of their disinterested position in this war and did not wish to be deprived of that pride. It would be difficult to persuade them that such a mandate was not a profit, but really a burden. Altogether he had shown himself very much opposed to any intervention on the part of the United States in these territorial questions.[23]

Equally, when asked about the provision of troops for Armenia, Wilson had been equivocal. Evidently, Curzon, having convinced himself that America probably would not assume a mandate, kept the suggestion alive as a tactical ploy. Apparently, when asked by Curzon if America would take either Constantinople or Armenia, Wilson had stated that he

should be led 'a little more slowly up to his fences; that, if the League
of Nations were once constituted and the Conference had been sitting
some time, the United States might possibly be less reluctant to consider
the question of mandatory intervention'.

To Curzon, Britain, not America, must dictate the peace. At the very
end of 1918, Curzon believed that his personal fortunes lay, as ever, in
the defence of British imperial interests. With the prodigious labours of
the Eastern Committee behind him, Curzon was anxious not to be in
the wilderness in the forthcoming negotiations.[24] The League of Nations
was not the kind of thing to thwart such hopes or to prevent the British
Empire from wielding its rightfully predominating influence in the final
settlement. Such, at least, was the message conveyed by Curzon to
Hankey in response to his request for advice as to whether he should
accept the job of Secretary of the League. Confessing his doubts
'whether the League . . . is going to be the great and potent and world
pacifying instrument that its creators desired', Curzon warned that
Hankey would 'be serving a multitude of masters', that the League
would 'experience many a great disappointment' and that it might, in
fact, fail to achieve its aims. To Curzon, distraught with avuncular concern, it seemed that Hankey might squander his talents if these were
pledged to 'anything so impersonal and soulless as an international
bureau'. As Curzon continued, there was a greater challenge nearer to
home:

> if you remain in England you will be mainly responsible for converting the
> War Cabinet into a Peace Cabinet, for constituting the Imperial Cabinet of
> the future, and for moulding the future organisation of the British Empire.
> These are great, imminent and inevitable problems. Their solution will be
> a signpost in the history of the Empire and in the progress of the world.[25]

The juxtaposition of these factors in Curzon's mind was the corner-
stone of his life's work and it was, equally, his primary concern at the
Imperial War Cabinet at the very end of 1918 when Lloyd George was,
in his opinion, in danger of attaching too much importance to American
opinion. This was true on a wide range of matters, yet Curzon, surprisingly perhaps, was much less outspoken than might have been
expected. Partly this was due to a fear of exclusion should his opinions
be regarded as politically incorrect, and to his confidence that if he bided
his time the League would fizzle out leaving a clear field for British
expansion. More obviously, Curzon had no reason to risk his neck
because many of his thoughts were articulated at length by Hughes, the

Australian leader, when the latter argued that Britain must avoid being 'dragged quite unnecessarily behind the wheel of President Wilson's chariot'. Hughes

> readily acknowledged the part which America had played in the war. But it was not such as to entitle President Wilson to be the god in the machine at the peace settlement, and to lay down the terms on which the world would have to live in the future. The United States had made no money sacrifices at all. They had not even exhausted the profits which they made in the first two and a half years of the war. In men, their sacrifices were not even equal to those of Australia. Relatively their sacrifices had been nothing like as much as those of Australia.

As Hughes implied, faced with American arrogance Britain and France might collude to achieve their respective national aims but 'give America the respect due to a great nation which had entered the war somewhat late but had rendered great service'. Moreover, Hughes felt that Wilson's conception of the League was both considerably vague and too inflexible. The first object must be to secure adequate rewards for the sacrifices made by the Empire. Then and only then should any remaining matters be passed to the League. As Hughes emphasised: 'Such a League must, however, be properly constituted, and one in which the British Empire occupied a place corresponding to its sacrifices in the war and its position in the world.'

Expressing his concurrence with Hughes's analysis, Curzon emphasised that Lloyd George would enter the Peace Conference with 'an authority fully equal, and indeed superior, to that of President Wilson'. This was true by virtue of the recent election, the sacrifices made by the Empire and the diverse imperial interests the world over. Whilst succumbing momentarily to temptation by admitting that although the 'fortunes of the world' depended upon Anglo-American co-operation and that, on some matters, Britain might have to side with France, Curzon was hastily rebuked, first by Reading, Britain's Ambassador in Washington, and then by Borden, the latter claiming that Canada would not support an Imperial policy which depended for its success on Britain co-operating with a European power against America. That influential colleagues such as Robert Cecil perceived the creation of the League as being the tangible expression of Anglo-American co-operation was no reason for despondency on Curzon's part. In any case, Cecil held that the Conference should pronounce on several important matters before the League had been established. As Curzon realised, all of this

MAP 4.   THE MIDDLE EAST

was highly speculative. Assuming it were achieved and, in accordance with Milner's views, the discussion then proceeded to an examination of what territorial responsibilities America might assume, then this haze of speculation became impenetrable. Such also was Amery's view, writing on December 20 in a highly imaginative memorandum entitled 'The United States and the Occupied Enemy Territories'. Adding his voice to the chorus, Amery suggested: 'To place Anglo-American relations on a permanent footing of mutual understanding and co-operation is the most important external object that the British Empire can aim at as the outcome of the war.' This might only be achieved if Britain and America assumed mandatory responsibilities in keeping with the wishes of the indigenous populations concerned. In Amery's view, when combined with strategic factors this would, realistically, present America with the option of Turkey, including Constantinople, and Belgian and Portuguese West Africa; failing which, she might obtain Armenia and territorial adjustments in West Africa or Central and South America. There was no question in Amery's mind of America partaking in the richer spoils of East Africa, Mesopotamia or Palestine.[26]

THE FUTURE OF PALESTINE

Discussions in the second half of 1918 about America assuming mandatory functions were partly occasioned by Sir Robert Borden. At meetings of the Imperial War Cabinet in the summer of 1918, Borden argued forcefully against Britain obtaining, either in fact or in appearance, large additions to her territory. In Borden's opinion, it would not be to Britain's advantage if America, with her vast potential and her increasing influence in international affairs, received nothing. Precisely how America might be included in the distribution of the spoils was unclear, but at the Imperial War Cabinet on 13 August, in suggesting that America might assume supervisory functions in Palestine, Lord Reading introduced one of the overriding factors in the debate.[27]

Quite where or how this idea originated is unclear. Possibly Mark Sykes, in attempting to escape from the consequences of internationalisation, was its first proponent. Writing to Picot in February 1917, in connection with a conversation with Sokolov, of the international Zionist movement, Sykes rejected internationalisation as unworkable. He then rejected, in turn, supervision by Belgium, Switzerland, Spain and the Scandinavian countries. As Sykes continued, American supervision, if attainable, would be convenient in terms both of inter-Allied relations and regarding 'internal questions of religious and racial importance'. Further, an American occupation of Palestine 'would have no immediate military importance, nor could it have any political or strategic sequellae that we need anticipate with apprehension'.

Although Sykes's letter is not clear on this point it seems that he envisaged a fifty-year occupation by America after which her position there would be re-examined. Such, along with various other provisos affecting the rights of the local populations and international interests, was the basis of Sykes's reasoning.[28]

The interest of several senior figures in the idea of an American mandate in Palestine upon Reading's resuscitation of it in August 1918 provoked energetic lobbying on the part of Leo Amery, to whom the proposal appeared thoroughly bad. During 1917 Amery had struggled to impress upon senior colleagues the need to retain Palestine under British control both as a means of thwarting *Drang nach Osten* and of securing the 'All-Red' route to India. By mid-1918, Amery had not developed that sensitivity to American opinion which, in future months, was to afflict most British strategists, himself included. Writing to Lloyd George on 8 June, Amery suggested that his leadership must reflect the traditions of the British people with their watchwords of 'the meek shall inherit the earth', the main-spring of British imperial expansion. To Amery it seemed that wartime expansion was incidental and would be brought about simply by Britain's efforts on behalf of the common cause in Europe and, elsewhere, in self-defence. As Amery continued, if the British Empire emerged stronger from the conflict, who had the right to complain?

> Not the peoples whom we shall guide instead of leaving them to German rule. Not our Allies for whom we have spent ourselves more unselfishly than, I believe, any nation has done in any war. Not America who, for all her professions, is never above a little quiet annexation, has in fact already occupied Hayti and San Domingo during this war without a word said to anyone, and will no doubt pick up a good many more trifles before the war is over.[29]

Amery's haste in dampening enthusiasm for Reading's proposal was indicative of the extent to which he believed American influence would destroy that southern British world which he aspired to create. On this basis Amery wrote to Smuts and Lloyd George on 16 August, arguing that to invite American involvement either in Palestine or East Africa would inevitably lead to friction.[30] Not only would America find herself unable to cope with 'an indigestible lump of unfamiliar problems at the other end of the world', but it disregarded the 'natural lines' along which Britain and America might respectively orientate their strategic doctrines. According to Amery several Monroe doctrines might be created; the British one extending from South Africa through Southern Asia to India. Given the potential gains open to a resurgent Germany, the wealth and physical scope of Lorraine and the actual and prospective American territorial gains, British ambitions, so described, appeared quite modest to Amery.[31]

Amery emphasised that he was, like Borden, averse to America's receiving nothing. For one thing America might be rendered amenable to important British gains if she obtained compensation herself. If, for humanitarian or other reasons, this ploy worked, then it seemed to Amery that America might be more inclined to swallow the bait if her imperial interests were first aroused by military involvement before the war's end and, especially, in territories close to home.[32] As 'hypothetical cases', Amery instanced Siberia and Mexico. Less intangible was Belgian restoration and the connected matter of the Congo, a prospect with the double appeal of greater accessibility than Palestine or East Africa and the fact that it would not require physical occupation by America – thereby removing the animus of annexation. Similar opportunities might also exist in West Africa. However, to attempt to interest America in areas conquered by Britain with which she had neither historic nor commercial links would, in Amery's view, simply alienate broad sections of opinion in America and the Dominions. In this preliminary counterblast Amery also defined specific reasons why America should not have Palestine.

Crucially, Amery argued that, in terms of culture, commerce and economics, Palestine could not be dissociated from surrounding Arab countries. Whilst Kantara on the Suez Canal would be the main port of Palestine, in the future it might also be the main outlet for the passenger traffic of Syria and Mesopotamia. To introduce American influence would, in Amery's opinion, compound the folly of meeting French claims in Syria but with the additional factor of American inexperience. Moreover, whilst Amery accepted that America, if installed in Palestine, might provide a buffer for Britain in Egypt, unlike proponents of this idea such as Hankey, Amery felt that the importance of imperial communications rendered its inclusion within the British sphere essential.[33] Amery advanced similar arguments on the subject of

East Africa but in both cases, it seems, he felt that it would be to Britain's financial advantage if her interests were arranged in economically and strategically interdependent blocks.[34]

With what success Amery impressed his views upon senior figures is difficult to measure with precision. However, Amery's arguments were not lost on Curzon and when reiterated by Curzon at the Eastern Committee and at the Imperial War Cabinet, in some cases in substantially the same form in which they were presented by Amery, they encountered little opposition.[35] Moreover, although Lloyd George played a more devious game, at meetings of the Imperial War Cabinet Curzon and Lloyd George claimed that whilst previously in favour of placing America in Palestine they were no longer so inclined.

Writing to Curzon and Lloyd George on 19 October Amery had re-emphasised that such was the interdependence of Palestine with surrounding countries, its problems could not be considered in isolation. For one thing, Amery held that racial affiliations rendered necessary the treatment on similar lines of Arabs and Jews throughout the Middle East. Notably, Amery anticipated that the question of Jewish settlement would quickly spread to the rest of the region. Amery then repeated earlier arguments about the necessity of incorporating Palestine into a broader regional economy, again alluding to the importance of Kantara being included within this and in the possession of the power entrusted with the development of Palestine. As Amery continued, on grounds of defence strategy the power controlling Egypt must also hold Palestine and, for purposes of mutual support and to outpace submarine warfare, a land through-route to Baghdad must be established. In America's possession, Palestine would not benefit from free commercial and other intercourse with neighbouring countries and, accordingly, neither Kantara nor Haifa would be fully developed. American inexperience in administering such territories would inevitably harm Anglo-American relations and, as Amery was envisaging the creation of a British protectorate in Palestine, he felt that American citizenship would not confer on the inhabitants of Palestine the same benefits as would incorporation into the heart of Britain's Empire in the Middle East. Amery's logic then took an intriguing turn. In his view, arguments for territorial contiguity rendered a French presence in Syria undesirable. Palestine might in the future depend more upon intercourse with Egypt, trans-Jordan and Mesopotamia than with Syria. However, as Amery suggested, to the extent that it did apply 'it is a strong argument for trying to induce the French to transfer their sphere of interest elsewhere'.[36]

If, as Amery continued, territory east of the Jordan were eventually incorporated into Palestine then this was added reason for the inclusion of both Palestine and Syria within the sphere of one power. Concluding his letter with a disclaimer against any outright demand by Britain to obtain the 'trusteeship' of Palestine as her part of the spoils, Amery invested his thoughts with broader appeal by suggesting that 'we should not pre-judge the settlement against ourselves by actively advocating an American solution. The really deciding factor ought in any case to be the wishes of the Arabs and Jews.'[37]

Curzon's response to Amery has not survived but a further letter from Amery written on 22 October, in which he sought to reassure Curzon as to the general direction of policy, suggests a substantial element of common ground. Rather than 'clamouring' to America 'for Palestine as well as all the territories which it is essential that we should retain control of after the war', Amery concurred in Curzon's view that Britain must instead rely upon the opinion of the Arabs and Jews. As Amery suggested, this would also scupper French ambitions in Syria. Having repeated the arguments in favour of directing American energies towards the West African seaboard or Eastern Siberia, Amery suggested that by the time peace discussions on outlying areas got underway 'President Wilson will have so much hay on his own fork that he won't take too pedantic a view of what we are doing'.[38]

Previously, Curzon and Amery had collaborated on the future of Palestine. As, respectively, Chairman and Secretary of the Territorial Committee, Curzon and Amery had gone some way to instilling in the psyche of Dominion leaders the importance of retaining Palestine within Britain's sphere. In fact, Curzon was hoping for rather more than that. At the third meeting of the Committee on 19 April 1917 he informed his colleagues that the Sykes–Picot Agreement had left the status of Palestine 'undetermined' and that France was 'very jealously attempting to peg out claims . . . by trying to send out a General of high rank to participate in our approaching campaign in that region'.[39] The minutes continue:

> In his [Curzon's] opinion the only safe settlement was that Palestine should be included in a British protectorate. He understood that the Zionists in particular would be very much opposed to Palestine being under any other flag or under a condominium. He considered that the British Government ought to make a very strong effort to secure a clear definition of our position in Palestine.[40]

Curzon would certainly have cause to regret the association of Zionism so strongly with a British protectorate. However, as Smuts told the Committee, on grounds of strategy and imperial communications British possession of Palestine was a prerequisite, and in the report of the Committee it was recommended that Britain should try to obtain modification of Sykes–Picot so as to obtain 'definite and exclusive control over Palestine'. A further clause suggested that a railway connecting Egypt, Palestine, Mesopotamia, and the Persian Gulf 'is an object to be kept steadily in view'.[41]

As Chairman of the Mesopotamian Administration Committee and of the bodies which replaced it, Curzon had ample opportunity to reflect on the increasingly sensitive and hotly contested issue of international rights in Palestine. Relations between Britain, France and Italy in Palestine were worsened by chauvinism and by rivalries over the possession of the Holy Places. When, early in 1918, Allenby was asked to appoint French and Italian officers to important positions on his staff, he had replied that it would be difficult to comply with this request at present but that there might be openings for Sanitary Officers.[42] Apparently dissatisfied with this reply the Middle East Committee, for 'diplomatic reasons', reissued the original instruction; whereupon Allenby again refused to comply with it.[43] Curzon's desire to see Britain installed in Palestine was seriously undermined by a catalogue of incidents which occurred during 1918. More importantly there was the question of Zionism, an issue of growing concern to Curzon from an early stage which led him periodically to question the wisdom of the British mandate.

In a memorandum entitled 'The Future of Palestine', dated 26 October 1917, Curzon questioned the nature of the commitments into which Britain was entering by virtue of her support for the creation of 'a National Home for the Jewish Race in Palestine'. In the first place it seemed to Curzon that there was considerable ambiguity both within and outside government circles about what was meant by this phrase. Broadly there were two groups, the first represented by those such as Sir Alfred Mond[44] who appeared to contemplate ' "an autonomous Jewish State" . . . ie., a political entity, composed of Jews, governed by Jews, and administered mainly in the interests of Jews'. Curzon's memorandum continued: 'Such a State might naturally be expected to have a capital, a form of government, and institutions of its own. It would possess the soil or the greater part of the soil of the country. It would take its place among the smaller nations of the earth.' This and other similar models suggested to Curzon that to some of its adherents Zionism meant the re-creation of Palestine as it was before the dispersion. The second body as defined by Curzon aspired to the creation in Palestine of a religious and cultural centre for Jewish people.[45]

Curzon simply was not convinced that Palestine in its present condition of physical ruin would be able to support a substantially increased population. Advisedly, perhaps, the comparison which sprang to Curzon's mind in arriving at this conclusion was that of Wales, slightly smaller in size than Palestine. At any rate there was much to be done in the way of afforestation and irrigation before any revival would be possible, and Curzon evidently had little time for the romanticised images of biblical Palestine held by Lloyd George and others:

> The scriptural phrase, a land 'flowing with milk and honey', which suggests an abounding fertility, must be read in relation to the desert features of Sinai, to which it stood in glowing contrast, and loses somewhat of its picturesque charm when we realise that the milk was that of the flocks of goats that roamed, and still roam, the hills, while the honey was the juice of the small grape that was used as a substitute for sugar and still makes a palatable wine.

In Curzon's view, the settlement of those accustomed to more northerly climates would only be possible in the higher parts of the country and Palestine was, moreover, badly affected by disease. Although sections of the country with suitable climate and adequate water supply produced excellent crops of wheat and barley, it was, Curzon argued, essentially a pastoral economy with no indigenous mineral resources:

> Such is the country – a country calling for prolonged and patient toil from a people inured to agriculture – and even so only admitting after generations of a relatively small population – that we are invited (if we can get hold of it, which we have not yet done) to convert into the national home of a people, numbering many millions, brought from other and different climates, and to a large extent trained in other industries and professions.

As to the existing population of Arabs, as Curzon suggested, they would not accept expropriation for the Jews nor would they be willing 'to act merely as hewers of wood and drawers of water to the latter'. Furthermore, the ethnography of Palestine appeared extremely complex to Curzon and this was compounded by competing religious claims.

Given the nature of the country Curzon doubted whether Britain should commit herself to any of the more expansive Zionist claims. Realistically, Britain might aspire to establish in Palestine a European, non-Jewish administration which would confer equal civil and religious rights on all elements of the population, Jews included. Moreover, provision might be made for land purchase and settlement for returning Jews, and steps should be taken to safeguard the integrity of, and order in, Jewish, Christian and Moslem Holy Places. Curzon concluded:

> If this is Zionism there is no reason why we should not all be Zionists, and I would gladly give my adhesion to such a policy, all the more that it appears to be recommended by considerations of the highest expediency, and to be urgently demanded as a check or counterblast to the scarcely concealed and sinister political designs of the Germans. But in my judgement it is a policy very widely removed from the romantic and idealistic aspirations of many of the Zionist leaders whose literature I have studied, and, whatever it does, it will not in my judgement provide either a national, a material, or even a spiritual home for any more than a very small section of the Jewish people.

Over a year later, at the Eastern Committee on 5 December 1918, as Curzon explained to his colleagues, his previous fears about the scope of Zionist ambitions and the friction to which they must lead had not been without foundation.[46] Since the Balfour Declaration it seemed to Curzon that Zionist aims had become daily more expansive. As Curzon observed: 'They now talk about a Jewish State. The Arab portion of the population is well-nigh forgotten and is to be ignored.' Not only did the Zionists 'claim the boundaries of the old Palestine', but they also proposed to colonise lands east of the Jordan.

Such ambitions were known to be causing concern among Faisal's followers but, more especially, among the Moslem population of Palestine who suspected Britain of duplicity, and were, in Curzon's view, leading to a 'situation which is becoming rather critical'. Especially worrying was that Faisal, whilst apparently willing to support limited Jewish immigration if Palestine were eventually entrusted to Britain, would 'back the Arabs [of Palestine] by all means in his power' if Britain were to have no further interests there. As Curzon observed, the antidote to such ills might be found, unexpectedly, in the Anglo-French Declaration which then appeared to threaten the prospect of Arabs and Jews playing off the Great Powers against each other.

Rejecting internationalisation as being 'singularly unsuited to the conditions of Palestine', Curzon proceeded to eliminate France as a possible tutelary power 'because . . . nobody wants her there', because this 'would be quite intolerable to ourselves, and . . . equally unwelcome to the people'. Confessing to previous sympathies for the idea of an American mandate, Curzon rejected the idea because of the friction which would arise between America and, on either side of her, France and Britain. As Curzon continued, besides delivering Palestine from the 'Crescent', Britain's occupation had been intended to enable the country to 'prosper and flourish under the Cross':

> If that is to be so, believe me, Palestine can only flourish and have any future before it if its interests – political, commercial, and otherwise – are considered in relation to the States that lie around it. You cannot treat Palestine as an insignificant little country – although it is nothing else really – which merely has to be kept from outside invasion; if you are to develop it you must develop it in connection with Syria in the north, Arabia on the east and Egypt on the south.

Again, recalling Amery's words, Curzon questioned whether America's being established in Palestine would not lead to constant friction with Britain in Egypt. Not only had America 'no experience of this sort of work or this kind of people', but her 'methods of work . . . [and] of handling Eastern people would be different from ours'.

To Curzon, Britain must therefore be prepared to consider assuming the Palestine mandate herself, especially as the commercial development of Palestine would be dictated by Egyptian factors. Given the condition of Palestine's ports, Curzon suggested that Palestinian trade would be directed through the Suez Canal and that Kantara would become the main commercial port. The argument for a British presence was strengthened by the need to regard Palestine as 'the strategical buffer of Egypt', the veracity of which had, in Curzon's view, been demonstrated by the war. However, as Curzon sought to explain, Britain must not be motivated purely by self-interest:

> Ought we not to try and keep the Arabs of Palestine in close touch with the Arabs of the country both to the east and to the north? If you, so to speak, segregate them under the charge of a separate Power which has no interests in those regions, you will really sterilize them and arrest their growth. On the other hand, our position and influence in the surrounding Arab areas must be always so great that the Arabs of Palestine would have, I think, a much better chance in our hands than in those of any others.

Most telling of all, Curzon held, was the 'conclusive' evidence that both Arabs and Zionists in Palestine wanted a British mandate and upon this essential point Britain should make her stand at the Peace Conference. Though a strong supporter of a British Palestine, Cecil did not wish entirely to discount the possibility of an American mandate. To Curzon's point that America probably would not assume any foreign commitments, Cecil replied that they might interest themselves in Constantinople or Palestine 'because of the great swagger of it'. However, when on 16 December the Eastern Committee discussed the resolutions on Palestine, Cecil dissociated himself from Balfour's objection to the clause which stated that, while Britain would not object to the selection of America, if Britain were to be asked then 'we ought not to decline'. Whilst Balfour feared that such an announcement might elicit accusations of acquisitiveness, Cecil felt that Britain's claim might have been expressed more strongly.[47]

LOST OPPORTUNITIES

Having striven successfully to obtain the support of his colleagues for a British mandate in Palestine, Curzon was particularly concerned by indications that the scope of Zionist ambitions might seriously jeopardise Britain's position in the country. It was precisely the danger of risking 'all that we have won' to which Curzon drew the attention of Balfour in mid-January 1919, when recalling an interview with the Chief Administrator of Palestine, Sir Alfred Money. According to Curzon, both Money and Allenby felt that Britain 'should go slow about the Zionist aspirations and the Zionist State'. If a Jewish government were introduced then, Curzon reported, an Arab rising would follow 'and the nine-tenths of the population who are not Jews would make short shrift with the Hebrews'. As Curzon stated, he had long shared this concern about 'the pretensions of Weizmann and Company' and a belief that they 'ought to be checked'.[48]

Evidence suggests that Curzon was giving expression to unease about Balfour's apparent lack of vigilance in his dealings with Weizmann; something which would also be commented upon by other senior figures later in 1919. In his response to Curzon's observation that had Balfour not thwarted a recent proposed declaration by the Zionists then considerable harm would have been done, Balfour replied that on his information Weizmann had 'never put forward a claim for the Jewish *Government* of Palestine'. Such a claim would, in Balfour's opinion, be 'inadmissible' and, in any case, as Balfour added, Britain should go no further than his original declaration to Rothschild.[49]

Curzon was not satisfied with this explanation, informing Balfour that he had 'no doubt' that in the near future Weizmann aspired to a Jewish government. As Curzon continued, this was clearly suggested in the language of the Declaration, which the latter had proposed to issue early in December 1918, in which Weizmann had employed the term 'commonwealth' interchangeably with 'National Home'. More seriously, when communicating to Eder, a member of the Zionist Commission,[50] the favourable results of discussions between Faisal and himself, Weizmann had spoken of the 'whole administration of Palestine' being so constituted as to make a Jewish Commonwealth under British trusteeship and that 'the Jews shall so participate in the administration as to assure this object'.[51] Moreover, according to Weizmann, Jews were to have 'extensive rights in regard to the taking over of land including the right of expropriating the effendis'.[52] To Curzon, continuing his letter to Balfour of 26 January, the import of this was clear:

> What all this can mean except Government I do not see. Indeed a Commonwealth as defined in every dictionary is a 'body politic', a 'state', an 'independent community', a 'republic'.
>
> I feel tolerably sure therefore that while Weizmann may say one thing to you or while you may mean one thing by a National Home, he is out for something quite different. He contemplates a Jewish State, a Jewish nation, a subordinate population of Arabs etc. ruled by Jews, the Jews in possession of the fat of the land, and directing the administration.
>
> He is trying to effect this behind the screen and under the shelter of British trusteeship.
>
> I do not envy those who wield the latter, when they realise the presence to which they are certain to be exposed.[53]

Curzon's disquiet regarding Zionism was understandable. Reliable information suggested that in Palestine the Jews were outnumbered by Arabs by approximately nine to one. Moreover, Curzon had been alerted to Faisal's attempts to enlist Jewish support in his struggle with France and this additional dimension assumed growing significance in the following months. Above all, Curzon wished to prevent the sanctioning by his colleagues in Paris of an announcement along the lines of the programme outlined by Weizmann in his letter to Eder. In Curzon's view, this would lead to 'disaster', to the establishing in Palestine of a 'Jewish Empire', and to the supplanting of Britain as the tutelary power.[54]

There was, in fact, good evidence to support Curzon's fears. Besides those of Weizmann's proposals already outlined, Eder had also been informed that Hebrew was to be the official language of the Jews in Palestine and that they would be allowed 'the widest practicable measure of self-government'. They would, moreover, have right of pre-emption of public works and a Jewish Congress would be established in Jerusalem. Included within the remit of that body would be land settlement and purchase, the promotion and organisation of immigration and, wherever possible, the supervision and control of concessions for public works. Weizmann also stipulated that Jews should have 'educational and cultural autonomy' and that the Sabbath and Jewish holidays should be legal days.[55] In January, Weizmann had complained to Kidston, of the Foreign Office, that in certain matters developments in Palestine were not consistent with the promises made by Balfour. Notably, Hebrew was not recognised as an official language and postage stamps still bore an Arabic (or Turkish) inscription. More seriously, Weizmann alleged that certain 'junior administrative officials', Storrs especially,[56] were 'showing signs of impatience with the Jews'. As Kidston recalled, he had pointed out that it was the Zionists rather than British officials who were guilty of impatience: 'Our Officers had many differing interests to reconcile and the Jews were making their task difficult by their importunity. They seemed to think that their national home must be handed over to them ready made at a moment's notice.'[57]

Equally aghast at Weizmann's proposals, G.F. Clayton had argued on the eve of 1919 that the 'rights of the voiceless many' must be preserved. In his view, Weizmann got the cart before the horse. The first step, according to Clayton, must be to create an administration in Palestine in such a way 'as to give practical effect to Mr Balfour's declaration and that Jews shall be increasingly employed therein'. This was predicated upon Clayton's belief that, in view of the overwhelming preponderance of non-Jews in Palestine, it would be 'highly injudicious to impose, except gradually, an alien and unpopular element which up to now has had no administrative experience'. In Clayton's view, the Zionists would establish themselves not by monopolising administrative positions but by contributing to the development of the country by means of the establishing of Jewish Colonies. Any thought of expropriating the larger Moslem landowners would lead to 'serious trouble' in Arab–Jewish relations.[58]

Further difficulties arose when it was revealed that Weizmann had obtained a paraphrase of Clayton's telegram and that he interpreted it as a sanction of his proposals by the Foreign Office.[59] Predictably, feeling within the Foreign Office unanimously favoured disabusing Weizmann of this illusion. Kidston was not immune to feelings of 'uneasiness' about Zionism, minuting on 27 February:

> It appears to be taken for granted that Great Britain is to be the tutelary power in that country. I venture to think that we shall never in any circumstances be the controlling power. Jewish aspirations, as may be seen from this and from all the other papers emanating from the Zionist Organisation, are unlimited, and the Jew will control his controller not only in Palestine but in every quarter of the Globe.[60]

If, as Kidston continued, Britain attempted to meet Zionist claims then this would arouse the hostility of France, of a revitalised Russia and would, moreover, as Kidston warned in true Buchanesque style, afford to Central Europe 'a nest in which to hatch out world-wide intrigues'. Alternatively, should Britain restrict Zionist ambitions, then it seemed likely to Kidston that Britain would simply turn the 'whole international machinery of Zionism . . . against us'. Moreover, it seemed to him that Britain could not now hope to escape responsibilities in Palestine. Any possibility of enticing the French into the country on grounds of it being 'an integral part of Syria' and under conditions imposed by the League of Nations appeared to have vanished. As Kidston recalled, whilst the French might previously 'have risen to the bait', they now realised 'that it contains a very sharp hook'. In fact, as Kidston observed, should Britain offer it to them, it 'would probably cause them very considerable embarrassment'.

In Kidston's view, Britain had also careered past a further escape route in failing to manipulate the supposed emotional susceptibility of America by means of 'a clever propaganda on sentimental and religious lines'.[61] With these options debarred there remained the unappetising possibility of reverting to an international solution.

To Curzon it was indeed a tale of lost opportunities. Recalling that he alone of the War Cabinet had opposed Zionism and had foreseen its dangers, Curzon noted that neither France nor America had seemed to be suitable neighbours for Britain in Egypt and, accordingly, as Curzon concluded, 'we must march up always with a self-imposed cross upon our shoulders'.[62] The spring of 1919 brought no relief in the Palestine question. In fact, it was with what Curzon termed 'a gloomy satisfaction' that on 25 March he wrote to Balfour recalling his previous warnings on the subject. Though it remained unclear who might replace Britain in Palestine, Curzon again expressed the hope that a proposed international investigatory commission[63] might relieve Britain of responsibilities there.[64] Conditions in Palestine worsened daily because of the activities of British officers who apparently acted in ignorance of the Balfour Declaration, and the public expression by Zionists of expansive ambitions was likely to fuel the flames.[65] With this in mind Curzon had reported to Balfour the published resolutions of a recent conference of Zionist leaders, which appeared to go further than previous expressions of Zionist ambitions and a considerable way towards the creation of the Jewish Empire which Curzon feared. Besides the official recognition of all Jewish holidays, the conference had agreed that there should be Jewish supervision of all educational institutions and that in all schools Hebrew should be the main language. With 'absolute control of immigration', 'immediate control of water-rights, carrying with it control of the land', the Jewish ascendancy would be established. This would be further assured by the Jewish nationalisation of all public land and of private estates of a certain size, and by complete control by Jews of all public works. It was, however, the prospect of the corresponding position of the native population and of the mandatory power attempting to fulfil its role which made Curzon 'shudder'.[66]

Balfour well knew that delays in the despatch of the international Commission compounded the situation. Both he and Curzon had received representations from Herbert Samuel to this effect, which also dwelt upon the unsympathetic attitude of British officers towards Zionism.[67] Whilst Balfour was endeavouring to have Palestine removed from the itinerary of the Commission, unease persisted about Balfour's relationship with the Zionist movement. Typical of this was Balfour's insistence, on the one hand, that Britain should not assume that she would obtain the Palestine mandate, and, on the other hand, his ambiguous position with regard to Zionist ambitions. To E.S. Montagu, an outspoken critic of the movement, there was considerable potential for harm in Balfour's unguarded remarks. Writing to him on 20 February, Montagu complained that Balfour, in an interview with the Palestinian Delegation, was alleged 'to have expressed [an] assurance that the perseverance of the Jews themselves with the support of Britain would overcome the difficulties in obtaining their object, and to have described their object as one of "reconstituting Palestine as the Jewish national home" '.[68] Montagu, to whom this statement appeared to exceed the Declaration of November 1917, could not accept Balfour's defence that Montagu's own argument was based upon 'a pointless literary distinction', and responded to this by saying that Balfour should bear in mind the distinction between Jewish Englishmen and English Jews.[69]

If further delays occurred before the despatch of the Commission and if nothing were done publicly to define Britain's relationship with Zionism, then exaggerated reports of the scope of that movement would continue to undermine Britain's position in the Middle East.[70] Similarly some, perhaps over-sensitive, officials feared that Zionism was inspired by Germany and that it would seep into Mesopotamia.[71] Thus it appeared to Kidston, who frankly admitted that the Eastern Department of which he was head was unable to cope with the issue. Not only was the necessary expertise lacking but the Department neither trusted nor was trusted by the Zionist leadership.[72] Curzon shared this distrust of the more prominent Zionists, informing Lord Derby, Britain's Ambassador in Paris, at the end of April that he was about to see Weizmann and that he would 'receive from me no sympathy with the advanced and aggressive aspirations in which Zionism, under his guidance, has lately shown an inclination to indulge'.[73] Curzon's keen displeasure was understandable, given that Zionism, even in a moderate form, would probably ensure that Britain would lose the support of the native population. According to Allenby, either America or France would be chosen and Clayton spoke of the military enforcement of the mandate by Britain should there be a Zionist Palestine.[74]

Curzon's refrain at this time that the Zionists 'had only themselves to blame if they lost the prize' or that they were 'reaping the harvest that they had sown' originated in his desire to see the demise of Zionist aspirations for political and religious control in Palestine by virtue of the unwisdom of their campaign.[75] However, whilst local intelligence confirmed the growing unpopularity of Zionism, such apparently was its attraction to British statesmen in Paris that considerable efforts were being made to guarantee its ascendancy. Writing to the Foreign Office on 7 May, Mallet observed that in fulfilling her pledges to the Zionists Britain must avoid any suggestion of conferring religious privileges on the Jews. Equally important, in view of the unpopularity of Zionism with the native population of Palestine, was that the British could not immediately 'fulfil their pledges of any form of political preference'. As Mallet continued:

> An increase in the numbers and economic influence of the Jews and steady colonisation must precede political favours. By this means the non-Jewish inhabitants of Palestine who fear the Jews primarily as a political and religious force may gradually come to welcome his presence, as they see the full advantages from the influx of Jewish money and the Jewish methods of developing the country.[76]

There was nothing here to which Curzon need have objected in principle, but he had to some extent become increasingly sensitive to any notion of affording preferential treatment to the Zionist cause. Mallet had written amid mounting interest among British firms in the commercial development of Palestine. According to Mallet, in her support for Zionism Britain was ensuring that Palestine would not be developed to the detriment of the country or its inhabitants by foreign concession hunters. Specifically, with the formation by the Zionists of a public utility company, and with Zionist control of immigration and land development, Mallet held that the interests of the Palestinian population would be preserved. Until the Peace Conference had pronounced on the future of the country and until Britain had calculated 'the full implication of their acceptance of a mandate for Palestine and of the policy of the national home for the Jews', Mallet believed that no commercial interests, British included, should establish themselves in Palestine.[77]

To Kidston, the proposal simply indicated a change of emphasis in policy which would confer political and possibly religious supremacy on the Jews by indirect means. Moreover, Kidston felt it unlikely that the non-Jewish majority would either obtain or expect to obtain material benefit from this arrangement and that it would, more probably, 'reduce them to a state of vassalage'. As Kidston pointed out, in Britain, in the House of Commons and in the Dominions, there were signs of a growing and 'regular movement . . . against handing over to exclusive exploitation by the Jews a country for which British, Canadian, Australian, and Indian soldiers had fought and died'.[78] To Curzon, Mallet's telegram simply revealed another hidden dimension of the Zionist evil, as he minuted despairingly on 10 May, that 'the national home is now seen to mean a monopoly of Jobs'.[79] Moreover, having rigidly played the game in Palestine, if the Zionists were to get preferential treatment then Curzon believed that Britain, as the proposed mandatory power, should begin developing the country.[80]

More annoying still was that the Zionist sympathies of Balfour and Lloyd George were perceived as preventing the alleviation of the position in Palestine. When asked at the end of May what might be done to mitigate the hostility of administrative authorities towards Zionism, Herbert Samuel, an influential Jew and a Liberal, recommended the issuing of a declaration whereby the extent and nature of Britain's commitments to Zionism were specifically defined. Whilst the British mandate would, according to Samuel, be based squarely upon the Balfour Declaration, it might also be made clear that under no circumstances would Arabs be 'despoiled of their land or required to leave the country', or that the majority would be ruled by the minority. With such guarantees, and further assurances about religious liberty and the retention of the Holy Places, Samuel felt that the Arabs should be told, and expected to accept, that Britain intended to fulfil her pledges of November 1917. An added incentive to Arab co-operation might be provided in the suggestion that the development of the country as a whole under the new regime would confer considerable material benefits on the population as a whole.[81] Once the international Commission was under way, the Eastern Department felt it unlikely that such a declaration would be sanctioned in Paris.[82]

To Curzon, any such re-affirmation of British sympathy towards Zionism seemed quite wrong and, irrespective of its wording, likely to feed Zionist ambitions. In addition, when the Commission examined conditions in Palestine it found, not surprisingly, that Zionism could only be implemented against the wishes of the people.[83] A further twist and one which had hitherto lain dormant was the attitude of France towards Zionism. Besides the position in Palestine, by mid-July it had also been disclosed, according to the findings of the Commission, that a French mandate in Syria could not be established without violence.[84] There was now the possibility, however, that France would manipulate the unpopularity of Zionism to undermine support for Britain in Syria. Further information received at the Foreign Office strengthened the conviction that Britain was heading for serious problems in Palestine. In Jerusalem, in particular, anti-Zionist agitation was adopting an anti-British stance and little could be done to rectify this.[85] As Curzon informed Balfour on 20 August, Britain had only one option:

> Personally, I am so convinced that Palestine will be a rankling thorn in the flesh of whoever is charged with its Mandate that I would withdraw from this responsibility while we yet can. There was a time when the soldiers told us that our possession of Palestine was necessary for the defence of Egypt, but they no longer hold this view. On the other hand, the difficulty of drawing a boundary between Syria and Palestine and of administering these two countries by separate European Powers is becoming more manifest every day; while the task of reconciling Zionist aspirations with Arab deserts in Palestine is one that the experience of the last six months has made all our administrators unwilling to undertake. The Prime Minister clings to Palestine for its sentimental and traditional value, and talks about Jerusalem with almost the same enthusiasm as about his native

hills. Others (of whom you would probably be one) think that, irksome as will be the burden, we cannot now refuse it without incensing the Zionist world.[86]

Subsequent developments confirmed Curzon's judgement. This was particularly so when, towards the end of September, there emerged concrete evidence that, as had been suspected at the Foreign Office for some time, Zionist ambitions were not restricted to Palestine. On 25 September, Kinahan Cornwallis, liaison officer between Faisal and Allenby, reported that, on the initiative of Weizmann, two meetings had occurred between the latter and Faisal. Apparently, in exchange for Faisal's support for the realisation of Zionist aims in Palestine, Weizmann had offered money and advisers for Faisal's Arab State, should they be necessary. According to Cornwallis, whilst Weizmann had suggested that he might succeed in persuading France to drop her claims to the Syrian hinterland, Faisal had not been satisfied with this desiring, instead, that the Zionists should 'throw in their lot with the Arabs against the French'. Upon this matter, Cornwallis stated, the talks had foundered as Faisal, though disposed to co-operate with the Zionists, regarded as unsatisfactory Weizmann's belief that France might be allowed to occupy the Syrian littoral with a view to her being 'squeezed out later'.[87]

To H.W. Young, Zionist involvement in Syria seemed preferable to a condominium of Anglo-French interests suggested by T.E. Lawrence; possibly on the grounds of his sensitivity to Arab nationalism and his belief that an early reconciliation between the Arabs and Zionists would be to Britain's advantage.[88] Such advanced thinking was disagreeable to Young's superiors. Kidston, Sir John Tilley, Acting Under-Secretary, and Hardinge firmly opposed any extension of Zionist influence and, inevitably, predicted that France would intervene and demand to know why Mesopotamia was being treated differently.[89] Moreover, as Hardinge observed, by virtue of Young's provision for the joint payment of the Hejaz subsidy by the 'Arab administration of Mesopotamia and Arab Syria', the Zionists might also secure a foothold in the Hejaz.[90] Curzon agreed, commenting on 3 October that it would be 'fatal' if Faisal were 'run by the Zionists'. As Curzon observed: '[w]ith the Zionists already in the ascendant in Palestine and financing, administering, arming and controlling Syria in addition – they would become one of the most formidable factors in the East. This would be the "new Jerusalem" with a vengeance.'

As Curzon concluded, such was the impression of Zionist aims derived by him at a recent interview with Weizmann when the latter, according to Curzon, had 'let the cat out of the bag'.[91] Weizmann had, in fact, been in the process of doing this for some time and there can be little doubt that, in his opposition to Zionism, Curzon, faced with Weizmann's persistent complaints, had personalised the matter. Writing to Balfour in August, Curzon had confessed his bewilderment on receipt of a letter from Weizmann 'in which that astute but aspiring person claims to advise us as to the principal politico-military appointments to be made in Palestine, to criticise sharply the conduct of any such officers who do not fall on the neck of the Zionists (a most unattractive resting place) and to acquaint us with the "type of man" whom we ought or ought not to send'. Weizmann, as Curzon continued, would 'be a scourge on the back of the unlucky mandatory', and it seemed necessary in Curzon's view for Balfour to 'drop a few globules of cold water on his heated and extravagant pretensions'.[92]

Curzon, though well aware that his views neither reflected those of Lloyd George nor of British policy as a whole, left Weizmann in no doubt as to his feelings on the matter. Commending to Balfour on 25 September the possibility of 'zionist support in the development and even administration of the Damascus region' and the introduction there of Zionist advisers, Weizmann had observed of Curzon:

> It is the position in the Foreign Office and Lord Curzon's relations to us and our movement which troubles me so much. So much can be done by one who is sympathetic and so much can be prevented by one who is indifferent. I am sorry to say that Lord Curzon takes the very short view of our question and he does not see the magnitude and perhaps the beauty of the problem.[93]

This was a reasonable and penetrating remark, yet it was as much an indictment of the disarray in British policy as a whole as of Curzon's personal involvement. Curzon's growing disenchantment with Zionism was understandable. Weizmann was well aware that he could undermine Britain's position in Mesopotamia either by rousing the Jewish population there or by playing upon Faisal's manipulation of the parity of Syria and Mesopotamia to obtain supremacy in Palestine and influence in the Syrian hinterland. Faced with this position and given his strong misgivings about Zionism, Curzon remained aloof and resolutely opposed to any further expression of sympathy for Zionism.[94] That movement was, in Curzon's view, simply one force which was actively undermining gains in the Middle East for which Britain had sacrificed so much. Describing to Balfour a series of Cabinet discussions on the Middle East which had occurred early in August, Curzon illuminated wide divergences within the Cabinet as to the apportioning of mandates. 'The jungle in which we wandered' – Curzon's description of those meetings – was peculiarly apt given that debate continued on the most fundamental points and that, in spite of his efforts, there remained considerable reluctance to tackling any aspects of the Middle Eastern question head on.[95] In any case, as Curzon had made plain, opinion on the future of Palestine was particularly diverse, and Balfour's own enthusiasm for Zionism was, Curzon suggested, perhaps not quite so unequivocal as it had once been.[96] Balfour, having escaped from the complexities of the issue and taken refuge at Whittingehame, when attempting to present a unified front to Rothschild at the end of September appeared simultaneously to absolve Curzon from any partiality and to wash his hands of the matter:

> There is no doubt that you and Doctor Weizmann are perfectly right in saying that there is a great deal of intrigue of one sort or another going on against Zionism. Nobody, however, has suggested to me that the Government should go back upon their declared policy. I also agree with Doctor Weizmann in earnestly desiring a good understanding with Feysal. The undoubted difficulties of the existing situation have almost entirely arisen from the long delay in settling problems connected with what was the Turkish Empire. For this I do not know that anybody is to blame – certainly not the British Government; and clearly nothing can be done until we know what issues from the American turmoil.
>
> In the meantime, I am, as you know, not the Acting [sic] for Foreign Affairs, and am not therefore at the moment in a position to take any steps in the matter, if steps there are which ought to be taken. My views on Zionism are, I need hardly say, quite unchanged, although the difficulties surrounding them have doubtless increased.[97]

And with this majestic swerve the bundle was passed to Curzon.

'THIS SYRIAN TANGLE'

'The Arab Difficulty'

By the late summer and autumn of 1918, British policy-makers had begun to take stock of Britain's position in the Arab Middle East. Partly, this analysis was occasioned by the Armistice of Mudros and the

ensuing discussion about British desiderata at the Peace Conference. For
some time before this, however, there had been ongoing debate about
the nature of Britain's engagements in the region both with her
European Allies and with the Arabs. This, in turn, originated in the
widespread dissatisfaction among senior British officials with the
Sykes–Picot Agreement. The momentum for its revision was sustained
during the first half of 1918 by periodic representations from Hussein
that, by virtue of the terms of that Agreement, his European Allies
appeared to be contemplating an imperialistic division of the region
without reference to the wishes of native opinion. There had, moreover,
since the previous winter, been continuing concern about the establishing in Palestine of an administration which, though not necessarily
'international' in the sense intended in Sykes–Picot, might give due
recognition to the rights of Britain's Allies to participate in it.

The debate got under way in earnest in mid-July at a meeting of
the Eastern Committee at which the assembled officials examined a
memorandum prepared by Mark Sykes which was intended, in
Curzon's words, to tackle the 'Arab difficulty'.[98] According to Sykes,
Allied unity might best be preserved by appointing a French and an
Italian adviser to serve under Allenby in order to preserve their respective national interests in Palestine.[99] Georges Picot, with whom Sykes
had spoken before writing the memorandum, was apparently in favour
of this arrangement.[100] Furthermore, Sykes believed that in the event of
British forces occupying areas of Syria, Britain must come to an understanding about the position of the French Commissioner, that is, the
head of the French Mission attached to the Egyptian Expeditionary
Force, Georges Picot.[101] Specifically, Sykes felt that in communications
between the EEF and the Syrians, the French Mission should be used as
the medium. Moreover, on 'military-political questions which directly
concern these regions', Sykes held that Allenby should regard Picot
as his adviser. If it proved necessary to establish a temporary administration in the course of the occupation then, according to Sykes, subject
to 'military decision' France should organise and control this administration. Though subject to Allenby's authority, the administrative
personnel would be French. Such measures were, in Sykes's opinion,
necessary to convince France that Britain did not herself intend to
establish a civil administration in Syria and, on the basis of the military
occupation, 'call it a military administration'. It seemed imperative to
Sykes that in the interests of the Entente and as a means of preventing
friction, Britain must remove any such suspicions.[102]

In spite of the strong feelings of the French Government on this matter, Macdonogh doubted if Allenby would find it acceptable to have a French administration in Syria and a British administration in Palestine aided by another Frenchman and an Italian. As Macdonogh protested, Sykes–Picot 'was founded on a pre-war basis without due consideration to a changing military situation'. Rather, Macdonogh continued, Allenby might be informed that upon the British entry into Syria France would be 'accorded certain privileges'. Balfour stated that if the French rejected this arrangement then it might be discreetly brought to their attention that Allenby need not enter Syria at all.[103]

In defining the arrangements for inter-Allied relations in Palestine and Syria, Sykes was attempting to foster inter-Allied unity. This, he claimed was essential to establish a 'stable and progressive state of affairs' in the Arab regions of the former Ottoman Empire, consistent with British strategic and economic interests. Neither objective could be obtained, however, unless France was made to realise that although the Syrian Arabs might assist an Anglo-French invasion of Syria, they certainly did not want a permanent British presence there. According to Sykes, if the Allies genuinely aspired to promote the 'Arab movement', then American complicity in this was desirable. American co-operation would not be forthcoming if Wilson felt he was 'entering a tangle of Old-World arrangements'. Sykes therefore proposed a joint Anglo-French memorandum in which it was suggested that the future well-being of the Arabs depended upon the development of self-government. Prevailing conditions necessitated an intervening tutelary period and, in Sykes's view, this function might best be undertaken 'on the sanction of the free nations of the world, and with the consent of the inhabitants of the areas concerned'.[104] Though progressive in that it presaged a definite and public re-emphasis in British policy, Sykes was introducing nothing new to the debate, merely giving substance to fears which had been current among some imperialists for several months. Rather more worrying was the second and more important plank of Sykes's plan to dismember his agreement of 1916.

As developments revealed, the reason for Sykes's activity in the summer of 1918 lay not so much in what Curzon termed the 'Arab difficulty' but, rather, in British relations with the Arabs and, in particular, with the Hashemite dynasty. Over the following months, senior British policy-makers attempted to reconcile Hashemite ambitions with those of Britain and France. As far as Sykes was concerned the scope of Hashemite ambitions, encompassing the titular chiefdom of the Arabic-speaking peoples, was of no concern to Britain. What was important was to convince Hussein that Britain and France had no imperialistic designs on Arab countries and thereby render his position stronger among his followers.[105] Sykes therefore suggested a further Anglo-French memorandum, sections of which might be publicised in the Middle East.[106]

The broad line of thought developed by Sykes was acceptable to the Eastern Committee primarily because it was seen to offer an antidote to the 'Arab difficulty', that is, Hussein's concern about the imperialistic intentions of his European Allies. As Curzon observed, the draft declaration prepared by Sykes closely resembled assurances which Wingate had intended to give to Hussein in January 1918. The essence of Sykes's draft was contained in the last two paragraphs of his memorandum and the excision of the first four paragraphs was agreed upon by the Eastern Committee as being less likely to sow doubt about Allied intentions. More significantly, when introducing the discussion, Curzon had pounced upon the proposed disclaimer against annexation, instancing the case of Basra for which a reservation had previously been claimed. Curzon's objection was apparently immediately upheld by the Committee and for the offending word was substituted an ordinance against 'the disposal of these [Arab] areas'.[107]

The issue of Britain's retention of Basra, though remaining important, had receded somewhat in the policy calculations of senior India Office officials. Of more immediate concern in the summer of 1918 was the enduring legacy of the meeting in May 1917 between Sykes, Picot and Hussein, at which the latter had accepted the idea of parity between Syria and Mesopotamia.[108] At the time this was vehemently opposed by officials in Cairo, principally because it appeared to confirm the French claim to Syria.[109] By the spring of 1918, it was generally acknowledged that, while in Mesopotamia Britain had gone a considerable way to achieving her aims, France had yet to obtain any of her desiderata in Syria. This factor might preclude a revision of Sykes–Picot. Several months later this discrepancy was, if anything, more pronounced and at the Eastern Committee on 18 July, Shuckburgh and Montagu expressed strong objections to any statement which might reinforce this parity. Considerable energy had been devoted to establishing a fabric of British control beneath the Arab façade in Mesopotamia and Shuckburgh, for one, shared the dislike of Sir Percy Cox for making Mesopotamia a 'pawn' in negotiations with Hussein. Continuing, Shuckburgh observed:

The language which it was now proposed to hold to the King might not go beyond what had already been said, but he considered a further formal undertaking, which the French Government were to be asked to counter-sign, quite unnecessary. By bringing in the French Government an entirely new element of complication was introduced. If Great Britain and France jointly undertook – as was proposed – that the future administration of Mesopotamia should be based on the 'principle of the consent of the governed', France might claim, with some show of reason, that she was entitled to see that the undertaking was duly fulfilled. To that extent we should be giving her an opening for intervening in Mesopotamian affairs.[110]

For India Office officials and for A.T. Wilson this aspect of British policy became a matter of considerable concern in the months ahead. However, at the Eastern Committee on 18 July, in response to Montagu's objection that the first paragraph of Sykes's draft declaration failed to preclude French interference in Mesopotamia, it was suggested that, in the context of the amended paragraph, such fears were groundless. If, however, the French succumbed to temptation then this 'would have to be met by the sharp rejoinder that it was no business of theirs'.[111]

Curzon's position on the Syrian issue was uncomfortable from the very outset. Though possessed of a fervent belief in the iniquity of Sykes–Picot, he was apparently unwilling or unable to set forth a plan of action which might lead to its revision. Possibly, by the summer of 1918 Curzon had, in the case of Syria, belatedly concluded that Britain must press the idea of self-determination. If so, then he failed to articulate these thoughts until later in the year. More seriously, Curzon erred fundamentally in entrusting to the Foreign Office the negotiations between Britain and France on the matter of French involvement in Syria. Quite why he did so is difficult to explain. Perhaps Curzon attached too much importance to the public acknowledgements by Sykes and Balfour that Sykes–Picot was 'dead' rather than to any detailed understanding of what exactly was meant by this.[112] On the other hand, Cecil, into whose hands the matter was placed, had clearly stated that Britain was bound by Sykes–Picot and that, according to his investigations, France had no intention of submitting to its revision.[113] Moreover, having received from Allenby a telegram embodying his understanding of the relations to be established with France in Syria, the Foreign Office had produced, as a basis for an understanding on this question with France, a draft agreement which accorded France political influence in Syria inconsistent with Allenby's telegram.[114] Curzon pointed out that the drafts deserved careful attention and at the meeting of the Eastern Committee on 26 September, and in view of Allenby's military successes, Curzon suggested that an understanding with France was 'of the utmost importance'; otherwise, as then appeared to be the case, the Foreign Office would continue to rely upon the Sykes–Picot Agreement.[115]

If Curzon felt no inclination to examine the motives of the Foreign Office hierarchy, then they were less disposed to give Curzon any room for manoeuvre. By the summer of 1918 it was almost certainly common knowledge that Curzon did not wish to see France established in area 'A' of Sykes–Picot. Admittedly, having launched an initial fusillade against that Agreement soon after its conclusion, Curzon apparently did not thereafter publicly air his views specifically on the subject of Syria. In fact, Curzon maintained his reserve until later in 1918 when, with more elements in play, the chances of ousting France seemed more propitious. Yet if there were any constants in his thinking, Curzon set great store in preserving complete freedom of action for Britain on the approaches to India, and that remained as true in 1918 as in 1916. Given the attitude of Cecil and Sykes towards Curzon and his committees, it seems that Cecil capitalised on Curzon's hesitancy and drew a departmental cloak over the matter. Such is the impression gained from a reading of Balfour's feeble explanation at the Eastern Committee on 26 September of what the Foreign Office had done to obtain an understanding with France. Cecil, who resumed the defence, stated that the drafts prepared by Sykes at his (Cecil's) instigation had been amended after scrutiny by 'various experts'. Cecil continued:

> Our view had been that it should be left to the French to make the first move, and matters had consequently been hung up until Allenby's recent victories.[116]

If Curzon had, inadvertently or otherwise, left the issues of Basra and Anglo-French co-operation dangling, then by the time of the meeting of the Eastern Committee on 3 October it became apparent to what extent the Foreign Office had capitalised on this. Confronted with the minutes of an Anglo-French Conference[117] on Syria held on 30 September at the Foreign Office and chaired by Cecil, it is difficult to gauge how angry Curzon was as he announced that

> the Eastern Committee had for a long time been proceeding on the hypothesis that the Anglo-French Agreement of 1916 was out of date and unscientific, and that it was desirable to get rid of it. The Committee had fre-

quently suggested that the agreement should be revised, but he feared that the Foreign Office had postponed any settlement of the question until we were now presented with something like a *fait accompli* in Syria.[118]

Sykes was unable to explain what had happened in terms of the revision of Sykes–Picot other than to point out that in July he had pressed for a decision as Picot had then been in England.[119] However, Sykes noted, he personally had never been instructed by the Foreign Office 'to do away with the agreement'.[120] Given that France might possibly misinterpret the draft agreement as confirming her right to the territories in Northern Mesopotamia conferred on her by Sykes–Picot, Sykes suggested that the case of Mesopotamia might be discussed with a view to its revision.[121]

Curzon's main objection to the draft agreement with France, and the reason why Cecil had been anxious to conclude it, was that, notwithstanding French unwillingness to participate militarily in the advance into Syria, the position conferred upon her there by Sykes–Picot was confirmed.[122] In accordance with previous discussions France was to be represented during the military occupation by Picot, who would act as Allenby's Chief Political Adviser. As such, and subject to Allenby's authority, Picot would act as 'sole intermediary' between Allenby and 'any Arab Government or Governments, permanent or provisional, which may be set up in Area A, and recognised under the terms of clause one of the Agreement of 1916'. Though explicitly denying Picot the right to participate in discussions pertaining to military matters, he would none the less receive from Allenby an account of any conversations on non-military matters held by him, personally, with any individual entitled to approach him through Picot. The draft then conferred on Picot the right to establish in the Blue area 'such provisional civil administration . . . as may be necessary for the maintenance of order and the facilitating of military operations'. The personnel for this administration, for Picot's role as intermediary and, more importantly, the advisory staff for the Arab Government or Governments of area 'A' under clause one of Sykes–Picot, would all be provided by Picot even if Allenby might ultimately have them removed.[123]

Whilst the draft agreement may have partially reduced friction between Britain and France it also seemed to highlight divisions among members of the Eastern Committee. Macdonogh, like Curzon, realised that the draft threatened to precipitate a French civil administration in Syria; something which he felt Allenby should not feel pressurised to implement but which France was eagerly awaiting an opportunity to establish.[124]

In the event, the stealthy approach of the Foreign Office did not find favour with Curzon. Rather than tackling the revision of Sykes–Picot head-on when, in accordance with his views and those of others, Britain might have ousted France from area 'A', it now seemed that France had been let in by the back door. Moreover, from her position of relative weakness, with important aspects of Sykes–Picot already in the melting-pot, Britain would now have to confront France with several other matters. Important among these, and an issue which Curzon had hoped it would be unnecessary to wrestle from France with her removal from Syria, was the inclusion within area 'A' of parts of the Tigris and Euphrates.[125] With the ball now rolling there had also to be considered the defunct claims of Russia and, as Sykes suggested, the issue of Italian desiderata which were based upon the provisions of that Agreement. Curzon remarked that besides the provisions of Sykes–Picot which related to the Blue area and area 'A', 'his main objections to the agreement lay in the surrender of a monopoly interest in Alexandretta, Mersina and Adana to the French, and he thought that the whole question of the future of Armenia should now be raised'.[126]

Cecil, faced with this bombardment, whilst willing to raise with France the issues mentioned by Curzon, had also capitalised on the latter's preoccupation in another respect. At the Anglo-French Conference of 30 September and at the instigation of the British delegates, it had been agreed to recommend the issuing of a declaration defining the attitude of Britain and France 'towards the Arab territories liberated from Turkish rule'. It was stated:

> Such a declaration should make it clear that neither Government has any intention of annexing any part of the Arab territories, but that in accordance with the provisions of the Anglo-French Agreement in 1916, both are determined to recognise and uphold an independent Arab State or Confederation of States, and with this view to lend their assistance in order to secure the effective administration of those territories under the authority of the native rulers and peoples.[127]

Clearly this disregarded the opposition expressed by Curzon, and apparently concurred with by the Eastern Committee of 18 July, to the disclaimer on annexation contained in Sykes's original draft declaration to King Hussein, because it failed to consider the exclusive position to which Britain aspired in Basra.[128] As Shuckburgh pointed out to the

Committee on 3 October, the question of the status of Basra had previously been reserved and before any further action was taken the matter should be discussed again.[129]

Cecil mustered some convincing arguments to justify what must have appeared to be a fairly bewildering and self-contradictory position. On the one hand, possibly in the interests of future Anglo-French co-operation, Cecil appeared to be working covertly for the introduction of French influence into Syria and for the implementation of Sykes–Picot. On the other hand, in defence of his position *vis-à-vis* the above quoted declaration, Cecil argued that France must not be allowed to annex any parts of area 'B'. This improbable contingency was followed by the more convincing argument that in order to enlist American help 'in settling the future of the occupied territories . . . we must declare against annexation'. Possibly Cecil was in his own way laying the foundations for the demise of French influence in Syria. As Cecil explained to the Committee, Britain and France must aim to establish 'independent Arab administrations in Areas "A" and "B", and to help the Arabs towards stable government'. In his opinion, this policy should be extended to the Blue and Red areas and this approach might be reflected in the final declaration. Yet even if, looking far ahead, Cecil believed that by encouraging self-determination the Syrian population might opt for severing the French connection, as Macdonogh pointed out, the question of Basra remained unresolved. Whilst Smuts and Montagu, when faced with Cecil's logic, were prepared to accept the possibility of a strong British presence without formal annexation, Macdonogh felt that it would be difficult to reconcile this with Cecil's proposed pledge of independence for Basra. Yet again it seems that Curzon was unsure of his ground, quoting to the assembled Committee from the minutes of a previous meeting when, in agreement with Sir Percy Cox, he had argued for the annexation of Basra. On that occasion, in responding to a suggestion by Sykes that a proclamation announcing the annexation of Basra might be unwise, Curzon had 'expressed the hope that a terminological variant, such as "perpetual lease" or "enclave" might be found, both to safeguard the reality which we must not abandon, and to save the appearances which the occasion might require'. However, early in October Curzon perceived Hussein's ambitions as the principal threat to Britain's position in Basra.

'THE PRIVILEGE OF THE CONQUERORS'

In spite of his efforts Cecil did not have things all his own way. Curzon, having reflected briefly on the discussion at the Eastern Committee of 3 October and on the results of Cecil's handiwork, attempted to clamber back behind the wheel of the Syrian negotiations. Without access to the original draft minutes of that meeting of the Eastern Committee it is difficult to assess with precision the role of the leading personae in the debate. The version of the conclusions of the meeting printed in January 1919 seems to reflect the sense of a minute by Crowe in which he took exception to certain aspects of 'the Chairman's last revise'.[130] The implication of Crowe's minute suggests that Curzon had misunderstood Cecil's line of thought. The latter, as previously stated, considered it possible that France might eventually be ousted from area 'A' by encouraging self-determination underpinned by American involvement. In other words, even if Britain might initially have to accept the introduction of French influence into Syria, in the long term France would find her position untenable. Apparently, Curzon had blundered into this tidy web and, in his haste to secure the cancellation of Sykes–Picot, he had confused the issue with the draft agreement on Syria which arose from the Anglo-French Conference of 30 September.

Cecil subsequently claimed that the Eastern Committee had agreed to ratify the draft agreement but that a letter should be written covering the ratification, in which France might be asked to accept the modification of the agreement on two counts.[131] Firstly, as Curzon had suggested, the Tigris and Euphrates Valleys must be excluded from area 'A' and, secondly, again in view of Curzon's representations, certain alterations must be made to the Palestinian frontier.[132] The conclusions of the Eastern Committee of 3 October raised rather broader issues. Far from suggesting a ratification of the draft the conclusions recommended the preparation of a 'revised draft . . . with the least possible delay . . . on the lines generally of the Conference at the Foreign Office as modified at the foregoing discussion'. However, whilst Cecil had agreed to discuss with France the future of 'lesser Armenia', the conclusions of the Committee stated baldly that when revising the results of the Foreign Office Conference, 'the future of Armenia should be provided for'.[133] The two previous 'special reservation[s]', namely, 'the exclusion of old Palestine from the blue area', and the limitation of the Blue area to 'Syria proper', appeared to Crowe to remove the gilt from the gingerbread. To attempt this and simultaneously to rush through an 'abrogation' of

Source: *Illustrated London News*

7. The Earl Curzon of Kedleston

Source: Illustrated London News

8. Lord Robert Cecil

Sykes–Picot as specified in the conclusions of the Committee seemed to Crowe to be 'exceedingly bad diplomacy' and likely to 'lead to our discomfiture'. A wiser course, he argued, would be to proceed with the 'acceptance of the provisional arrangement subject to certain reservations, as agreed upon by the Committee' (presumably according to Cecil's version of events). As to the broader issues raised in the conclusions, which were designed to supplant Sykes–Picot, Crowe implied that these had first been defined as a '*later* elaboration of our proposals for a fresh agreement'. In his view it would be unwise to approach this task with haste. Rather, Crowe believed that these proposals must be 'allowed to emerge eventually in the course of discussion, and possibly after fresh communication with Italy and perhaps with America'.[134] Whether or not Crowe's interpretation of these proposals amounted simply to the 'modification' of Sykes–Picot suggested by Cecil in his note, in which he dissented from the 'abrogation' of Sykes–Picot suggested in the printed minutes, is difficult to judge.

In the event a compromise was reached on the basis of a memorandum written by Cecil after having discussed the Syrian question with Pichon, the French Foreign Minister.[135] Whilst Curzon expressed his willingness to accept the draft agreement devised by the Anglo-French Conference, he did so on the understanding that, as enumerated by Cecil in his memorandum, the agreement would apply only to those territories occupied or to be occupied by the EEF. Moreover, Curzon was satisfied with Cecil's statement that, whilst for various reasons Britain regarded the provisions of Sykes–Picot as being unsuited 'to present conditions', it would be pointless to settle them at present. Accordingly, Cecil suggested, and Curzon accepted, that they might be raised at a later date when, besides France and Britain, America and Italy might be asked to participate.[136]

The lull in the debate was short-lived. Within two days of the acceptance of Cecil's memorandum by Curzon and the War Cabinet, the Eastern Committee again turned to the Syrian question; on this occasion with reference to a declaration to King Hussein drafted by Sykes in accordance with the provisions of the draft agreement of 30 September.[137] In this instance the lines of battle were drawn rather differently. Converted by Cecil's argument of the need to enlist American sympathy and conscious of the original purpose of the declaration, Smuts and Montagu detected some ambiguity in the wording of the draft declaration in so far as it pronounced against annexation by Britain or France, or 'in the event of the inhabitants . . . desiring annexation by a third Power'. Crowe, who had attended the Conference, opposed an irreversible declaration against annexation and, in support of this, instanced the inconvenience caused by a similar self-denying ordinance in the case of Muscat. When the discussion was resumed on the following day, Crowe, defending a new draft declaration which he had drawn up with Sykes, suggested that by virtue of this amended declaration Britain might freely annex any areas should Germany or Turkey attempt to annex or impose a protectorate in any area of the former Ottoman Empire.[138] The revised declaration, which replaced a negative declaration against annexation with a positive statement in favour of the establishment of independent rule, patently owed more to Crowe's thinking than to that of Sykes.[139]

By this stage Curzon was beginning to feel rather concerned. Faced with the prospect of relinquishing close control over Basra should Sykes's previous draft be accepted, the alternative provided by Crowe, though ingenious, apparently held no appeal for Curzon. Faced with two limiting alternatives, Curzon darted up a blind alley, suggesting that it might be best to limit the declaration to Syria alone.[140] Cecil parried the blow by recourse to the argument about the parity of Mesopotamia and Syria and the inevitable unwillingness of France to accept in Syria what Britain would not accept in Mesopotamia.[141] Faced with unanimous concern among officials attached to the Eastern Committee about the need to avoid giving a wrong impression to America or the Arabs, Curzon was forced to tread the path of self-determination, being entrusted by the Committee to approve on their behalf a further draft declaration which was simultaneously to excise any mention of annexation while 'emphasizing Arab rights and claims'.[142]

Having once let the French in, unexpectedly perhaps, Curzon found himself taking to self-determination in Syria rather well, and for the simple reason that a variety of developments rapidly favoured the eventual removal of French influence at least from area 'A'. Amid representations that the terms of Sykes–Picot and the Declaration to the Seven were mutually contradictory, T.E. Lawrence had suggested that the latter 'would be regarded as binding'.[143] By the terms of that Declaration the areas liberated by Arab arms would have independence. As Lawrence informed the Eastern Committee on 29 October, at the time of his departure from Syria, Faisal had been in occupation of Damascus and this, clearly, would restrict the intention of French officials, 'to build up a colonial empire in the East'. As if to confirm Curzon's belief in the necessity of undoing the provisions of Sykes–Picot relating to Northern Mesopotamia, Lawrence reported that the Kurds, while willing to join any confederation backed by the British, would not accept French rule in any form. Lawrence continued:

> whoever controlled Lower Mesopotamia must also control the upper waters of the Euphrates, as it would be possible to utilise the whole of the water of the Euphrates for irrigating the plain of Aleppo by draining it off between Birejik and Rakka. The Arabs of North Mesopotamia were distinguished for their extreme nationalism, and they had deduced from the attitude of the French during this war, wherever they had come into contact with them, that the French were inimical to the movement for national independence. The French were getting into Syria under General Allenby's wing, and although he did not like it, Faisal would probably be content to leave Beirut and the Lebanon to French tutelage provided that there was no question of French annexation.[144]

However, in Lawrence's view, the economic needs of Syria were such that the Arab State must have access to the sea, preferably at Tripoli, because of the commercially important Tripoli–Homs railway. Also, Lawrence reported that the Arabs wanted an outlet at Arsus in the south of Ayas Bay. To Lawrence it seemed essential that no one power should obtain control of the entire bay. Rather, a section of it, including Adana, Mersina and Port Ayas, might form part of an Armenian State which, Lawrence felt, must 'be near the sea and modest in size'. Concluding his remarks, Lawrence reported that Picot had informed him that France meant to introduce French advisers to Faisal's Syrian State but that Faisal maintained that he might 'choose whatever advisers he liked'. Lawrence added: 'He [Faisal] was anxious to obtain the assistance of British or American Zionist Jews for this purpose. The Zionists would be acceptable to the Arabs on terms.'[145]

Similar views about the future of Syria, Cilicia and Northern Mesopotamia were expressed at this time by Macdonogh and Hogarth. Both envisaged a small Armenian State centred on Sivas and Cilicia and including some measure of control in Ayas Bay.[146] In Iraq, Macdonogh proposed a single state from north of Mosul to the Gulf under Abdullah and with a 'direct British administration under the British Resident at Baghdad'. In Jezireh, Macdonogh suggested there might be a separate state under British influence. In Syria proper, Macdonogh envisaged that the Arab State in the Syrian hinterland would have within its borders the coastal strip between Tripoli and Arsus and that the state would be under a British minister installed at Damascus.[147] Hogarth agreed, generally, that the Arab claims to the Syrian coast must not be disregarded and that the position conferred on France in Mosul by Sykes–Picot was no longer tenable.[148]

Amid such evaluations more explicit pronouncements in favour of British control in Syria were made. Writing on 19 November Cornwallis observed:

> I have always acted on the supposition that Great Britain has neither the ambition nor the wish to extend her influence to Syria but if in the next two months the population shows an unmistakable preference for her help, it will be most difficult to refuse without incurring the charge of abandoning a nation which has during the last three years looked to us as its saviour.[149]

Growing evidence of the unpopularity in Syria of France, in particular, but also of the Hashemite dynasty, was of considerable value to Curzon when, early in December, he attempted to argue conclusively that France must not be permitted to establish herself in Syria.[150] Having reiterated his opposition to the position conferred on France in Northern Mesopotamia by Sykes–Picot, Curzon castigated the Agreement for the 'most fantastic and incredible line of division' which it established between areas 'A' and 'B'. In fact, Curzon argued, if Sykes–Picot stood it would be 'a source of incessant friction' between the French, British and Arabs.[151]

According to Curzon, developments on the ground were conspiring to undo the Agreement. The Arabs, who had contributed much more to the liberation of the territories than France, had established native government in major towns of area 'A' including Damascus, Homs, Hama and Aleppo. In coastal Syria, Curzon added, 'some form of native institutions' had been constituted by the Arabs. Continuing, Curzon observed: 'Meanwhile, the French, taking full advantage of the terms of the Sykes–Picot Agreement, have sought to push in their Governors and their functionaries everywhere, only being restrained by the fact of the military situation and the control which General Allenby has been in a position to exercise.' However, the French were viewed with suspicion by the Arabs and, as Curzon remarked, if asked 'to choose a single Great Power as their tutelar Power in the future, they would be much more likely to choose Great Britain than France'.[152]

In Curzon's opinion Britain had two options. On the one hand, she might decide to accept the 'complicated and dangerous system of partition' which would emerge if French and Arab claims were realised. In this eventuality an Arab coastal strip including Tripoli and Latakia would be hemmed in on either side by France in the Lebanon and in Alexandretta. On the other hand, if Britain remained in Palestine or on the basis of her position in Egypt alone, it seemed to Curzon that most people would support the removal of France from Syria.[153] Faced with the choice of backing either the French or the Arabs and in the event of America refusing to wipe the slate clean in terms of inter-Allied agreements, Curzon postulated a middle course:

> our line of action probably should be this, to back Faisal and the Arabs as far as we can, up to the point of not alienating the French, the bent of whose ambitions turns towards the East and a future French sphere in those regions. For the safety of our Eastern Empire I would sooner come to a satisfactory arrangement with the Arabs than I would with the French, but I would not carry the arrangement with the Arabs to the point of quarrelling with the French. Secondly, if that be our line of action as regards Faisal, ought we not to play the policy of self-determination for all it is worth? When we made the Anglo-French declaration in November last, I think, as often happens, we hardly realised what its full purport and bearing might be. Perhaps I am interested in the matter, perhaps I am inclined to value the argument of self-determination, because I believe that most of the people would determine in our favour.[154]

Somewhat incredulous, Cecil pointed out that, in connection with the Anglo-French Declaration, this had been his assumption all along.[155] However, whilst Cecil, like Balfour, was prepared to use self-determination as a means to an end, he was none the less aware that if it were used unwisely and simply as a means for Britain to avoid her treaty arrangements, then it would cause trouble. Although France had agreed to reconsider the Sykes–Picot Agreement, she had subsequently attempted to withdraw her consent and, in any case, Cecil believed that France would not 'give up the whole of Syria without the most tremendous convulsion'.

> They would rather give up anything in the world than give up that claim to Syria; they are mad about it, and Cambon himself is quite insane if you suggest it. I am sure you will never get them out of Syria, and we ought to make up our mind to go for some settlement which will give them some position in Syria, however unpleasant it may be to have them there.

At the very least, Cecil suggested, France must be given Beirut 'and a bit of the Lebanon'.[156] There was, moreover, the possibility of inducing in the French a reasonable attitude in regard to Syria by raising the issue of her ambitions in Alsace-Lorraine.[157] Disappointed by Cecil's suggestion that self-determination might limit but not remove Sykes–Picot, Curzon again pointed to the undesirability of leaving Faisal's Syria landlocked and was supported in this by T.E. Lawrence who, on grounds of French control of customs receipts and railway dues, argued that Syria as defined in Sykes–Picot 'is an impossible country'. Isolated from the Mediterranean, from Mesopotamia and from Arabia it would be a perpetual 'source of discord'. In view of the growing nationalist movement in Syria, Lawrence was prepared to recommend to Faisal that if it were offered he should accept the possession of one port only, Tripoli, as a starting point.[158]

The final resolutions of the Eastern Committee on Syria revealed broad agreement with the approach suggested by Curzon and endorsed, albeit reluctantly, by T.E. Lawrence. The overall effect of the resolutions if implemented would be radically to reduce the scope for French expansion in the Middle East. As a matter of principle it was deemed necessary to 'cancel' Sykes–Picot. More specifically, the resolutions proposed that French rights in area 'A' and in the Syrian portion of the Blue zone might be cancelled. Within area 'B', Britain might support the French claim to 'a special political position in the Lebanon and Beirut' and at Alexandretta. In order to conform with the Anglo-French Declaration, in neither case would France be permitted to fortify the port. Beyond this, French expansion might be held in check by the provision of an outlet, probably at Tripoli, for the 'autonomous Arab State' established under Faisal and by a general clause in which it was stated 'that no foreign influence other than that of Great Britain should be predominant in areas A and B'.[159]

'THE REFLECTIONS OF AN OUTSIDER'

Developments in British policy in the Middle East in the first months of 1919 were deeply disappointing to Curzon. Not only was his own authority ill-defined but he felt increasingly isolated from decision making and unable to ensure the implementation of the broad policy which he had very skilfully elucidated at meetings of the Eastern Committee. Worse still, misguided colleagues were, in their confusion, actively undoing his good work. Curzon, writing on 24 March for his Cabinet colleagues in a paper entitled 'A Note of Warning About the Middle East', maintained that Britain and her Allies were unduly preoccupied with the German peace. In the east, Curzon argued, British diplomacy was being conducted on the unsure foundations of the

Turkish Armistice which, in his view, had not been sufficiently 'comprehensive and severe'. Instead of conducting her diplomacy from a position of military ascendancy at the capital of Ottoman power, Britain's standing in Constantinople had, in Curzon's words, 'rested more upon the calculating self-interest of the Turks on the one hand, and bluff on our part on the other'. Besides the local difficulties to which this led, the Turkish Government was successfully playing off Britain against France. The strength of the CUP[160] in the former Ottoman Empire was undiminished and, so Curzon held, British prestige was being undermined, among other things, by developments in Egypt, by Britain's proposed departure from the Caucasus, by Bolshevik successes in the Ukraine, and by on-going debate among the Allies about Greek and Italian landings in Asia Minor. The future of Palestine had also to be considered and 'squabbling' over the future of Syria persisted between Britain and France. Far from beholding the 'conclusion and celebration of a speedy and glorious peace', Curzon perceived a more foreboding prospect:

> The above is the picture upon which the Old Turk, who still hopes to re-establish the former regions, and the Young Turk, who means to cheat us if he can of the spoils of victory, look out from the trembling watch-towers of Stambul. Both are probably aware that they cannot escape the loss of Mesopotamia, of Arabia, and the Holy Places . . . of Palestine and in Europe of Eastern Thrace. But when they realise that they are to be deprived altogether of Armenia, that they are to be turned out of Constantinople and of Europe, and that even their reduced patrimony in Asia Minor and Anatolia is either to be parcelled out between enemies (Greece and Italy) whom they abhor, or is to be patronised by some foreign mandatory Power who will equally be anathema to them, I sometimes ask myself – what will they do? Will they once more bow to Kismet? Or will they think it worth while to strike another blow . . . for Islam and the few remaining vestiges of their freedom?
>
> I suggest to the military and naval authorities that they should not ignore these possibilities; and I point out to my colleagues, not as a prophecy but as a warning, that fresh trouble may even now be brewing in the East, which may disarrange some of our best laid plans.[161]

Curzon's frustration was to some extent understandable. At meetings of the Eastern Committee he and his colleagues had thrashed out the various options in terms of mandatory control. Had the resolutions of the Committee been adopted, and had Curzon's colleagues entrusted with the negotiations in Paris been equally committed to maintaining the forward momentum established by Curzon, then Britain might reasonably have hoped to obtain mandatory control in Mesopotamia, Syria, the Caucasus, Persia and, possibly, in Palestine. Instead, debate about mandatory responsibilities continued, fuelled both by the inability of the Allies to elicit a decision from the United States and by the on-going assessments of the interplay of strategic factors in the division among the Allies of the former Ottoman Empire. Shortly after the convening of the Peace Conference the discussion had become extremely tangled.

The fundamental problem remained, as ever, the cancellation of Sykes–Picot. As Robert Cecil had suggested to the Eastern Committee, the Anglo-French Declaration had not been designed to achieve this but merely to weaken it.[162] Faced with demands by Foch that France might now be allowed to occupy area 'A', Lloyd George and Sir Henry Wilson pressed for a speedy decision on mandates.[163] However, as Wilson noted in his diary early in February, Balfour was then unable to present a scheme for the unravelling of Sykes–Picot, something which was inextricably linked with such a decision, and there was, in any case, the problem of American indecision.[164] The broad consensus was that France must be induced to forgo her rights in area 'A' of Sykes–Picot and the bait was to be Constantinople and Thrace. This idea was supported by Sir Henry Wilson, Cecil, Smuts and Montagu and had the advantage that it would enable Britain to establish America in Armenia as a buffer between British and French interests.[165] The main drawback of this exchange, besides French opposition, was that America might express an interest in Constantinople, thus creating a double hurdle before France might be ejected from Syria. Moreover, whilst agreeing with this solution initially, both Balfour and Lloyd George apparently had second thoughts and by the end of February 1919 were opposed to it.[166]

Evidence is lacking on what exactly Curzon might have done to extricate Britain from the tangle. His 'Note of Warning', though reflecting deeply held concerns about the position in Asia Minor, was in other respects something of a knee-jerk reaction to developments in the Middle East as dictated by policy formulation in Paris. Of these developments Curzon was not kept as fully informed as he would have wished. Some insight into Curzon's thoughts is provided by a letter from Balfour to Curzon of 20 March and by Curzon's reply of 25 March.[167] Balfour's letter was provocative and the timing of Curzon's 'Note of Warning' suggests that it was intended to stiffen Balfour.

In his letter, and in reply to a representation from Curzon on the matter, Balfour had dismissed the issue of Italian landings in Adalia as being 'out of all proportion to any effects which, as far as I can see, it is likely to have'. It was in any case, as Balfour added, something which could only be dealt with in London. On the broader Middle Eastern question Balfour confessed his anxiety, remarking that a 'satisfactory solution' of the question, and indeed the 'machinery' by which such a solution might be obtained, had so far proved impossible to devise. Part of the problem, Balfour confided, was that Lloyd George was conducting negotiations

> and, while I entirely agree with what I understand to be his main objects, I am by no means sure that he has thought out the question as a whole; or that, in more or less informal conversations with this or that Member of the Conference, he may give away to one Power what ought to be reserved for another.[168]

Curzon, among others, shared this suspicion of Lloyd George's diplomacy but, couched in such vague terms, and unable as Curzon was directly to influence events, Balfour's account did little to smooth Curzon's plumage.[169] Balfour then gave a brief outline of the triangular Middle Eastern problem which consisted of American wishes, Allied ambitions and the unravelling of Sykes–Picot. Central to this was the willingness of America to consider a mandate not only for Constantinople but also for a Greater Armenia including Cilicia, something incompatible with French claims in Sykes–Picot. Balfour continued:

> Again, the P.M. has so far come to no arrangement with the French about Syria. Clemenceau, in London, asked him what he wanted, and he answered, 'Mosul'. Clemenceau replied, 'Then you shall have it'. If 'Mosul' can be interpreted to mean the upper regions of Mesopotamia this, in my opinion, might give us all we really want; but it by no means gives us all that Faisal thinks we ought to have; and leaves Damascus and Aleppo, etc. in the French sphere, which Feisal swears he will on no account tolerate.[170]

Deprived of these towns Syria would not, in Foch's opinion, be of any use to France. Besides her historical claims, Balfour added, French claims in Syria rested upon the Sykes–Picot Agreement. This had been modified by the Anglo-French Declaration and, as Balfour reported, Faisal maintained that if that document meant what it said then the French could not possibly have influence in the Syrian hinterland.[171]

With this broad and unscientific appraisal of the Syrian 'impasse', Curzon calculated for himself the time which had elapsed between the wresting from France of Mosul and the passing of this knowledge to him. More bitter still was Balfour's disclosure that Lloyd George had stated 'that under no circumstances' would Britain accept the Syrian mandate. Moreover, a commission was to be despatched to Syria, Mesopotamia and Armenia to establish the wishes of the peoples of those countries. These revelations, delivered in Balfour's almost conversational tone, and coming almost simultaneously with the suggestion of an Italian mandate in the Caucasus, gave Curzon plenty to chew on.[172]

The first blast of the 'strong cool breeze' was not long in coming. Not surprisingly the idea of a commission did not appeal to Curzon. Replying to Balfour on 25 March, Curzon pointed out that the Commission, if it were necessary, should have been sent long since, permitting an early decision. Instead, Curzon observed, 'the entire Middle Eastern question seems to have been avoided at Paris as if it was the plague'. He continued:

> Now let us see what this Commission will do. It may give, it probably will give, an opinion in favour of Great Britain as the mandatory of Mosul and Mesopotamia. It will probably do this because it could do nothing else, and because, as far as I know, no one is able or willing to step into our shoes in that part of the world. But meanwhile its appearance upon the scene will cause a great deal of unrest and commotion there, will arouse all sorts of aspirations, disturb a good deal of the existing progress, postpone the institution of the new regime, and very likely render our task (when we have taken it up) a great deal more difficult.[173]

Curzon returned to the question of the Commission repeatedly and controversially in following weeks. Continuing his letter to Balfour, Curzon pointed out that if the Commission reported in favour of a French mandate in Syria it would have to disregard popular opinion and, by implication, prevailing notions of self-determination. Conversely, if it reported against a French mandate, it left unresolved the question of French claims. Moreover, Curzon postulated, if the Commission supported the creation of a Greater Armenia under American control, what would be the attitude of France towards her claims in Cilicia?[174] Curzon had difficulty in conceiving of a unanimous decision among the Commissioners. Also, the disorder to which he believed the delays entailed in the investigations would lead in Mesopotamia might, in his view, spread to the region as a whole.[175]

Concluding his letter Curzon uttered a final resonant warning against

Allied policy in Asia Minor where Greece, France and Italy were being allowed to 'gallop about' uncontrolled:

> From such knowledge of the East as I possess, I cannot help thinking that this great pack of cards which is being reared will, almost at the first blow, tumble in fragments to the ground.
>
> These, however, are only the reflections of an outsider who is at some distance from the scene; and it may be that, if I had been upon the spot, my policy would not have been any more sound or effective.[176]

During the remainder of 1919 Curzon would have frequent cause to reconsider his concluding remark.

'PLAYING THE GAME': MESOPOTAMIA 1919

By the beginning of 1919 the future development of Mesopotamia in all its aspects had been entrusted to members of the Inter-Departmental Conference on the Middle East. Curzon's efforts to absorb the implications of international opinion rendered him more sensitive to the diffusion of power occasioned by the Peace Conference. Certainly Curzon was determined to maintain a close personal control of Mesopotamian policy; especially, perhaps, in view of the disbanding of the Eastern Committee, the loss of executive functions to its successor, and also in view of the ambiguous nature of his position at the Foreign Office. During 1919 Curzon maintained that rigidity of outlook which had previously shaped his perception of events in Mesopotamia and which had identified him in the minds of several senior officials with a policy which was seen to be retarding the development of the country. Increasingly, perhaps, as important matters were inevitably submitted to the Acting Foreign Secretary rather than being dealt with, sometimes covertly, by senior officials delegated to the Eastern Committee, Curzon came to be identified, personally, with the range of maladies which afflicted Mesopotamia. The position of Curzon and various officials who acted to postpone the development of the country was largely determined by delays in the official apportioning of mandates. At the India Office, however, and in Mesopotamia, such delays were with few exceptions regarded as justification for quite a different approach. The year 1919 was to be critical in the development of Mesopotamia, when the accumulated efforts of Hirtzel and others would be fully exposed to the elements which, at the interdepartmental and international level, shaped events. Moreover, the period between the Armistice of Mudros and Curzon's permanent tenure of the Foreign Secretaryship in October 1919 was fraught with debate about the whole orientation of British Policy in Mesopotamia.

THE CONSTITUTION

In April 1919 and in response to a directive prepared in Whitehall in February 1919, A.T. Wilson produced a draft constitution for Mesopotamia. His draft took cognisance both of the views of political officers on the ground and of those measures outlined by his predecessor, Sir Percy Cox, for the administrative corpus of the new state; measures which had, since the spring of 1918, been evolved and in some measure sanctioned by means of correspondence between the Political Office, Baghdad, and Whitehall.[177]

Wilson's deliberations took place against the backdrop of the discussions of the Eastern Committee and his investigations, on the basis of instructions from that body, to elicit local opinion on the future of the country. The ambiguous picture which emerged was none the less clear enough, regarding a possible Amirate, to convince Wilson that such a figurehead was not possible.[178] There was also a growing concern among the most acute observers that the Sherifian cause and that of Arab nationalism might be more forcefully argued than previously anticipated. Hirtzel, attached to the British Delegation early in 1919 and more sensitive, perhaps, to international currents than colleagues in London, established the parameters of debate when drafting the original telegram to Wilson, in which the latter was asked his views on a constitution.[179] In framing a constitution, Hirtzel maintained, Wilson must forge a balance between, on the one hand, the 'necessity of effective and indisputable British control' and, on the other, the Anglo-French Declaration, whereby Britain was pledged to create an indigenous administration.[180] In view both of international opinion, embodied in the League of Nations, and of growing nationalist tendencies emanating from Baghdad, Hirtzel advised that the constitution should provide for a workable degree of Arab involvement in the administration, something which might increase in time, and sufficient Arab participation in government to prevent the alienation of nationalist elements.[181]

Curzon, to whom the draft was referred, shared the widely held view that Wilson was faced with a very difficult task – especially, as Curzon observed, because of the enormous cultural variety of Mesopotamia.[182] Wilson was therefore requested to formulate a 'flexible constitution' and one which might give play to those forces outlined by Hirtzel.[183] In framing his reply to the telegram of 14 February, Wilson had consulted the seventeen Political Officers who, under his supervision, ran the divisional administrative units of Mesopotamia. Wilson's formula was, in his words, 'framed on the most liberal basis compatible with the maintenance during the next few stormy years of public order'.[184] Implicit in this was that Arab involvement would gradually increase and that Wilson was a reluctant adherent to the Anglo-French Declaration.

To a considerable extent Wilson was merely taking on the baton from Sir Percy Cox who, in April 1918, and when attempting to reconcile ambitious plans for future British control in Mesopotamia with the policy of the 'Arab façade', had spoken of establishing 'a protective British supervision'. Again, this was compatible, in Cox's view, with the proclamation of March 1917 whereby Britain invited the Arabs of Mesopotamia to participate in the administration. According to Cox this supervision might best be exercised by a British High Commissioner, 'assisted by a Council, formed partly of the Heads of the most important Departments of State, and partly of representative non-official members from among the inhabitants'. Failing this, Cox envisaged the appointment of a titular native ruler; the main disadvantage of this being the loss of exclusive British control of capitulations. Whilst perceiving sufficient material for the lower ranks of the administration, Cox believed that unless and until native Arabs of a calibre suited to the more senior posts materialised, these would continue to be filled by young British officers. As Cox argued, local opinion preferred this to the employment of administrators 'saturated with the evil traditions of the regime in which they had been brought up and trained'.[185]

On 10 November, in view of increased international pressure occasioned by the Anglo-French Declaration, Wilson attempted to put flesh on these bones with the creation of Municipal Councils in the Baghdad and Basra Vilayets, and by means of resuscitating Divisional Councils.[186] In both cases Wilson intended to keep a tight rein and was assisted in this by the continuing absence of suitable native material for senior positions.[187] In the case of the Municipal Councils, whilst they would, according to Wilson, exercise important financial functions, the highest office holders would be British officials and the Council would be part nominated.[188] Exercising comparable functions in rural areas, members of the Divisional Councils would all be nominated by the respective Political Officers. However, the new state would be strongly imbued with British influence; both the Municipal and Divisional Councils pro-

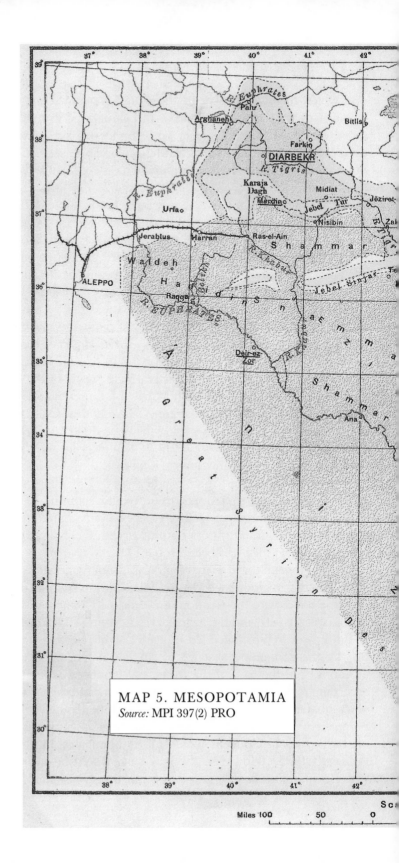

MAP 5. MESOPOTAMIA
Source: MPI 397(2) PRO

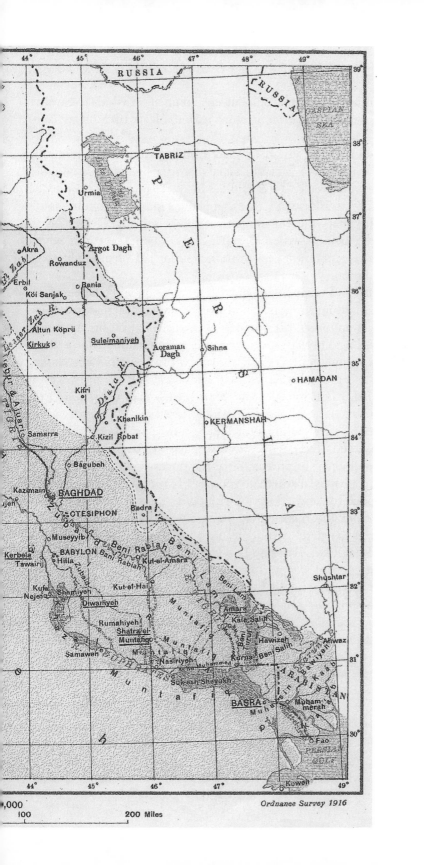

viding, in Wilson's opinion, a suitable environment in which to nurture delegates 'chosen' to serve on a future national legislative or advisory body.[189]

Besides the increasing emphasis placed on international opinion, the main developments since Cox laid initial plans for the administration in April 1918 were twofold. Firstly, the Mosul Vilayet had now to be included in any arrangements that were to be made. Secondly, assets enjoyed by the military administration – railways, bridges, docks, electric plant – were being transferred to the civil domain; something which reflected a more general transfer from the end of 1918 from military to civil administration.

By April 1919, Wilson maintained that only by introducing Arab blood into the administration would lasting nationalist resentment be avoided. Yet, if anything, his proposals back-pedalled on previous pronouncements. Local investigations revealed general support for a single British High Commissioner for the whole of Mesopotamia. Beneath him would be four, presumably British, Commissioners in the provinces of Basra, Baghdad, the Euphrates and Mosul, each area containing Provincial Councils selected by the Divisional Councils. The latter, however, were to be entirely nominated and non-executive bodies because, as Wilson observed, 'Experience shows that elective bodies are unsuited to present conditions.' In pursuance of the policy of introducing Arab blood, Wilson proposed to create an Arab hybrid, 'carefully selected Arabs of good birth and education belonging to Iraq by birth'. Such men, raised from the dust, would have few problems in identifying British interests as their own. Wilson conceded the point that the Governors of Baghdad, Basra and Amara would be Arabs drawn from this class, but even they would be advised by a British official.[190] The objections to this idea raised by British officials in Mesopotamia led Wilson to postpone its implementation. With minor deviations, such also were the views of the Political Officers who had assented to Wilson's constitution as 'the limit to which we can safely go at present . . . i.e. . . . , the maximum for which local opinion is prepared and of which local personnel is capable'.[191]

BRINGING IN THE DESERT

I

As noted in chapter 4, the momentum of British imperialism in Mesopotamia was sustained, in part, by the relationship which evolved between senior India Office officials and their subordinates in Mesopotamia. More specifically, there was Sir Arthur Hirtzel, with his acute understanding of the local view, his correspondence with Sir Arnold Wilson and, as time passed, his highly developed sensitivity to international opinion.[192]

Towards the end of 1918, as the Eastern Committee grappled with the complexities of Britain's case for the retention of Mesopotamia, there were more pronounced indications than before of a clash between A.T. Wilson and his superiors in London. By November 1918, British forces were in occupation of Mosul. For a considerable period many senior British officials remained ignorant of Lloyd George's success in persuading Clemenceau to concede control of that Vilayet to Britain. Moreover, both British and French personnel in Mesopotamia were apparently unaware of this development and, consequently, the peculiar interaction of international and local conditions, of personalities and motives, which together had previously ensured British predominance in Basra and Baghdad, continued to shape events in Northern Mesopotamia. Efforts by the French to cling to the position of ascendancy in Mosul created by Sykes–Picot served merely to strengthen the opposition to this among those responsible for the development of Mesopotamia.

Amid requests from Cambon in November 1918 that the French Consul at Basra and a Commander Sciard might be permitted to proceed to Mosul to distribute alms, Shuckburgh remained unflinching in his Francophobia:

> Every telegram we receive from Baghdad strengthens the case for getting the French out of Mosul, where it is evident that nobody wants them and that their presence will inevitably be a source of constant friction . . . The position, thanks to the Sykes–Picot Agreement, is a delicate one; and it has been found necessary, quite recently, to warn Col. Wilson against acting or appearing to act in disregard of French rights in the Mosul Vilayet; and he has been instructed to restrict political action in the French sphere to the actual requirements of the military administration.[193]

Likewise information that Sciard might attempt to raise a battalion of the Orient Legion in Mosul led Shuckburgh to respond bluntly that British military occupation of the country rendered this impossible.[194]

During the autumn and winter of 1918, A.T. Wilson on several occasions gave expression to the expansionist urges which had secured the Basra and Baghdad Vilayets. On 14 November he raised the question of railway surveys into Kurdish areas.[195] Shuckburgh and

H.V. Cox wished to sanction this, provided that the work would not impinge on the area reserved for France by the Sykes–Picot Agreement.[196] General agreement on the desirability of extending the Baghdad–Tekrit line was tempered on Shuckburgh's part by an eagerness not to be cowed by French prickliness over the fulfilling of Sykes–Picot.[197] At the Foreign Office Balfour was 'firmly opposed' to impinging on Area 'A' of that Agreement but, as Shuckburgh noted, 'The *whole* of the Mosul Vilayet is not in Area "A" (French sphere). Let us be careful to restrict our self-denying ordinance only to *those parts of the Vilayet in which the French (unfortunately) can establish claims.*'[198]

In mid-October, A.T. Wilson had expressed more than simply paternal feelings towards the Kurds of Eastern Mosul.[199] In his view tribes east of the Lesser Zab were anxious for British protection:

> The re-occupation of Kirkuk would bring them all in to us. The larger migratory tribes who spend part of their time in the Persian hills and part on the border of [the] Mesopotamia plain Dargai Jaf are showing a friendly disposition and a readiness to obey orders given to them . . .
>
> Politically as well as strategically there is much to be said for adopting of line of lesser Zab as the frontier of the Iraq State, including in the latter Altun Zupri, Sulaimaniyah and Penjwin: the rich districts of Sulaimaniyah and Halebja are susceptible to great development, and their products are essential to industries and general well-being of Iraq, viz, petroleum, coal, seed-wheat, gell, nuts and tanned material and tobacco. The first two in particular, as His Majesty's Government are aware, are of great potential value.[200]

Regardless of how policy-makers planned to secure Britain's future in Mesopotamia, by the end of 1918 there existed a broad consensus that American opinion would be of considerable, possibly cardinal, importance. An awareness of this was implicit in Hirtzel's methods; yet having failed to have these adopted as official policy by the Eastern Committee, it became of great importance to ensure at least that the outward image created by the British administration in Mesopotamia might reflect an understanding of the sensitivity of international opinion.

In taking the initiative and pronouncing on matters of policy, A.T. Wilson threatened to expose British aims at a crucial moment. That, occasionally, he merely reiterated earlier objectives did not particularly matter. The context in which Wilson expressed his thoughts had changed; this had been brought to his attention, yet he continued to transgress the new confines within which policy was defined. Moreover, he remained unrepentant, writing to Hirtzel on 20 November that whilst he had spoken freely it was his duty 'to represent the local view as fully as possible'. The problem, as Wilson continued, was that although Government was responsible for the future of the country, he remained 'in the dark as to real policy'. In fact, as Wilson concluded, Britain apparently had no policy in Northern Mesopotamia.[201]

There was, in fact, very little disagreement between Wilson, his colleagues in Mesopotamia and his superiors in London regarding the direction of policy. On 5 November, Robert Cecil, who to the last maintained that Britain was still bound by the Sykes–Picot Agreement, requested of Smuts that he might resuscitate the question of an investigatory commission at the Eastern Committee. In Cecil's view, Britain must discover the truth about the administration, whether it was as 'wooden and . . . unpopular' as alleged, what the relationship should be between the Mosul and Baghdad Vilayets and, lastly, it was necessary to know more of Southern Kurdistan and whether it might be possible to administer it as part of Mesopotamia.[202] This anxiety to establish what the population of Northern Mesopotamia wanted and, more especially, the urge to expand the area under British occupation was fairly widespread at the time.[203] There were also specific issues relating to the future administration of the country to be resolved.

II

Besides expansion of British control in a northerly and north-easterly direction, on 24 November A.T. Wilson informed the India Office of a request by the people of Abu Kemal and Dair uz Zor on the Euphrates for the despatch there of a political officer. Without official approval Wilson sanctioned the move to Abu Kemal and, provisionally, to Dair.[204]

Then, on 4 December, came further confirmation that Wilson had not grasped the importance of avoiding any infringement of Area 'A'. Reporting the views of the Kurdish chiefs at Sulaimaniyah, Wilson stated that there was a 'substantial unanimity' in favour of British protection. In response to a formal request for British protection and association with Iraq from a number of those Sheikhs, Wilson reported:

> I signed a document stating any Kurdish tribes from Greater Zab to Diala (other than those in Persian territory) who of their own free will accepted leadership of Sheikh Mahmoud would be allowed to do so, and that latter would have our moral support in controlling the above area on behalf of [the] British Government, whose orders he undertook to obey.

Wilson's actions accorded with the spirit if not the letter of British policy. Yet, as he noted, he had appointed a representative of Britain in the person of Sheikh Mahmoud in Southern Kurdistan. Moreover, he had contracted on behalf of the British Government to sustain this 'confederation' with at least moral support.[205] As Shuckburgh noted in a footnote marked 'very confidential' to a draft reply to Wilson's telegram, these actions had to be seen in the context of the Sykes–Picot Agreement and in view of the possibility of French tenacity being increased by actions which plainly contravened that Agreement. It therefore followed, as Shuckburgh noted, that the advance of the Political Officer at Abu Kemal to Dair should be disallowed 'unless there are strong reasons to [the] contrary based on [the] needs of [the] military administration'.[206]

Within three days of Shuckburgh writing, the threatened massacre of Armenian refugees in the vicinity of Dair gave Hirtzel, Shuckburgh and Eyre Crowe a pretext to avoid this narrow ordinance.[207] A political officer was to proceed to Dair 'in a purely military capacity to rescue [the] Armenians and [to] buy supplies'.[208] Whilst his administrative activities would be confined to the execution of those duties, this advance was of more than symbolic importance. As Wilson observed, Britain's position in Mosul was strong, as much could be accomplished on the basis of military needs in these unstable tribal territories.[209]

The discussion of British policy in the upper valley of the Euphrates was to be sustained by three factors. Broadly, the advance to Dair and the imminence of peace discussions occasioned a general debate on Mesopotamia's frontiers. This, in turn, necessitated a detailed discussion about the future of the Kurds, an issue which bedevilled British policy throughout 1919 and beyond. Of more immediate concern in December 1918 was that Faisal, apparently on the instructions of Allenby's command in Egypt, had despatched a number of his followers who had proceeded to occupy Dair.[210] This and subsequent military endeavours to secure Anah and Abu Kemal met with incredulity at the India Office where, besides Faisal's claim to control Syrian territory up to the Khabur river, little was known of any legitimate Hashemite claim to towns at more northerly points on the Euphrates.[211] The response of the Foreign Office to India Office representations – that the matter was one of purely military significance – merely compounded anxieties.[212] Whilst the conflicting claims of Faisal and Wilson persisted into 1920, during the first half of 1919 India Office officials were fully occupied with other aspects of British policy on the Euphrates.

On 27 January Wilson reported that the newly established political officer in Dair, having secured that town, now contemplated the seizure of Rakka further up the Euphrates.[213] Shuckburgh, who was disinclined to sanction the extension of British influence in that direction, questioned the military justification of this 'ominous' advance.[214] Curzon, newly installed at the Foreign Office, agreed, now possibly more alert to the consequences of being seen to be land-grabbing.[215]

This particular aspect of British policy towards Mesopotamia's borders then took a rather unexpected twist. On 22 February Balfour, then in Paris, conveyed to Wilson a private telegram from Hirtzel in which the latter posed the idea of extending the northern boundaries of Mesopotamia to include the entire Diarbekir basin. As Hirtzel continued, this move had been portrayed as essential in order to secure the full volume of water on the Tigris and Euphrates.[216] Though not explicitly stated, it seems possible that Hirtzel was toying with the idea of a northern Kurdish entity under British tutelage.

Hirtzel's intervention in the question of Mesopotamia's frontiers was unexpected if only because his previous communications from Paris suggested that conditions there militated against further British territorial gains. His attitude was determined by a number of factors. Notably, American opinion appeared to favour the extension of the northern boundary of Mesopotamia towards the frontier of the proposed Armenian State.[217] It may also be that Hirtzel got wind of Lloyd George's success in obtaining a renunciation of French rights in Mosul. There was certainly considerable evidence that French officers on the ground and their political masters still coveted the exclusive position conferred on them in Mosul by Sykes–Picot, and with it the immense mineral riches of the region. Besides American opinion, Hirtzel perceived the makings of further British expansion readily to hand.

In the initial discussions of Mesopotamia's frontiers which arose towards the end of 1918, the Foreign Office had recommended a more generous extension of British responsibilities in Northern Mesopotamia than was envisaged by A.T. Wilson.[218] In North-Eastern Mesopotamia this extension was due to the Foreign Office wishing to create a separate Nestorian enclave, Assyria, within the area which it defined as Southern Kurdistan.[219] The physical definition of Kurdistan by the Foreign Office and A.T. Wilson differed slightly but, simply stated, the Foreign Office, India Office and Baghdad alike envisaged an autonomous 'Southern' Kurdistan included within the frontiers of Mesopotamia.[220]

In suggesting the inclusion of the Diarbekir basin within those frontiers in February 1919, Hirtzel appeared to be endorsing the frontier proposed by the Foreign Office in November 1918. The Foreign Office boundaries had been communicated to Wilson on 13 December and in response he expressed doubts, on grounds of ethnography, about the feasibility of establishing a Nestorian enclave within Southern Kurdistan.[221] Instead, he suggested the creation of another area, lying mainly between his own north-eastern boundary and that proposed by the Foreign Office, in which the Christian peoples of that region might gather and, like the Kurds in Southern Kurdistan, constitute a separate enclave within Iraq with some measure of autonomy. Though not explicitly stated, the implication of this was that Wilson would accept the extension of Mesopotamia's frontiers to include a large swathe of territory stretching towards Diarbekir and Van (see Map 5). As to the north-western frontier, Wilson was equivocal. He made vague reference to reasons for adhering to the boundary which he had previously out-lined from Karadja to east of Rakka.[222] However, somewhat reluctantly it seems, Wilson was prepared to contemplate the inclusion within Mesopotamia of the area extending north beyond Diarbekir and west towards Marash, i.e., the Belikh Basin, something to which he had pre-viously objected on tribal grounds.[223] When commenting on Wilson's proposal A.J. Toynbee agreed with this logic on the grounds that the completion of the Baghdad Railway would draw this territory into close commercial relations with Syria.[224] In January 1919, Toynbee was also willing to consider some form of autonomy within the Mosul Vilayet for the Assyrian population of the Tur Abdin.[225] This, and Hirtzel's attempt to sustain Wilson's proposal for a separate Assyrian enclave further east, was symptomatic of the awareness among British officials of the problems posed by the Kurdish national movement; problems which ultimately defied Hirtzel's efforts to have Britain adopt a definite policy towards them. Bombarded by pleas from the Comité de l'Independence Kurde, Kidston employed a colourful metaphor to illustrate Britain's predicament:

> The Kurds now ask Great Britain to be a mother to them. I don't know how many similar applications to be adopted we have now had, but they are becoming alarmingly numerous and the resulting family promises to be hopelessly turbulent as well as quite impossibly expensive. Great Britain threatens to become like the old woman who lived in a shoe and that lady's methods with her offspring seem worthy of imitation in the case of most of these candidates for adoption.[226]

The root of the problem, as Toynbee observed, was the impossibility, on grounds of ethnography, geography, administration and the need to respect Persian integrity, of creating a single state which might include all of the Kurds.[227]

Responding to Hirtzel's suggestion about the inclusion of the Diarbekir basin, on 24 February, A.T. Wilson cast doubt on the necessity, in terms of irrigation requirements, for further territorial gains on the Tigris beyond the limits of the proposed Mosul Vilayet.[228] This apparently contradicted the sense of the telegram of 15 December in which he contemplated the posting of political officers to places such as Amadia which lay within the Diarbekir Basin.[229] Concluding his reply Wilson had rather more to say on the proposal:

> It would be necessary to constitute the new area into a fourth Vilayet, vis Diarbekir. It would apparently add considerably to our military liabilities. On local political grounds there is much to be said for strengthening non-Arab elements in the new state, but I confess I view with some apprehension the prospect of assuming further territorial responsibilities upon the somewhat nebulous basis indicated in the Secretary of State's telegram of 14 February and in current Reuters telegrams regarding mandatory States; on the basis of a British protectorate backed up by a virile Home Government I should not be afraid to do so.[230]

Wilson was not alone in his desire for a British protectorate pure and simple. D.G. Hogarth and General Marshall, among others, had spoken in this sense.[231] Yet Hirtzel's efforts to restrain Wilson were understandable, given that by swimming against the current of international opinion, the Civil Commissioner might seriously jeopardise Britain's future in Mesopotamia. This was to be the key factor in the deterioration of the relationship between Hirtzel and Wilson and was accentuated by the unease felt by Wilson about his position, something which he confided to his mother in mid-December 1918:

> My position is extraordinarily difficult in some ways. His Majesty's Government consider me as responsible to them for all political matters from Mosul to the Indian frontier, including the Gulf and Central Arabia, and consult me very freely. The Government of India regard me as 'too junior' (which is true) and are unwilling to accord me full recognition, which the Secretary of State for India gives. I have repeatedly run counter to the Government of India and have been supported by the Secretary of State: I have run counter to the Secretary of State and have induced him to modify his views, without getting any support from India. I have little or no expert advice at this end and have to rely on my wits and on the

general opinion of my colleagues: they are absolutely with me on all matters of importance. The Political Service is united and all of one mind.[232]

Wilson had conveyed similar concerns to Hirtzel a few weeks previously, protesting that his views on Mesopotamia, strong as they were, merely reflected opinion on the ground, which it was his duty to report.[233] To Wilson, there appeared to be no settled policy, and when eventually this was articulated, it took the 'nebulous' form of a directive rooted in the terminology of the Anglo-French Declaration.[234] More serious was Wilson's perception of his own position, a perception which in time became self-fulfilling as his instincts led him to champion the virile policies in which he believed and the effect of which he summarised in a letter written to his mother in January 1919:

> The truth is that I am partly responsible in the eyes of the Government for creating in these regions a political Frankenstein Monster and His Majesty's Government as far as I can see look to me (whether in a controlling or subordinate capacity I cannot say) to remain on the spot and harness it.[235]

A few days later Wilson brought the monster to life by suggesting that Muscat should be controlled from Baghdad.[236] Then, on 7 February, Wilson observed that the nominal sphere for which he was responsible and which, in his view, stretched from 'the Indian frontier westward to the border of Syria and includes Maskat and Central Arabia' should be placed under a single authority at Baghdad.[237] To Shuckburgh this was a further example of Wilson's tendency 'to "spread himself out" at times', and, accordingly, submitted that Wilson might 'contract his wings' as there was sufficient to occupy his attention in Mesopotamia.[238]

Ironically, Hirtzel's attempts to sustain the momentum of British territorial gain in Mesopotamia encountered opposition nearer to home. Shuckburgh, commenting early in March on the possible inclusion within the Mesopotamian mandate of the Diarbekir Basin, observed: 'On every ground it appears desirable not to extend unnecessarily our responsibilities in this region, or to push forward into areas far removed from our bases which we should have great difficulty in either administering or defending.'[239] Holderness, somewhat unhelpfully, suggested that the possibility of a limitrophe power controlling the upper reaches of the Tigris and Euphrates might be met by a discussion between Britain and that power.[240] This was precisely the mentality to which A.T. Wilson took exception and which seemed to preclude the possibility of forward moves on Mesopotamia's frontiers. In his telegram of

24 February, Wilson argued that for reasons connected with irrigation the Dair uz Zor region must be retained within Mesopotamia.[241] At the end of May and amid considerable debate about the definition of the Syrian/Mesopotamian border, Wilson resumed the charge, suggesting that the inclusion of Dair necessitated the acquisition of Rakka and Bilikh. Failing this, Wilson observed, Dair might as well be left to France, leaving Abu Kemal as the most advanced post on the Euphrates.[242]

Wilson wrote in response to a confusing telegram despatched to Allenby by the War Office which, in attempting to define the frontiers of the French mandate in Syria, appeared to Wilson to shore up in an unacceptable fashion homogeneous tribal areas.[243] Moreover, Wilson was concerned that the isolation of Dair rendered its administration from Baghdad impossible.[244] On grounds of ethnography and administration Hogarth accepted Wilson's view, suggesting, on the assumption that Britain obtained Palmyra, an extension of the frontier to Rakka.[245] Hirtzel agreed, partly because in Paris the War Office had asked that the frontier might include Birejik.[246] However, if the War Office failed to secure the inclusion of Palmyra within Palestine, then both Hirtzel and Hogarth would accept Abu Kemal as the most advanced point.[247] Besides the advantages conferred on irrigation by an advance beyond Abu Kemal, the main importance to Britain of this frontier lay in the eventual alignment of the proposed rail-link between Mesopotamia and the Mediterranean. As Shuckburgh noted there was one further consideration: that in retreating from Dair 'we should be abandoning a place . . . which we have already brought within our political influence at the request of the inhabitants . . . and which is of some importance as the centre of a fertile district, said to be specially rich in timber'. However, for the 'prudential reasons' which had previously led him to veto further territorial extensions, Shuckburgh preferred Abu Kemal.[248]

If the efforts of those who sought to restrain Wilson were understandable, then so, too, in some measure, were Wilson's efforts to evade those constraints. The continuing ambiguity surrounding the fate of Mesopotamia and, in particular, of the Mosul Vilayet affected every aspect of the administration. In the various schemes put forward for the Mesopotamian frontiers and in Wilson's draft constitution, it was assumed that the area of French influence in Mosul apportioned to her in the Sykes–Picot Agreement would be significantly reduced in scope. Towards the end of 1918, Wilson had been told that it was hoped to induce France to forgo her claims in Mosul but, like many of his superiors in London, Wilson remained ignorant of Lloyd George's success in obtaining Mosul well into 1919, learning of this, it seems, on his trip to Paris in the spring.[249] For much of 1919, however, Curzon prevented Wilson from making an announcement about the future of Mosul or Mesopotamia as a whole, something which Wilson regarded as a prerequisite to the implementation of his draft constitution. Curzon had also applied the brakes in another area.

In view of French sensibilities regarding the future of Mosul, at an Inter-Departmental Conference held on 11 January 1919 at which Curzon presided, it was decided that whilst the survey of the prospective rail-link to Mosul via Kifri might proceed, no further additions would be made to the Baghdad–Tekrit line.[250] Moreover, in communicating this instruction to Marshall, the War Office also suspended rail extensions on the Euphrates beyond Hit.[251]

As we have seen, A.T. Wilson had been a keen advocate of surveys into Kurdish territory and in this he had the qualified support of Shuckburgh and Hirtzel.[252] Writing at the end of November 1918, in connection with the Shoreimiyeh–Mosul line, Wilson noted that any sudden decision to cease construction would be interpreted as a sign that Britain did not intend to retain the Mosul Vilayet. Without some form of railway connection with Mosul, Wilson considered it 'almost impossible to develop and administer Mosul in harmony with [the] rest of Irak'.[253] Though sympathetic to this argument, senior India Office officials felt that the line could not be justified on military grounds. More broadly, Hirtzel confessed to having anxieties 'about Captain Wilson's "forward" policy in Mosul. We all want to get the French out, but fear we shall only put their backs up if we Anglicise it before coming to terms with them. That is what they clearly suspect us of trying to do in Syria.'[254]

Much the same view prevailed at the Foreign Office where, in February 1919, a request was received from Marshall via the War Office that a light gauge line of 2 feet 6 inches should be extended to Mosul from the standard gauge railhead.[255] The request was made on the grounds of the inadequacy of road transport for the supply of the garrison in Mosul. For this reason, it seems, the DMO was prepared to support the idea, observing that the line could, if necessary, be easily removed.[256] Hubert Young disagreed and in this had the concurrence of Kidston who noted that the proposal was in contravention of both the spirit and the letter of Sykes–Picot.[257] As Kidston explained, by article ten of that 'intolerable instrument', the railway on the Tigris was not to be extended beyond Samara.[258] A day later the idea was put to Curzon, who minuted with some acerbity: 'Just as an Archdeacon is a person who performs Archdiaconal functions so a railway is a line that performs railway functions even though it be 2.6 instead of 4.8. Disallow for present.'[259] By mid-April, however, under sustained pressure from Wilson and Marshall, Curzon was obliged to reverse this decision due to concerns about 'public order and future pacification' raised by unrest in Kurdistan.[260]

Continuing disorder in Southern Kurdistan and the revelation of Lloyd George's success in obtaining the cession of Mosul to Britain ensured that the extension of the line towards Mosul remained an important issue in the summer of 1919. On 1 June, McMunn, the new GOC, argued for a further extension from Kizil Robat in order to hold and pacify Kurdistan.[261] Hirtzel apparently favoured a metre gauge line via Kizil Robat, Kifri, Kirkuk, Altun-Keupri and Erbil for reasons which related primarily to long-term economic alignments but also to immediate military and civil needs.[262] The policy of occupying strategic centres suggested by McMunn was referred to the Inter-Departmental Conference on the Middle East but, in view of the absence of expert military advice, when the question was discussed at the meeting on 28 July a decision was deferred.[263] Having subsequently discussed the issue with Montagu, Major-General Radcliffe and Shuckburgh, Curzon sanctioned a telegram prepared by Shuckburgh in which it was suggested that as Britain would only ever exercise a 'loose political supervision' in Southern Kurdistan, any measures which appeared to suggest a permanent military occupation should be avoided. As Shuckburgh continued, the extension of British influence in that region had been undertaken in the belief that the inhabitants wanted it. They now appeared to be 'actively hostile' to the extent that strategic railways were necessary. 'In these circumstances', Shuckburgh concluded, 'might it not be a better course to withdraw our political officers, etc., and leave [the] Kurds to their own devices? [The] alternative of maintaining order by force among recalcitrant mountain tribesman opens up [the] prospect of military commitments which His Majesty's Government contemplates with [the] gravest apprehension. [The] last thing they desire is to create a new North West frontier problem on the North Eastern borders of Iraq.'[264]

SWORDS INTO PLOUGHSHARES

I

To Hirtzel no aspect of British policy in Mesopotamia had been of greater significance during 1918 than the development of commerce. As we have seen, Islington agreed, and thus encountered the opposition of Shuckburgh and Holderness who held that until the political future of Mesopotamia was clearer, preferential treatment should not be given to British companies ahead of their foreign rivals. Increasingly, Shuckburgh was motivated by a desire to avoid responsibility for failed ventures in the unsettled conditions which prevailed. By 12 November, amid representations from companies directed through the British Trade Corporation, some definition had been given to British policy in a draft reply to one such company, Messrs Forbes Forbes Campbell & Co. Limited:

> While it is impossible at the present stage to give anything in the nature of definite assurances in regard to future commercial facilities in the occupied territories, His Majesty's Government will be ready, as soon as circumstances permit, to give all possible encouragement to British firms of good standing seeking to interest themselves in the development of the country after the war.[265]

During the following months the same factors influenced thinking at the India Office, although Montagu at least was prepared to sanction investigatory measures, if nothing more, by a mission of the British Trade Corporation, something which had first been suggested in May 1918.[266] Somewhat reluctantly, Shuckburgh accepted this, adding that it would be necessary to avoid opening the flood gates to companies if this had a deleterious effect on civil administration and development. In any case, Shuckburgh observed, the fate of the country had yet to be decided and it would therefore be unjust to allow British firms to acquire interests if Britain could not protect them. Further, as Shuckburgh continued, 'it may tend to discredit our professions in the eyes of the world if, during a period in which the future of Mesopotamia is *ex hypothesi* still an open question, we are found to be busily engaged in building up a strong commercial position for ourselves on the spot'.[267]

In two separate ordinances of 6 January and 17 February 1919, the Board of Trade opened the trade of Mesopotamia, along with that of many other countries, to individuals and institutions resident in the United Kingdom.[268] In spite of this, difficulties remained. Continuing ambiguity about the future of the Mosul Vilayet, and the likelihood that any forward moves there by Britain inconsistent with the needs of the military occupation would provoke French protests, meant that Curzon was unwilling to declare the Vilayet in friendly occupation, thereby permitting the resumption of trade with other areas of the country.[269]

In the winter of 1918–19, Hirtzel was less enthusiastic about a cautious policy than many other officials. Admittedly, exposure to the atmosphere of the Peace Conference rendered him more acutely aware of the need to avoid any action which appeared publicly to assume a British mandate in Mesopotamia. In certain contexts this required tactical backtracking. Writing privately to Shuckburgh from Paris in January 1919, Hirtzel advised that, if it was still proposed to publish the report of the Mesopotamian Trade Commissioners, then it was essential to omit any suggestion of the exclusion of foreigners or of preference being given to British trade 'in any shape or form. All ideas of that kind will have to go, and absolute freedom of transit and transport and equality of treatment is the order of the day.'[270] On the other hand, in the detailed discussion which arose on the associated matter of banking, Hirtzel was equally convinced that measures which might facilitate discreet commercial and civil development under British auspices should not be delayed either by an unwillingness to delegate to Wilson the power to select which institution he wished to invite into Mesopotamia, or by excessive caution in Whitehall.[271] In Hirtzel's view, Mesopotamia must above all else be 'sufficiently "banked"'.[272] Against this, specifically, was a fairly broad awareness of the importance of banking as the forerunner of commercial exploitation in the future of Mosul. The disinclination of the Foreign Office to sanction the opening at Mosul of a branch of the Eastern Bank was, in any case, endorsed by Wilson who believed that, as regards the needs of the military occupation, the provisions of the Imperial Ottoman Bank in Mosul were sufficient.[273] By June 1919, in relation to this particular question, the risk of British trade being disadvantaged by Britain, in Montagu's words 'playing the game', had diminished.[274] And in Wilson's absence E.B. Howell, Wilson's deputy, had sanctioned the opening of a branch of the Eastern Bank in Mosul.[275]

In spite of their awareness of the French acquiescence in the cession of Mosul to Britain, for much of 1919 the Foreign Office acted persistently to put a brake on the commercial development of Mesopotamia. Indeed, notwithstanding the representation by many firms that the Board of Trade licence which permitted trade with Mesopotamia was retarding trade with Mosul, and that Mosul might henceforth be included under the proclamation of 1915, the Foreign Office made a concession, reluctantly, in December 1919. Curzon decreed that circumstances militated against 'any public declaration indicating a change of status of the Vilayet of Mosul'. However, he was prepared to sanction, discreetly, facilities 'for the resumption of trade with that district'. Accordingly, enquirers were to be told that they might act 'as if the Vilayet of Mosul had been declared friendly territory within the meaning of the Trading with the Enemy (Occupied Territory) Proclamation 1915'.[276]

During 1919 a parallel debate had arisen on the question of land leases to private individuals and commercial enterprises. Whilst applications from prospective Indian settlers had been turned down by Wilson, towards the end of June 1919 he recommended that 25-year leases be granted to officers and men of Force 'D', adding that local landowners who had been consulted on this were favourably disposed.[277] Personally, Montagu strongly opposed the granting of leases to white Britons if Indians were to be excluded.[278] Also, in granting land in military occupation, there was no existing authority empowered to transfer the ownership of land. Though aware of the potential for attracting investment by the sale of land in private ownership, Montagu considered this inconsistent with 'the spirit of the obligations which a mandatory power will undertake'.[279] Predictably, the Foreign Office agreed, defending the veto in such a way as to preclude the sale of either state or privately owned lands to outside persons until the political future of Mesopotamia had been decided at the Peace Conference.[280]

A.T. Wilson, concerned by the effect of such strictures on the fortunes both of local and foreign interests had, by November 1919, elicited some sympathy at the India Office. C.C. Garbett,[281] minuting on 1 November, suggested that the acquisition of land by firms with a commercial orientation, and which had Wilson's backing, might be put to the Foreign Office.[282] As to the related matter of commercial concessions Garbett felt that, with the exception of oil exploration, the need for such authorisation might be waived. Curzon's typically bland response – that 'international considerations' precluded either the granting of concessions in Mosul on anything other than exceptional lines after reference to London, or granting of commercial concessions anywhere in Mesopotamia 'pending the final settlement' – served merely to convince Hirtzel of Curzon's blind ignorance to the inevitable effect of his actions, which was summarised thus by Hirtzel in February 1920: 'I believe there is a real danger of a public demand that we should clear out of Mesopotamia when it is realised how much it is going to cost before the country begins to pay.'[283]

II

By the end of 1918, A.T. Wilson was encountering difficulties in the attitude of the military authorities regarding the transfer to civil government of departments such as agriculture, medical services and, in particular, irrigation.[284] There was an awareness both in Mesopotamia and in London that the handling of this transfer would have a lasting effect on Britain's popularity with the indigenous population, but it was felt in some quarters that the move to civil administration should await the decision of the proposed international Commission. Such was the view of the ever-cautious Holderness, who had also expressed himself similarly on the matter of contracts for civil administration staff in Mesopotamia.[285] Ironically, the War Office, in particular, was concerned about the loss of technical expertise which would occur if, as Curzon desired, only temporary contracts were to be issued on account of the uncertainty of the country's future.[286] For his part, Holderness pointed to the great expense involved, in terms of local revenues, if longer contracts were issued.[287] Eventually the Foreign Office was persuaded to extend these to three years; A.T. Wilson's argument that, exceptionally, 10-year contracts might be sanctioned was rejected.[288]

The discussion had arisen in the first months of 1919 in the context of concerted efforts by Wilson to accelerate the transfer to civil control of many aspects of administration entrusted to military control. Amid accusations that the administration was already 'preposterously large' and 'complex' and that Wilson had overestimated the deleterious effect of short, temporary contracts, Wilson was willing to accept that some 'quasi civil' departments which had been organised on military lines would remain until the military occupation ended.[289] On the other hand, General Marshall, the then GOC, with whom Wilson enjoyed relatively good relations, had, in March 1919, expressed a willingness to see the transfer to civil control of several departments.[290] Moreover, as Wilson noted, there were certain financial advantages in such a course:

> All I have asked to do is to take over existing machinery and adopt it, by drastic reduction, to civil needs, during the next twelve months: this will involve a deficit of between one and two million pounds on what is

nominally the civil administration budget, but it will save a much larger
sum on the military budget and will facilitate demobilisation and the
growth of civil government.[291]

Wilson's mounting frustration during the following months was
understandable. According to his interpretation of events, the only effective antidote to the increasing turbulence of the country was either a
proclamation announcing the permanence of the British connection –
something to which the Foreign Office objected throughout 1919 – or
some tangible evidence of this on the ground. Such evidence might be
provided by the expansion of the civil administration into areas previously controlled by the military. Yet, in spite of the cancellation of the
international Commission in its original form, Wilson perceived the attitude of the home authorities as being fundamentally at odds with the
best interests of Mesopotamia. There was, moreover, the deteriorating
relationship with the military to be considered, and it was in this connection that Wilson directed his frustration, passing to Hirtzel in a letter
dated 3 June, marked 'private and personal', a communiqué from the
Political Officer, Basra, A.S. Meek, in which the latter observed:

> Army rule has been immensely unpopular in the Basrah Division. The
> private soldier and his Officer cannot conceive how an alien race so many
> of whom, of the Koi Poloi, [sic] have grown rich in their connection with
> themselves can be so ungrateful as to dislike them. But the Army and all
> its ways is held in very strong dislike by the whole of upper class
> Mohammadan Society and generally speaking by the whole people . . .
> This may provoke a smile as being a little out of proportion. But the thing
> is a fact. People have been impatiently waiting the advent of a Civil
> Regime, misgiving the continuation of Military Control.

To enforce his point Meek complained of the unpopularity of
McMunn's announcement that he proposed to continue controlling the
civil government of the country for three years.[292] To ensure that this
volley went home, on the same day Wilson had also written to Gertrude
Bell, then in Europe, whose indiscretion could be counted upon, complaining specifically of McMunn's inflexibility in the matter of the
transfer to civil control. Moreover, Wilson added, according to some
reports McMunn had announced the indefinite continuation of civil
control and had, allegedly, 'broadly hinted' about his desire to be
the first High Commissioner.[293] In spite of Wilson's awareness of the
enormity of the task entrusted to him, his conception of his own destiny
was somewhat different from that with which his superiors, as career

officials, could readily empathise. Accordingly, he did not regard McMunn's ambitions as anything in the manner of a personal challenge. To Wilson, the General's intrigues merely undermined the imperial edifice which he had painstakingly erected; something which, in his view, was also occurring due to the perceived buckling of his mentor, Hirtzel, under the strain of negative advice. However, at least McMunn's ambitions, which according to Hirtzel lay rather in the direction of a military governorship, were equally unacceptable to the latter.[294]

By mid-1919 Hirtzel was beginning to perceive the incompatibility between Wilson's personality and the task which confronted him, even if he remained ignorant of the source from which this sprung in the mind of the Civil Commissioner. That Hirtzel was prepared to indulge Wilson was a measure of his esteem for the latter. Yet in the ominous tone which Hirtzel reserved for errant subordinates, in a letter dated 16 July, he had issued a caution which amounted to a final warning because, Hirtzel observed, 'I do not wish to see you run your head into a wall'. More tenderly, Hirtzel had directed the attention of the Civil Commissioner to a particularly important aspect of policy and, in its precise summary of the issue, Hirtzel's letter is worth quoting at some length. Commenting on two telegrams sent by Wilson, Hirtzel observed:

As regards Arab nationalism, I think you will soon find yourself in pretty deep water, and, to be frank, I do not feel that you are going the right way to work with it . . . You appear to be trying, impossibly, to stem the tide instead of guide it into the channel that would suit you best. You are going to have an Arab State whether you like it or not, whether Mesopotamia wants it or not . . . There is no getting out of it, and it is much easier to face the fact. Moreover, you are also going to have a lot of people in Mesopotamia whose heads will be full of absurd ideas from Syria and heaven knows where, and a room and a use must be found for them . . . All these things are going to be contrary to our most cherished hopes, and nothing that you or I say will alter them. I hoped that you would have realised all that when you were over here – that the idea of Mesopotamia as the model of an efficiently administered British dependency or protectorate is dead (the same idea is dying in India, and is decomposing in Egypt), and that an entirely new order of ideas reigns. No doubt we must do what we can to put on the brake, and save all we can out of the wreck. But it is no use to shut our eyes to the main fact. We must adapt ourselves and our methods to the new order of ideas, and find a different way of getting what we want. You are still young enough to do this wholeheartedly, and your success in life whether in Mesopotamia or elsewhere depends on the measure in which you do. With which parental advice I leave this thorny subject.[295]

Hirtzel was referring in particular to the increasingly contentious issue of the return to Mesopotamia of Baghdadi officers who had served in Faisal's army. Hirtzel had been conscious of the sensitivity of the issue for some time. By May 1919, there was growing concern among senior India Office officials at the prospect of such officers returning to Mesopotamia and spreading nationalist ideas. This was compounded by A.T. Wilson's announcement in Paris that in the future such officers might return to Mesopotamia – something which had the support of T.E. Lawrence – and his uncompromising hostility to the idea thereafter.[296] In July 1919, Kidston viewed the issue as a struggle personified by Wilson and Lawrence, the former regarding the officers as 'dangerous propagandists sent by Faisal and Hussein to undermine British authority and advocate the inclusion of Mesopotamia in an independent Arabia'. In Kidston's view an impasse could only be avoided by a decision as to mandates by the Peace Conference.[297]

Symptomatic of Hirtzel's increasing concern about Wilson's attitude towards Arab nationalism was an incident involving the expulsion of some boys from a Mosul school for wearing 'Arab colours'.[298] When tackled on the issue, Wilson had raised the question of a flag for Mesopotamia claiming, with Shuckburgh's concurrence, that so long as the military occupation persisted, the only permissible flag was the Union Jack.[299] Hirtzel was not so easily deceived, minuting angrily in August:

> We were not talking about flags, and Colonel Wilson has used reference to a Mesopotamian flag as a red-herring to put us off the scent – after his manner. The real question was whether in a country in which (though it may be under military occupation) we are publicly pledged to set up an Arab Government it is wise or proper to expel schoolboys for wearing Arab colours. I maintain that it is grossly stupid and improper, and if Colonel Wilson and his 'Education Department' cannot see that, it seems to me to show how disastrous even to the Civil mind is the effect of wearing the hobnails of 'military occupation'.

As Hirtzel noted, the issue was not so much one of Wilson's views about the establishing of an Arab State, but rather one of the 'spirit' in which the administration was conducted, and one of which the foregoing was indicative.[300] Stronger misgivings about the spirit of Wilson's regime were expressed by officials at the Foreign Office. Hubert Young,

minuting in September on Wilson's request that a prominent nationalist, Yasin Pasha, be excluded from Mesopotamia, observed that any
such efforts designed permanently to exclude nationalists would generate a powerful anti-British nationalism with which Indian sedition would
not compare. Young continued:

> If our administrative methods in Mesopotamia are such that they cannot
> be reconciled with Arab ideas, they must be wrong, and should be altered.
> It is no argument to point to the acquiescence of Arab Sheikhs and culti-
> vators in our methods. The people whom we must conciliate are those who
> think they know better than we do what the people want, and the way to
> show them that we are right – is to take them round by the hand, and make
> them realise that they cannot suggest any improvement on our methods.[301]

Young's views thus expressed tallied in some measure with Hirtzel's
thinking. However, whilst Hirtzel did not regard as inevitable any
diminution in British influence in Mesopotamia, Young increasingly
viewed concessions to the nationalists as a precursor to a more limited
role for Britain in the future of Mesopotamia.[302] There was a general
awareness that much of the trouble in Mesopotamia stemmed from a
fear that the Anglo-French Declaration would not be implemented, but
responses to this at the Foreign and India Offices differed. This impression was derived from Wilson's response to Hirtzel's letter of 16 July, in
which the latter stated that Wilson's constitution, which had on Hirtzel's
admission been approved, would on the cessation of the military occupation have to be replaced.[303] To Hirtzel, in the fraught atmosphere of
mid-1919, the most glaring omission in that document was its failure
adequately to provide for real Arab participation in the operation of
central government.[304] Mounting unrest in Mesopotamia rendered the
issue one of some importance and Wilson's defiant response, justified as
he was in claiming that his draft constitution had been accepted, was ill-
considered. According to Wilson, whilst the constitution was still open
to adaptation, on local grounds he was convinced that 'we are on
the right lines and that we cannot move more rapidly without the risk
of untoward events which would set the clock back'.[305] If Wilson's
personality rendered him a wayward, not to say defiant, oracle of
Government policy, then inevitably the cumulative effect of this was
ultimately to undermine his credibility among senior figures. Hirtzel was
no exception and, possibly as a result of Wilson's telegram of 21 July,
he came down firmly in favour of the return of Sir Percy Cox as being
'*urgently necessary*'.[306]

The context of Hirtzel's remark was a discussion which arose on the subject of a proposal by Wilson that before any final decision was reached by the home authorities about the future of Mesopotamia, an officer of 'reputation and of experience' should tour the country and acquaint himself and officials in London with conditions on the ground.[307] Amid speculation as to why Wilson had suggested the idea and as to possible candidates, Hirtzel supported the proposal on the grounds that it was essential to know of conditions in Mesopotamia before a mandate was prepared. Failing this, Hirtzel added, it would be drawn up 'in Paris or Sutherland House' with undue emphasis on France and Syria, something which might affect the interests of Mesopotamia. On the subject of Cox's return, Hirtzel continued: 'The Agreement with Persia should be signed this week, and therewith we shall have turned the corner. But in Mesopotamia the corner is ahead of us, and we shall need the oldest political hand if it is to be turned without a smash.'[308] There were few dissenting voices at the Foreign Office on the matter of Cox's return. However, in the debate which arose about a suitable candidate to conduct the investigation and in spite of Hirtzel's enthusiasm for the project, Curzon delivered the *coup de grâce* by indicating his belief that further investigation of the country should not be undertaken until the mandate had been obtained.[309]

The prospect of Cox's return and an announcement of this, something which it was hoped might have had a steadying effect, also enabled Curzon and senior Foreign Office officials to frustrate India Office plans in another related matter. For some time Wilson had been requesting permission to make an announcement about the future of Mesopotamia and, in particular, of Mosul.[310] Prior to this the India Office had, somewhat reluctantly, yielded to the steadfast refusal of the Foreign Office to entertain the idea. By August 1919, with the cancellation of the international Commission, the postponing of the decision on mandates and what Shuckburgh termed 'the highly unsatisfactory, not to say dangerous, state of affairs that is being allowed to develop', it was decided to make a stand.[311] Shuckburgh, who drafted a telegram to the Foreign Office, assessed the problem in the following terms:

> We cannot of course allow Colonel Wilson to tear up the Declaration of November. But the situation is an exasperating one. No one really wants to turn us out of Mesopotamia, and our disappearance would do no good to anybody. Yet we are not allowed to say that we are going to stay; and our silence is beginning to create serious suspicion as to our intentions, leading to unrest, organised sedition (fomented from outside) and the

murder of our political officers in outlying districts. All of this we might stop merely by *saying* that we intend to do what everybody knows we must and ought to do.[312]

Naturally this was acceptable to Hirtzel who, like Shuckburgh, though aware of Curzon's obstructiveness, was not above quoting the latter to illustrate that the real problem lay in Paris where Lloyd George's efforts to secure a British mandate in Mesopotamia were insufficient.[313] Hirtzel, sensibly perhaps, given the weight of opposition to any forward moves, felt it necessary to tone down the draft declaration which it was intended should be sent to Wilson, and which Shuckburgh had prepared and enclosed in his telegram to the Foreign Office. Whilst Shuckburgh proposed and Hirtzel accepted the need for an announcement which might give effect to the intention of the Anglo-French Declaration to provide 'support and effective assistance' to the local administration, Hirtzel's alterations reflected his belief both that much needed to be done to increase Arab involvement in the administration and that, conversely, the nature and duration of British involvement must reflect this.[314]

Responding to this idea the Foreign Office stated that Curzon, having discussed the idea with the British Delegation in Paris, was unwilling to sanction an announcement; and this was understandably regarded as contemptuous by Shuckburgh.[315] Curzon strongly resented interference by India Office officials who were not acting on his instructions via the Inter-Departmental Conference on the Middle East which, in any case, Curzon was unwilling to convene on a daily basis.[316] Moreover, even if he and his officials shared the sense of frustration occasioned by the delay in Paris, they were, unlike their counterparts at the India Office, willing to run the risks entailed in 'playing the game'. The most significant of these was the prospect of alienating France; something which, it might be added, was not considered by Vansittart[317] in Paris as being of sufficient magnitude to preclude his acceptance of the India Office announcement in diluted form.[318]

'A POLICY OF SCUTTLE': THE CAUCASUS, 1919

As we have seen in chapter 5, during the debates at the War Cabinet and Imperial War Cabinet on British policy in Russia, Curzon exercised considerable restraint. Partly this was owing to his desire to avoid charges of conducting an anti-Bolshevik crusade. Also, during December 1918, as Chairman of the Eastern Committee, Curzon was hard at work directing that body to the production of desiderata for the Peace Conference. He was, moreover, greatly preoccupied with discussions of the future of the Caucasus, with Britain's role in this, and with the various elements which, if properly handled, might provide for a significant British presence in the region.

At the fortieth meeting of the Eastern Committee on 2 December, Curzon attempted to define British strategic interests in the Caucasus:

> The whole experience of the war has taught us the supreme importance of this region, with a view to the countries further east, over which it is essential, in the interest of India and our Empire, that we should exercise some measure of political control. A hostile force in possession of this region of the Caucasus would turn the flank of the British position in Asia, as it very nearly did in Persia and Trans-Caspia in the course of the past six months. Further, anybody can easily see how a state of chronic disorder among the people in this area, many of whom are hereditary enemies, would immediately turn the Caucasus into an Asiatic Balkans threatening the peace of that part of the world, as the similar jealousies and ambitions of the Balkans have done in the eastern part of Europe. Any sort of anarchy, disorder, or Bolshevism there must inevitably react upon our whole position in Persia and the countries lying to the east of Persia.

To Curzon's mind there were also important economic considerations, both British and 'international'. The opening of the Dardanelles would make Batum the major port for Persian trade but also, by virtue of the Batum–Baku Railway, of increased importance in the export of oil. It would, in fact, in Curzon's words, become 'the emporium for the central parts of Asia'. In the case of Baku, a cosmopolitan and sophisticated city, there was the major international concern of the oil wells, the safety of which rendered it essential, from Britain's perspective, that no unstable political element should obtain permanent control there.[319]

Curzon proceeded to describe the other states 'creeping into existence' to the south of the Caucasus range, namely, Daghestan, Russian Armenia and Azerbaijan. The peculiar conditions of each, geographical, historical and religious, rendered them more or less likely, in Curzon's view, to be of use in deterring possible military threats to Britain's position in the east.[320] One such threat, Curzon noted, was the resuscitation of 'Russian' power in the region, something which would have obvious implications for the future independence of those states:

> Russia has spent millions of money and 60 or 70 years of fighting in order to get them. Will she abandon that quest altogether? Is it possible that a

reconstituted Russia of the future will once again get the Caucasus under her sway? I cannot answer that question; and in all probability what we ought to do, without forming any opinion upon it at all, is to refrain from taking any step that would prevent a resuscitated Russia from resuming her connection with that part of the world. But for the time being it is clear, from all the information we have, that these rising Republics are furiously anti-Bolshevik, and we ought to do nothing whatever to lead them to suppose that we are ignoring their claims to independence in favour of a possible revival of Russia in the future.[321]

Beyond this, Curzon believed that Batum must become a free port and that Britain should secure the Batum–Baku Railway. Baku, in turn, should be internationalised. Contemplating the future assumption of responsibilities by France or America in the Caucasus, and having out-lined British and international interests there, Curzon magnanimously and somewhat circuitously, postulated a temporary British occupation:

> we have to look to peace and order in that country. Is it not desirable to contemplate a temporary occupation there which might even take the form in most circumstances thoroughly to be deprecated – of international control? . . . I suggest to the Committee . . . that we should contemplate for the time being an Allied occupation of this country, an Allied occupation which might be undertaken by ourselves, the French, and the Americans, or in the last resort by ourselves alone, which would involve the holding of Batum, Tiflis, and Baku, the policing of the line, the control of railways, telegraphs, and so on, and, in fact, the giving of some kind of backbone and stability which will enable these rather rudimentary States, on either side of the line, to make their way into existence. I merely throw that out as a suggestion, because whether America or France ultimately takes it up there must be an interval before they can do so, and in that interval everything is tottering. You want the presence of some Power to keep order now, and you want to secure in the future that there shall be a free way from the Black Sea to the Caspian.[322]

Curzon had a strong hand and had prepared himself thoroughly for the discussions at the Eastern Committee relating to the Caucasus. Introducing the subject in the context of a proposed American relief mission to Armenia, Curzon juxtaposed the idea of suspicion of foreign interests in the region with the need for Britain to take a more active role there. Whilst concerned that if America staged a relief mission it might impinge upon areas in Syria conferred upon France in the Sykes–Picot Agreement, Curzon emphasised that in his opinion the French and Russian spheres in Armenia created by that Agreement had lapsed.[323]

Curzon was, moreover, extremely anxious to avoid giving the Americans the impression that France had any legitimate claims in Armenia or the Caucasus. To his mind, the argument that France might be enticed from Syria by an offer of an Armenian mandate was based upon the false premise that Sykes–Picot still held good. However, alongside other arguments used to oppose French involvement, there was the inescapable logic that if Sykes–Picot were binding and if France were to obtain Syria, then, if the Caucasus were of military value to Britain, the British presence there should continue. In the context of Armenian relief Curzon, though ultimately willing like the Foreign Office to accept the offer of help, had expressed misgivings about the scope of American aims. Suspicion of the composition of the proposed American mission was compounded by an awareness of the mining interests of the sponsor of the programme, E.J. Hoover. On the broader issue of America as a possible mandatory in Armenia, Curzon raised the possibility that the origins of this idea lay in a Committee of Union and Progress plot to save the former Ottoman Empire by supporting a temporary American supervision of its component parts.[324] In any case, Curzon objected, would not the War Office regard the presence of America in Armenia as a military threat to British interests? If the relief mission were to proceed, then, Curzon argued, it must be accompanied by several British Officers 'keeping a watch' on American activities.[325] Having started the hares of French and American involvement in the Caucasus, Curzon, with considerable elegance, proceeded in the course of the following weeks to run them to ground, occasionally lashing out powerfully in an effort to end the chase.

Indicative of this was his argument that the power which held Armenia must also hold the Caucasus. By Armenia, Curzon had in mind not the six vilayets but a very much smaller entity centred on Sivas and conforming to the ideas of authorities such as D.G. Hogarth.[326] Against this were Montagu, Robert Cecil and several Foreign Office officials who believed that by excluding Lazistan from Armenia, pan-Turanian schemes would be aided by the resulting territorial connection between Turkey proper and the Caucasus.[327] There was, moreover, in Cecil's mind, the repugnant idea of changing Armenia's borders on the basis of Turkish atrocities.[328] In any case, if, as Curzon argued, the trusteeship of Armenia and the Caucasus were inseparable, then would France or the United States still be interested in such an undertaking? According to Cecil, America would not.[329] As far as Armenia itself was concerned, it was necessary, in Curzon's opinion, both to create a 'palisade' against pan-Turanianism or the aggression of a third power, and to fulfil Britain's stated aim of creating an independent Armenian State. Given the factors which militated against American involvement there and in the Caucasus then, unless America or France would undertake supervisory functions, as Curzon observed, 'we have an absolutely free hand'.[330]

Other minds were working along very different lines. Montagu, like Cecil, believed in the necessity of creating a large Armenia, comprising the six vilayets, but felt America probably would not assume such a responsibility. Accordingly, and in view of French interest in the Anatolian Railway and her ability to garrison the region, Montagu considered France 'the natural Power to undertake it'.[331] Cecil agreed with this logic and with Curzon's conviction in the indivisibility of Armenia and the Caucasus. Tempted by the riches of this vast region, it was Montagu's belief that 'the most commercially minded nation in the World', that is France, would find this prospect difficult to resist.[332] Conversely, it was precisely the kind of entanglement in nationalist feuds which such responsibilities would inevitably involve to which Cecil pointed when arguing against the assumption of such a position by Britain.[333] However, Cecil conceded Curzon's point that there would be an interim period before France, or any other candidate, intervened. According to Curzon, Britain was already closely involved in the politics of the Caucasus; not least by virtue of the presence of her troops on the Batum–Baku Railway, an international rail-line.[334]

As we have noted the thinking of men such as Cecil, who favoured a French presence in the Caucasus, was predicated upon the belief that only by such means might Britain evade the Sykes–Picot Agreement. Smuts for his part felt it possible that France might occupy the Caucasus and then refuse to evacuate Syria.[335] In strategic and commercial terms that contingency was unacceptable even to Cecil. If, Cecil agreed, Sykes–Picot were to stand, then America, not France, should be invited in.[336] Discussion of French interests in the Caucasus by the Eastern Committee revealed deep-rooted animosities to French imperialism among several senior figures. To what extent undue emphasis was placed upon such animosities as a means to an end is unclear. However, those officials who voiced such opinions did not attempt seriously to resist the logic of Curzon's thoughts – that if America would not go into the Caucasus – then only Britain remained. In opposing a French mandate Curzon was also helped by a fairly widespread concern that the rapid easterly movement of a hostile military force, in the manner of

Drang nach Osten, might be repeated if France were in possession of
Batum and Baku. This concern was expressed most forcibly by senior
War Office officials and by H.V. Cox; and it was in response to such a
remark by Cox at the Eastern Committee on 2 December that Curzon
fanned the flames of Francophobia across the dry embers of the
Caucasus. Observing that much of his public life had centred on the
'political ambitions of France', and that her 'national character' and
'political interests' were frequently at odds with those of Britain, Curzon
observed:

> I am seriously afraid that the great Power from whom we may have most
> to fear in the future is France, and I almost shudder at the possibility of
> putting France in such a position. She is powerful in almost all parts of the
> world, even around India. Are we to place her in a position to control this
> railway from Batum to Baku? Batum is one of the main approaches to
> India. France is a highly organised State, has boundless intrepidity, imagi-
> nation, and a certain power of dealing with Eastern peoples; and the idea
> that she would sit quietly there simply for the purpose of allowing
> Azerbaijan and the other States to constitute themselves a strong people is
> out of the question, for the French are born intriguers . . . I can only say
> that I should be most reluctant to lend a hand to a scheme which would
> place France in a position of political authority in this region, and that I
> would sooner the States fought it out among themselves, and that Russia
> ultimately came back.[337]

Curzon's efforts to slay the idea of a French mandate were helped considerably by the weaknesses in the presentation of the case by proponents of the scheme. Both Cecil and Curzon knew that America was
most unlikely to take on the Caucasus. As Cecil observed, they 'would
be mad to do it'.[338] If, however, America was somehow induced to
assume responsibilities there, as Cecil argued, their presence would only
be of a temporary nature; and in the event of a revival of Russian
strength British possessions would be unprotected.[339] This was hardly a
positive recommendation of a French mandate. Nor was Cecil's belief
that if France were to retain Syria then an American presence in the
Caucasus was to be preferred. Added to this was Curzon's belief that
whereas France probably would not represent an actual military danger
to British interests, she might none the less intrigue against these interests. Cecil agreed that France would be a formidable rival in the
Caucasus.[340] This admission was to be of some importance when, in presenting his provisional summary of recommendations to the Committee, Curzon suggested a British mandate. To this Cecil objected that, if

France were to have responsibility for an Armenian State centred on Sivas, then the duties incumbent upon Britain in connection with the defence of the Caucasian Republics would lead to unremitting friction with France.[341]

At least some of Curzon's arguments were intended to counter the views of Smuts who, on 2 December, argued forcefully for an American presence in the Caucasus.[342] Smuts was motivated partly by a deep antipathy towards French polices world-wide; something to which he gave expression in a paper written on the following day, the crucial section of which read:

> France was a very bad neighbour to us in the past . . . I am afraid her arrogant diplomacy may be revived by the great change which has come over her fortunes. She has always been very ambitious, is militant and imperialist in temperament, and her politics leave generally a nasty trail of finance and concession-hunting behind them. I fear we shall find her a difficult if not an intolerable neighbour.
>
> We have been most generous to her. We have handed over to her two of the best tropical colonies of Germany; and in the fatal Sykes–Picot agreement we have made her the principal heir to the Turkish estate. In this agreement, with its natural corollary in the preposterous claims of Italy, I see the seeds of future trouble for Europe, and I think no effort should be left untried to get out of this hopeless blunder in policy. But France will not let us off; she will hold on grimly to the reversion of Syria and Asia Minor and Upper Mesopotamia, and will ask us an important price for any relaxation of her claims.[343]

Smuts's mistrust of France was sufficient to preclude the possibility of Britain luring her out of Syria with an offer of the Caucasus, and to this extent his views coincided with Curzon's thinking. From an imperialist angle Smuts then went badly astray arguing, in tones which in other contexts might have been acceptable to Cecil, that in order to evade Sykes–Picot and in the broader framework of international relations, Britain must befriend America. This was necessary, Smuts observed, partly to counter French selfishness and greed, and partly in view of the need to establish a League of Nations and with it a system of mandatory control in the countries of the former Ottoman Empire, in Persia and the Caucasus. Smuts's intentions became clearer during the following weeks, but it was evident even at this stage that his belief that 'our programme is an unselfish one' and his conviction that America must be courted were bound to restrict the more expansive ambitions of his colleagues.[344]

The pro-French stance adopted by Cecil and Montagu, who for reasons connected with the pan-Turanian threat also favoured a French presence in the six vilayets and in the Caucasus, encountered powerful and decisive opposition from senior War Office officials. At successive discussions of the Caucasus at the Eastern Committee, playing upon fears embedded in the official psyche, the War Office argued that to place any western power in this strategically important region would seriously jeopardise British interests in the east. On 2 December, Major-General Thwaites, DMO, argued that having created a new line of communications with India which encompassed Malleson's[345] troops in Trans-Caspia, Britain could neither permit another power to establish itself there nor allow disorder to prevail.[346] Moreover, there were other matters, such as the enforcement of the Turkish Armistice which, together, would probably require a prolonged British presence in the region. Firstly, Thwaites argued, as part of her effort to safeguard her position on this new line of communications, Britain must control the Caspian. Secondly, Thwaites could not conceive of America assuming responsibilities in the Caucasus.[347] Macdonogh resumed the charge on behalf of the War Office at the next meeting of the Committee arguing that, by virtue of the Anglo-French Agreement of 23 December 1917, Britain had a valuable bargaining tool with which to undo Sykes–Picot. Robert Cecil, who agreed with Macdonogh, interpreted the value of that Agreement somewhat differently, namely as a means of levering French interests further to the north.[348] Curzon's efforts to oppose Cecil and Montagu received a boost from Sir Henry Wilson. Reiterating the view in a paper for the Eastern Committee that for reasons of strategy Britain could not tolerate the presence of France in the Caucasus, Wilson added that Turkish and Russian Armenia must be separated. This was necessary, firstly, for ethnographic reasons and, secondly, to prevent France obtaining access to the oil of Baku and to the Caspian by virtue of the interests of Russian Armenians in the oil situated in the vicinity of Baku.[349]

Whilst Curzon emphasised that he envisaged only a temporary British occupation of the Caucasus, both he and War Office officials were keenly aware that the nature of the task as it evolved during the occupation might dictate a longer occupation. In fact, Curzon was willing to conceive of some measure of civil administration in the region. Cecil and Montagu objected to this reasoning, observing that Britain might be drawn into a prolonged commitment if she were to stay until the Caucasian States could stand alone or until France, established in

Armenia, were no longer a threat. In Cecil's opinion, Britain might safeguard her essential interests by controlling the Black and Caspian Seas and, as a minimum, the former alone. Possession of the intervening states was unnecessary.[350] Curzon and Sir Henry Wilson, whilst accepting Cecil's premise about the control of the seas, believed that in order to do this Britain must possess the major ports on each; something which necessitated the holding of the Caucasian Republics.[351]

Curzon, having assessed the issue from the purely British perspective, and in attempting to refute Montagu's allegations of Britain 'drifting' into an acceptance of the logic that Britain alone was fitted to the task of maintaining order in every corner of the Middle East, then assessed the issue of Britain's responsibilities in a broader context:

> so far from claiming it as our desire to become the mandatory or tutelary Power of these regions, in some cases we cannot possibly escape it, and as to others, we have gone so far as to say that we would gladly accept any foreign Power of the first order, so long as we are not ourselves involved and thus incur the very suspicions which Mr Montagu fears. For instance, when we discussed Armenia and Caucasia, a very strong feeling was expressed here that it would be well, both on grounds of broad policy and also on the narrow ground of expediency, to interest France in Armenia. I think at the present moment the proposition is that the tutelary powers should be exercised by France in the case of Armenia, and preference was expressed at this table for a larger rather than a smaller Armenia to be handed over to France. Then when we came to the Caucasus, it was only by what Mr Montagu calls the irrefutable processes of logic that we gradually came to the conclusion that, willing as we were to take France, and even more so America, the larger political and strategical considerations to which the Chief of the Imperial General Staff has drawn attention must surely drive us to another conclusion. Even if we do arrive at that conclusion surely behind it all lies the double protection, first, of that principle of self-determination upon which we have relied and upon which we are quite content to rely; secondly, the possibility of a League of Nations which should itself ask us to act as the mandatory. Therefore, so far from contemplating that we should appear at the Peace Conference, or anywhere, with proposals that Great Britain should do this or that, I think, on the contrary, that we ought to start in the other way and trust to the inevitable process of events and the insurmountable logic of the situation to prove that, in the last resort, we shall be bound to assume certain responsibilities.

Concluding his observations, Curzon could frankly admit that at some stage Britain must take stock of her position and arrive at some decision 'as to whether or not the burden is really too heavy'.[352] Until such a time, however, Curzon remained confident that the arguments which he had presented to the Eastern Committee would be borne out by developments in the Caucasus and in Paris.

'FROM THE BLACK SEA TO THE CASPIAN'

In arguing for a British presence in the Caucasus, Curzon's logic rested squarely upon the ideas mustered by the General Staff to support the contention that, in view of her Indian Empire, Britain had a vital strategic interest in preventing other powers from establishing themselves in that region. Balfour was totally unconvinced, observing at the Eastern Committee on 9 December:

> Every time I come to a discussion – at intervals of, say, five years – I find there is a new sphere which we have got to guard, which is supposed to protect the gateways of India. Those gateways are getting further and further from India, and I do not know how far west they are going to be brought by the General Staff.[353]

Balfour contended that when in the past Russia had been established in the Caucasus with great military resources and, unlike France, not militarily vulnerable or separated by great distances from her home base, Britain 'did not tremble'. Moreover, he observed, *Drang nach Osten* was no longer a threat, the possibility of a revival of Russian strength in the region was remote and a French presence there would be unmanageable.[354]

Balfour's reasoning, that the defence of India should be mounted closer to India, was strongly contested by Curzon at the Eastern Committee. In his view the war had shown that Britain might again have to contemplate the defence of India far to the west. Just as the establishing of a cordon from Hamadan to the Caspian had been necessary so, in the future, Britain might have to defend India in the Caucasus. Far from desiring a permanent British presence there, Curzon noted, he simply wanted a continuation of the British presence in order 'to give the people a chance'. Implicit in this was that Curzon perceived a Russian revival in the region as a greater threat than did Balfour and that partly for this reason, and in spite of the additional commitments which it would involve, if asked by the Peace Conference, Britain could not refuse. Curzon continued:

> I think by the process of exhaustion, if by no other means, it must come to

us, because nobody else has any interest there in the future, unless it be an aggressive interest. In the last resort they will come and say, 'You are already there; we want you to stay; take charge of these people, and set them on their legs.' I do not think anything will alter the fact that somebody must be there; and, if so, I do not see why we should wring our hands, our interests being so closely involved, and propose anybody but ourselves. Are we so unsuspicious that we are prepared to let the French, the most imperialistic people in [the] world . . .[355]

Curzon resumed his train of thought later at the same meeting in response to Balfour's remark that the Caucasian peoples should be allowed to regress into disorder and cut each other's throats. Montagu had then inquired about the actual military danger of France being established in the Caucasus. As it was, Curzon noted, France was already to receive Arab territories to which she had little real claim. Her acquisition of Armenia was to take place by default and by virtue of the fact that nobody else wanted it. Curzon objected:

> Having got her into Armenia you want to give her the Black Sea, and not only the six vilayets but something more. Having given her that, you say we must be disinterested, everybody suspects us, and therefore you propose to clap on to the French this area in which she is not interested, and to which she has no claim, and which she may use to our disadvantage.

In the event of an Anglo-French war Curzon had no doubt that France would use her position in this way. There was, moreover, the matter of oil and, as Sir Henry Wilson remarked, the issue of whether this should be given to France. To Curzon it seemed that France might gain 'very considerable profit' from it and that the Batum–Baku oil-line, 'a great international concern', must be preserved as such and, in all probability, by Britain.[356]

The arguments deployed by Curzon against Cecil and Montagu in their support for the assumption by France of responsibilities in the Caucasus were not sufficient to divert them from their path. In conjunction with the arguments about oil, however, they were apparently sufficiently convincing to invest Balfour with some caution about the possibility of France obtaining a strategic foothold in the Caucasus. Moreover, Balfour was at least willing to consider that France might be bought off elsewhere.

The final resolutions of the Eastern Committee on the Caucasus and Armenia represented, to all intents and purposes, a victory for Curzon. Admittedly, uncertainties remained about the size of the Armenian State to be created: whether or not it would include all of the six vilayets and, therefore, Russian Armenia. To Curzon this issue was of less importance than before. If possible, it was argued that the prospect of a French presence in this Armenian State should be contemplated as a means of revising Sykes–Picot. The crucial point, resolution seven, read:

> If it be decided at the Peace Conference, either as the result of a request from the States, or at the instance of the League of Nations (should such be set up), that the services of a Great Power are required for a period to protect international interests in the areas concerned, the selection of America would be preferable to that of France, but is not in itself desirable. The selection of France would on broad grounds of policy and strategy be undesirable. Only in the last resort, and reluctantly if pressed to do so, might Great Britain provisionally accept the task.[357]

That some power vested with authority need be there at all was ensured by other clauses regarding the need to ensure free transit on the Batum–Baku rail-line and to safeguard 'international interests' in Baku and its oilfields. On the basis of the decision of the Committee that Britain should retain control of the Caspian, and by virtue of the arguments presented by Sir Henry Wilson, it followed that Britain should assume the responsibility. Curzon was obliged to dilute the conclusions which he had previously suggested both by accepting a disclaimer on the part of Britain to any commitments involving permanent large-scale operations in the region and on the basis that Britain, if she were selected, might have a specific mandate relating to the protection of international interests, and defined by the League of Nations. The force of the arguments presented by Curzon and the General Staff effectively eliminated France or America from this role. In any case, in December 1918 Curzon was confident that the League would never come to fruition and that Britain's role in the region would not be confined to the protection of purely international interests. Rather, as we have seen, Curzon was well aware that British involvement in the region would develop a momentum of its own.

HOLDING THE MARCHES

In mid-May 1919, Curzon recalled with dismay the factors which, in his view, had conspired to derail his plans for a prolonged British presence in the Caucasus. Foremost among these was the 'insistence' of Lloyd George.[358] Next, Curzon cited the concurrence in this of Balfour, Cecil and Montagu and the 'conversion' of Sir Henry Wilson. There was, moreover, the fact that when in December 1918 the question of a British mandate was discussed, it was felt that Britain could not spare the troops for two divisions. Nor, as Curzon recounted, was the Treasury willing to foot the bill. More broadly, there was the strategic argument that 'the Caucasus is neither the corridor to India nor a part of the glacis of the Indian fortress'.[359]

Broadly speaking this was a fairly accurate assessment. At meetings of the Eastern Committee, Curzon had developed a powerful argument in favour of British supervision and his opponents were, ultimately, unable entirely to reject it. Admittedly, in the final resolutions presented by the Committee it was stated that 'Only in the last resort, and reluctantly if pressed to do so, might Great Britain provisionally accept the task'.[360] Yet the alternatives, as Curzon's expositions had shown, were quite unrealistic. Thus, even if Curzon had not obtained the explicit concurrence of his colleagues, he none the less created a theoretical climate in which the self-fulfilling logic of his argument might take root.

The defection *en masse* of the War Office, which at the Eastern Committee had endorsed Curzon's geopolitical assessment, and of Balfour, Cecil and Montagu, was occasioned by Lloyd George's belated contribution to the debate. At successive meetings of the Imperial War Cabinet, Lloyd George, arguing emphatically against any British military activity which might be perceived as being directed towards the destruction of Bolshevism, presented an umbrella to those who felt uncomfortable with the consequences of Curzon's thinking.[361]

These factors counted heavily against Curzon throughout the protracted debate about the Caucasus during 1919. Although Sir Henry Wilson never entirely abandoned his conviction that Britain had important interests in the Caucasus, he was equally aware that, failing support for Denikin, only a full-scale occupation of the region by Britain would suffice to protect those interests. As Wilson well knew, Britain could not afford such a commitment nor could she therefore, as Wilson desired, effectively deal with Bolshevism militarily. The allure of Lloyd George's argument was that it rendered Curzon impotent. For those who regarded Curzon's thinking as too expansive it was a short step to argue that there was in fact little to be feared from Bolshevism if Denikin were given support. Others took this logic further and, like Churchill and Cecil, questioned the existence of British strategic interests in the Caucasus. Curzon was, therefore, placed in the impossible position of having to withhold his strongest card, namely the threat of Bolshevism;

something which he knew could only serve to consolidate the position of his opponents if used unwisely. Worse still, Lloyd George was aware of this.

This sparring between Lloyd George and Curzon had been demonstrated in a particularly revealing manner at a meeting of the Imperial War Cabinet on 23 December 1918, when it was decided to push forward feelers for a possible understanding with the Bolsheviks. This in itself was indicative of the speed and success with which Lloyd George had acted and was further illustrated by Milner's protest that while 'quite opposed to aggressive action against Bolshevism . . . he did not wish the fire to spread; he wished to confine it to the area it had already ravaged'. However, Milner continued, as 'the greatest danger of the civilised world', it was essential 'to hold the marches'.[362]

Espying the trip-wire, Curzon 'pointed out that the above considerations did not apply to the Caucasus; this was not a Bolshevik area, we were concerned in it by reason of our position in the East'.[363] Curzon then rehearsed the geopolitical factors which rendered the Caucasus of strategic importance to the British Empire, using as his model the enduring threat posed by *Drang nach Osten*. With only a minor slip of the tongue, a passing reference to Russian history, Curzon proceeded:

> The problem there was not one of Bolshevik and anti-Bolshevik, but one of nascent native States not Russian in nationality . . . These areas have been [*sic*] conquered by the Russians after a century's hard fighting. The States forming there were constantly appealing to us to back them at the Peace Conference: they wished to hold their own against the world.

As Curzon noted, British troops were the only forces to hand and, if they were withdrawn prematurely, the hopes of the Republics would be dashed. At the very least, Curzon concluded, a force should be left on the line Batum–Baku until a mandatory was appointed.[364]

Gently prodding Curzon towards the noose, Lloyd George asked by whom the Republics expected to be attacked. Feebly, Curzon instanced Bicharakoff[365] who, according to him, had been instructed thus by the Russian Government at Omsk. With evident relish Lloyd George delivered the *coup de grâce*, observing 'that we appeared committed not only to fight the Bolsheviks, but also anti-Bolsheviks'.[366] Possibly Montagu and Milner missed the significance of this particular encounter, but the underlying point was that in bringing most of his colleagues to his position of unflinching opposition to Britain assuming, in relation to Bolshevism, a hostile military role in the Caucasus, Lloyd George sustained an essentially disingenuous policy for much of 1919. In this he was helped, not least, by Curzon's willingness to speak out against British 'intervention' in Russia proper – a distinction which others disregarded – on the grounds that it would have to be a solo effort.[367] Also, there was the flaccid posturing of Balfour who, while admitting that in view of the prevalence of Bolshevism in the Caucasus something must be done, was prepared to accept as an adequate response the supporting of Denikin.[368]

By a series of well-timed and carefully executed interventions at meetings of the Imperial War Cabinet in December 1918, Lloyd George steered the emphasis of debate from the springboard provided by Curzon in his Eastern Committee resolutions to a contemplation of the bare minimum that Britain might conceivably undertake in the Caucasus. He achieved this by fuelling the uncertainties of several senior colleagues about the ability of Britain to restrict her involvement, about her ability to extract her troops, about the connected repercussions on the domestic political front, about the 'advantage' to be gained by Britain being there and even about the relatively innocuous threat of Bolshevik ambitions when compared with those of Tsarist Russia.[369]

Although the policy of supporting Denikin appeared to offer a convenient solution, it was founded upon the hypocrisy of those who, while admitting that Britain had a common interest with countries with whom they had previously co-operated and who were now exposed to 'external aggression', were not prepared to offer military support. So long as Denikin survived then British strategic interests which, by implication of the above, did exist, would be safe. That it was a faint-hearted, stillborn policy, which overlooked Denikin's politically unfashionable ambitions in the Caucasus and a policy which was, moreover, divisive, was neglected in the interests of false economy.

The cracks began to show when senior figures such as Lloyd George and, albeit reluctantly, Sir Henry Wilson, lent their support to Italian intervention and continued to do so publicly in spite of the outcry from various experts. No doubt the insertion of a buffer between increasingly endangered British interests and the Bolshevik army appealed, yet it is questionable and probably highly doubtful if there was ever any expectation at the highest levels that Italy either would or could take on the Caucasus. Lloyd George, having embarked upon a course of avoiding the inevitable and of buying time, compromised to the extent of admitting, though much too late in the day, that the prospect of a reunified Russia comprising all of those elements to which Britain had lent her support was, from the point of view of Britain's eastern Empire, a worrying prospect.[370] By the late summer of 1919 Lloyd George had begun to have doubts about the chances of Denikin reaching Moscow.[371] Within a month the offensive had begun to crumble and, amid the terror evoked by Bolshevik advances, Curzon, again unsuccessfully, made a bid for a permanent British presence in the Caucasus and on the Caspian Sea.

After Lloyd George's hijacking of the Caucasian issue in December 1918, Curzon had little chance of influencing the debate until the autumn of 1919 when discussion about the retention of troops in Batum got under way. Though frank about his belief that Britain would find it difficult to extricate her troops after their deployment in the Caucasus, there was a profound uncertainty about the extent of Curzon's ambitions. Within the Foreign Office there was little agreement about what political formations were likely to emerge in Russia proper and its hinterlands. Early in 1919 Curzon found himself unable to direct policy in the Caucasus for a whole variety of reasons. He was deprived of vital telegrams and the War Office, which, unlike the Foreign Office, already had representatives in the region, appeared to be pursuing a forward policy for which he, Curzon, might ultimately be held responsible. There was no Caucasian 'expert' within the Eastern Department of the Foreign Office to whom Curzon, in his ambiguous position at the time as Acting Foreign Secretary, might turn. This ambiguity and that which, to all except Curzon, appeared to surround the functions of the Inter-Departmental Conference on the Middle East, was, needless to say, of not inconsiderable value to those anxious to restrict Curzon's contribution to the Caucasus issue.

NOTES

1. Cox to Curzon, 13 January 1919, British Legation, Tehran, Curzon Papers F112/209.
2. Ibid. Cecil to Curzon, 10 January 1919, British Delegation, Paris, confidential.
3. Ibid.
4. Entry of 13 January 1919, Chelwood Papers, Cecil Diaries, Add. Ms 51131 (British Library); the combination of disarray at the Foreign Office and Curzon's disenchantment with his position early in 1919 was commented upon elsewhere by Cecil: ibid., entries of 15 January 1919; also entry of 2 January, Barnes and Nicholson, *The Leo Amery Diaries*, vol. 1; see also Hardinge to Graham, 20 January 1919, British Delegation, Paris, private, Hardinge Papers /40; entries of 1 February 1919, Diaries of Field Marshal Sir Henry Wilson, reel 8.
5. Milner to Lloyd George, 9 June 1918, 17 Great College Street, SW, very confidential, F/38/3/37.
6. Ibid.
7. Ibid. Memorandum by L.S. Amery, 'War Aims and Military Policy', 15 June 1918, F/2/1/25.

8. Amery to Smuts, 1 November 1918, Supreme War Council, British Section, Versailles, W.K. Hancock and J. Van Der Poel, *Selections from the Smuts Papers* (Cambridge, 1963), vol. 3, no. 848, pp. 682–4; Amery to Wilson, 22 December 1918, Offices of the War Cabinet, 2 Whitehall Gardens, SW, Papers of Field Marshal Sir Henry Wilson 2/8.

9. Ibid. Amery to Smuts.

10. Ibid. Amery to Smuts, 19 October 1918, Offices of the War Cabinet, no. 846, pp. 678–9.

11. Ibid. See also, Amery to Smuts, 25 September 1918, Offices of the War Cabinet, 2 Whitehall Gardens, SW, no. 842, p. 673.

12. Amery to Lloyd George, 19 October 1918, Offices of the War Cabinet, 2 Whitehall Gardens, SW, Lloyd George Papers F/2/1/31; Amery to Curzon, 19 October 1918, Offices of the War Cabinet, Curzon Papers F112/267.

13. See n. 8, Amery to Smuts.

14. Entry of 6 October 1918, Versailles, Hankey Diaries 1/4 (Churchill College, Cambridge).

15. Ibid. Reporting the same discussion to Balfour, Robert Cecil recalled Lloyd George as having been 'in a very exalté frame of mind'; that having slept on the matter 'After a warm argument of some length', Lloyd George confessed that he, Cecil, had been right. As Cecil continued: 'All the same the incident disquiets me. He was really at his very worst yesterday – a tricky attorney negotiating about an unsavoury county court case could scarcely have been worse.' Cecil to Balfour, 7 October 1918, British Embassy, Paris, private, Balfour Papers FO 800/201, f. 320 (PRO).

16. Memorandum by Smuts, 'Our Policy at the Peace Conference', 3 December 1918, p. 39, P Memoranda, CAB 29/2.

17. Minutes of the Imperial War Cabinet, 20 December 1918, IWC 44, CAB 23/42.

18. Ibid.

19. Ibid.

20. Ibid. See E. Goldstein, 'British Peace Aims and the Eastern Question: The Political Intelligence Department and the Eastern Committee, 1918', *Middle Eastern Studies*, 23, p. 434.

21. Ibid. Milner's performance on this occasion rendered him 'wobbly' in Sir Henry Wilson's estimation; entry of 20 December 1918, Diaries of Field Marshal Sir Henry Wilson, reel 8.

22. Minutes of the Imperial War Cabinet, 30 December 1918, IWC 47, CAB 23/42. Unless otherwise stated the remaining material in this section relates to the minutes of this meeting.

23. See G. Egerton, 'Britain and the "Great Betrayal": Anglo-American Relations and The Struggle for United States Ratification of the Treaty of Versailles, 1919–20', *Historical Journal*, 21, 4 (1978), p. 887. As Curzon pointed out, the Eastern Committee had only discussed this as a possibility.

24. Curzon had been aware of Cecil's intention to quit the Foreign Office from at least some point in November 1918. His contributions at meetings of the Eastern Committee had been formulated on the basis of his desire to replace him as Balfour's deputy and heir apparent. It seems possible that with Cecil's departure Curzon hoped to increase his authority in eastern matters and it may even be that Curzon aspired to create a Middle Eastern Department at the Foreign Office under his control. These elements are suggested in a letter from Hankey to Curzon, which was written in reply to a letter from Curzon on the future of the Eastern Committee. It has proved impossible to locate Curzon's letter; Hankey to Curzon, 2 January 1919, 10 Downing Street, Curzon Papers F112/212a.

25. Curzon to Hankey, n.d., 1 Carlton House Terrace, private, Hankey Papers 4/11 (Churchill College, Cambridge). Not only did Hankey accept Curzon's advice but he appears to have swallowed whole Curzon's distrust of the League; see Egerton, op. cit., pp. 888–9, 911.

26. Memorandum by Amery, 'The United States and the Occupied Enemy Territories', 20 December 1918, enclosed in Amery to Wilson, 22 December 1918, Offices of the War Cabinet, 2 Whitehall Gardens, SW, Papers of Field Marshal Sir Henry Wilson 2/8; Amery to Bonar Law, 20 December 1918, Offices of the War Cabinet, 2 Whitehall Gardens, SW, Bonar Law Papers 84/4/14.

27. Minutes of the Imperial War Cabinet, 13 August 1918, IWC 30, CAB 23/42; for a discussion of this meeting see W. Stivers, *Supremacy and Oil: Iraq, Turkey, and the Anglo-American World Order, 1918–30* (Ithaca and London, 1982), pp. 29–31.

28. Sykes to Picot, 28 February 1917, 9 Buckingham Gate, London, Sykes Papers DR588.4 32B (St Antony's College, Oxford). The suggestion of Sykes as the originator of the idea of

America assuming supervisory functions in Palestine is advanced by Christopher Sykes in an undated footnote on this letter; see also, J. Nevakivi, *Britain, France and the Arab Middle East*, p. 51.

29. Amery to Lloyd George, 8 June 1918, Offices of the War Cabinet, 2 Whitehall Gardens, Lloyd George Papers F/2/1/24.

30. Ibid. Amery to Lloyd George, 16 August 1918, enclosing memorandum by Amery, 'The United States and British War Aims', 15 August 1918, F/2/1/29; Amery to Smuts, 16 August 1918, Barnes and Nicholson, *The Leo Amery Diaries*, vol. 1, pp. 233–4.

31. Ibid.

32. Ibid. Memorandum by Amery, 15 August 1918.

33. Ibid. See also entry of 26 August 1918, Hankey Diaries 1/5 (Churchill College, Cambridge).

34. Ibid. Memorandum by Amery, 15 August 1918.

35. Minutes of the Imperial War Cabinet, 20 December 1918, IWC 44, CAB 23/42; Minutes of the Eastern Committee, 5 and 16 December 1918, *EC* 41, *EC* 43, CAB 27/24.

36. See n. 12.

37. Ibid.

38. Amery to Curzon, 22 October 1918, Offices of the War Cabinet, Curzon Papers F112/267. As J.S. Galbraith suggests, Curzon was quite prepared to use 'idealistic arguments to adorn his security objectives'. Galbraith, *JICH*, 13, p. 34.

39. Minutes of the Territorial Committee, 19 April 1917, third meeting, CAB 21/77.

40. Ibid. See Kedourie, *The Chatham House Version*, p. 29.

41. Territorial Committee, Report on Terms of Peace, 28 April 1917, p. 16.

42. Minutes of the Middle East Committee, 12 January 1918, eleventh meeting, secret, CAB 27/22.

43. Ibid. Minutes of the second meeting (new series), 26 February 1918, CAB 27/23.

44. At this time Mond was an influential Jewish industrialist and financier, a Liberal MP and first Commissioner of Works.

45. Memorandum by Curzon, 'The Future of Palestine', 26 October 1917, G.T. 2406, CAB 24/30. Unless otherwise stated the remaining material in this section relates to this memorandum.

46. Minutes of the Eastern Committee, 5 December 1918, *EC* 41, secret, CAB 27/24. Curzon's fears about indigenous opposition to Jewish settlement were vindicated; see Kedourie, *England and the Middle East*, p. 153. Unless otherwise stated the remaining material in this section relates to this meeting of the Eastern Committee.

47. Minutes of the Eastern Committee, 16 December 1918, *EC* 43.

48. Curzon to Balfour, 16 January 1919, Foreign Office, London, SW1, Balfour Papers FO 800/215, f. 91 (PRO).

49. Ibid. Balfour to Curzon, 20 January 1919, British Delegation, Paris (draft reply), f. 115.

50. Led by Weizmann, the Commission, which was created early in 1918, was composed of representatives of British and other Zionist organisations and was intended to pave the way for the implementation of the Balfour Declaration. See Fromkin, *A Peace to End All Peace*, pp. 323ff.

51. Curzon to Balfour, 26 January 1919, 1 Carlton House Terrace, SW, private, Balfour Papers FO 800/215, f. 136 (PRO).

52. Weizmann to Eder, 17 December 1918, FO 371/4170, pp. 151–2.

53. See n. 51; also Gilmour, *Curzon*, p. 521.

54. Minute by Curzon, 30 January 1919, FO 371/4153, p. 70.

55. See n. 52.

56. As Governor of Jerusalem, Storrs was by no means a 'junior' official.

57. Minute by Kidston, 25 January 1919, FO 371/4153, p. 91.

58. Telegram from Clayton, 31 December 1918, no. 259, FO 371/4170, p. 153.

59. Ibid. Minute by Kidston, 27 February 1919, pp. 256ff.

60. Ibid.

61. Ibid.

62. Ibid. Minute by Curzon, 28 February 1919, p. 258.

63. See pp. 242–3.

64. Curzon to Balfour, 25 March 1919, Foreign Office, SW1, private and confidential, Balfour Papers FO 800/215, f. 365ff.

65. Samuel to Balfour, 7 April 1919, 31 Porchester Terrace, Hyde Park, W2, Balfour Papers Add. Ms 49745, f. 196 (British Library).
66. See n. 64.
67. See n. 65.
68. Montagu to Balfour, 20 February 1919, India Office, Whitehall, SW, private, Balfour Papers Add. Ms 49754, 184ff. (British Library).
69. Balfour to Montagu, 25 February 1919, private, copy, Balfour Papers FO 800/215 f. 277 (PRO); Montagu to Balfour, 26 February 1919, British Delegation, Paris, Balfour Papers Add. Ms 49745, f. 188ff. (British Library).
70. Minute by M.D. Peterson, 24 March 1919, FO 371/4179/44731, p. 226.
71. Ibid. Minute by Kidston, 29 March 1919, pp. 304–5.
72. Minute by Kidston, 31 March 1919, FO 371/4167 p. 435.
73. Curzon to Derby, 30 April 1919, Curzon Papers F112/196, f. 49.
74. Clayton to War Office, 2 May 1919, no. C155, WO 106/190, f. 12.
75. Minutes by Curzon, 1 April 1919, FO 371/4153 p. 439; 3 July 1919, FO 371/4181, p. 347.
76. Mallet to Curzon, 7 May 1919, Paris, no. 678, FO 371/4215, p. 478.
77. Ibid.
78. Ibid. Minute by Kidston, 10 May 1919, pp. 476–7.
79. See n. 76 and minute by Curzon, 10 May 1919.
80. See, for example, minute by Curzon, 2 September 1919, FO 371/4211, p. 297.
81. Samuel to Foreign Office, 5 June 1919, Hotel Piaza, Paris, 76242/M.E./44, enclosed in Weizmann to Tyrrell, 6 June 1919, Zionist Delegation, Paris, FO 371/4181, p. 37.
82. Ibid. Minute by M.D. Peterson, n.d., p. 33.
83. Col. French to Curzon, 19 July 1919, FO 371/4182, p. 91.
84. Ibid.
85. Ibid. Minute by W.S. Edmunds, 8 September 1919, 125609, p. 347.
86. Curzon to Balfour, 20 August 1919, Foreign Office, SW1, Balfour Papers Add. Ms 49734, f. 154 (British Library); see Mejcher, *JCH,* 8, p. 67.
87. Note by Cornwallis, 25 September 1919, Carlton Hotel, Pall Mall, London FO 371/4183, p. 218.
88. Ibid. T.E. Lawrence to Curzon, 25 September 1919, pp. 240ff; 'Note on Colonel Lawrence's Proposals', 30 September 1919, H.W. Young, pp. 230ff.
89. Ibid. Minutes by Kidston, 29 September 1919, p. 229; J.C. Tilley, 2 October 1919, Hardinge, n.d., 134231, p. 237.
90. Ibid. Minute by Hardinge, n.d., p. 237.
91. Ibid. Minute by Curzon, 3 October 1919.
92. Curzon to Balfour, 9 August 1919, Balfour Papers Add. Ms 49734, f. 141 (British Library).
93. Weizmann to Balfour, 25 September 1919, 67 Addison Road, Kensington, Balfour Papers /5 (Scottish Record Office).
94. Minutes by Curzon, 30 October and 5 November 1919, FO 371/4184, pp. 377–8.
95. See n. 86.
96. Ibid.
97. Balfour to Rothschild, 29 September 1919, Whittingehame, private, Balfour Papers /5, f. 54 (Scottish Record Office).
98. Minutes of the Eastern Committee, 11 July 1918, *EC* 19, secret, CAB 27/24; Memorandum by Sir Mark Sykes on a private and personal conference with Picot, 3 July 1918, EC 766 CAB 27/28.
99. Ibid. Memorandum by Sykes.
100. Ibid. Minutes of the Eastern Committee.
101. Ibid.
102. Ibid. Memorandum by Sykes, 6 July 1918, Foreign Office, Annex (A), Memorandum on M. Picot's Position in Palestine, attached as Appendix to *EC* 21, 18 July 1918, secret, CAB 27/24.
103. Ibid. *EC* 21, pp. 3–4.
104. Ibid. Memorandum by Sykes.
105. Ibid.
106. See Appendix 9.

107. Minutes of the Eastern Committee, 11 July 1918, *EC* 21.
108. Arab Bureau, Report by Sir Mark Sykes on meeting between himself, Hussein, Picot, 19 May 1917, secret, FO 882/16, f. 98ff.
109. See p. 90.
110. Minutes of the Eastern Committee, 18 July 1918, *EC* 21, secret, CAB 27/24.
111. Ibid.
112. Ibid., p. 3.
113. Ibid., p. 4.
114. Ibid. *EC* 22, 29 July 1918, secret, p. 1; *EC* 23, 8 August 1918, secret, appendix, EC 953.
115. Ibid. *EC* 23, p. 2; *EC* 33, 26 September 1918, p. 9.
116. Ibid. *EC* 33, pp. 8–9.
117. The Conference was said to have produced a 'draft agreement' and the terms are hereafter referred to interchangeably.
118. Minutes of the Eastern Committee, 18 July 1918. *EC* 34, 3 October 1918, secret, p. 2; see also appendix A, EC 1769.
119. Ibid. *EC* 34, p. 6.
120. Ibid., p. 2.
121. Ibid., p. 3.
122. Ibid., pp. 2 and 4.
123. Ibid. Appendix A.
124. Ibid. *EC* 34, p. 3.
125. Ibid.
126. Ibid., p. 4.
127. Ibid. Appendix A.
128. Ibid. *EC* 21, 18 July 1918, pp. 5–6.
129. Ibid. *EC* 34, p. 4. The remaining material in this section relates to the minutes of this meeting.
130. Minute by Crowe, 9 October 1918, FO 371/3384/16919.
131. *EC* 34, 3 October 1918, secret, note by Secretary, p. 6, CAB 27/24 (printed January 1919).
132. Ibid., p. 6.
133. Ibid.
134. Ibid. See also n. 130.
135. Ibid. G.T. 5955, appendix to WC 485, 14 October 1918, CAB 23/8; appendix to *EC* 35, 17 October 1918.
136. Ibid. See also WC 485.
137. Memorandum by Sir Mark Sykes, EC 1944 CAB 27/34.
138. *EC* 35 and *EC* 35a, 17/18 October 1918, secret, CAB 27/24.
139. Ibid. Appendix B.
140. Ibid. *EC* 35, p. 8.
141. Ibid., p. 9.
142. Ibid. Sluglett, *Britain In Iraq*, pp. 23–4, suggests that the Anglo-French Declaration might be seen 'as a sop to the Americans', or as 'an attempt on the part of the two Allies to present a common front, an appearance of solidarity in their Middle Eastern Policy'. Possibly it was both of these things but, more than anything, it represented an attempt to reconcile British imperialism with Wilsonian principles and to ensure British ascendancy in the east by means of camouflage.
143. Ibid. *EC* 37, 29 October 1918, secret, p. 2.
144. Ibid., p. 3.
145. Ibid.
146. Memorandum by G.S. Macdonogh, 28 October 1918, 'A Note on Policy in the Middle East', EC 2133 CAB 27/35; memorandum by Hogarth, 'Memorandum on Certain Conditions of Settlement of Western Asia', EC 2302 CAB 27/36.
147. Ibid. EC 2133.
148. Ibid. EC 2302.
149. Arab Bureau, Note by Cornwallis, 19 November 1918, FO 882/13, f. 170.
150. *EC* 41, 5 December 1918, pp. 6ff.
151. Ibid., pp. 7–8.

152. Ibid., p. 8.
153. Ibid., p. 9.
154. Ibid., p. 10; see Goldstein, *MES*, 8, p. 425.
155. Ibid.
156. Ibid., p.12
157. Ibid., p. 13.
158. Ibid., pp. 15–16.
159. *EC* 43, 16 December 1918, p. 3; see also Eastern Committee Resolutions on Syria, EC 2716A, CAB 27/38; see Goldstein, op. cit.
160. Committee of Union and Progress.
161. Memorandum by Curzon, 'A Note of Warning About the Middle East', 24 March 1919, G.T. 7037, CAB 24/77.
162. Minutes of the Eastern Committee, 5 December 1918, *EC* 41, secret, CAB 27/24, p. 10.
163. Entry of 1 February 1919, Diaries of Field Marshal Sir Henry Wilson, reel 8.
164. Ibid.
165. Ibid. Entry of 4 February 1919; see also entries of 4 and 25 February 1919, Chelwood Papers, Cecil Diaries, Add. Ms 51131 (British Library).
166. Ibid. Entry of 25 February 1919, Cecil Diaries. Curzon was resolutely opposed to the idea, writing to Mallet, who had produced a memorandum on the proposal, that he was 'greatly startled' by the suggestion which, in his view, had 'nothing to recommend it'. Curzon continued:

> In the first place, it would convert France at once into a formidable mid-Eastern Power. Secondly, all the Balkan States would press round her and begin the old intrigues again. Thirdly, from Constantinople she could not be prevented from interfering across the Straits. She would become a sort of informal protecting Power of the Turk and would have her finger in every Asia Minor pie.

However, as Curzon concluded, in an interview with the French Ambassador, Cambon, the latter had, quite unexpectedly, stated officially that such also were the views of the French Government; Curzon to Mallet, 13 March 1919, Foreign Office, confidential, Curzon Papers F112/213a, f. 35.
167. Balfour to Curzon, 20 March 1919, private, Balfour Papers FO 800/215, f. 343; ibid., Curzon to Balfour, 25 March 1919, Foreign Office, SW1, private and confidential, f. 365.
168. Ibid. Balfour to Curzon, 20 March 1919.
169. See, for example, entry of 4 February 1919, Chelwood Papers, Cecil Diaries, Add. Ms 51131 (British Library).
170. See n. 167. Precisely what passed between Lloyd George and Clemenceau remains unclear. Certainly before the meeting Lloyd George had evinced some enthusiasm for Britain obtaining Palestine and Mosul and it was subsequently claimed by France that in return for the cession of those regions to Britain she was to have secured direct control of the Syrian hinterland. Some authors claim that, by virtue of this meeting, France was also to obtain the Lebanon and Cilicia; see, for example, L. James, *The Life and Times of Field-Marshal Viscount Allenby 1861–1936* (London, 1993), p. 183.

However, as France had already obtained those territories by virtue of Sykes–Picot, it seems highly unlikely that she would seek to re-obtain them when the feeling prevailed in France that Sykes–Picot remained binding. The belief that France had obtained the right to occupy the Syrian hinterland was to be an important factor in discussions of the Syrian question in Paris.

What is clear, however, and contrary to Gilmour's recent assessment, is that in December 1918 Lloyd George had no desire to 'extend' Sykes–Picot; see Gilmour, *Curzon*, p. 519. At the War Cabinet on 3 October 1918, Lloyd George felt Sykes–Picot to be 'most undesirable'. By February 1919, according to Riddell, Lloyd George considered Sykes–Picot was 'causing all the trouble with France'. Minutes of a meeting of the War Cabinet, 3 October 1918, WC 482a, CAB 23/14; E. Kedourie, *England and the Middle East*, p. 136. It is conceivable that, in order to obtain Mosul and Palestine, Lloyd George, consciously or otherwise, played upon the desire of France to adhere to those portions of the Agreement which related to the Syrian littoral and the hinterland as it would scarcely have been possible to discuss the region without some reference to it however fleeting and reluctant. A.S. Klieman, *Foundations of British Policy*,

p. 35, provides a sounder interpretation of the meeting suggesting that Lloyd George's request was 'based on an expanding conception of Britain's strategic needs' and originated in 'what Hogarth termed the "passion of possession" following conquest'.

171. Balfour to Curzon, 20 March 1919, private, Balfour Papers FO 800/215.
172. Ibid.
173. Ibid. Curzon to Balfour, 25 March 1919. Curzon's displeasure with the manner in which the decision to send the Commission was taken was widely shared by members of the British Delegation. This was certainly true of Hirtzel who, writing on 29 March with Montagu's concurrency, observed:

> The procedure adopted in this case seems to me extraordinary and contrary to the public interests. The 'representatives' of the four Powers take what has every appearance of being a 'snap' decision, and their officials (or the officials of His Majesty's Government at all events) are left to glean what they can from gossip – the only authoritative statement of the facts being destined for Lord Curzon's 'personal information'. This is open diplomacy with a vengeance. But why are we wasting our time and the public money in Paris?

According to Kedourie, *England and the Middle East*, p. 139, Curzon's apprehensions were shared by Gertrude Bell and T.E. Lawrence.

174. Curzon to Balfour, 25 March 1919.
175. Ibid. A.J. Toynbee apparently shared this concern: minute by Toynbee, 29 March 1919, FO 608/86/5570, p. 33.
176. Curzon to Balfour, 25 March 1919.
177. 'Mesopotamia: Future Constitution', secret, Wilson, to S/S, 6 April 1919, Annex and draft reply to S/S's telegram of 14 February 1919, embodying the Commissioner's proposals, L/P+S/10/757 B317; note by Sir Percy Cox, 'The Future of Mesopotamia', 22 April 1918, EC 173 CAB 27/25; see Kedourie, *England and the Middle East*, p. 177.
178. Ibid. Annex (embodying Commissioner's proposals).
179. Draft S/S to Civil Commissioner, 14 February 1919, L/P+S/10/755, p. 353.
180. Ibid. See also S/S to Civil Commissioner, 14 February 1919, P551, p. 9.
181. Ibid. Draft, S/S to Civil Commissioner.
182. Ibid. Minute by Curzon, (?8) February 1919.
183. See n. 180.
184. See n. 177, Wilson to S/S, 6 April 1919, B317.
185. Ibid. EC 173, 22 April 1918.
186. See n. 177, Wilson to S/S, 6 April 1919; enclosure no. one, Civil Commissioner to S/S, 10 November 1918, no. 9695.
187. Ibid. Also enclosure no. two, Civil Commissioner to S/S, 10 November 1918, no. 9696.
188. See n. 186.
189. See n. 187.
190. See n. 178.
191. See n. 177, Wilson to S/S, 6 April 1919, B317.
192. In a tribute to Hirtzel in *The Times* of 6 January 1937 by Sir Percy Cox, entitled 'Whitehall and The Man on the Spot', Cox recalled his good fortune in having benefited invariably from good relations with his superiors in London. Cox continued: 'But in the gallery of my memory Arthur Hirtzel will always figure on a pedestal by himself. He had an exceptional capacity, partly based of course on a thorough knowledge of the problem he was dealing with of getting into the mind of the man on the other end of the line.'
193. Minute by Shuckburgh, 13 December 1918, L/P+S/11/141 P5076.
194. Ibid. Also, S/S to Civil Commissioner, Baghdad, draft, 17 December 1918.
195. Pol. Baghdad to S/S, 14 November 1918, L/P+S/10/723 P5099.
196. Ibid. Minutes by Shuckburgh, 21 November 1918, and H.V. Cox, 22 November 1918.
197. Ibid. Minute by Shuckburgh, 17 December 1918, P5099.
198. Ibid.
199. Refer to Map 5.
200. Pol. Baghdad to S/S, 15 October 1918, L/P+S/10/755 P4610.
201. Wilson to Hirtzel, 20 November 1918, Baghdad, Wilson Papers vol. 2, f. 63 (London Library).

202. Cecil to Smuts, 5 November 1918, Foreign Office, Cecil Papers FO 800/198, f. 206 (PRO).
203. See n. 231.
204. Civil Commissioner to S/S, 24 November 1918, L/P+S/10/769 P5593.
205. Ibid. Pol. Baghdad to S/S, 4 December 1918, no. 10628; also at EC 2630 CAB 27/38.
206. Ibid. Draft telegram to Baghdad, 9 December 1918, L/P+S/10/769 P5426.
207. Ibid. Minutes by Shuckburgh, 12 December 1918, Hirtzel, 12 December 1918, and Crowe, 13 December 1918, P5202.
208. Ibid. Pol. Baghdad, 11 December 1918, no. 10,974; draft telegram to Baghdad by Shuckburgh, 13 December 1918, P5593.
209. Ibid. Pol. Baghdad.
210. Ibid. Pol. Baghdad to S/S, 18 December 1918, no. 11252, P5654; also at EC 2789 CAB 27/38, p. 251.
211. Ibid. Minute by Shuckburgh, 18 December 1918; Shuckburgh to US/S Foreign Office, 21 December 1918.
212. Ibid. Tyrrell to US/S India Office, 3 January 1919.
213. Ibid. Pol. Baghdad, 27 January 1919.
214. Ibid. Minute by Shuckburgh, 30 January 1919.
215. Ibid. Minute by Curzon, c. 31 January 1919.
216. Ibid. Cypher telegram from Mr Balfour to His Majesty's Representative, Baghdad, 22 February 1919, no. 3, enclosing private message from Hirtzel.
217. Crowe to Curzon, 12 October 1919, British Delegation, no. 1939, FO 371/4193.
218. Memorandum on Future Frontiers of Mesopotamia by A.J. Toynbee, 11 December 1918, with reference to telegrams from Baghdad 10852 and 10853 of 8 December 1918, L/P+S/10/769 P5202/18; PID memorandum, 21 November 1918, 'The Settlement of Turkey and the Arabian Peninsula', CAB 24/72.
219. Ibid. PID memorandum. Of course, as the joint author of this (PID) memorandum, along with Eyre Crowe, in his memorandum of 11 December Toynbee was commenting upon his own previous assessment of the issue. E. Goldstein, *MES*, 23, p. 420, appears to suggest that the memorandum was produced by Toynbee alone. Joint authorship, or collaboration of some nature between Toynbee and Crowe, was suggested by Robert Cecil at the Eastern Committee on 16 December 1918: Minutes of the Eastern Committee, *EC* 43, secret, CAB 27/24, p. 23.
220. Ibid. Also 'Note on Kurdistan', 4 December 1918, by Shuckburgh, also at EC 2765 CAB 27/38.
221. Ibid. Private telegram to Baghdad, 13 December 1918; Pol. Baghdad to S/S, 15 December 1918, private, no. 11163, L/P+S/10/769 5202/18.
222. Ibid. Pol. Baghdad to S/S.
223. Ibid. Memorandum by A.J. Toynbee.
224. Ibid.
225. Minute by A.J. Toynbee, 19 January 1919, FO 608/82, p. 2.
226. Minute by Kidston, 10 January 1919, FO 608/95, p. 19.
227. Ibid. Minute by Toynbee, 27 January 1919, p. 23.
228. Pol. Baghdad to Sir Arthur Hirtzel, 24 February 1919, L/P+S/10/769.
229. Ibid. Pol Baghdad to S/S, 15 December 1918, private, no. 11163.
230. See n. 228.
231. General Marshall to his brother (Jack), 1 January 1919, GHQ Mesopotamian Expeditionary Force, Marshall Papers; Arab Bureau Memorandum by D.G. Hogarth, 30 December 1918, FO 882/13.
232. A.T. Wilson to his mother, 14 December 1918, Baghdad, Wilson Papers, vol. 2, f. 62 (London Library).
233. Ibid. Wilson to Hirtzel, 20 November 1918, f. 63.
234. See n. 228.
235. Wilson to his mother, 11 January 1919, H.T. 'North Point', Wilson Papers, vol. 2 (London Library).
236. Pol. Baghdad to S/S, 21 January 1919, no. 843, L/P+S/11/146.
237. Ibid. Pol. Baghdad to S/S, 7 February 1919.
238. Ibid. Minutes by Shuckburgh, 22 January 1919, P385; 27 January 1919, P450.
239. Minute by Shuckburgh, 3 March 1919, L/P+S/10/769.

240. Ibid. Minute by Holderness, 4 March 1919.
241. See n. 228.
242. Pol. Baghdad to Sir Arthur Hirtzel, 31 May 1919, L/P+S/10/769.
243. Ibid. WO to GOC-in-C Egypt, 23 May 1919, WO78285.
244. See n. 242.
245. Hogarth to Hirtzel, 12 June 1919, Ashmolean Museum, Oxford, L/P+S/10/769.
246. Ibid. Minute by Hirtzel, (?13) June 1919.
247. Ibid. Also n. 245.
248. Ibid. Minute by Shuckburgh, 9 June 1919.
249. Wilson to Sir Percy Cox, 9 May 1919, Offices of the Civil Commissioner, private and personal, Wilson Papers Add. Ms 52455a, f. 51ff. (British Library). It seems that Wilson was informed of the _intention_ to obtain from France the renunciation of her claims in Mosul in December 1918; see S/S to Pol. Baghdad, 9 December 1918, draft, L/P+S/10/769.
250. Revised minutes of Inter-Departmental Conference on Mesopotamian Railways and their extension, 11 January 1919, L/P+S/10/723 P5372.
251. Ibid. WO to GOC Mesopotamia, 13 January 1919, secret, no. 73864, P307/1919.
252. See nn. 207, 208
253. Pol. Baghdad to S/S, 29 November 1918, no. 10.443, L/P+S/723 P5372.
254. Ibid. Minute by Hirtzel, 5 December 1918.
255. GOC Mesopotamia, 4 February 1919, no. X5272, in DMO to Hardinge, 10 February 1919, War Office, FO 371/4148, p. 224.
256. Ibid. DMO to Hardinge, 10 February 1919, War Office, no. 121/3/1302 (MO2), p. 223.
257. Minutes by H.W. Young and Kidston, 12 February 1919, FO 371/4148, p. 222.
258. Ibid. Minute by Kidston.
259. Ibid. Minute by Curzon, 13 February 1919.
260. FO to Sec. Army Council, 15 April 1919, L/P+S/10/723 P2032.
261. GOC Mesopotamia, 1 June 1919, no. X7049, L/P+S/11/156 P5283.
262. Ibid. Memorandum by Hirtzel, 'Mesopotamian Railways', 21 July 1919.
263. Ibid. Minute by Shuckburgh, 28 July 1919.
264. Ibid. Draft telegram to Pol. Baghdad, prepared by Shuckburgh, 22 August 1919.
265. Draft reply to Messrs Forbes Forbes Campbell and Co. Ltd, 12 November 1918, L/P+S/10/368/P4920, p. 230.
266. Ibid. Minute by Montagu, n.d., P5469.
267. Ibid. Minute by Shuckburgh, 27 December 1918, p. 218.
268. Minutes by Wakely, 20 May 1919, and Kershaw, 23 May 1919, L/P+S/10/572/P2603.
269. Ibid. Spicer to US/S, India Office, 27 February 1919, Foreign Office, confidential, no. 23241/C/144 P1167
270. Minute by Shuckburgh on private letter from Hirtzel to Shuckburgh, 6 February 1919, L/P+S/10/367, pt.3 P582.
271. Minutes by Hirtzel, 9 November 1918, and 16 April 1919, L/P+S/10/531, pt.5.
272. Ibid. Minute by Hirtzel, 6 April 1919, P1857.
273. Minute by Shuckburgh, 12 April 1919, pt.6 P1863.
274. Ibid. Minute by Montagu, 15 April 1919.
275. Ibid. Memorandum by E.B. Howell for D.A.G., GHQ, Baghdad, Offices of the Civil Commissioner, Baghdad, 21 March 1919, no. 8835/77/3 P5463.
276. Montgomery to US/S India Office, 12 December 1919, Foreign Office, L/P+S/10/572.
277. A.T. Wilson to S/S, 27 June 1919, Offices of the Civil Commissioner, Baghdad, L/P+S/10/847/P4613.
278. Ibid. Minute by Montagu, 8 September 1919, draft.
279. Ibid. IO to FO, 10 September 1919, draft.
280. Ibid. Wakely to US/S India Office, 19 September 1919, Foreign Office, P5754.
281. Garbett, who had worked under Wilson's direction in the civil administration in Mesopotamia, was attached to the India Office in an unknown capacity during 1919. Wilson was to place him in the ranks of the enemy who were actively undermining his work.
282. Minute by C.C. Garbett, 1 November 1919, L/P+S/10/847 P6435.
283. Ibid. Tilley to India Office, 22 December 1919, P8379; ibid., Minute by Hirtzel, 10 February 1920, P8002.

284. Wilson to Hirtzel, 20 November 1918, Baghdad, Wilson Papers, vol. 2, f. 63 (London Library).
285. Minute by Holderness, 27 March 1919, L/P+S/11/146 P359.
286. Ibid. Cubitt to US/S India Office, 11 February 1919.
287. See n. 285.
288. Wellesley to US/S India Office, 24 October 1919, Foreign Office, no. 142042/M.E./44.A, L/P+S/11/146.
289. Ibid. Note by A.T. Wilson, 31 March 1919, British Delegation, Paris; minute by A.H. Grant, 26 March 1919.
290. Ibid. Note by Major-Gen. Sir W.R. Marshall, KCB, 19 March, Naval and Military Club.
291. See n. 289, note by A.T. Wilson.
292. A.S. Meek (P.O. Basra) to Wilson, 18 May 1919, in Wilson to Hirtzel, 3 June 1919, private and personal, Wilson Papers Add. Ms 52455c (British Library).
293. A.T. Wilson to Bell, 3 June 1919, Offices of the Civil Commissioner, Baghdad, A.T. Wilson Papers 69/79/1 (Imperial War Museum).
294. Hirtzel to Wilson, 16 July 1919, private, Wilson Papers Add. Ms 52455c (British Library).
295. Ibid.
296. Minutes by (unknown author) 21 June, and Hirtzel, 23 June 1919, L/P+S/11/140 4937 3322.
297. Minute by Kidston, 31 July 1919, FO 371/4231/109379.
298. Major Gillan to US/S, India Office, Office of the Civil Commissioner, Baghdad, 29 May 1919, no. 16039/107/88, L/P+S/11/154 P3860.
299. Ibid. Pol. Baghdad to S/S, 6 August 1919, no. 8763 P4709; minute by Shuckburgh, 13 August 1919.
300. Ibid. Minute by Hirtzel, (?14) August 1919.
301. Minute by H.W. Young, 17 September 1919, FO 371/4150/129808, pp. 67–8. On Young's Arab sympathies, see Kedourie, *England and the Middle East*, p. 180.
302. See, for example, minute by H.W. Young, 7 July 1919, FO 371/4181, pp. 360ff.
303. See n. 294; also Pol. Baghdad to S/S, 21 July 1919, no. 8165, L/P+S/10/757 P4265.
304. Ibid., n. 294.
305. Ibid. Pol. Baghdad to S/S.
306. Minute by Hirtzel, 3 August 1919, L/P+S/10/686 P4142, p. 8.
307. Ibid. Pol. Baghdad to S/S, 19 July 1919, no. 8106.
308. See n. 306.
309. Minute by Shuckburgh, 11 August 1919, L/P+S/10/686, p. 6.
310. Pol. Baghdad, 7 June 1919, no. 6403, enclosed in IO to FO, 23 June 1919, FO 371/4149, pp. 179–80.
311. Minute by Shuckburgh, 14 August 1919, L/P+S/10/757, p. 25.
312. Ibid. IO to FO, 19 August 1919, draft, p. 23; also at FO 371/4149, p. 416.
313. Ibid. Minute by Hirtzel, 15 August 1919, L/P+S/10/757.
314. Ibid. IO to FO, 19 August, draft, corrections by Hirtzel.
315. Ibid. Wellesley to US/S India Office, Foreign Office, 26 September 1919, 118150/ME.44a; minute by Shuckburgh, 6 October 1919, P5962.
316. Minute by Curzon, ?25 July 1919, FO 371/4149/103288, p. 234.
317. Vansittart, who was an Assistant Clerk, was attached to the Foreign Office Section of the British Delegation, but was quite junior at this stage in his career.
318. Minutes by H.W. Young, Kidston and Tilley, 23 September 1919, FO 371/4149; ibid., minutes by Hardinge, n.d., and Curzon, 24 September 1919; ibid., Vansittart to Kidston, 15 September 1919, P414. H.W. Young was to suggest retrospectively that Curzon's adherence to the rules was reluctant and, certainly, it would appear to have contradicted his previously opportunistic and devious involvement in Mesopotamian affairs; see H.W. Young, *The Independent Arab* (London, 1933), p. 291.
319. Minutes of the Eastern Committee, 2 December 1918, EC 40, secret, CAB 27/24, pp. 15–16.
320. Ibid., pp. 16–17.
321. Ibid., p. 17. This striking self-contradiction may have arisen from Curzon's desire to avoid any suspicions of conducting an anti-Bolshevik crusade.
322. Ibid., pp. 17–18.
323. Ibid., p. 5.

324. Ibid., p. 7.
325. Ibid., p. 8.
326. Memorandum by D.G. Hogarth, 'Memorandum on Certain Conditions of Settlement of Western Asia', 15 November 1918, General Staff, War Office, EC 2302, CAB 27/36.
327. *EC* 40, CAB 27/24, pp. 14, 19, 22.
328. Ibid., p. 14.
329. Ibid.
330. Ibid., p. 5.
331. Ibid., p. 19.
332. Ibid., pp. 19–20.
333. Ibid., pp. 18–19.
334. Ibid., p. 19.
335. Ibid. *EC* 42, 9 December 1918, p. 16.
336. Ibid. *EC* 40, p. 21.
337. Ibid., p. 22; see Goldstein, MES, 23, p. 424.
338. *EC* 41, 5 December 1918, CAB 27/24, p. 20; Goldstein, op. cit.
339. *EC* 40, p. 21.
340. Ibid., p. 22.
341. Ibid. *EC* 42, 9 December 1918, p. 8.
342. Ibid. *EC* 40, pp. 20ff.
343. Memorandum by Smuts, 'Our Policy at the Peace Conference', 3 December 1918, CAB 29/2.
344. See n. 342
345. See p. 192, n. 117.
346. *EC* 40, CAB 27/24, p. 24.
347. Ibid.
348. Ibid. *EC* 41, pp. 5–6.
349. General Staff Memorandum, 'Future Settlement of Trans-Caucasia: the military aspect of the case', EC 2632, CAB 27/38, pp. 46ff. J.D. Rose might be clearer on the fact that Sir Henry Wilson came to support the proposals of Churchill for withdrawal from the Caucasus only by default: J.D. Rose, 'Batum as Domino, 1919–1920: The Defence of India in Trancaucasia, International History Review, 11, 1 January 1980, p. 267.
350. *EC* 42, 9 December 1918, CAB 27/24, pp. 8–9.
351. Ibid., pp. 9ff.
352. Ibid., p. 4.
353. Minutes of the Eastern Committee, *EC* 42, 9 December 1918, secret, p. 12; see Goldstein, op. cit., p. 443.
354. *EC* 42, 9 December 1918, pp. 12–13.
355. Ibid., p. 13.
356. Ibid., p. 14.
357. Ibid. *EC* 43, 16 December 1918, p. 2; for a broadly similar analysis of the discussions on the Caucasus at the Eastern Committee and Imperial War Cabinet see B.C. Busch, *Mudros to Lausanne*, pp. 110ff. However, whilst Busch may be correct to suggest that, in a purely technical sense, Curzon believed a temporary occupation of Batum–Baku to be possible, the whole thrust of his argument at the Eastern Committee was that if Britain became involved it would be extremely difficult for her to extricate herself.
358. Minute by Curzon, 14 May 1919, FO 371/3662/7172, p. 39. Whether or not, as Curzon alleged, Lloyd George had a 'grudge' against the Caucasus, it was true that, as Rose claims, both Lloyd George and Balfour were unwilling to accept the strategic analysis developed by Curzon, by virtue of which, the Caucasus was perceived as being on the glacis of India; D. Gilmour, *Curzon*, p. 514; Rose, op cit., p. 284.
359. Minute by Curzon, 14 May 1919.
360. *EC* 43, 16 December 1918, secret, CAB 27/24.
361. See, especially, minutes of the Imperial War Cabinet, 12, 23 and 31 December 1918, IWC 42, 45, 48, CAB 23/42.
362. Ibid. IWC 45.
363. Ibid. In his assessment of Curzon's adherence to the 'essentially . . . negative domino theory' throughout 1919, in justifying British imperialism in the Caucasus, Rose fails to acknowledge

the fact that in the atmosphere of retrenchment any 'positive' and manifestly acquisitive motives would have been rejected out of hand. This was particularly so in view of Curzon's reputation as a forward thinker. Moreover, Rose neglects Curzon's difficulty in being unable to introduce the Bolshevik factor into discussions; something which occurred later in 1919. When it was openly discussed then, as Klieman suggests, the strategic analysis formulated by Curzon, either with reference to Mesopotamia or the Caucasus was bound to find favour. That it did not do so with Winston Churchill who was entrusted with the rationalisation of British overseas commitments was due, not to any fundamental divergence of views on the desirability of retaining an extensive eastern empire, but to Churchill's awareness of what was possible. Of course, Churchill had expressed himself in favour of establishing a permanent British presence in Trans-Caspia if this were practicable; Rose, *IHR*, p. 272; Klieman, *Foundations of British Policy*, p. 25.

364. See n. 362.
365. See p. 192, n. 94.
366. See n. 362.
367. Ibid. IWC 48, 31 December 1918, p. 5.
368. Ibid. IWC 42, 12 December 1918.
369. See n. 361 and, in particular, regarding those meetings, respectively, pp. 5–6; pp. 5, 10; pp. 4–5.
370. Minutes of the War Cabinet, 25 July 1919, CAB 23/11; Minutes of the War Cabinet, 25 September 1919, WC 624a, CAB 23/15.
371. Ibid. Minutes of the War Cabinet, 12 August 1919, CAB 23/11.

Conclusion

I N THE COURSE of 1919 Curzon revived efforts to secure an exclusive position for Britain in the Hejaz. However, the Eastern Committee resolutions on the Arabian Peninsula and the Hejaz of December 1918 involved a greater compromise on Curzon's part than did those relating to any other area. Partly this related to a fear that, if Britain pressed for a recognition of her exclusive position at the wrong moment, then the nature of her predominance in the Peninsula would be drawn into the wider debate about the apportioning of territories. Also, such a course might jeopardise the possibility of obtaining from France and Italy a recognition of Britain's political predominance in the Peninsula both outside and within the Hejaz by means of *ad hoc* bargaining.

In the long term Curzon had little doubt that traditional threats to British predominance in 'the Curzon lake', as the Persian Gulf came to be known after 1903, would revive.[1] In the meantime there was much to be made from inter-Allied rivalries in creating an atmosphere in which Britain might strengthen her position. The relative neglect of the issue by historians reflects the extent to which these rivalries have been perceived merely as shadow boxing. Yet the fact it was taken seriously at the time was reflected in the firm opposition of the Eastern Committee to bringing the issue of Britain's position in the Peninsula before the Conference.[2] Similarly, though Balfour and Cecil opposed efforts to gain a recognition of British predominance in the Hejaz, they did support the idea of a British 'Monroe doctrine' in the Peninsula.[3] This distinction, or, more properly, Curzon's inability to distinguish between what might appear as naked acquisitiveness and camouflage, was the reef on which his career foundered during World War I. The strength of opposition to Curzon's involvement in foreign affairs within the Foreign and India Offices was indicative of the extent to which his policies were identified with a bygone era of British imperialism in the east. Certainly, Curzon could be relied upon to capitalise on the fortunes of war. Besides inter-Allied rivalries there was the matter of Turco-German ambitions.

By December 1917 *Drang nach Osten* represented, in Curzon's estimation, not only a threat to Britain's possessions in the east, to mankind, or even to the world, but to the 'universe' itself. Of course, as Curzon added, the recapture of Baghdad by the enemy, an important step in this scheme, was unlikely to happen.[4] It was hardly surprising, therefore, that, for many, Curzon appeared as the high priest of war imperialism. This image was reinforced by Curzon's tendency to perceive international affairs in the east in the manner of a chessboard; something which was undoubtedly useful in illustrating the need to fight for complete victory.[5] Yet it was also a severely limiting framework and one which failed to acknowledge that American involvement in the war and the future of transatlantic co-operation rendered this traditional concept largely redundant. In practice, new methods had to be found to sustain old rivalries and this would account for the diverse manifestations of War Imperialism in the Middle East. It is partly this diversity which renders difficult any overall assessment of the parameters of this phenomenon or of Curzon's significance in its development.

From an early stage any notion of a strictly defensive war in the east was abandoned and the prospect of British gains was welcomed by many politicians not normally associated with acquisitive policies. However, when seen in the context of inter-Allied rivalries, of *Drang nach Osten*, of pan-Islamism and of a possible Russian revival, the notion of a defensive war rapidly came to be associated with 'defensive security'. According to the immediacy of those threats, or the success of officials in portraying them in excessively lurid terms, some measure of forward momentum was sustained. War Imperialism in the east clearly was not synonymous with the eastern mind. Possibly, the urge to avoid wasteful strategies in the west might have taken Britain to Constantinople, to Jerusalem or Baghdad, but it certainly would not have secured Mosul for Britain, inspired efforts to obtain Syria, and a privileged position in the Hejaz, or laid the foundations for further expansion in the Caucasus or Trans-Caspia.[6]

Montagu's depiction of the 'rounded' Lord Curzon with an unhealthy appetite for the acquisition of new territories 'for diplomatic, economic, strategic and telegraphic reasons', has tended to stick.[7] John Mack speaks of Curzon and Cromer as bedfellows in the 'old colonialism of the nineteenth century' and, more recently, Goldstein has placed Curzon in the school of the 'old style imperialists'.[8] However, Montagu, wisely, was careful to distinguish Curzon from the 'flag wagging type of honest Briton' and, as we have seen, Curzon's perception of international affairs obtained considerable support in the definition of British desiderata in the east for the Peace Conference.[9] On this basis, and as War Imperialism was a much broader phenomenon than simply Curzon's thinking alone, it is highly doubtful it should be seen in the terms suggested by Sykes in connection with Arabian affairs, as a confluence of 'out-of-date minds'.[10] Equally, an assessment of War Imperialism is rendered difficult by the hypocrisy of senior figures who, while willing to accept the logic of the war imperialists, were not then prepared to follow these policies through. Nevakivi has, amongst others, spoken of Sykes–Picot as being at odds with the spirit of the age and with the notion of the consent of the governed.[11] Yet if such a thing were possible it might be thought that the spirit was in contradiction with the age. As Amery suggested, the Americans, in their imperial activities in Central America, were every bit as land-grabbing as the British could hope to be and, in any case, it is highly doubtful that Anglo-French co-operation in the east was ever feasible unless predicated upon an essentially selfish division of territories.[12] It was, however, an essential feature of War Imperialism that expansive designs should remain covert and that, characteristically, they would find expression alongside notions of delivering the populations of the Middle East from the Turk, of rejuvenating ancient civilisations and prosperity, or even of feeding the world.[13]

Besides the broader issues of retrenchment and sensitivity to international opinion which affected the deliberations of policy-makers in 1919, several things might be said to explain the apparent failure, or only partial success, of Curzon in the role of high priest of the imperialists. As we have seen in a whole range of matters Curzon was kept in the dark from 1916 onwards. In the case of Arabian affairs he was deliberately misled by colleagues. On Mesopotamian policy he was deliberately marginalised by Foreign and India Office officials. On questions relating to the Caucasus and Syria, Foreign Office advice was systematically ignored by the British Delegation in Paris throughout 1919. In Palestinian matters it may well be, as Gilmour has alleged, that Curzon was misled by Balfour and that, as the latter confessed, a national home for the Jews always meant a Jewish State.[14] On the other hand, such were the limitations of Curzon's understanding of the 'spirit' of the age that for him the 'international' administration envisaged by Sykes–Picot in Palestine had no real meaning, and to the

Territorial Committee and, later, to the Eastern Committee, Curzon stated that the fate of Palestine had been left undecided.[15]

Similarly, regarding Arab nationalism, Curzon was not the moving figure at the Foreign Office in attempts to reconcile Britain's post-war presence in the east with native opinion. Quite simply, that phenomenon, like many others, was perceived by Curzon to be an impediment to capitalising on a victor's peace.[16] In Mesopotamia especially, by the beginning of Curzon's Foreign Secretaryship proper, fierce debate raged about the revision of Wilson's constitution and the means whereby greater Arab participation might be permitted. Of course, Curzon was not alone in being caught by the turning of the tide. By the late summer of 1919 A.T. Wilson well knew that trends in international affairs must inevitably lead to his departure from Baghdad. For Hirtzel even, who had done so much to channel Wilson's 'exaggerated virtues', adaptation to the conditions of 1920 proved to be a difficult task.[17] For Curzon, such adaptation had proved impossible throughout the war and, as Egerton has written, in attempting to achieve his aims, Curzon turned to traditional methods.[18] Most obviously, this was demonstrated in his efforts to re-establish his executive powers in connection with the Inter-Departmental Conference on the Middle East. Repeatedly, Curzon urged upon subordinates in the Foreign Office that they desist from drawing a distinction, either in name or function, between the Conference and its predecessor the Eastern Committee.[19] However, given Curzon's general unwillingness to sanction development in Mesopotamia before America had stated her intentions and before Britain had definitely obtained the Mesopotamian mandate, the deliberations of the Inter-Departmental Conference were, from Curzon's point of view, in some measure superfluous. Naturally, these discussions remained important to those who, like Hirtzel and Shuckburgh, were possessed of a detailed understanding of the need to define the nature of post-war development in the east and to reconcile it with international trends.[20]

Justly or otherwise Curzon had come to be associated with outdated notions of imperialism. Tempting as it is to challenge the burgeoning stack of evidence which leads to this conclusion, there remains the insoluble matter of why, if the foregoing treatment of the evidence is wrong and if no concerted attempts were made to exclude Curzon, his counsel was not actively sought on vital matters such as the cession of Constantinople to Russia or the Sykes–Picot Agreement. Assuming efforts were made to exclude him from foreign policy formulation throughout the period 1915–19, then clearly there were many factors involved above and beyond Curzon's conception of international affairs: notably, Curzon's manner, and his failure, in the opinion of Lord Crawford, a prominent Tory Peer, to 'cut ice', perhaps, as Crawford suggested, owing to an excessively didactic and professorial demeanour.[21] Certainly, Curzon's frequent references to his own travels in the east became increasingly meaningless when international trends rendered conditions in the Arab Middle East, excepting the Trucial States, radically different. On the other hand, where Curzon's imperial convictions found their most uninhibited expression – in Peninsular Arabia and in the Caucasus – his belief in the endurance of ancient rivalries was largely vindicated by events. By the end of 1919 and the beginning of 1920, both Italy and France had begun to renew their intrigues in Peninsular Arabia. Equally, with the onset of 'The Red Terror' in the east, a temporary measure of support was secured for the forward strategies evolved by Curzon at the Eastern Committee.[22] The irony of Curzon's position was that throughout 1919 both he and his most outspoken opponent, Churchill, feared Bolshevik hostility above all else. Publicly, Curzon played this down right to the end of 1919, constrained by the 'aura of luxury' which afflicted the Caucasus by mid-1919.[23] At the outset of 1920, however, with what Curzon termed the dawn of a new era in international affairs, that is, lip-service to the League of Nations, there was in the public mind the appalling vision of 'The Horrors of Bolshevism' to keep alive the spectre of shadows lurking in the Himalayas.[24]

In 1918 Balfour had, typically, questioned the need for Britain to have a policy in the Caucasus.[25] Shuckburgh, on behalf of the India Office, confirmed that from the Indian perspective the region was regarded as somewhat remote.[26] More recently Gilmour has, by implication, castigated Curzon for aspiring to expand the Empire in a region fitted only 'for Greenmantle and those obscure heroes of the Great Game'.[27] Equally, in the context of Enver's 'Caucasian fantasies', the region has been relegated to a terrestrial no-man's land by Alan Palmer.[28] Faced with a strategic problem which, as Sir Henry Wilson admitted, required a full-scale British occupation, it is neither surprising nor reprehensible that Curzon sought to achieve some measure of strategic security on the basis of traditional concepts of the defence of India, which no one had disproved and for which Curzon's colleagues were quite unable to find an alternative. Whilst Curzon's approach to the problems of Mesopotamia and Syria and the broader lines of eastern policy were by no means vindicated, the handling of those questions by colleagues in Paris and by the British Delegation bordered on incompetence, and in the summer of 1919 the Cabinet turned to Curzon to lead them from the jungle.[29] This, surely, was the most glaring indictment of any notion of inter-Allied or international co-operation or of a new age in world affairs. As Curzon confided to Milner early in 1920, little had changed:

> these Eastern peoples with whom we have to ride pillion have different seats from Europeans, and it does not seem to me to matter much whether we put them on the saddle in front of us or whether they cling on behind and hold us round the waist. The great thing is that the firm seat in the saddle shall be ours.[30]

NOTES

1. See Gilmour, *Curzon*, p. 370.
2. Minutes of the Eastern Committee, 26 December 1918, EC 47, secret, CAB 27/24.
3. Ibid., pp. 10ff.
4. Memorandum by Curzon, 'German and Turkish Territories Captured in the War', 5 December 1917, G. 182, CAB 24/4, p. 2.
5. See, for example, A. Verrier, *Francis Younghusband And the Great Game* (London, 1991), p. ix; Curzon to Crewe, 3 December, 1914, Hackwood, private, Crewe Papers I/20/3. Curzon certainly appeared thus to A.T. Wilson who was to write in 1930: 'Before the Great War my generation served men who believed in the righteousness of the vocation to which they were called, and we shared their belief. They were the priests, and we the acolytes, of a cult – pax Britannica – for which we worked happily, and if need be, died gladly. Curzon at his best, was our spokesman and Kipling, at his noblest, our inspiration.' Quoted in B.C. Busch, *Britain and the Persian Gulf*, p. 388.
6. Writing to Gertrude Bell in a repentant vein in April 1920, Hogarth was to reflect:

   > The empire has reached its maximum and begun the descent. There is no more expansion in us . . . and that being so we shall make but a poor Best of the Arab Countries. Had the capture of Baghdad ended the War we could have done much; but the rest of 1917 and all of 1918 and 1919 have lowered our vitality permanently. We started in 1914 young and vigorous and we have come out in 1919 to find we are old and must readjust our ideas.

   Quoted in Klieman, *Foundations of British Policy in the Arab World*, p. 28. J.E. Mack is quite wrong to suggest that the 'old colonialism of Curzon and Cromer might have been contrasted with the views of Hogarth and Storrs representing 'the liberal strain in British politics . . . [which] dreamed of Arab independence and unity under British guidance'. Whilst Hogarth, like many of his colleagues in the Arab Bureau, may have identified the need to build an Arab façade, throughout the war both he and Storrs were exponents of a British protectorate in Syria and Mesopotamia; hence the high regard in which Hogarth was held by Curzon; see J. E. Mack, *A Prince of Our Disorder*, p. 123.
7. Montagu to Balfour, 20 December 1918, India Office, Whitehall, SW1, private and personal, secret, Balfour Papers Add. Ms 49748 (British Library); see Galbraith, *JICH*, 13, p. 25. On this theme see K. Neilson, 'For Diplomatic, Economic, Strategic and Telegraphic Reasons: British Imperial Defence, the Middle East and India, 1914–18', in *Far Flung Lines: Essays in Honour of Donald Mackenzie Schurman*, ed. G. Kennedy and K. Neilson (London, 1997).
8. See n. 6; also Goldstein, *MES*, 23, p. 419.
9. See n. 7.
10. Sykes to Drummond, 20 July 1917, Office of the War Cabinet, 2 Whitehall Gardens, London, SW, Sykes Papers DS 42.1 68 (St Antony's College, Oxford).

11. See Nevakivi, *Britain, France and the Arab Middle East*, p. 50.
12. Amery to Lloyd George, 8 June 1918, Office of the War Cabinet, 2 Whitehall Gardens, Lloyd George Papers, F/2/1/24.
13. Such sentiments were expressed by Curzon early in 1915 in connection with Mesopotamia: 'This country once waved with corn and was occupied by a large and prosperous population, but it is now a desert . . . I hope that under the new conditions it may recover its prosperity and that the desert may again blossom as the rose.' See A.T. Wilson, *Loyalties: Mesopotamia, 1914–17* (Oxford, 1930), p. 103. Wilson himself had related precisely the same ideas to his father in December 1915: Wilson to his father, 27 December 1915, Basra, A.T. Wilson Papers, vol. 2 (London Library). Hirtzel indulged in similar thoughts, speaking to Wilson in January 1917 of the 'necessity in the interest of humanity' that public opinion should be reconciled to the dismemberment of the Ottoman Empire: Hirtzel to Wilson, 18 January 1917, India Office, private, A.T. Wilson Papers Add. Ms 52455c (British Library).
14. See Gilmour, *Curzon*, p. 521.
15. Minutes of the Territorial Committee, 19 April 1917, third meeting, CAB 21/77; minutes of the Eastern Committee, 5 December 1918, *EC* 41, secret, CAB 27/24.
16. See Galbraith, op. cit., p. 42. It certainly seemed thus to Curzon in his address to the King in November 1918, when he observed that the enemy were 'fugitives on the face of the earth'. As Curzon continued amid much cheering:

> We might also congratulate ourselves on the part that the British Empire had played in this struggle and on the position it filled at the close . . . and we might say that the British flag never flew over a more powerful or a more united Empire than now. Britain had never had better cause to look the world in the face and never did our voice count for more in the councils of the nations or in determining the future destinies of mankind.

See *The Times*, 19 November 1918.
17. Perhaps this was expressed most succinctly in the reluctance of officials such as H.V. Cox and Sir Percy Cox to endorse the use of the aeroplane as the main plank in Churchill's schemes for future British control in Mesopotamia. To Hirtzel, who vested so much importance in establishing a close relationship with his subordinates in the Middle East, the aeroplane was the harbinger of unwanted change:

> The strength of our administration or political control in the past has generally lain in the relations built up by a succession of individual officers with the people among whom they lived. This great asset will disappear when the Political Officer flashes in and out again in an aeroplane or motor. The *deus in machina* is useful in his place, but is out of place in the day-to-day administration.

Minute by Hirtzel, 16 August 1920, L/P+S/10/766.
18. See Egerton, *HJ*, 21, p. 910.
19. See, for example, minute by Curzon, 29 September 1919, FO 371/4183, pp. 243–4.
20. It is extremely doubtful if it is possible to speak as M. Kent does (Kent, in Hinsley, p. 443) of 'Indian opinion'. Certainly, as Mejcher has shown, on the overriding question of the creation of a new Middle Eastern Empire, the India Office, generally, diverged sharply from the Government of India in believing Indian control of Mesopotamia to be impossible. Connected with this was the important divergence of opinion on the issue of support for the Arab movement. It is notable that, in their assessment of the nature of the relationship between powerful Secretaries of State and their subordinate permanent officials, Galbraith and Huttenback omit any reference to such relationships at the India Office; see Galbraith and Huttenback, in Ingram, p. 104. Of the three war-time Secretaries of State for India, Crewe, Chamberlain and Montagu, the last alone might be said to have been particularly outspoken, yet even Montagu was unable or unwilling to alter the fundamental nature of India Office policy in the Middle East; a policy which, in large measure, was devised and sustained by senior officials and, in particular, by Hirtzel. Hirtzel's conception of the post-war Middle East was, in turn, considerably broader than any notion of purely 'Indian', Government of India or departmental brief; see Mejcher, *JCH*, 8, pp. 83–4.
21. See Gilmour, *Curzon*, p. 511; this aspect of Curzon's character had been commented upon some years before by Alan Lascelles; see *End of an Era: Letters and Journals of Sir Alan Lascelles*,

1887–1920, ed. Duff Hart-Davis (London, 1986), entry of 28 April 1910, pp. 77–8. H. Rider-Haggard, a long-standing friend and correspondent of Curzon's said of Curzon on his death that 'he had not the art of popularity'. D. S. Higgins, ed., *The Private Diaries of Sir Henry Rider Haggard, 1914–1925* (London, 1980), entry of 26 March 1925, p. 284.

22. See *The Times*, 16 January 1920.
23. Ibid., 5 November 1919; see J. D. Rose, *IHR*, 11.
24. *The Times*, 8 January 1920.
25. Minutes of the Eastern Committee, 9 December 1918, EC 42, secret, CAB 27/24, p. 16.
26. See B.C. Busch, *Mudros to Lausanne*, p. 122.
27. See Gilmour, op. cit., p. 519.
28. See Alan Palmer, *The Decline and Fall of The Ottoman Empire* (London, 1992), p. 241.
29. Curzon to Balfour, 20 August, 1919, Foreign Office, Balfour Papers, Add. Ms 49734, f. 154 (British Library). Curzon was not officially to take charge at the Foreign Office until October and, for some time, it appears that Balfour had not dealt with Foreign Office matters in Paris other than those which arose in inter-Allied sessions at the Quai d'Orsay. According to Balfour, the delay in transferring the Foreign Secretaryship to Curzon was at Lloyd George's behest and for political reasons. Quite where authority lay in this intervening period is difficult to judge; see Balfour to Long, 22 September 1919, Whittingehame, Prestonkirk, North Berwick, private and confidential, Long Papers Add. Ms 62403 (British Library); see Gilmour, op. cit., p. 505.
30. See J.G. Darwin, 'The Fear of Falling: British Politics and Imperial Decline Since 1900', *Transactions of the Royal Historical Society*, 1986, p. 35.

Appendices

Sykes–Picot Agreement

Sir Edward Grey to M. Cambon

(Secret)
Your Excellency,   *Foreign Office*, May 16, 1916.

I HAVE the honour to acknowledge the receipt of your Excellency's note of the 9th instant, stating that the French Government accept the limits of a future Arab State, or Confederation of States, and of those parts of Syria where French interests predominate, together with certain conditions attached thereto, such as they result from recent discussions in London and Petrograd on the subject.

I have the honour to inform your Excellency in reply that the acceptance of the whole project, as it now stands, will involve the abdication of considerable British interests, but, since His Majesty's Government recognise the advantage to the general cause of the Allies entailed in producing a more favourable internal political situation in Turkey, they are ready to accept the arrangement now arrived at, provided that the co-operation of the Arabs is secured, and that the Arabs fulfil the conditions and obtain the towns of Homs, Hama, Damascus and Aleppo.

It is accordingly understood between the French and British Governments –

1. That France and Great Britain are prepared to recognise and uphold an independent Arab State or a Confederation of Arab States in the areas (*a*) and (*b*) marked on the annexed map [reproduced as Map 2], under the suzerainty of an Arab chief. That in area (*a*) France, and in area (*b*) Great Britain, shall have priority of right of enterprise and local loans. That in area (*a*) France, and in area (*b*) Great Britain, shall alone supply advisers or foreign functionaries at the request of the Arab State or Confederation of Arab States.

2. That in the blue area France, and in the red area Great Britain, shall be allowed to establish such direct or indirect administration or control as they desire and as they may think fit to arrange with the Arab State or Confederation of Arab States.

3. That in the brown area there shall be established an international administration, the form of which is to be decided upon after consultation with Russia,

and subsequently in consultation with the other Allies, and the representatives of the Shereef of Mecca.

4. That Great Britain be accorded (1) the ports of Haifa and Acre, (2) guarantee of a given supply of water from the Tigris and Euphrates in area (*a*) for area (*b*). His Majesty's Government, on their part, undertake that they will at no time enter into negotiations for the cession of Cyprus to any third Power without the previous consent of the French Government.

5. That Alexandretta shall be a free port as regards the trade of the British Empire, and that there shall be no discrimination in port charges or facilities as regards British shipping and British goods; that there shall be freedom of transit for British goods through Alexandretta and by railway through the blue area, whether those goods are intended for or originate in the red area, or (*b*) area, or area (*a*); and there shall be no discrimination, direct or indirect, against British goods on any railway or against British goods or ships at any port serving the areas mentioned.

That Haifa shall be a free port as regards the trade of France, her dominions and protectorates, and there shall be no discrimination in port charges or facilities as regards French shipping and French goods. There shall be freedom of transit for French goods through Haifa and by the British railway through the brown area, whether those goods are intended for or originate in the blue area, area (*a*), or area (*b*), and there shall be no discrimination, direct or indirect, against French goods on any railway, or against French goods or ships at any port serving the areas mentioned.

6. That in area (*a*) the Bagdad Railway shall not be extended southwards beyond Mosul, and in area (*b*) northwards beyond Samarra, until a railway connecting Bagdad with Aleppo via the Euphrates Valley has been completed, and then only with the concurrence of the two Governments.

7. That Great Britain has the right to build, administer, and be sole owner of a railway connecting Haifa with area (*b*), and shall have a perpetual right to transport troops along such a line at all times.

It is to be understood by both Governments that this railway is to facilitate the connection of Bagdad with Haifa by rail, and it is further understood that, if the engineering difficulties and expense entailed by keeping this connecting line in the brown area only make the project unfeasible, that the French Government shall be prepared to consider that the line in question may also traverse the polygon Banias-Keis Marib-Salkhad Tell Otsada-Mesmie before reaching area (*b*).

8. For a period of twenty years the existing Turkish customs tariff shall remain in force throughout the whole of the blue and red areas, as well as in areas (*a*) and (*b*), and no increase in the rates of duty or conversion from *ad valorem* to specific rates shall be made except by agreement between the two Powers.

There shall be no interior customs barriers between any of the above-mentioned areas. The customs duties leviable on goods destined for the interior shall be collected at the port of entry and handed over to the administration of the area of destination.

9. It shall be agreed that the French Government will at no time enter into any negotiations for the cession of their rights and will not cede such rights in the blue area to any third Power, except the Arab State or Confederation of Arab States, without the previous agreement of His Majesty's Government, who, on their part, will give a similar undertaking to the French Government regarding the red area.

10. The British and French Governments shall agree that they will not themselves acquire and will not consent to a third Power acquiring territorial possessions in the Arabian peninsula, nor consent to a third Power constructing a naval base on the islands of the east coast of the Red Sea. This, however, shall not prevent such adjustment of the Aden frontier as may be necessary in consequence of recent Turkish aggression.

11. The negotiations with the Arabs as to the boundaries of the Arab State or Confederation of Arab States shall be continued through the same channel as heretofore on behalf of the two Powers.

12. It is agreed that measures to control the importation of arms into the Arab territories will be considered by the two Governments.

I have further the honour to state that, in order to make the agreement complete, His Majesty's Government are proposing to the Russian Government to exchange notes analogous to those exchanged by the latter and your Excellency's Government on 26th April last. Copies of these notes will be communicated to your Excellency as soon as exchanged.

I would also venture to remind your Excellency that the conclusion of the present agreement raises, for practical consideration, the question of the claims of Italy to a share in any partition or rearrangement of Turkey in Asia, as formulated in article 9 of the agreement of 26th April, 1915, between Italy and the Allies.

His Majesty's Government further consider that the Japanese Government should be informed of the arrangements now concluded.

I have, &c.

E. GREY

Note: Reproduced more fully in J.C. Hurewitz, ed., *The Middle East and North Africa in World Politics: A Documentary Record*, vol. 2, no. 16.

Proclamation of Lieutenant-General Sir Stanley Maude at Baghdad

Lieutenant-General Sir Stanley Maude has issued a proclamation at Baghdad, of which the following is the English text:–

'To the People of Baghdad Vilayet

1. In the name of my King, and in the name of the peoples over whom he rules, I address you as follows:–

2. Our military operations have as their object the defeat of the enemy, and the driving of him from these territories. In order to complete this task, I am charged with absolute and supreme control of all regions in which British troops operate; but our armies do not come into your cities and lands as conquerors or enemies, but as liberators.

3. Since the days of Halaka your city and your lands have been subject to the tyranny of strangers, your palaces have fallen into ruins, your gardens have sunk in desolation, and your forefathers and yourselves have groaned in bondage. Your sons have been carried off to wars not of your seeking, your wealth has been stripped from you by unjust men and squandered in distant places.

4. Since the days of Midhat, the Turks have talked of reforms, yet do not the ruins and wastes of to-day testify the vanity of those promises?

5. It is the wish not only of my King and his peoples, but it is also the wish of the great nations with whom he is in alliance, that you should prosper even as in the past, when your lands were fertile, when your ancestors gave to the world literature, science, and art, and when Baghdad city was one of the wonders of the world.

6. Between your people and the dominions of my King there has been a close bond of interest. For 200 years have the merchants of Baghdad and Great Britain traded together in mutual profit and friendship. On the other hand, the Germans and Turks who have despoiled you and yours, have for 20 years made Baghdad a centre of power from which to assail the power of the British and the Allies of the British in Persia and Arabia. Therefore the British

Government cannot remain indifferent as to what takes place in your country now or in the future, for in duty to the interests of the British people and their Allies, the British Government cannot risk that being done in Baghdad again which has been done by the Turks and Germans during the war.

7. But you people of Baghdad, whose commercial prosperity and whose safety from oppression and invasion must ever be a matter of the closest concern to the British Government, are not to understand that it is the wish of the British Government to impose upon you alien institutions. It is the hope of the British Government that the aspirations of your philosophers and writers shall be realised and that once again the people of Baghdad shall flourish, enjoying their wealth and substance under institutions which are in consonance with their sacred laws and their racial ideals. In Hejaz the Arabs have expelled the Turks and Germans who oppressed them and proclaimed the Sherif Hussein as their King, and his Lordship rules in independence and freedom, and is the ally of the nations who are fighting against the power of Turkey and Germany; so, indeed, are the noble Arabs, the Lords of Koweyt, Nejd, and Asir.

8. Many noble Arabs have perished in the cause of Arab freedom, at the hands of those alien rulers, the Turks, who oppressed them. It is the determination of the Government of Great Britain and the great Powers allied to Great Britain, that these noble Arabs shall not have suffered in vain. It is the hope and desire of the British people and the nations in alliance with them, that the Arab race may rise once more to greatness and renown among the peoples of the earth, and that it shall bind itself together to this end in unity and concord.

9. O people of Baghdad remember that for 26 generations you have suffered under strange tyrants who have ever endeavoured to set one Arab house against another in order that they might profit by your dissensions. This policy is abhorrent to Great Britain and her Allies, for there can be neither peace nor prosperity where there is enmity and misgovernment. Therefore I am commanded to invite you, through your nobles and elders and representatives, to participate in the management of your civil affairs in collaboration with the political representatives of Great Britain who accompany the British Army, so that you may be united with your kinsmen in North, East, South, and West in realising the aspirations of your race.'

19th March 1917.

Source: Curzon Papers F112/256.

The London Agreement

ART. 1. A military convention shall be immediately concluded between the General Staffs of France, Great Britain, Italy and Russia. This convention shall settle the minimum number of military forces to be employed by Russia against Austria-Hungary in order to prevent that Power from concentrating all its strength against Italy, in the event of Russia deciding to direct her principal effort against Germany.

This military convention shall settle question of armistices, which necessarily comes within the scope of the Commanders-in-chief of the Armies.

ART. 2. On her part, Italy undertakes to use her entire resources for the purpose of waging war jointly with France, Great Britain and Russia against all their enemies.

ART. 3. The French and British fleets shall render active and permanent assistance to Italy until such time as the Austro-Hungarian fleet shall have been destroyed or until peace shall have been concluded.

A naval convention shall be immediately concluded to this effect between France, Great Britain and Italy.

ART. 4. Under the Treaty of Peace, Italy shall obtain the Trentino, Cisalpine Tyrol with its geographical and natural frontier (the Brenner frontier), as well as Trieste, the counties of Gorizia and Gradisca, all Istria as far as the Quarnero and including Volosca and the Istrian islands of Cherso and Lussin, as well as the small islands of Plavnik, Unie, Canidole, Palazzuoli, San Pietro di Nembi, Asinello, Gruica, and the neighbouring islets.

NOTE. The frontier required to ensure execution of Article 4 hereof shall be traced as follows: –

From the Piz Umbrail as far as north of the Stelvio, it shall follow the crest of the Rhetian Alps up to the sources of the Adige and the Eisach, then following the Reschen and Brenner mountains and the Oetz and Ziller heights. The frontier shall then bend towards the south, cross Mt. Toblach and join the present frontier of the Carnic Alps. It shall follow this frontier line as far as Mt. Tarvis and from Mt. Tarvis the watershed of the Julian Alps by the Predil Pass, Mt. Mangart, the Tricorno (Terglu) and the watersheds of the Podberdo, Podlaniscam and Idria passes. From this point the frontier shall follow a south-easterly direction towards the Schneeberg, leaving the entire basin of the Save and its tributaries outside Italian territory. From the Schneeberg the frontier shall come down to the coast in such a way as to include Castua, Mattuglia and Volosca within Italian territory.

ART. 5. Italy shall also be given the province of Dalmatia within its present administrative boundaries, including to the north Lisarica and Tribania; to the south as far as a line starting from Cape Planka on the coast and following eastwards the crests of the heights forming the watershed, in such a way as to leave within Italian territory all the valleys and streams flowing towards Sebenico – such as the Cicola, Kerka, Butisnica and their tributaries. She shall also obtain all the islands situated to the north and west of Dalmatia, from Premuda, Selve, Ulbo, Scherda, Maon, Pago and Patadura to the north, up to Meleda to the south including Sant' Andrea, Busi, Lissa, Lesina, Tercola, Curzola, Cazza and Lagosta, as well as the neighbouring rocks and islets and Pelagosa, with the exception of Greater and Lesser Zirona, Bua, Solta and Brazza.

To be neutralized: –

(1) The entire coast from Cape Planka on the north to the southern base of the peninsula of Sabbioncello in the south, so as to include the whole of that peninsula; (2) the portion of the coast which begins in the north at a point situated 10 kilometres south of the headland of Ragusa Vecchia extending southward as far as the River Voïussa, in such a way as to include the gulf and ports of Cattaro, Antivari, Dulcigno, St. Jean de Medua and Durazzo, without prejudice to the rights of Montenegro consequent on the declarations exchanged between the Powers in April and May 1909. As these rights only apply to the present Montenegrin territory, they cannot be extended to any territory or ports which may be assigned to Montenegro. Consequently neutralisation shall not apply to any part of the coast now belonging to Montenegro. There shall be maintained all restrictions concerning the port of Antivari which were accepted by Montenegro in 1909; (3) finally, all the islands not given to Italy.

NOTE. The following Adriatic territory shall be assigned by the four Allied Powers to Croatia, Serbia and Montenegro: –

In the Upper Adriatic, the whole coast from the bay of Volosca on the borders of Istria as far as the northern frontier of Dalmatia, including the coast which is at present Hungarian and all the coast of Croatia, with the port of Fiume and the small ports of Novi and Carlopago, as well as the islands of Veglia, Pervichio, Gregorio, Goli and Arbe. And, in the Lower Adriatic (in the region interesting Serbia and Montenegro) the whole coast from Cape Planka as far as the River Drin, with the important harbours of Spalato, Ragusa, Cattaro, Antivari, Dulcigno and St. Jean de Medua and the islands of Greater and Lesser Zirona, Bua, Solta, Brazza, Jaclian and Calamotta. The port of Durazzo to be assigned to the independent Moslem State of Albania.

ART. 6. Italy shall receive full sovereignty over Valona, the island of Saseno and surrounding territory of sufficient extent to assure defence of these points (from the Voïussa to the north and east, approximately to the northern boundary of the district of Chimara on the south).

ART. 7. Should Italy obtain the Trentino and Istria in accordance with the provisions of Article 4, together with Dalmatia and the Adriatic islands within the limits specified in Article 5, and the Bay of Valona (Article 6), and if the central portion of Albania is reserved for the establishment of a small autonomous neutralised State, Italy shall not oppose the division of Northern and Southern Albania between Montenegro, Serbia and Greece, should France, Great Britain and Russia so desire. The coast from the southern boundary of the Italian territory of Valona (see Article 6) up to Cape Stylos shall be neutralised.

Italy shall be charged with the representation of the State of Albania in its relations with foreign Powers.

Italy agrees, moreover, to leave sufficient territory in any event to the east of Albania to ensure the existence of a frontier line between Greece and Serbia to the west of Lake Ochrida.

ART. 8. Italy shall receive entire sovereignty over the Dodecanese Islands which she is at present occupying.

ART. 9. Generally speaking, France, Great Britain and Russia recognise that Italy is interested in the maintenance of the balance of power in the Mediterranean and that, in the event of the total or partial partition of Turkey in Asia, she ought to obtain a just share of the Mediterranean region adjacent to the province of Adalia, where Italy has already acquired rights and interests which formed the subject of an Italo-British convention. The zone which shall eventually be allotted to Italy shall be delimited, at the proper time, due account being taken of the existing interests of France and Great Britain.

The interests of Italy shall also be taken into consideration in the event of the territorial integrity of the Turkish Empire being maintained and of alterations being made in the zones of interest of the Powers.

If France, Great Britain and Russia occupy any territories in Turkey in Asia during the course of the war, the Mediterranean region bordering on the Province of Adalia within the limits indicated above shall be reserved to Italy, who shall be entitled to occupy it.

ART. 10. All rights and privileges in Libya at present belonging to the Sultan by virtue of the Treaty of Lausanne are transferred to Italy.

ART. 11. Italy shall receive a share of any eventual war indemnity corresponding to her efforts and her sacrifices.

ART. 12. Italy declares that she associates herself in the declaration made by France, Great Britain and Russia to the effect that Arabia and the Moslem Holy Places in Arabia shall be left under the authority of an independent Moslem Power.

ART. 13. In the event of France and Great Britain increasing their colonial territories in Africa at the expense of Germany, those two Powers agree in principle that Italy may claim some equitable compensation, particularly as regards the settlement in her favour of the questions relative to the frontiers of the Italian colonies of Eritrea, Somaliland and Libya and the neighbouring colonies belonging to France and Great Britain.

ART. 14. Great Britain undertakes to facilitate the immediate conclusion, under equitable conditions, of a loan of at least 50,000,000*l.* to be issued on the London market.

ART. 15. France, Great Britain and Russia shall support such opposition as Italy may make to any proposal in the direction of introducing a representative of the Holy See in any peace negotiations or negotiations for the settlement of questions raised by the present war.

ART. 16. The present arrangement shall be held secret. The adherence of Italy to the Declaration of the 5th September, 1914, shall alone be made public, immediately upon declaration of war by or against Italy.

After having taken act of the foregoing memorandum, the representatives of France, Great Britain and Russia, duly authorised to that effect, have concluded the following agreement with the representative of Italy, also duly authorised by his Government: –

France, Great Britain and Russia give their full assent to the memorandum presented by the Italian Government.

With reference to Articles 1, 2 and 3 of the memorandum, which provide for military and naval co-operation between the four Powers, Italy declares that she will take the field at the earliest possible date and within a period not exceeding one month from the signature of these present.

Source: J.C. Hurewitz, ed., *The Middle East and North Africa in World Politics: A Documentary Record,* vol. 2, no. 10.

The St Jean de Maurienne Agreement

1. Preliminary Decisions Taken at Saint-Jean de Maurienne, 19 April 1917

M. Ribot made objections regarding assignment of Mersina and Adana to Italy, but admitted facilities should be granted to commerce of the Interior in the direction of Mersina as in the case of Alexandretta and Haifa. The Italian zone will commence at a point to be determined west of Mersina.

Baron Sonnino asked for the inclusion in Italian zone of occupation of everything which so figures on Mr. Balfour's map. He asked, besides, that the northern part of the vilayet of Smyrna be also included. Mr. Lloyd George and M. Ribot undertake to submit this claim to their Governments.

It was agreed that the interests of the other Powers already established in the different zones shall be scrupulously respected, but that the Powers concerned in these interests shall not make use of them as a means of political action.

An exchange of views took place as to the situation which might result for the Allied Powers at the moment of peace with respect to the Ottoman Empire. After the discussion, Mr. Lloyd George made the following proposal, which was accepted: –

It is agreed that if, at the time when peace is made, the total or partial possession of territories contemplated in the agreements concluded between France, Great Britain, Italy and Russia, as regards attribution to them of a part of the Ottoman Empire, could not be granted entirely to one or several of the Powers in question, then the interests of those Powers would be taken afresh into equitable consideration....

In a general way, the Ministers undertook to recommend the above decisions to their Governments.

2. Agreement Approved in London, 18 August 1917

Subject to Russia's assent.

1. The Italian Government adheres to the stipulations contained in articles 1 and 2 of the French–British [Sykes–Picot] agreements of 9 and 16 May 1916. For their part, the Governments of France and of Great Britain cede to Italy,

under the same conditions of administration and of interests, the green and 'C' zones as marked on the attached map [omitted here].

2. Italy undertakes to make Smyrna a free port for the commerce of France, its colonies and its protectorates, and for the commerce of the British Empire and its dependencies. Italy shall enjoy the rights and privileges that France and Great Britain have reciprocally granted themselves in the ports of Alexandretta, of Haifa, and of St. Jean d'Acre, in accordance with article 5 of the said agreements. Mersina shall be a free port for the commerce of Italy, its colonies and its protectorates, and there shall be neither difference of treatment nor advantages in port rights which may be refused to the navy or the merchandise of Italy. There shall be free transit through Mersina, and by railroad across the *vilâyet* of Adana, for Italian merchandise bound to and from the Italian zone. There shall be no difference of treatment, direct or indirect, at the expense of Italian merchandise or ships in any port along the coast of Cilicia serving the Italian zone.

3. The form of international administration in the yellow zone [same as Sykes–Picot brown zone] mentioned in article 3 of the said agreements of 9 and 16 May shall be decided together with Italy.

4. Italy, insofar as she is concerned, approves the provisions on the ports of Haifa and of Acre contained in article 4 of the same agreements.

5. Italy adheres, in that which relates to the green zone and zone 'C,' to the two paragraphs of article 8 of the French–British agreements concerning the customs regime that shall be maintained in the blue and red zones, and in zones 'A' and 'B.'

6. It is understood that the interests that each Power possesses in the zones controlled by the other Powers shall be scrupulously respected, but that the Powers concerned with these interests shall not use them as means for political action.

7. The provisions contained in articles 10, 11, and 12 of the French–English agreements, concerning the Arabian Peninsula and the Red Sea, shall be considered as fully binding on Italy as if that Power were named in the articles with France and Great Britain as a contracting party.

8. It is understood that if, at the conclusion of peace, the advantages embodied in the agreements contracted among the allied Powers regarding the allocation to each of a part of the Ottoman Empire cannot be entirely assured to one or more of the said Powers, then in whatever alteration or arrangement of provinces of the Ottoman Empire resulting from the war the maintenance of equilibrium in the Mediterranean shall be given equitable consideration, in conformity with article 9 of the London agreement of 26 April 1915.

9. It has been agreed that the present memorandum shall be communicated to the Russian Government, in order to permit it to make its views known.

Source: J.C. Hurewitz, ed., *The Middle East and North Africa in World Politics: A Documentary Record,* vol. 2, no. 23.

The Cherchali Note

(100065).

COMMUNICATED BY FRENCH AMBASSADOR
Ambassade de France
à Londres.

Confidentiel.

Dans une note précédente, en date de ce jour, l'Ambassadeur de France a exposé au Gouvernement britannique les affaires purement musulmanes faisant l'objet principal de la mission de M. Cherchali au Hedjaz.

Il a toutefois paru préférable au Gouvernement français de prévoir, au cours des relations qui vont s'établir entre l'envoyé français et le Grand Chérif la possibilité de conversations politiques.

M. Cherchali doit s'attacher, le cas échéant, à prévenir tout malentendu sur l'attitude de la France en Arabie et dans les régions limitrophes de la péninsule.

En ce qui concerne plus particulièrement la Syrie, la chérif doit connaître (peut-être inexactement) la substance de l'entente intervenue entre la France et l'Angleterre. Le silence observé jusqu'ici à La Mecque à ce sujet n'a plus aujourd'hui de raison d'être. Il fait le jeu en Arabie et dans les milieux syriens de ceux qui représentent la France soit comme se désintéressant de l'avenir de la Syrie, soit au contraire comme faisant obstacle aux desseins d'expansion formés par le Chérif. Le Gouvernement français a tout intérêt à mettre fin à ces légendes: il lui semble possible de le faire, sans divulguer les accords eux-mêmes, et en se bornant à laisser connaître le sens général de l'arrangement franco-britannique.

M. Cherchali n'aura d'ailleurs aucune initiative à prendre à cet égard. Il a été invité seulement à ne pas décourager les demandes d'informations qui lui seraient présentées par le Chérif. Si ce souverain l'interrogeait sur la politique éventuelle de la France en Syrie, l'envoyé français ne lui répondrait qu'après en avoir référé à M. Ribot.

Voici d'ailleurs le texte même des instructions complémentaires du Gouvernement français à M. Cherchali:

'*En Arabie*, la France, en plein accord avec l'Angleterre, ne tient qu'à maintenir, d'une part, l'indépendance du Chérif, et d'autre part, l'intégrité des possessions de ce Souverain. Nous estimons, comme nos Alliés, qu'aucune Puissance européenne ne saurait exercer d'influence dominante ou même prépondérante dans les Lieux Saints de l'Islam et nous sommes résolus à ne point intervenir dans les questions politiques de la péninsule arabique.

En pleine union avec nos Alliés, nous considérons en outre qu'aucun Gouvernement européen ne saurait acquérir de nouvel établissement en Arabie.

C'est pour fournir au Chérif les moyens de protéger son indépendance et l'intégrité de ses états contre tout retour offensif des Turcs, que la France a envoyé auprès de lui une mission militaire destinée à procurer aux Chefs des colonnes arabes des conseillers en même temps que des techniciens.

Tout en estimant qu'aucune Puissance ne saurait obtenir ni territoire nouveau, ni prestige politique en Arabie, le Gouvernement français reconnait que la proximité des côtes égyptiennes d'un côté et du Golfe Persique de l'autre créent toutefois en faveur des intérets commerciaux de nos Alliés anglais une situation dont vous devez tenir compte. Je verrais donc avantage, toutes les fois que des questions de cet ordre seront agitées devant vous, à ce que vous réserviez votre opinion jusqu'à la réception d'instructions que vous demanderez soit au Département, soit à notre Ministre au Caire, et qui seront concertées avec le Gouvernement britannique.

En ce qui concerne la Syrie et son arrière-pays, la France ne saurait laisser à d'autres le soin d'assurer le développement de ces régions. D'une part, le Gouvernement français n'a jamais cessé de s'intéresser au sort des populations qui les habitent et nous pouvons, à cet égard, invoquer les plus anciennes et les plus constantes traditions. D'autre part, l'établissement d'entreprises importantes a marqué dans ces dernières années le souci que nous avions de collaborer à la mise en valeur de cette partie de l'Asie Mineure. Désireux non d'asservir les habitants de ces contrées, mais, au contraire, de faciliter leur évolution, le Gouvernement de la République, en plein accord avec le Gouvernement anglais, serait disposé à leur reconnaître des régimes adaptés aux conditions spéciales aux diverses régions.

C'est ainsi que dans les provinces où domine l'élément arabe, la France encouragerait la création d'émirats à Alep, Damas, Mossoul, etc., dont les souverains auraient des liens avec le roi du Hedjaz. Il est bien entendu que le Gouvernement français se réserverait le droit de fournir seul les conseillers dont les émirs pourraient avoir besoin pour mener à bonne fin leur oeuvre de civilisation. De même, c'est à la France que devraient être demandés les capitaux nécessaires à la mise en valeur du pays, tandis que nous assumerions la charge des grandes entreprises destinées à assurer le développement économique de ces régions.

Sur le front de mer où les populations sont plus mélangées, la nécessité d'un régime spécial s'impose qui leur serait accordé sous l'égide directe du Gouvernement français.

En ce qui concerne Jérusalem et la Palestine, on étudierait un modus vivendi de nature à garantir le respect de toutes les religions, et le Chérif ne serait pas écarté de cette étude.

Vous n'avez point à prendre l'initiative de faire connaître au Malek ces projets du Gouvernement français. Mais comme il est à penser qu'il a été mis au courant, inexactement peut-être, du sens général de notre entente avec l'Angleterre, il est probable qu'il vous entretiendra à ce sujet. Vous lui marquerez que vous n'en avez qu'une notion imparfaite, mais que vous êtes prêt à transmettre au Gouvernement français une demande d'information et à communiquer au Chérif la réponse de la France. Je vous indiquerai dans ce cas, s'il y a lieu pour vous de complêter ou de réduire l'exposé ci-dessus. Mais, vous pouvez déjà, sans avoir besoin de m'en référer, opposer un démenti autorisé aux affirmations qui représenteraient la France soit comme se désintéressant du sort de la Syrie, soit au contraire comme faisant obstacle aux desseins d'expansion du Chérif. Vous déclarerez que la France est disposée à en tenir largement compte.

Parmi les autres questions politiques qui pourront faire l'objet d'entretiens avec le Chérif figure celle de la création d'un établissement de banque franco-britannique à Djeddah.

Depuis 1913, la Banque ottomane possédait une agence à Djeddah. Bien que cet établissement eut rendu et fut appelé encore à rendre des services aux pélerins et au commerce au Hedjaz, sa dénomination de 'Banque impériale ottomane' lui donna aux yeux du Gouvernement chérifien l'apparence d'une institution officielle ottomane.

Tenant compte de cette situation, le Directeur de l'agence, M. Aboucassem, après avoir pris l'avis des directions de la Banque à Paris et à Londres, se montra disposé à modifier le titre de l'établissement financier de Djeddah et à le transformer en une banque autonome, qui pourrait rendre au Gouvernement chérifien de précieux services et qui jouirait de la confiance des deux pays alliés, la France et l'Angleterre.

A la suite de la reconnaissance par les Gouvernements anglais et français du Grand Chérif comme Malek, le Gouvernement hachimite parut prêt à accepter une entente sous la condition que la Banque prendrait, par exemple, le titre de 'Banque arabe du Hedjaz' et qu'elle se soumettrait à la juridiction des tribunaux religieux.

Cependant au début de Décembre 1916, le Directeur de l'agence était avisé que les pourparlers devaient être différés. Quelques semaines plus tard, il lui était notifié, par lettre officielle, que le Gouvernement hachimite refusait de reconnaître son établissement et qu'il déclinait toute responsabilité sur les conséquences de son maintien à Djeddah.

Il y aurait lieu de ne pas laisser ignorer au Malek la pénible impression que ce changement d'attitude a laissée aux deux Gouvernements français et anglais. Ces deux Gouvernements veulent croire que la situation nouvelle provient d'un malentendu, car le Malek Houssein avait reconnu antérieurement les services que serait appelé à rendre au développement économique du nouvel état l'établissement financier franco-anglais, qui devait être substitué à l'agence de la Banque ottomane. Pour maintenir le crédit du nouvel état, pour assurer dans des conditions satisfaisantes son organisation financière, le concours de cet établissement sera nécessaire au Malek, qui doit envisager les conséquences graves qu'entraînerait l'influence des notables de Djeddah, qui se livrent à des opérations de prêts et de changes de monnaies, dans des conditions usuraires. Les pélerins musulmans et les Gouvernements ayant des sujets musulmans doivent être assurés de posséder à Djeddah un établissement financier sérieux et honnête, capable d'inspirer confiance au dedans et au dehors. Des questions de détail peuvent sans doute être l'objet de négociations, mais il ne semble pas possible qu'étant donné les avantages politique et économiques que le Malek doit en retirer pour son pays le principe de la création d'un établissement financier france-anglais ne soit pas admis par lui.'

Source: Curzon Papers F112/277.

Projet d'Arrangement, Paris, 3 October 1917

This Document is the Property of His Britannic Majesty's Government

SECRET

[191542]

PROJET D'ARRANGEMENT

LES développements de la lutte poursuivie par les Arabes contre les Turcs et la nécessité d'aider le Roi du Hedjaz à les libérer du joug ottoman ayant amené les Gouvernements anglais et français à accuser leur action au Hedjaz, les deux Gouvernements ont reconnu l'opportunité de préciser les termes des accords conclus par eux en mai 1916, en ce qui concerne les pays arabes. En conséquence, les deux Gouvernements se mettent d'accord sur les principes suivants:

1. En raison du caractère sacré reconnu par les musulmans au territoire du Hedjaz, les deux Gouvernements sont résolus à maintenir l'indépendance entière de ce royaume et l'intégrité de ses limites conformément à la carte annexée au présent arrangement, étant entendu qu'aucune Puissance quelconque ne pourra exercer une influence dominante ou même intervenir de quelque façon que ce soit dans l'administration ni dans les affaires intérieures de ce royaume.

2. Au cas où des concessions de toute nature seraient offertes à un particulier, à un groupement ou à une société ressortissant à l'une des deux Puissances contractantes, le Gouvernement français et le Gouvernement britannique s'engagent respectivement à ne pas donner leur agrément à l'entreprise envisagée avant d'avoir prévenu l'autre partie et s'être assurée qu'une coopération des ressortissants des deux pays n'est pas réalisable.

3. Il est entendu qu'en ce qui concerne la zone (A) le Gouvernement français

et en ce qui concerne la zone (B) le Gouvernement anglais seront seuls qualifiés pour traiter avec le Roi du Hedjaz toutes les questions intéressant la souveraineté arabe sans aucune intervention de l'autre Puissance.

4. Jusqu'à la fin des hostilités les Gouvernements anglais et français continueront à assurer au Roi du Hedjaz l'aide qui lui est nécessaire conformément aux méthodes suivies jusqu'ici.

5. Le Gouvernement de Sa Majesté britannique fait valoir que les relations de voisinage avec ses possessions, l'importance qu'il y a pour lui à éliminer toutes causes de troubles dans la péninsule arabique lui ont créé des intérêts politiques spéciaux. Le Gouvernement français est prêt à reconnaître ces intérêts spéciaux et renouvelle sa ferme intention de ne rechercher aucune influence politique dans ces régions. Il reste bien entendu que le Gouvernement britannique emploiera l'influence qu'il peut acquérir sur les chefs locaux à assurer au commerce licite et à la navigation français un traitement aussi avantageux que celui fait au commerce licite et à la navigation britanniques. Comme il est de la plus haute importance pour les deux pays contractants de mettre un terme aux trafics pouvant favoriser les troubles – tels que le trafic des armes et munitions de guerre, vente des esclavages, &c. – les deux Gouvernements conviennent que le Gouvernement britannique fera le nécessaire pour faire interdire ces trafics par les autorités locales, auxquelles il pourra prêter le concours de ses forces navales pour faire la police des eaux territoriales.

Paris, le 3 octobre, 1917.

Source: Curzon Papers F112/277.

Anglo-French Declaration, 7 November 1918

The object aimed at by France and Great Britain in prosecuting in the East the War let loose by the ambition of Germany is the complete and definite emancipation of the peoples so long oppressed by the Turks and the establishment of national governments and administrations deriving their authority from the initiative and free choice of the indigenous populations.

In order to carry out these intentions France and Great Britain are at one in encouraging and assisting the establishment of indigenous Governments and administrations in Syria and Mesopotamia, now liberated by the Allies, and in the territories the liberation of which they are engaged in securing and recognising these as soon as they are actually established.

Far from wishing to impose on the populations of these regions any particular institutions they are only concerned to ensure by their support and by adequate assistance the regular working of Governments and administrations freely chosen by the populations themselves. To secure impartial and equal justice for all, to facilitate the economic development of the country by inspiring and encouraging local initiative, to favour the diffusion of education, to put an end to dissensions that have too long been taken advantage of by Turkish policy, such is the policy which the two Allied Governments uphold in the liberated territories.

Source: J.C. Hurewitz, ed., *The Middle East and North Africa in World Politics: A Documentary Record*, vol. 2, no. 28, p. 112.

The Russian Situation:
Memorandum by Lord Curzon

(*This Document is the Property of His Britannic Majesty's Government*)
SECRET
G.T.4046.

WAR CABINET

THE RUSSIAN SITUATION

Memorandum by Lord Curzon

While great events are happening in France, we seem to be in some danger of losing sight of what is going to happen in Russia.

It is difficult to keep pace with all the telegrams, but the following appears to be the situation:–

On the one hand, we have Mr. Lockhart at Moscow acting in the closest collaboration with Trotsky and repeating to us daily with increasing passion the Trotzky [*sic*] formulas of

(a) Creation of a new Russian revolutionary army
(b) Allied assistance in this undertaking
(c) No Allied or Japanese intervention at Vladivostock
(d) No Allied or British intervention at Murmansk or Archangel.

This, it is true, is a policy, but so far at any rate it has not got beyond the region of declamation.

As against this, we know that there is no Russian Army because it has disappeared: and that there is not likely to be any new Russian Army because no one means to fight. The majority of our advisers tell us that to hope to create a new State or a new Army in Russia out of the shattered debris of Bolshevism is a fantastic dream.

Meanwhile we have General Poole advising the occupation of Murmansk and Archangel. We find opinion even among Russians (M. Maklakoff himself is a convert) veering round in the direction of Japanese intervention in Siberia. But there seems to be a general consensus that if this takes place, it should be, not as an independent movement, or a movement made at the request or with the consent of the Allies, but a step taken with their actual and visible co-operation. Hitherto Japan is believed to have refused this condition. Will she persist in that attitude? It is the sole policy which America seems at all likely to favour.

Ought we not to decide between the two policies? To believe in one, while we pursue the other, or to believe in neither, but to pursue both, seems equally to lead to destruction.

(Intd.) C. of K.

26th March 1918.

Source: CAB 24/46.

Declaration to the King of Hedjaz

ANNEX (C)*

Declaration to the King of Hedjaz

The Governments of Great Britain and France desire jointly to inform the Government of Hejaz that their policy in regard to the Arabic-speaking peoples of Arabia, Syria, Jazirah, and Irak is as follows:–

1. In such areas as were free before the war the Governments recognise and reaffirm the existing freedom and independence of the inhabitants.

2. In such areas as have been liberated since the war by the efforts of the inhabitants, the two Governments recognise the complete and sovereign independence of the inhabitants of those regions.

3. With regard to such areas as are now occupied by the Allied forces, it is the intention and desire of the two Governments that these areas should be permanently delivered from the oppression under which they formerly suffered, and that their future government should be based upon the principle of the consent of the governed.

4. With regard to areas still subject to Ottoman oppression, it is the desire of the two Governments that the inhabitants of these areas should be delivered from the oppression to which they are now subjected, and that the inhabitants should be put in a position to decide upon forms of government which appear most suitable for the various regions with due regard to the maintenance of security and order.

5. The two Governments desire to make it clear to the Government of Hejaz and to the Arabic-speaking peoples above-mentioned that on the part of neither Government has there ever been any intention of annexing these areas nor of disposing of them, nor allowing them to be disposed of by any other party, in any way other than is desired by the populations thereof.

6. The two Governments further wish to make it clear that they desire to facilitate to the utmost co-operation, alliance, and unity of purpose among the the various elements of the Arabic-speaking peoples in the regions mentioned

in the first paragraph, with a view to the ultimate restoration of the liberty and prosperity which these areas formerly enjoyed.

*Attached to Memorandum by Sir Mark Sykes, 6 July 1918, Foreign Office, EC 825, appendix of *EC* 21, 18 July 1918, CAB 27/24.

Bibliography

MANUSCRIPT SOURCES

Bodleian Library, Oxford
Asquith Papers
Bryce Papers
Inverchapel Papers
Milner Papers

British Library
Balfour Papers
Bertie Papers
Cecil of Chelwood Papers
Long Papers
Robertson-Murray Correspondence
A.T. Wilson Papers

Cambridge University Library
Hardinge Papers
Crewe Papers

Churchill College, Cambridge
Esher Papers
Hankey Papers
Lloyd Papers
Page-Croft Papers
Wemyss Papers

House of Lords Record Office
Bonar Law Papers
Lloyd George Papers

Imperial War Museum
Diaries and Correspondence of Field Marshal Sir Henry Wilson
A.T. Wilson Papers

King's College, London
Akaba Papers

Lister Papers
Marshall Papers
Maurice Papers
Milne Papers
Poole Papers
Queripel Papers

Lambeth Palace Library
Davidson Papers

London Library
A.T. Wilson Papers

National Maritime Museum
Norris Papers

Oriental and India Office Collections
Political and Secret Department:
  L/P+S/10 (subject files) series
  L/P+S/11 (annual files) series
  L/P+S/18 (memoranda) series
Military Department:
  L/MIL/5 (compilations and miscellaneous) series
  L/MIL/17 (Military Department Library)
European Manuscripts:
  Bailey Collection
  Barrow Collection
  Butler Collection
  Chelmsford Collection
  Curzon Collection
  Hamilton Grant Collection
  Walter Lawrence Collection
  Keyes Collection
  Monro Collection
  Montagu Collection
  Reading Collection
  Seton Collection
  Willingdon Collection

Pembroke College, Cambridge
Storrs Papers

Public Record Office
Admiralty Files ADM 116– Admiralty Case Files

Cabinet Office Papers:
CAB 1 – Cabinet Office, Miscellaneous Records
CAB 2 – Committee of Imperial Defence, minutes
CAB 4 – Committee of Imperial Defence, memoranda: miscellaneous
CAB 17 – Committee of Imperial Defence, correspondence and miscellaneous papers
CAB 21 – Cabinet Office: registered files
CAB 23 – War Cabinet Minutes
CAB 24 – Cabinet Memoranda
CAB 25 – Supreme War Council, 1917–1919
CAB 27 – Committees General Series to 1939
CAB 28 – Allied Conferences
CAB 29 – Peace Conference and other International Conferences
CAB 42 – List of Cabinet Papers 1915 and 1916; Papers of the War Council, Dardenelles Committee and the War Committee
CAB 63 – Hankey Papers

Foreign Office Papers:
FO 95 – Miscellanea Series 1
FO 248 – Embassy and Consular Archives, Persia
FO 263 – Embassy and Consular Archives, Japan
FO 350 – Jordan Papers
FO 371 – Foreign Office: Political Departments: General Correspondence
FO 373 – Peace Conference Handbooks
FO 608 – Peace Conference of 1919–1920 Correspondence
FO 686 – Jedda Agency Papers
FO 882 – Arab Bureau Papers
FO 899 – Cabinet Papers
FO 800 – Private collections: Ministers and Officials, Balfour Papers, Bertie Papers, Cecil Papers, Cromer Papers, Crowe Papers, Grey Papers, Langley Papers, Mackinder Papers, Nicolson Papers

Public Record Office Classes:
PRO 30/30 Milner Papers
PRO 30/57 Kitchener Papers

War Office Papers:
WO 32 – Registered files: General Series
WO 106 – Directorate of Military Operations and Intelligence

Scottish Record Office
Balfour Papers
Lothian Papers (including those of Professor J.Y. Simpson)

Somerset Record Office
Herbert Papers

St Antony's College, Oxford
Hogarth Papers

Sykes Papers
Young Papers

Wiltshire Record Office
Long Papers

PRINTED ORIGINAL SOURCES

The Leo Amery Diaries, ed. J. Barnes and D. Nicholson, 2 vols (London, 1980).
The Letters of Gertrude Bell, ed. Lady Francis Bell, 2 vols (New York, 1927).
The Letters of T. E. Lawrence, ed. M. Brown (Oxford, 1991).
G. N. Curzon, *Persia and the Persian Question*, 2 vols (London, 1966).
M. Gilbert, *Companion Volume Four, The Stricken World, 1916–1922*, parts 1 and 2 (Boston, 1978).
Selections From The Smuts Papers, ed. W. K. Hancock and J. Van Der Poel, 7 vols (Cambridge, 1963–73).
End of an Era: The Letters and Journals of Sir Alan Lascelles, 1887–1920, ed. Duff Hart Davis (London, 1986).
The Middle East and North Africa in World Politics: A Documentary Record, ed. J. C. Hurewitz, 3 vols (New Haven, CT/London, 1975–79).
The Military Correspondence of Field Marshal Sir Henry Wilson 1918–22, ed. K. Jeffrey (London, 1985).
Thomas Jones Whitehall Diary, ed. K. Middlemas (London, 1969).
Mark Sykes: His Life and Letters, S. Leslie (London, 1923).
Records of the Emirates, 1820–(1960), ed. P. Tuson (Archive Editions, 1992).
The Diaries of Parker Pasha, War in the Desert 1914–18 Told from the Secret Diaries of Alfred Chevalier Parker, Nephew of Lord Kitchener, Governor of Sinai, and Military Intelligence Chief in the Arab Revolt, ed. H. V. F. Winstone (London, 1983).
Documents on British Foreign Policy 1919–1939, first series, ed. E. L. Woodward and R. Butler, 24 vols (London, 1947).

NEWSPAPERS

The Times
The New York Times

BOOKS

R. Adelson, *Mark Sykes: Portrait of an Amateur* (London, 1975).
–, *London and the Invention of the Middle East: Money, Power and War, 1902–1922* (New Haven, CT/London, 1995).
L. S. Amery, *My Political Life,* 3 vols (London, 1953–55).
C. M. Andrew and A. S. Kanya-Forstener, *The Climax of French Imperial Expansion 1914–1924* (Stanford, CA, 1981).
R. Bidwell and G. R. Smith, *Arabian and Islamic Studies* (London/New York, 1983).

K. C. Bourne and D. C. Watt, eds, *Studies in International History, Essays Presented to W. Norton Medlicott* (London, 1967).

E. Brémond, *Le Hejaz dans la guerre mondiale* (Paris, 1931).

D. Bullock, *Allenby's War: The Road to Damascus 1916–18* (Poole, 1987).

B. C. Busch, *Britain and the Persian Gulf 1894–1914* (Berkeley and Los Angeles, 1967).

–, *Britain, India and the Arabs, 1914–1921* (Berkeley, 1976).

–, *Hardinge of Penshurst, A Study in the Old Diplomacy* (Hamden, CT, 1980).

–, *Mudros to Lausanne: Britain's Frontier in West Asia 1918–1923* (New York, 1976).

D. Cannadine, *Aspects of Aristocracy* (New Haven, CT, 1994).

Cecil, Viscount of Chelwood, *All the Way* (London, 1949).

J. Charmley, *Churchill: The End of Glory* (London, 1993).

S. Cohen, *British Policy in Mesopotamia 1903–14* (London, 1976).

J. Darwin, *Britain, Egypt, and the Middle East: Imperial Policy in the Aftermath of War, 1918–1922* (New York, 1981).

D. Dilks, *Curzon in India*, 2 vols (London, 1969–70).

M. L. Dockrill and J. D. Goold, *Peace Without Promise: Britain and the Peace Conferences 1919–1923* (London, 1981).

C. H. Ellis, *The Transcaspian Episode: 1918–1919* (London, 1963).

A. G. S. Enser, *A Subject Bibliography of the First World War*, 2nd edn (Hants/Vermont, 1990).

L. Evans, *United States Policy and the Partition of Turkey, 1914–1924* (Baltimore, MD, 1965).

M. R. D. Foot, *War and Society: Historical Essays in Honour of J. R. Western, 1928–71* (London, 1973).

I. Friedman, *The Question of Palestine, 1914–1918, British–Jewish–Arab Relations* (London, 1973).

D. Fromkin, *A Peace to End All Peace: Creating the Modern Middle East 1914–1922* (London, 1989).

T. G. Fraser, *The Middle East, 1914–1979* (London, 1980).

L. E. Gelfand, *The Inquiry: American Preparations for Peace, 1917–1919* (London/New Haven, CT, 1963).

M. Gilbert, *The Challenge of War: Winston S. Churchill, 1914–1916* (London, 1990).

–, *The World in Torment: Winston S. Churchill, 1917–1922* (London, 1990).

E. Goldstein, *Winning the Peace, British Diplomatic Strategy, Peace Planning, and the Paris Peace Conference, 1916–1920* (Oxford, 1991).

D. Gilmour, *Curzon* (London, 1994).

A. M. Gollin, *Proconsul in Politics* (London, 1964).

W. Gottlieb, *Studies in Secret Diplomacy During the First World War* (London, 1957).

J. Grigg, *Lloyd George: From Peace To War, 1912–1916* (London, 1985).

P. Guinn, *British Strategy and Politics, 1914–1918* (Oxford, 1965).

K. Hamilton, *Bertie of Thame: Edwardian Ambassador* (Woodbridge, 1990).

W. K. Hancock, *Smuts*, 2 vols (Cambridge, 1962–68).

Hankey, Lord Maurice, *The Supreme Command 1914–1918,* 2 vols (London, 1961).

Hardinge, Lord Charles, *Old Diplomacy: The Reminiscences of Lord Hardinge of Penshurst* (London, 1947).

C. Hazlehurst, *Politicians at War, July 1914 to May 1915* (London, 1971).

P. C. Helmreich, *From Paris to Sèvres: The Partition of the Ottoman Empire at the Peace Conference of 1919–1920* (Columbus, OH, 1974).

F. H. Hinsley, ed., *British Foreign Policy Under Sir Edward Grey* (Cambridge, 1977).

D. Holden and R. Johns, *The House of Saud: The Rise and Fall of the Most Powerful Dynasty in the Arab World* (New York, 1981).

P. Hopkirk, *On Secret Service East of Constantinople* (London, 1994).

–, *Setting the East Ablaze* (London, 1984).

E. Ingram, *National and International Politics in the Middle East, Essays in Honour of Elie Kedourie* (London, 1986).

L. James, *Imperial Warrior: The Life and Times of Field Marshal Viscount Allenby* (London, 1993).

K. Jeffrey, *The British Army and the Crisis of Empire, 1918–1922* (Manchester, c. 1984).

D. Judd, *Lord Reading, Rufus Isaacs, First Marquess of Reading, Lord Chief Justice and Viceroy of India, 1860–1935* (London, 1982).

F. Kazemzadah, *The Struggle for Transcaucasia, 1917–1921* (New York/Oxford, 1952).

E. Kedourie, *The Chatham House Version and Other Middle-Eastern Studies* (London, 1970).

–, *England and the Middle East: the Destruction of the Ottoman Empire, 1914–1921* (Sussex, 1978).

–, *In the Anglo-Arab Labyrinth: The McMahon–Husayn Correspondence and its Interpreters 1914–1939* (Cambridge, 1976).

G. Kennedy and K. Neilson, eds, *Far Flung Lines: Essays on Imperial Defence in Honour of Donald Mackenzie Schurman* (London, 1997)

M. Kettle, *The Allies and the Russian Collapse March 1917–March 1918* (London, 1981).

P. King, *The Viceroy's Fall: How Kitchener Destroyed Curzon* (London, 1986).

A. S. Klieman, *Foundations of British Policy in the Arab World: The Cairo Conference of 1921* (Baltimore, MD, and London, 1970).

J. Lees-Milne, *The Life of Reginald, 2nd Viscount Esher* (London, 1996).

J. N. Lockman, *Meinertzhagen's Diary Ruse: False Entries on T. E. Lawrence* (Michigan, 1995).

J. Lord, *Duty, Honour, Empire: The Life and Times of Colonel Richard Meinertzhagen* (London, 1971).

W. R. Louis, *In the Name of God Go! Leo Amery and the British Empire in the Age of Churchill* (New York/London, 1992).

J. Mack, *A Prince of Our Disorder: The Life of T. E. Lawrence* (Boston/Toronto, 1976).

P. Magnus, *Kitchener: Portrait of an Imperialist* (London, 1968).

P. Mansfield, *A History of the Middle East* (London, 1991).

J. Marlowe, *Late Victorian: The Life of Sir Arnold Talbot Wilson* (London, 1967).

E. Mawdsley, *The Russian Civil War* (Cambridge, MA, London, 1989).

H. Mejcher, *Imperial Quest for Oil, Iraq 1910–1928* (London, 1976).

E. Monroe, *Britain's Moment in the Middle East 1914–1920* (London, 1969).

L. Mosley, *Curzon: The End of an Epoch* (London, 1961).

H. Nicolson, *Curzon: The Last Phase 1919–1925: A Study in Post-War Diplomacy* (London, 1934).

T. H. O'Brien, *Milner* (London, 1979).

W. J. Olson, *Anglo-Iranian Relations During World War I* (London, 1984).

–, *Britain's Elusive Empire in the Middle East 1900–1921* (New York/London 1982).

A. Palmer, *The Decline and Fall of the Ottoman Empire* (London, 1992).

Petrie, Sir Charles, *The Life and Letters of Sir Austen Chamberlain*, 2 vols (London, 1939–40).

Y. Porath, *The Emergence of the Palestinian–Arab National Movement 1918–1929* (London, 1974).

K. Robbins, *Sir Edward Grey* (London, 1971).

Ronaldshay, Earl of, *The Life of Lord Curzon*, 3 vols (London, 1928).

N. Rose, *Churchill: An Unruly Life* (London, 1994).

–, *Vansittart: Study of a Diplomat* (London, 1978).

V. Rothwell, *British War Aims and Peace Diplomacy, 1914–1918* (Oxford, 1971).

H. M. Sachar, *The Emergence of the Middle East: 1914–1924* (New York, 1969).

M. L. Sandars and P. M. Taylor, *British Propaganda During the First World War* (London, 1982).

R. B. Sergeant and R. Bidwell, *Arabian Studies* (Cambridge, 1990).

P. Sluglett, *Britain in Iraq, 1914–32* (London, 1976).

S. R. Sonyel, *Turkish Diplomacy, 1918–1923: Mustafa Kemal and the Turkish National Movement* (London/Beverly Hills, 1975).

F. Stanwood, *War Revolution and British Imperialism in Central Asia* (London, 1983).

W. Stivers, *Supremacy and Oil: Iraq, Turkey and the Anglo-American World Order 1918–1930* (London, 1982).

E. Tauber, *The Arab Movement in World War I* (London, 1993).

A. L. Tibawi, *Anglo-Arab Relations and the Question of Palestine, 1914–1921* (London, 1977).

U. Trumpener, *Germany and the Ottoman Empire, 1914–1918* (Princeton, NJ, 1968).

R. H. Ullman, *Anglo-Soviet Relations, 1917–1921,* 3 vols (Princeton, NJ, 1961–72).

Vansittart, Lord, *The Mist Procession* (London, 1958).

D. Walder, *The Chanak Affair* (London, 1969).

S. D. Waley, *Edwin Montagu: A Memoir and an Account of His Visits to India* (London, 1964).

F. G. Weber, *Eagles on the Crescent: Germany, Austria, and the Diplomacy of the Turkish Alliance 1914–1918* (Ithaca/London, 1970).

B. Westrate, *The Arab Bureau: British Policy in the Middle East 1916–20* (University Park, PA, *c.* 1982).

T. Wilson, *The Myriad Faces of War: Britain and the Great War 1914–1918* (Cambridge, 1986).

H. V. F. Winstone, *The Illicit Adventure: The Story of Political and Military Intelligence in the Middle East from 1898–1926* (London, 1982).

–, *Gertrude Bell* (London, 1983).

–, *Captain Shakespear: A Portrait* (London, 1976).

M. Yapp, *The Making of the Modern Middle East 1792–1923* (London, 1987).

H. Young, *The Independent Arab* (London, 1933).

ARTICLES

S. A. Cohen, 'Sir Arthur Nicolson and Russia: The Case of The Baghdad Railway', *The Historical Journal*, 18, 4 (1975).

–, 'The Genesis of the British Campaign in Mesopotamia, 1914', *Middle Eastern Studies*, 12 (1976).

–, 'Mesopotamia in British Strategy, 1903–1914', *Middle Eastern Studies*, 9 (1978).

J. G. Darwin, 'The Fear of Falling: British Politics and Imperial Decline Since 1900', *Transactions of the Royal Historical Society* (1986).

Sir William Deakin, 'Imperial Germany and the "Holy War" in Africa, 1914–1918', *University of Leeds Review*, 28 (1985/86).

G. W. Egerton, 'Britain and the "Great Betrayal": Anglo-American Relations and the Struggle for United States Ratification of the Treaty of Versailles, 1919–1920', *The Historical Journal*, 21, 4 (1978).

J. Fisher ' "On the Glacis of India": Lord Curzon and British Policy in the Caucasus, 1919', *Diplomacy & Statecraft*, 8, 2 (1997).

–, ' "The Safety of Our Indian Empire": Lord Curzon and British Predominance in the Arabian Peninsula, 1919', *Middle Eastern Studies*, 33, 3(1997).

T. G. Fraser, 'Germany and the Indian Revolution, 1914–18', *Journal of Contemporary History*, 12 (1977).

–, 'India in Anglo-Japanese Relations During the First World War', *History*, 12 (1977).

D. French, 'The Dardanelles, Mecca and Kut: Prestige as a Factor in British Eastern Strategy, 1914–1916', *War and Society*, 5, 1 (May 1987).

I. Friedman, 'The McMahon–Hussein Correspondence and the Question of Palestine', *Journal of Contemporary History*, 5, 2 (1970).

J. S. Galbraith, 'No Man's Child: The Campaign in Mesopotamia, 1914–1916', *The International History Review*, 6, 3 (August 1984).

–, 'British War Aims in World War I: A Commentary on "Statesmanship" ', *Journal of Imperial and Commonwealth History*, 13 (1984–85).

E. Goldstein, 'British Peace Aims and the Eastern Question: The Political Intelligence Department and the Eastern Committee, 1918', *Middle Eastern Studies*, 23, 4 (1987).

D. Goold, 'Lord Hardinge and the Mesopotamia Expedition and Inquiry, 1914–1917', *The Historical Journal*, 19, 4, (1976).

J. B. Kelly, 'The Legal and Historical Basis of the British Position in the Persian Gulf', *St Antony's Papers*, no. 4, *Middle Eastern Affairs*, no. 1 (London, 1958).

A. S. Klieman, 'Britain's War Aims in the Middle East in 1915', *Journal of Contemporary History*, 13 (1968).

D. Lee, 'Notes and Suggestions: The Origins of Pan-Islamism', *American Historical Review*, 47 (1942).

A. L. Macfie, 'The British Decision Regarding the Future of Constantinople, November 1918–January 1920', *The Historical Journal*, 18, 2 (1975).

H. Mejcher, 'British Middle East Policy, 1917–21: The Inter-Departmental Level', *Journal of Contemporary History*, 8 (1973).

K. Neilson, 'Kitchener: A Reputation Refurbished?', *Canadian Journal of History*, 15, 2 (1980).

J. D. Rose, 'Batum as Domino, 1919–1920: The Defence of India in Transcaucasia', *The International History Review*, 11, 1 (January 1980).

V. H. Rothwell, 'Mesopotamia in British War Aims, 1914–1918', *The Historical Journal*, 13, 2 (1970).

B. Schwarz, 'Divided Attention: Britain's Perception of a German Threat to Her Eastern Position in 1918', *Journal of Contemporary History*, 28 (1993).

J. K. Tanenbaum, 'France and the Arab Middle East 1914–1920', *The American Philosophical Society*, 68, 7 (1978).

A. J. Toynbee, 'The McMahon–Hussein Correspondence: Comments and a Reply', *Journal of Contemporary History*, 5, 4 (1970).

R. Warman, 'The Erosion of Foreign Office Influence in the Making of Foreign Policy 1916–18', *Historical Journal*, 15 (1972).

Index